TRAVELING with the INNOCENTS ABROAD

Mark Twain's Original Reports from Europe and the Holy Land

Edited by
Daniel Morley McKeithan

NORMAN : UNIVERSITY OF OKLAHOMA PRESS

By Daniel Morley McKeithan

*A Study of the Debt to Shakesfeare in the Beaumont and Fletcher Plays (*Austin, 1938*)*
*A Collection of Paul Hamilton Hayne Letters (ed.) (*Austin, 1944*)*
*Selected Letters of John Garland James (ed.) (*Austin, 1946*)*
*Traveling with the Innocents Abroad (ed.) (*Norman, 1958*)*

Library of Congress Catalog Card Number 58-6858

ISBN: 978-0-8061-4332-3 (paper)

The paper in this book meets the guidelines for permanence and durability of the Committee on Production Guidelines for Book Longevity of the Council of Library Resources, Inc.

To B. H. M.

MARK TWAIN's second book, and his most interesting book of foreign travel, was *The Innocents Abroad, or The New Pilgrims' Progress; Being Some Account of the Steamship Quaker City's Pleasure Excursion to Europe and the Holy Land, with Descriptions of Countries, Nations, Incidents and Adventures, as They Appeared to the Author* (Hartford, American Publishing Company, 1869). He wrote the book in the spring and early summer of 1868, basing it on his notebook and the letters which he had contributed to the San Francisco *Daily Alta California,* the *New York Tribune,* and the *New York Herald* concerning the *Quaker City* pleasure excursion to Europe, the Holy Land, and Egypt in 1867.

Twain was thirty-one when, on December 15, 1866, he sailed from San Francisco to return to the East after five and one-half years of exciting adventure in the West—three years in Nevada, two in San Francisco, and four months in the Hawaiian Islands. He had already served an impressive apprenticeship in the writing profession, beginning at least as early as 1852. After his piloting days on the Mississippi (1857–61) and his mining days in Nevada, he had served on the staff of the *Territorial Enterprise* of Virginia City, Nevada, and the San Francisco *Morning Call,* written letters to the New York *Sunday Mercury,* contributed articles and sketches to the *Golden Era* and the *Californian,* published the Jumping Frog story in the New York *Saturday Press* (November 18, 1865), visited and reported on the Sandwich (Hawaiian) Islands for the Sacramento *Union,* gotten an article into *Harper's Magazine* (December, 1866),[1] and had agreed to permit C. H. Webb to collect some of his tales and sketches for his first book (*The Celebrated Jumping Frog of Calaveras County, and Other Sketches,* New York, C. H. Webb, 1867). He had also completed a successful lecture tour of California and Nevada.

Twain sailed from San Francisco to Nicaragua on the steamer

[1] On the *Hornet* disaster. Unfortunately, his name appeared in the magazine as Mark Swain.

America with Captain Ned Wakeman, whom he later described as Ned Blakely in *Roughing It,* Captain Hurricane Jones in *Some Random Notes of an Idle Excursion,* and Captain Stormfield in *Captain Stormfield's Visit to Heaven.* He arrived in New York near the middle of January, and before going home to visit his mother and other relatives in St. Louis, Hannibal, and Keokuk, he heard of the *Quaker City* pleasure excursion to Europe and the Holy Land which was to begin in June. Before he left California, he had secured a position with the *Daily Alta California* as special traveling correspondent and had been toying with the idea of making a trip around the world. Now, however, he persuaded his editors to pay his fare on the *Quaker City* voyage ($1,250) and continue to accept travel letters. He made his visit to the Middle West early in March and returned to New York by the middle of April to await the departure of the pilgrims, in the meantime reporting to the *Alta* on various aspects of life in New York. He also lectured at Cooper Union and several other places in and near New York. These early *Alta* letters were collected and edited by Franklin Walker and G. Ezra Dane (*Mark Twain's Travels with Mr. Brown,* New York, Alfred A. Knopf, 1940). Before he sailed, he made arrangements to contribute a few letters to the *New York Tribune.*

The *Quaker City,* eighteen hundred tons, using steam and auxiliary sails, was under the command of Captain C. C. Duncan, who took his family along for the trip. The ship sailed from New York on June 8, 1867 (although it dropped anchor within the harbor for the night because of rough weather outside), and returned to New York over five months later, on November 19. There were about seventy-six passengers, including children and the captain's family. Twain had a "splendid, immoral, tobacco-smoking, wine-drinking, godless roommate" named Dan Slote of New York. Henry Ward Beecher and General Sherman, who had been advertised as passengers, did not go, but there were Moses S. Beach of the New York *Sun,* his seventeen-year-old daughter, Emma, and Mrs. A. W. Fairbanks of Cleveland, all of whom became lifelong friends of Twain. Other good traveling companions were John A. Van Nostrand of New Jersey, Dr. A. Reeve Jackson, the ship's surgeon, Colonel W. R. Denny of Virginia, J. W. Davis of New York, Julius Moulton of St. Louis, and Dr. G. B. Birch of Hannibal, Ohio. William F. Church of Cincinnati was one of the pious pilgrims. Dr. E. Andrews of Albany was the Oracle, and Bloodgood H. Cutter, a Long Island farmer, was the Poet Lariat. A young passenger of eighteen, Charles J. Langdon of Elmira, New York, showed Twain a picture of his sister Olivia and became Twain's brother-in-law several years later.[2]

Twain visited Horta, on Fayal Island in the Azores, Gibraltar, Tangier, Marseilles, Paris, Versailles, Genoa, Milan, Lake Como, Venice, Florence, Pisa, Leghorn, Civita Vecchia, Rome, Naples, Athens (under cover of darkness because the ship had been quarantined), Constantinople, Sebastopol, Odessa, Yalta, Smyrna, Syria and Palestine (making the "long trip" from Beirut to Jerusalem by horseback in the scorching summer heat), Egypt, Spain, and Bermuda.

Of the fifty-eight letters which he wrote concerning the trip, all of which are included in the present volume, fifty were written for the San Francisco *Daily Alta California.* These were numbered by Twain as follows: 1–39, 43–48, and 51–54 (the last letter, written after the return of the *Quaker City* to New York, was not numbered). Numbers 40–42, 49, and 50 are missing, possibly because Twain got his numbering confused—he was constantly moving, the weather was almost unbearably hot in the Holy Land, and he was sometimes irritated by guides, hostile natives, swarms of beggars, and even by the pious pilgrims themselves. Of course it is also possible that a few letters were lost or that the *Alta* editors decided not to publish several of them. The amazing thing is that he was able to write so many letters and so well—including the best writing he had done so far. Letter 13 was written for the Naples *Observer* but was reprinted by the *Alta.* Letter 58 was written for the *New York Herald* upon the return of the *Quaker City*. The other six letters (2, 12, 23, 26, 38, and 56) were written for the *New York Tribune.*

Twain's *Alta* letters were headed thus:

> [Entered according to Act of Congress, in the year 1867, by Fred'k MacCrellish & Co., in the Clerk's Office of the District Court for the District of California.]
>
> THE HOLY LAND EXCURSION.
>
> LETTER FROM "MARK TWAIN."
>
> [SPECIAL TRAVELLING CORRESPONDENT OF THE ALTA.]

[2] My chief sources for biographical details are A. B. Paine, *Mark Twain: A Biography* (3 vols., New York and London, Harper and Brothers, 1912) and Paine, *Mark Twain's Letters* (2 vols., New York and London, Harper and Brothers, 1917).

There usually followed the number of the letter and a list of subjects treated in it. The headings of the *Tribune* letters varied according to the place and contents. The *Herald* letter was prefaced by an editorial note headed "The Quaker City Pilgrimage," and the letter itself was headed "The Cruise of the Quaker City."

The newspapers' headings at the top of each letter have for the most part been retained in this book, although they sometimes were altered to give some indication of the subject matter. Where brackets were used by Twain or by the newspapers, they have been changed to parentheses, in order to avoid confusion with the brackets used by the editor. Otherwise, the letters are reprinted just as they appeared in the newspapers, retaining the subheads and Twain's sometimes erratic spelling and punctuation. The letters have been renumbered so that the various cities are described by Twain in the order in which they were visited by the pilgrims. However, Twain's original number for each letter may be found in the note following it.

On November 21, 1867, Elisha Bliss, Jr., manager of the American Publishing Company of Hartford, wrote Twain that he wanted to publish a book of his, "perhaps compiled from your letters from the past, etc., with such interesting additions as may be proper. . . . If you have any thought of writing a book, or could be induced to do so, we should be pleased to see you, and will do so." Twain replied on December 2 that he could make a book out of the *Alta* and *Tribune* letters.

> I could weed them of their chief faults of construction and inelegancies of expression, and make a volume that would be more acceptable in many respects than any I could write now. When those letters were written my impressions were fresh, but now they have lost that freshness; they were warm then, they are cold now. I could strike out certain letters, and write new ones wherewith to supply their places.

After delays and further correspondence, Twain went to Hartford in the latter part of January, 1868, to confer with Bliss about the details of the book. Bliss offered him either $10,000 cash for his copyright or a royalty of 5 per cent. Twain wisely accepted the latter and promised to deliver the manuscript of the book to the publisher by the end of July. He returned to Washington, where he was doing journalistic work, and started writing the book. Trouble developed, however, when he learned, through Joe Goodman, his old friend of the *Territorial Enterprise*, that the *Alta* editors had copyrighted his letters and were planning to publish them in a book. (Twain should have known about the copyright because of the notice printed at the head of each letter.) Correspondence proving slow and unsatisfactory, Twain decided to go to San Francisco for a personal interview. He sailed for Aspinwall (Colón), crossed the isthmus, and sailed for San Francisco with Captain Ned Wakeman again, who told him of his wonderful dream of heaven which Twain used in *Captain Stormfield's Visit to Heaven* (first written in 1868 but not published until forty years later). He easily persuaded the *Alta* editors to release publication rights to him, finished his book in about two months, made a lecture tour of California and Nevada, left both for the last time in his life, sailed from San Francisco on July 6, reached New York on July 28, and handed the manuscript to Bliss in Hartford at the end of the month.

In the meantime he had met and fallen in love with Olivia Langdon of Elmira, and the readers of *The Innocents Abroad* may be in her debt, for, according to A. B. Paine, she read the proofs with Twain and may have helped him make further revisions. If she made any suggestions, they were probably wise, for her taste and literary judgment were good. Twain rightly valued her criticism of much of his later writing. She may have refined her Samson a little, but there is no evidence that she cut his hair. Nearly every revision which Twain made in the letters when writing the book was an improvement (although some of the parts that he added should have been revised too). An exception is the passage concerning the Roman soldier who perished at his post at Pompeii.[3]

The Innocents Abroad was published in July, 1869, and since that time it has been the most popular book of foreign travel ever written by any American. In the preface to the book Twain wrote:

> This book is a record of a pleasure trip. . . . Yet notwithstanding it is only a record of a picnic, it has a purpose, which is, to suggest to the reader how *he* would be likely to see Europe and the East if he looked at them with his own eyes instead of the eyes of those who traveled in those countries before him. . . .
>
> I offer no apologies for any departures from the usual style of travel-writing that

[3] For a single eloquent and moving sentence he substituted an inflated passage which he then deflated with a joke. See Letter 14 and Chapter IV of the second volume of *The Innocents Abroad.* Professor Leon T. Dickinson feels that the original sentence was a bit turgid and grandiloquent too, that Twain decided to deflate it with a joke, and that he further inflated it as a build-up. See "Mark Twain's Revisions in Writing *The Innocents Abroad,*" *American Literature*, Vol. XIX (May, 1947), 152n.

may be charged against me—for I think I have seen with impartial eyes, and I am sure I have written at least honestly, whether wisely or not.

In this volume I have used portions of letters which I wrote for the *Daily Alta California*, of San Francisco, the proprietors of that journal having waived their rights and given me the necessary permission. I have also inserted portions of several letters written for the New York *Tribune* and the New York *Herald*.

In the notes following the letters I have tried to indicate what use Twain made of these letters and what his revisions and deletions were. He, indeed, made tremendous use of all these letters, with the exception of a few which repeated ideas that had already been expressed more appropriately in other letters. Several passages which had been written too hurriedly or too flippantly—such as the stories of Joseph and the Prodigal Son—were deleted. Many chapters were made up almost entirely of one or more of the letters. It should be stressed, however, that Twain did not reprint a single letter verbatim. He went through every letter with careful scrutiny—deleting, substituting, revising, often toning down harsh passages, making others more accurate, or moderating praise that seemed too high when read calmly a year later in San Francisco. He was also, as Bernard DeVoto says, an artist interested in his tools, and he improved diction or style in nearly every paragraph.

Twain expressed a desire to see the Holy Land in springtime, before the burning droughts of summer had scorched the life out of it. If he had seen it in that pleasanter time, he might have revised some of his harsher judgments, both of the land and of the people. He said the people were naturally intelligent and goodhearted and might do well under better government.

The best discussions which I have found of the use that Mark Twain made of the letters in writing *The Innocents Abroad* are by DeLancey Ferguson[4] and Leon T. Dickinson.[5] "It is a commonplace of criticism," writes Professor Ferguson, "that Mark Twain's mature style is first established fully in *The Innocents Abroad*. But what is really remarkable is that it appears almost equally in the *Alta* letters from which the book was compiled." He also believes that "the passages newly written for the book display no advance in taste and judgment. Some are good; some are bad." He clarifies and qualifies these statements by indicating that while Twain made many improvements in the letters, some of the

[4] *Mark Twain: Man and Legend* (Indianapolis and New York, The Bobbs-Merrill Company, 1943).

[5] "Mark Twain's Revisions," 139–57.

newly written parts needed improvements too. There is convincing evidence that Twain was capable of self-criticism, but it is only natural that at times he could read more critically what he had written several months earlier than what he had just written.

Comparing the amount of new matter with that taken from the letters, Professor Ferguson states that the letters "made up considerably more than half the book." The first ten chapters contain the descriptions of the Azores, Tangier, and Gibraltar from the letters—the rest is new. Twain greatly expanded the material on France and doubled that on Italy, but since "the letters to the *Alta* carried the trip no further than Jerusalem and the Dead Sea," "the concluding chapters, from Alexandria onward, were wholly new"—except, of course, for the summarizing letter written after his return to New York. The most eloquent passage in the book—the description of the Sphinx—was, one might add, in this new part. According to Professor Ferguson, Twain followed the letters closely from the ascent of Vesuvius through his account of the Holy Land, adding little except the strictures on J. C. Prime's *Tent Life in the Holy Land.*

The letters, Professor Ferguson says, "had blemishes which were later deleted" and "were more or less revised." Brown disappeared, along with some of his remarks showing bad taste. Other comments of his were transferred to the doctor, Blucher, or Twain himself. In the book, Ferguson says, Twain toned down mockery, criticism, and skepticism concerning relics, miracles, the church, and Biblical stories and moderated his praise of Napoleon III. Twain eliminated "most of the slang," much of the "small-town humor," "a few passages," superfluous and commonplace words, and "comparisons aimed at Pacific Coast readers." He improved the diction, and "stylistically the revisions were usually improvements."[6] There can be little doubt, I think, that nearly all of the revisions were improvements, although Twain sometimes went astray when he inserted something new.

I would have qualified Professor Ferguson's statement that "there remained whole chapters, such as the descriptions of the Parthenon and the ruins of Baalbec, in which scarcely a word was altered,"[7] for no letter was reproduced without change.

Professor Dickinson writes: "He revised in the light of two facts: (1) he was addressing a different audience from the one he had ad-

[6] *Mark Twain,* 121–37.

[7] *Ibid.,* 136–37.

dressed in his newspaper letters, and (2) he was now writing, not newspaper articles, but a book." It was the purpose of his study "to show how the book differs from the letters and what exactly Clemens did to make it different." Dickinson discusses the revisions under the headings of clarity, variety, propriety, and humor and gives examples of each. A summary of his discussion follows.

"In the first place, *The Innocents Abroad* is clearer than the *Alta* letters." For the benefit of his larger audience he removed references to the West Coast. Twain improved his expression, clarified references, avoided redundancies, inserted words to improve coherence and "whole passages in an effort to preserve the continuity of the journey," reorganized a number of passages, shifted material to more appropriate places in the narrative, improved the order of details, and corrected some misstatements.

"Besides being in many ways clearer than the *Alta* letters, *The Innocents Abroad* is considerably more varied." More variety of expression and of subject matter was necessary in a book than in weekly letters. He eliminated certain words which had been used too often or too close together. He made the contents more varied by introducing new subject matter and by arranging his material "to produce a motley effect."

"A number of significant changes were made for the sake of decorum. The book was intended to sell primarily in the East, and Eastern taste was quite different from Western. Clemens recognized the difference." He tried to adapt his writing to his new readers "by purifying his expression, by deleting or modifying coarse passages, and by altering his remarks in order to avoid the charge of blasphemy." He made the language less colloquial and somewhat more formal, reduced the number of slang words and put some of them in quotation marks, and raised the general level of his diction. Although the book contains outspoken criticism both of the church and of the pilgrims, it is "more temperate than the newspaper version." Some changes were made to avoid charges of irreverence, profanation, or flippancy.

"Perhaps the most notable difference between *The Innocents Abroad* and the *Alta* letters is the book's superior humor." One reason why he eliminated some of the satire was his feeling that it was inappropriate in a book predominantly humorous. Some of the weak or broad humor was cut out, and Twain substituted humor of a richer, more discriminating quality. Some of the humorous situations in the letters were sketchy, and he developed them for the book. Moreover, he added new quips and several humorous anecdotes.[8]

The text of *The Innocents Abroad* referred to in my notes is the Author's National Edition, in two volumes. Twenty-seven chapters appear in volume I, and volume II contains thirty-three numbered chapters, "A Newspaper Valedictory," and "Conclusion." The first edition of the book, mentioned in my first paragraph, contains sixty-one numbered chapters and a "Conclusions," in one volume.

I obtained photostats of all these letters from the Library of Congress, and I am grateful to Donald C. Holmes, chief of the Photoduplication Service, for patiently answering many questions concerning them. Typed copies of the letters were made from the photostats by Mrs. R. C. Stephenson.

[8] "Mark Twain's Revisions," 139–49.

Daniel Morley McKeithan

Strasbourg, France
February 1, 1958

CONTENTS

Introduction vii
1. The Azores 3
2. Adventures in Horta 10
3. Gibraltar 18
4. Tangier 25
5. The Ways of the Moors 30
6. Versailles and Paris 36
7. Genoa 41
8. Milan 48
9. Lake Como 53
10. Venice 59
11. Florence 66
12. Civita Vecchia 72
13. Quarantined in Naples Harbor 74
14. The Buried City of Pompeii 76
15. Ascent of Mount Vesuvius 83
16. More on Ascent of Mount Vesuvius 89
17. Descent of Mount Vesuvius 95
18. Ancient Athens 100
19. Arrival at Constantinople 110
20. The Cripples of Constantinople 115
21. Morals of the Mohammedans 120
22. The Dogs of Constantinople 123
23. A Genuine Turkish Bath 128
24. Sebastopol 132
25. Arrival in Odessa 137
26. A Visit to the Emperor of Russia 142
27. More About Alexander II 150
28. Guests of the Grand Duke 157
29. Smyrna 163
30. Smyrna's Lions 168
31. Bygone Magnificence 173

32. Camping Out 178
33. All About Joshua 183
34. Portrait of a Syrian Village 188
35. Damascus the Eternal 193
36. More of Damascus 198
37. South to Banias 204
38. First Day in Palestine 209
39. Ancient History of Dutch Flat 213
40. The Fall and Rise of Joseph 219
41. Famous Holy Places 225
42. Pious Enthusiasm of the Pilgrims 229
43. The Apparition 236
44. Mount Tabor and the Prodigal Son 242
45. Nazareth 248
46. Jezreel and Samaria 254
47. A Curious Remnant of the Past 260
48. Exploring Jerusalem 266
49. More Biblical Landmarks 272
50. A Holy Place 277
51. The Wandering Jew 281
52. Enough of Sights 287
53. Threatened With Attack 291
54. Bethlehem, the Dead Sea 296
55. Palestine Scenery 302
56. American Colony in Palestine 306
57. Home Again 309
58. Summing Up the Excursion 313
Index 320

Frontispiece: Mark Twain
of the *Quaker City*

Traveling with the Innocents Abroad

Mark Twain's Original Reports from Europe and the Holy Land

1. The Azores

Horta, Fayal, June 19th

After ten days of strong head winds that retarded our progress, and a heavy sea that kept about twenty of the passengers sea-sick all the time, we hove in sight of this almost unknown land this morning early.

The Azores Islands lie on nearly the same parallel of latitude as San Francisco and New York, and are 2,400 miles straight east of the latter city. They are nine or ten in number. The extent of this island of Fayal (pronounced Fy-all) is about 28,000 acres—too large for one farm and not large enough for two. The islands belong to the Crown of Portugal, and were discovered about four hundred and fifty years ago. They are composed of volcanic hills and mountains, and of course the soil is very rich. The hills are carefully cultivated clear to their summits, and so are the mountains up to an altitude of eight or nine hundred feet. Every farm is cut up into innumerable little squares, by walls of lava, built to protect the growing products from the rude winds that blow here, and this gives a hill-side the semblance of a vast checker-board. All the landscape is green and beautiful; but it is a quiet, pastoral sort of beauty, for there are no rugged features about the mountains—all their outlines are soft and gently curved. Even the Great Pico rises up out of the sea with a smooth unbroken swell to the height of 7,613 feet—a colossal pyramid of softest green, without break or breach of any kind to mar its exquisite symmetry.

There is a Civil Governor here, but, to use the language of the vulgar, there is a Military Governor who "holds the age" on him, and can retire him and suspend the civil law whenever in his judgment it is proper to do so.

Going Ashore

This town of Horta sits in the lap of a cluster of cultivated hills, and its snowy houses peep out everywhere from a mass of bright vegetation which is almost tropical in its variety and luxuriance. A little stone fort, armed with a dozen small cannon, commands the harbor, but I suppose our navy could take it if it were necessary. Two of the guns are two hundred and fifty years old. If they ever touch a match to them they will explode and destroy the garrison.

The moment our anchor was dropped we were surrounded by a swarm of chattering, gesticulating, dark-skinned, piratical looking Portuguese boatmen, who could not make us understand what they wanted, and were as unable to understand what we said in reply. I thought there must necessarily be a Californian in the party, though, and so it proved. I found one, and then we were all right. He had served the devil in San Francisco, and could speak our language well enough for purposes of lying and swindling, and we engaged his boat and went ashore.

A crowd of bare-footed and ragged and dirty vagabonds, of both sexes, received us on the wharf, and with one hospitable impulse held out their hands. With one grateful impulse we seized the hands and shook them. And then we saw that their hospitality was a vain delusion—they only extended their hands to beg.

Noted Americans

We ploughed through, and like dutiful citizens went to pay our respects to the American Consul, Mr. Dabney. His house is commodious, and stands in the midst of a forest of rare trees and shrubs, and beautiful plants and flowers. The grounds contain eighteen acres and are laid out with excellent taste. The Dabney family are from New England, and have lived here and held this Consulship, father and son, for sixty years. They have grown to be almost the wealthiest people in the island, and are perhaps altogether the most influential and the best beloved. The common people reverence them as their protectors and their truest friends.

Two of the junior Dabney's married daughters of Professor Webster, who was executed in Boston twelve or fifteen years ago, for the murder of Dr. Parkman. The girls were very young then, but highly educated and accomplished. The Webster family removed to Fayal immediately after their great misfortune came upon them, to hide their sorrows from a curious world, and have remained here in exile ever since. I remember a print of that day which pictured the young Webster girls in Court at the trial of their father, but I did not recognize them in the fine, matronly, dignified ladies we saw to-day. Their exile was well chosen. In no civilized land could they have found so complete a retirement from the busy, prying world. This island is almost unknown in America—and everywhere else, no doubt. There is scarcely anything about it in print anywhere, and when you ask a wise and well-read man what its condition and characteristics are, he answers with prompt decision that he don't know. The island exports nothing to speak of, and does not import more than double that much. Nobody comes here, and nobody goes away. News is a thing unknown in Fayal. A thirst for it is a passion equally unknown. A Portughee of average intelligence inquired to-day if our civil war was over? because, he said, somebody had told him it was—or at least it ran in his mind that somebody had told him something like that! And when a passenger gave an officer of the garrison copies of the *Tribune*, the *Herald* and *Times*, he was surprised to find later news in them from Lisbon than he had just received by the little monthly steamer. He was told that it came by cable. He said he knew they had tried to lay a cable ten years ago, but it had been in his mind, somehow, they they hadn't succeeded!

Slumberdom

It is a mighty slow place—slow and dull and sleepy. They plough with a wooden plough, such as old Abraham used; they put only one grain of corn in a hill, and don't make any hills, either; they have three holidays a week, and loaf the balance of the time; they scorn threshing-machines and all other unholy inventions with the true Jesuit wisdom, which says that ignorance is bliss and progress is sedition. So an ox tramps out their wheat on a threshing-floor, after the fashion of the time of Moses, when it was commanded that the ox that trod out the grain should not be muzzled. But altogether the slowest and funniest thing is the windmill they grind their corn with. It grinds about ten bushels a day; the shelled corn is put into a hopper, from which it flows down a trough and into the mill-stones—and a lazy lout of a Portughee leans on those stones all day long, and keeps the corn back with his hand and permits only a proper quantity to fall upon the stones at a time. Now, how long do you suppose a Yankee would stand there before he would invent some way of making that trough shake, and feed the mill intelligently itself? Half the mill is stone—ten feet of it—and the upper half is heavy woodwork, and to it is attached the sails; when the wind don't blow right they hitch on some jackasses and slew the whole upper story around till the sails are brought in proper position! How is that for inspired stupidity? They don't even know enough to make the sails movable, instead of the house. I suppose if they were to build an observatory they would make the telescope stationary and turn the edifice to suit the position of the stars.

The only species of vehicle they have is a cumbersome cart with a great wicker-work body on it and solid wheels cut from the ends of logs, and the axle is made fast in the wheel and both turn together. They have no stoves and no chimneys. They build their fires in the centre of the single room a family occupies, and build it on the floor—some of the smoke escapes through channels built in the walls, and a good deal of it don't. Most freight transportation is done on little donkeys considerably larger than a cat, but not larger than an ordinary calf. The donkey and the balance of the family all eat and sleep in the same room. The grass intended for the donkey's breakfast is made into a pallet for him to sleep on, and if he gets hungry in the night he eats up his pillows, bolster, bedding and everything else. The donkey is not so ignorant as his master, has less vermin, is not so uncleanly, is better informed and more dignified, and is altogether the most worthy and respectable of the two. Neither are allowed to vote, and, doubtless, neither desire it. Laborers' wages are twenty to twenty-six cents a day, and those of mechanics from forty to sixty. It is enough to exist on, and that is all these people care for. Laborers do not get suddenly rich here, it is said.

Jesuit Church

It is in communities like this that Jesuit humbuggery flourishes. We visited a Jesuit cathedral nearly two hundred years old, and found in it a piece of the veritable cross upon which our Savior was crucified. It was polished and hard, and in as excellent a state of preservation as if the dread tragedy on Calvary had occurred yesterday instead of nearly twenty centuries ago. But these confiding people believe in that piece of wood unhesitatingly.

In a chapel of the cathedral is an altar with facings of solid silver—at least they call it so, and I think myself it would go a couple of hundred to the ton—and before it is kept forever burning a small lamp. A devout lady who died, left money and contracted for unlimited masses for the repose of her soul, and also stipulated that this lamp should be kept lighted always, day and night. She did all this before she died, you understand. It is a very small lamp, and a very dim one, and I don't think it would set her back much if it went out on her.

The great altar of the cathedral, and also three or four minor ones, are a perfect mass of gilt jim-cracks and gingerbread, and reminded me of the tawdry trumpery of the Chinese Temple in San Francisco. And they have got more old rusty apostles standing around the filagree work, some on one leg and some with one eye out, but a gamey look in the other, and some with two or three fingers gone, and some with not enough nose left to blow—all of them crippled and discouraged, and fitter subjects for the hospital than the cathedral.

The walls of the chancel are of porcelain, all pictured over with figures of almost life size, very elegantly wrought, and dressed in the fanciful costumes of two centuries ago. The design was a history of something or somebody, but none of us were learned enough to read the story. The old father, reposing under a stone close by, dated 1686, might have told us if he could have risen. But which he didn't.

Donkey Riding

As we came down through the town, we encountered a squad of little donkeys ready saddled for use. The saddles were peculiar, to say the least. They consisted of a sort of saw-buck, with a small mattress on it, and this furniture covered about half the donkey. There were no stirrups, but really such supports were not needed—to use such a saddle was the next thing to riding a dinner table—there was ample support clear out to one's knee joints. A pack of ragged Portuguese muleteers crowded around us, offering their beasts at half a dollar an hour—more rascality to the stranger, for the market price is sixteen cents. Half a dozen of us mounted the ridiculous affairs, Brown among the number, though he inveighed bitterly against the indignity of being compelled to make such a figure of himself through the principal streets of a town of 10,000 inhabitants.

We started. It was not a trot, a gallop, or a canter, but a regular stampede, and made up of all possible or conceivable gaits. No spurs were necessary. There was a muleteer to every donkey and a dozen volunteers beside, and they banged the donkeys with their goad-stocks [sticks], and pricked them with their spikes, and shouted something that sounded like "*Sekki-yah!*" and kept up a din and a racket that was worse than Bedlam itself. These rascals were all on foot, but no matter, they were always up to time—they can outrun and outlast a jackass. Altogether ours was the liveliest and the queerest procession I ever witnessed, and drew crowded audiences to the balconies wherever we went.

Brown could do nothing at all with his donkey. The brute scampered zigzag across the road and the others ran into him; he scraped Brown against carts and the corners of houses; the road was fenced in with high stone walls, and the donkey gave him a polishing first on one side and then on the other, but never once took the middle; he finally came to the house he was born in and darted into the parlor, scraping Brown off at the doorway. After remounting, Brown said to the muleteer, "Now, that's enough, you know; you go slow hereafter." But the fellow knew no English and did not understand, so he simply said, "*Sekki-yah!*" and the donkey was off again like a shot. He turned a corner suddenly, and Brown went over his head. And, to speak truly, every mule stumbled over the two, and the whole cavalcade was piled up in a heap. No harm done. A fall from one of those donkeys is of little more consequence than rolling off a sofa. The donkeys all stood still after the catastrophe, and waited for their dismembered saddles to be patched up and put on by the noisy muleteers. Brown was pretty angry, and wanted to swear, but every time he opened his mouth his animal did also, and let off a series of brays that drowned all other sounds. Of course, this made Brown furious; but when he stooped down to pick up his hat and the donkey hit him behind, he just became a maniac. He waltzed into the midst of those donkeys and drivers, and in two minutes he had cleared a space around him large enough to review an army in, almost.

It was jolly, clattering around the breezy hills and through the beautiful cañons. There was that rare thing, novelty, about it; it was a fresh, new, exhilarating sensation, this donkey riding, and worth a hundred worn and threadbare home pleasures.

Where the Russ Pavement Comes from

The roads were a wonder, and well they might be. Here was an island with only a handful of people in it—25,000—and yet such superb roads do not exist in the United States outside of Central Park.

Everywhere you go, in any direction, you find either a hard, smooth, level thoroughfare, just sprinkled with black lava sand, and bordered with little gutters neatly paved with small smooth pebbles, (a counterfeit of the Central Park roads,) or compactly paved ones like Broadway. They talk much of the Russ pavement in New York, and call it a new invention—yet here they have been using it in this remote little isle of the sea for two hundred years! Every street in Horta is handsomely paved with the heavy Russ blocks, and the surface is neat and true as a floor—not marred by holes like broadway. And every road is fenced in by tall, solid lava walls, which will last a thousand years in this land where frost is unknown. They are very thick, and are often plastered and whitewashed, and capped with projecting slabs of cut stone. Trees from gardens above hang their swaying tendrils down, and contrast their bright green with the whitewash or the black lava of the walls, and make them beautiful. The trees and vines stretch across these narrow roadways sometimes, and so shut out the sun that you seem to be riding through a tunnel. On each side of these Russ roads, also, is a little gutter, paved with small round pebbles. The pavements, the roads and the bridges, are all government work.

The bridges are of a single span—a single arch—of cut stone, without a support, and paved on top with flags of lava and ornamental pebble work. Everywhere are walls, walls, walls—and all of them tasteful and handsome—and eternally substantial; and everywhere are those marvellous pavements, so neat, so smooth, and so indestructible. And if ever roads and streets, and the outsides of houses, were perfectly free from any sign or semblance of dirt, or dust, or mud, or uncleanness of any kind, it is Horta, it is Fayal. The lower classes, in their persons and their domiciles, are dirty—but there it stops—the town and the island are miracles of cleanliness.

I think Horta was not built for a day, but for all time. The houses are made of thick walls of lava, plastered outside and whitewashed till they gleam among the green vegetation like snow—and they are roofed with imperishable tiles. There is nothing about them that can burn—even the floors are of packed earth or paved with stone.

Back Again

Well, we arrived home again after a ten-mile excursion, and the irrepressible muleteers scampered at our heels through the main street, goading the donkeys, shouting the everlasting *"Sekki-yah,"* and singing:

We 'ang Jeffah Davis on sowlah applah tree,
We 'ang Jeffah Davis on sowlah applah tree,
We 'ang Jeffah Davis on sowlah applah tree,
So we go molloching on!

When we were dismounted and it came to settling, the yelling and jawing, and swearing and quarrelling among the muleteers and with us, surpassed any row I have listened to yet. One fellow would demand a dollar an hour for the use of his donkey; another claimed half a dollar for pricking him up, another a quarter for helping in that service, and about fourteen guides presented bills for showing us the way through the town and its environs; and every devil of them was more vociferous, and more vehement, and more frantic in gesture than his neighbor. Finally, we paid one guide, and paid for one muleteer to each donkey, and told the others to go to the hottest place they could find in the other world. They probably did not start then, but there is no question that they will some day.

This letter, numbered one by Twain, appeared in the *Daily Alta California* on August 2, 1867. The parts of the letter containing information repeated in Letter 2 were omitted from *The Innocents Abroad.* Most of the other parts were used (Volume I, Chapters V and VI), with little change, such as the descriptions of the cathedral, the donkey ride, and the roads, bridges, and walls. The book does not mention the consul or his family, the boatman who had lived in California, or the Chinese temple in San Francisco. Twain changed "Portughee" to "Portuguese" and "Brown" to "Blucher" (the name used in Letter 2). The book mentions the muleteers' "singing 'John Brown's Body' in ruinous English," but does not quote any of it. In the book Twain says it was early on the morning of June 21 that they first sighted the Azores, but he was probably misled by an entry in his journal beginning thus: "June 21st, Azores. Daylight. Arrived at the port of Horta" (*Mark Twain's Notebook*, New York and London, Harper and Brothers, 1935, p. 61). Probably June 21 was the date of the entry, not of the arrival. The same entry mentions the ten-mile ride by jackass and the dinner for eight. Moreover, a brief letter which he wrote his mother from Fayal was dated June 20 (*Mark Twain's Letters*, I, 129).

2. Adventures in Horta

At Sea, June 23, 1867.

We had a pleasant ten days' run from New-York to the Azores Islands—not a fast run—for the distance is only 2,400 miles straight east

—but an exceedingly pleasant one. We had balmy Summer weather, and the nights were even finer than the days. We had the phenomenon of a full moon located just in the same spot in the heavens at the same hour every night. The reason of this singular conduct on the part of the moon did not occur to me at first, but it did afterward when I reflected that we were gaining about twenty minutes every day because we were going east so fast—we gained just about enough every day to keep along with the moon—it was becoming an old moon to the friends we left behind us, but to us Joshuas it stood still in the same place, and remained always the same.

Young Wm. Blucher, who is from the far West, and is on his first voyage, was a good deal bothered by the constantly changing "ship-time." He was proud of his new watch at first, and used to haul it out promptly when eight bells struck at noon, but he came to look after a while as if he were losing confidence in it. Seven days out from New-York he came to me, and said with great decision:

"Thish-yer's a swindle!"

"What is a swindle?"

"Why, this watch. I bought her out in Illinois—give $150 for her—and I thought she was good. And, by George, she is good on shore, but somehow she don't keep up her tick here on the water—gets sea-sick, may be. She skips, she runs along regular enough till half-past eleven, and then, all of a sudden, she lets down. I've set that old regulator up faster and faster, till I've shoved it clear around, but it don't do any good; she just cleans out every watch in the ship, and clatters along in a way that's astonishing till it is noon, but then them eight bells always gets in about ten minutes ahead of her anyway. I don't know what to do with her now. She's doing all she can—she's going her best gait, but it won't save her. I'll bet there ain't a watch in the ship that's making better time than she is, but what does it signify? When you hear them eight bells you'll find her just about ten minutes short of her score, sure." The ship was gaining a full hour every three days, and that fellow was trying to make his watch go fast enough to keep up with her. But as he had said, he had shoved the regulator up as far as it would go, and the watch was on its best gait, and so nothing was left him but to fold his hands and see the ship beat the race. I sent him to the captain, and he explained to him the mystery of "ship-time," and set his troubled mind at rest. This is the young man who asked so many questions about sea-sickness before we left, and wanted to know what its characteristics were, and how he was to tell when he had it. He found out.

We saw the usual sharks, blackfish, porpoises, &c., and large schools of Portuguese men-of-war were added to the regular list of sea wonders. Some of them were white and some of a brilliant carmine color. The nautilus is nothing but a transparent web of jelly, that spreads itself to catch the wind, and has fleshy-looking strings a foot or two long dangling from it to keep it steady in the water. The nautilus is an accomplished sailor, and has good sailor judgment. It reefs its sail when a storm threatens or the wind blows pretty strong, and furls it entirely and goes down when a gale blows. Ordinarily it keeps its sail wet and in good sailing order by turning over and dipping it in the water for a moment. Seamen say the nautilus is only found in these waters between the 35th and 45th parallels of latitude, and one of them told Blucher that when the rare pink or carmine ones showed themselves to a ship when she was on the 40th parallel that ship was doomed to disaster, and would go down in some far ocean solitude and never be heard of more. The fact that we were just on the 40th parallel gave the story a vital interest for Blucher, and made him unhappy till the new wonder of a flying fish that darted on board and was captured drew his mind from it.

At 3 o'clock on the morning of the 10th [19th] of June, we were awakened and notified that the Azores Islands were in sight. I had only been in bed an hour and a half, and did not take any interest in islands. But another persecutor came, and then another and another, and finally, believing that the general enthusiasm would permit no one to slumber in peace, I got up and went sleepily on deck. It was 5½ o'clock, and a raw, blustering morning. The passengers were huddled about the smoke-stacks and fortified behind ventilators, and all were wrapped in wintry costumes, and looking sleepy and unhappy in the pitiless gale and the drenching spray. The island in sight was Flores. It seemed only a mountain of mud standing up out of the dull mists of the sea. But as we bore down upon it, the sun came out and made it a beautiful picture. It was a mass of green farms and meadows that swelled up to a h[e]ight of 1,500 feet, and mingled its upper outlines with the clouds. It was ribbed with sharp, steep ridges, and cloven with narrow canyons, and here and there on the h[e]ights, rocky upheavals shaped themselves into mimic battlements and castles, and out of rifted clouds came broad shafts of sunlight, that painted summit, and slope, and glen with bands of fire, and left belts of somber shade between. The aurora borealis of the frozen pale [pole] exiled to a Summer land. We skirted around two-thirds of the island, four miles from shore, and all the opera-glasses in the ship were called into requisition to settle disputes as to whether mossy spots on the uplands were groves of trees or groves of weeds, or whether the white villages down by the sea were really villages or only the clustering tombstones of cemeteries. Finally, we stood to sea and bore away for San Miguel, and Flores shortly became a dome of mud again, and sank down among the mists and disappeared. But to many a sea-sick passenger it was good to see the green hills again, and all were more cheerful after this episode than anybody could have expected them to be, considering how sinfully early they had gotten up.

But we had to change our notions about San Miguel, for a storm came up, toward noon, that so pitched and tossed the vessel that common sense dictated a run for shelter. Therefore we steered for the nearest island of the group—Fayal (the people there pronounced it Fy-all, and put the accent on the first syllable.) We anchored in the open roadstead of Horta, half a mile from the shore. The town has 8,000 to 10,000 inhabitants. Its snow-white houses nestle cosily in a sea of fresh green vegetation, and no village could look prettier or more attractive. It sits in the lap of an amphitheater of hills which are from 300 to 700 feet high, and carefully cultivated clear to their summits—not a foot of soil left idle. Every farm and every acre is cut up into little square inclosures by stone walls, whose duty it is to protect the growing products from the destructive gales that blow there. These hundreds of green squares, marked by their black lava walls, make the hills look like vast checker-boards.

The islands belonged to Portugal, and everything in Fayal has Portug[u]ese characteristics about it. But more of that anon. A swarm of swarthy, noisy, lying, shoulder-shrugging, gesticulating Portug[u]ese boatmen, with brass rings in their ears, and fraud in their hearts, climbed the ship's sides, and various parties of us contracted with them to take us ashore at 25 cents a head—silver coin of any country. We landed under the walls of a little fort, armed with batteries of 12 and 32 pounders, which Horta considers a most formidable institution, but if we were ever to get after it with one of our turreted monitors they would have to move it out in the country if they wanted it where they could go and find it again when they needed it. The group on the pier was a rusty one—men and women, and boys and girls, all ragged, and barefooted, and uncombed, and dirty, and by instinct, education, and profession, beggars. They trooped after us, and never more, while we tarried in Fayal, did we get rid of them. We walked up the middle of the principal street, and these vermin surrounded us on all sides, and glared upon us; and every moment excited couples shot ahead of the gang to get a good look back, just as village boys do when they accompany the elephant on his advertising trip from street to street. It was very flattering for me to be part of the material for such a sensation. Presently an old woman, with a fashionable Portuguese hood on, approached me. This hood is of thick blue cloth, attached to a cloak of the same stuff, and is a marvel of ugliness. It stands up high, and spreads far abroad, and is unfathomably deep. It fits like a circus tent, and a woman's head is hidden away in it like the man's who prompts the singers from his tin shed in the stage of an opera. There is no particle of trimming about this monstrous *capote*, as they call it—it is just a plain, ugly, dead-blue mass of sail, and a woman can't go within eight points of the wind with one of them on; she has got to go before the wind or not at all. The general style of the capote is the same in all the islands, and will remain so for the next 10,000 years, but each island shapes its capotes just enough differently from the others to enable an observer to tell at a glance what particular island a lady hails from. Well, as we came along we overhauled a bent, wrinkled, and unspeakably homely old hag, with her capote standing high aloft. She was becalmed. Or rather, she was laying-to, around a corner, waiting for the wind to change. When she saw me she drifted out and held out her hand. Such friendliness in a strange land touched me, and I seized it. I shook it cordially, and said.

"Madame, I do not know your name, but this act has graven your —your—peculiar features upon my heart, and there they shall remain while that heart continues to throb."

She drew her hand away and said something which I could not understand, and then kissed her palm to me and curtsied. I blushed and said:

"Madame, these attentions cannot but be flattering to me, but it must not be—alas, it cannot be—I am another's!" (I had to lie a little, because I was getting into a close place.)

She kissed her hand again and murmured sweet words of affection, but I was firm. I said:

"Away, woman—tempt me not! Your seductive blandishments are wasted upon one whose heart is far hence in the bright land of America. The jewel is gone—you behold here naught save the empty casket—and empty it shall remain till grim necessity drives me to fill the aching void with vile flesh, and drink, and cabbage. Avaunt, temptress!"

But she would not avaunt. She kissed her hand repeatedly and curtsied over and over again. I reasoned within myself, This unhappy woman loves me: I cannot reciprocate; I cannot love a foreigner; I cannot love a foreigner as homely as she is—if I could, I would dig her out of that capote and take her to my sheltering arms. I cannot love her, but this wildly beautiful affection she has conceived for me must not go unrewarded—it *shall* not go unrewarded. And so I said, "I will read to her my poetic paraphrase of the Declaration of Independence."

But all the crowd said, "No—shame, shame, shame!—the poor old woman hasn't done anything!"

And they gave the old hag some Portuguese pennies like shuffle-board blocks, and hustled her away, averring that she was begging, and not making love, and thus, by the well-meaning stupidity of my comrades I was prevented from implanting a sweet memory in the soul of one who may now go down to the grave with no sacred thing upon the altar of her heart but the ashes of a hopeless passion—and yet a stanza or two would have made her so happy!

Speaking of those prodigious Portuguese pennies reminds me that it takes 1,000 *reis* (pronounced rays,) to make a dollar, and that all financial estimates are made out in reis. We did not know this until after we had found it out, and we found it out through Blucher. Blucher said he was so happy and so grateful to be on solid land once more, that he wanted to give a feast—said he had heard it was a cheap land, and he was bound to have a grand banquet. He invited nine of us, and we ate an excellent dinner at the principal hotel. In the midst of the jollity produced by good cigars, good wine, and passable anecdotes, the landlord presented his bill. Blucher glanced at it and his countenance fell. He took another look to assure himself that his senses had not deceived him, and then read the items aloud, in a faltering voice, while the roses in his cheek turned to ashes:

" 'Ten dinners, at 600 reis, 6,000 reis!' Ruin and desolation!"

" 'Twenty-five cigars at 100 reis, 2,500 reis!' Oh my sainted mother!"

" 'Eleven bottles of wine at 1,200 reis, 13,200 reis.' Be with us all! 'Total, 21,700 reis!' Great Caesar's ghost, there ain't money enough in the ship to pay that bill! Go—leave me to my misery, boys, I'm a ruined community." I think it was the blankest looking party I ever saw. Nobody could say a word. It was as if every soul had suddenly been stricken dumb. Wine-glasses descended slowly to the table, their contents untasted. Cigars dropped unnoted from nerveless fingers. Each man sought his neighbor's eye, but found in it no ray of hope, no encouragement. At last the fearful silence was broken. The shadow of a desperate resolve settled down upon Blucher's countenance like a cloud, and he rose up and said: "Landlord, this is a wretched, mean swindle, and I'll never, never stand it. Here's $150, Sir, and it's all you'll get—I'll swim in blood, Sir, before I'll pay a cent more!"

Our spirits rose and the landlord's fell—at least we thought so; he was confused at any rate, notwithstanding he had not understood a word that had been said. He glanced from the little pile of gold pieces to Blucher several times, and then went out. He must have visited an American, for, when he returned, he brought back his bill translated into a language that a Christian could understand—thus:

10 dinners, 6,000 reis, or	$ 6.00
25 cigars, 2,500 reis, or	2.50
11 bottles wine, 13,200 reis, or	13.20
Total, 21,700 reis, or	$21.70

Happiness reigned once more in Blucher's dinner party. More refreshments were ordered.

I think the Azores must be very little known in America. Out of our whole ship's company there was not a solitary individual who knew anything whatever about them. Some of the party, well read concerning most other lands, had no other information about the Azores than that they were a group of nine or ten small islands far out in the Atlantic, something more than half-way between New-York and Gibraltar. That was all. These considerations move me to put in a paragraph of dry facts, just here, which I might not venture to if I were writing about worn-out and written-out Europe.

The community is eminently Portuguese—that is to say, it is slow, poor, shiftless, sleepy and lazy. There is a civil government appointed by the King of Portugal, and a military governor, who can assume supreme control and suspend the civil government at his pleasure. The islands contain a population of about 200,000, almost entirely Portuguese. Everything is staid and settled, for the country was 100 years old when Columbus discovered America. The principal crop is corn, and they raise it and grind it just as their great-great-great-grandfathers did. They plow with a board slightly shod with iron; their trifling little harrows are drawn by men and women; small wind-mills grind the corn, ten bushels a day, and there is one assistant superintendent to feed the mill and a general superintendent to stand by and keep him from going to sleep. When the wind changes they hitch on some donkeys, and actually turn around the whole upper half of the mill till the sails are in proper position, instead of fixing the concern so that the sails could be moved instead of the mill. Oxen tread the wheat from the ear, after the fashion prevalent in the time of Methuselah. There is not a wheel-barrow in the land—they carry everything on their heads, or on donkeys, or in a wicker-bodied cart, whose wheels are solid blocks of wood and whose axles turn with the wheel. There is not a modern plow in the Islands, or a threshing machine. All attempts to introduce them have failed. The good Catholic Portughee crossed himself and prayed God to shield him from all blasphemous desire to know more than his father did before him. The climate is mild; they never have snow or ice, and I saw no chimneys in the town. The donkeys and the men, women and children of a family, all eat and sleep in the same room, and are unclean, are ravaged by vermin, and are truly happy. The people lie, and cheat the stranger, and are desperately ignorant, and have hardly any reverence for their dead. That latter trait shows how little better they are than the donkeys they eat and sleep [with]. The only well-dressed Portuguese in the camp are the three or four well-to-do families, the Jesuit priests and the soldiers of the little garrison. The wages of a laborer are 20 to 24 cents a day, and those of a good mechanic about twice as much. They count it in reis at a thousand to the dollar, and this makes them rich and contented. Fine grapes used to grow in the islands, and an excellent wine was made and exported. But a disease killed all the vines 15 years ago, and since that time no wine has been made. The islands being wholly of volcanic origin, the soil is necessarily very rich. Nearly every foot of ground is under cultivation, and two or three crops a year of each article are produced, but nothing is exported save a few oranges—chiefly to England.

The mountains on some of the islands are very high. We sailed along the shore of the Island of Pico, under a stately green pyramid that rose up with one unbroken sweep from our very feet to an altitude of 7,613 feet, and thrust its summit above the white clouds like an island adrift in a fog!

We got plenty of fresh oranges, lemons, figs, apricots, &c., in these Azores, of course. But I will desist. I am not here to write Patent-Office reports.

We are on our way to Gibraltar, and will reach there five or six days out from the Azores.

This letter was printed in the *New York Tribune* on July 30, 1867. Nearly all of it was used in the book (Volume I, Chapters V and VI), with little change. There are a few slight revisions and additions, and at one point a long passage from Letter 1 was inserted. The only important omission is the episode concerning the beggar woman, who is not mentioned in the book, although the women's hoods are described in much the same language.

3. Gibraltar

Gibraltar, June 30th.

All hands were called on deck at ten o'clock this morning by the news that land was in sight. Within the hour we were fairly within the Strait of Gibraltar, with the tall yellow-splatched [-splotched] hills of Africa on our right, with their bases vailed [veiled] in a blue haze and their summits swathed in clouds—the same being according to Scripture, which says that "clouds and darkness are over the land." The words were spoken of this particular portion of Africa, I believe. On our left were the granite-ribbed domes of old Spain. The Strait is only thirteen miles wide in its narrowest part.

At short intervals, along the Spanish shore, were quaint-looking old stone towers—Moorish, we thought—but learned better afterwards. In former times the Morocco rascals used to coast along the Spanish Main in their boats till a safe opportunity seemed to present itself, and then dart in and capture a Spanish village, and carry off all the pretty women they could find. It was a pleasant business, and was very popular. The Spaniards built these watch-towers on the hills to enable them to keep a sharper lookout on the Moroccan speculators.

It was a bright, breezy morning, and the picture on either hand was very beautiful to eyes weary of the changeless sea. The ship's company were uncommonly cheerful. But while we stood admiring the cloud-capped peaks and the lowlands robed in misty gloom, a finer picture burst upon us and chained every eye like a magnet—a stately ship, with canvas piled on canvas till she was one towering mass of bellying sail! She came speeding over the sea like a great bird. Africa and Spain were forgotten. All homage was for the beautiful stranger. While everybody gazed, she swept grandly by and flung the Stars and Stripes to the breeze! Quicker than thought, hats and handkerchiefs flashed in the air, and a cheer went up! She was beautiful before—she was radiant now. Many a one on our decks knew then for the first time how tame a sight his country's flag is at home compared to what it is in a foreign land. To see it is to see a vision of home itself and all its idols, and feel a thrill that would stir a river of sluggish blood.

The Pillars of Hercules

We were approaching the famed Pillars of Hercules, and already the African one, "Ape's Hill," a grand old mountain with summit streaked with granite ledges, was in sight. The other, the great Rock of Gibraltar, was yet to come. The ancients considered the Pillars of Hercules the head of navigation and the end of the world. The information the ancients didn't have, was very voluminous. Think of the Children of Israel poking around in the desert forty years instead of cutting across; think of Peter trying to walk on the water when he had never practiced; think of Joseph getting his brothers into his power after they had treated him so shabbily and then not hanging them a little. The ancients didn't know much. Even the prophets wrote book after book and epistle after epistle, yet never once hinted at the existence of a great continent on our side of the water, yet they must have known it was there, I should think. They knew beforehand what was going to happen, and surely they ought to have known what already existed. But no, they left the ancient public to believe that the Pillars of Hercules was the head of navigation, and Columbus was the first practical prophet to come out and tell them any better.

The Rock of Gibraltar

In a few moments a lonely and enormous mass of rock, standing seemingly in the centre of the wide strait and apparently washed on all sides by the sea, swung magnificently into view, and we needed no tedious travelled parrot to tell us it was Gibraltar. There could not be two rocks like that in one kingdom.

The Rock of Gibraltar is about a mile and a half long, I should say, by 1,400 to 1,500 feet high—is a quarter of a mile wide at its base. One side and one end of it come about as straight up out of the sea as the side of a house, the other end is irregular and the other side is a steep slant which would be very hard for an army to climb. At the foot of this slant is the walled town of Gibraltar—or rather the town occupies part of the slant. Everywhere—on hillside, in precipice, by the sea, on the heights,—everywhere you choose to look, Gibraltar is clad with masonry and bristling with guns. It makes a striking and lively picture, howsoever you look at it. It is shoved out into the sea on the end of a flat, narrow strip of land, and is suggestive of a "gob" of mud on the end of a shingle. A few hundred yards of this flat ground at its base belongs to the English, and then, extending across the strip from the Atlantic to the Mediterranean, a distance of a quarter of a mile, comes the "Neutral Ground," a space two or three hundred yards wide, which is free to both parties.

Tiresome Repetition

"Are you going through Spain to Paris?" That question was bandied about the ship day and night from Fayal to Gibraltar, and I thought I never could get so tired of hearing any one combination of words again, or more tired of answering, "I don't know." At the last moment six or seven made up their minds to go, and did go, and I felt a sense of relief at once—nobody could ask me the worn-out old question any more. But behold how annoyances repeat themselves. We had no sooner gotten rid of that Spain nuisance than the Gibraltar guides started another: "That high hill yonder is called the Queen's Chair; it is because one of the Queens of Spain placed her chair there when the French and Spanish troops were besieging Gibraltar, and said she would never move from the spot till the English flag was lowered from the fortresses. If the English hadn't been gallant enough to lower the flag for a few hours one day, she'd have had to break her oath or die up there."

We rode on asses and mules up the steep, narrow streets and entered the subterranean galleries the English have blasted out in the rock. These galleries are like spacious railway tunnels, and at short intervals in them great guns frown out upon sea and town through portholes five or six hundred feet above the ocean. There is a mile or so of this subterranean work, and it must have cost a vast deal of money and labor. The gallery guns commanded the peninsula and the harbors of both oceans, but they might as well not be there, I should think, for an army could not climb the perpendicular wall of the rock anyhow. Those lofty portholes afford superb views of the sea, though. At one place, where a jutting crag was hollowed out into a great chamber, whose furniture was huge cannon and whose windows were portholes, a glimpse of the Queen's Chair, and the inevitable old story was repeated and respectfully submitted to.

On the topmost pinnacle of Gibraltar we halted a good while, and no doubt the mules were tired. They had a right to be. The military road was good, but rather steep, and there was a good deal of it. The view from the narrow ledge was magnificent; from it ships that looked like the tiniest little toy-boats were turned into noble ships by the telescopes, and other ships that were fifty miles away, and even sixty, they said, and invisible to the naked eye, could be clearly distinguished through those same telescopes. Below, on one side, we looked down upon an endless mass of batteries, and on the other straight down into the sea. The Queen's chair was near at hand, and we heard the old story over again.

Geologic Theories

Gibraltar has stood several protracted sieges, one of them of nearly four years duration (it failed), and the English only captured it by stratagem. The wonder is that anybody should ever dream of trying so impossible a project as taking it by assault—and yet it has been tried more than once.

The Moors held the place twelve hundred years ago, and a staunch old castle of theirs of that date still frowns from the middle of the town, with moss-grown battlements and sides well scarred by shots fired in battles and sieges that are forgotten now. A secret chamber, in the rock behind it, was discovered some time ago, which contained a sword of exquisite workmanship, and some quaint old armor of a fashion that antiquaries are not acquainted with, though it is supposed to be Roman. Roman armor and Roman relics, of various kinds, have been found in a cave in the sea extremity of Gibraltar; history says Rome held this part of the country about the Christian era, and these things seem to confirm the statement.

In that cave, also, are found human bones, crusted with a very thick, stony coating, and wise men have ventured to say that those men not only lived before the flood, but as much as ten thousand years before it. It may be true—it looks reasonable enough—but as long as those fellows can't vote any more the matter can be of no great public interest. In this cave, likewise, are found skeletons and fossils of animals that exist in every part of Africa, yet within memory and tradition have never existed in any portion of Spain save this lone peak of Gibraltar! So the theory is that the channel between Gibraltar and Africa was once dry land, and that the low, neutral neck between Gibraltar and the Spanish hills behind it was once ocean, and of course that these African animals, being over at Gibraltar (after rock, perhaps—there is plenty there), got closed out when the great change occurred. The hills in Africa, across the channel, are full of apes, and there are now, and always have been, apes on the rock of Gibraltar—but not elsewhere in Spain! The subject is an interesting one.

Personnel of Gibraltar

There is an English garrison at Gibraltar of 6,000 or 7,000 men, and so uniforms of flaming red are plenty; and red and blue, and undress costumes of snowy white, and also the queer uniform of the bare-kneed Highlander; and one sees soft-eyed Spanish girls from San Roque, and veiled Moorish beauties (I suppose they are beauties) from Tarifa, and turbaned, sashed and trowsered [trousered] Moorish merchants from Fez, and long-robed, bare-legged, ragged Mohammedan devils from Petouan [Tetuán] and Tangier, some brown, some yellow and some as black as virgin ink—and Jews from all around, in gaberdine, skull cap and slippers, just as they are in pictures and theatres, and just as they were three thousand years ago, no doubt. You can easily understand that a crowd like ours, made up from fifteen or sixteen States of the Union, found enough to stare at in this shifting panorama of fashion to-day. They were constantly exclaiming, "How like Mr. Forrest's Othello that big turbaned, wide-trowsered black African is!—and the long-bearded Jew yonder, in his full robe, looks like all the Shylocks I ever saw!" I was so busy looking that I hardly ever asked any questions. Occasionally my conscience smote me, but I quieted it with the reflection that I had taken pains to give Brown the strictest instructions to ask questions and find out everything—to pry into all matters that presented themselves and leave nothing undiscovered that could be of lively interest to the public of the Pacific coast.

One or Two of Our Own Party

We have got one or two people in our party who are an eternal annoyance to everybody. I do not count the Oracle in that list. I will explain that the Oracle is an innocent old ass, who doesn't know enough to come in when it rains, but who eats for four, and is vulgar, and smells bad, and looks wiser than the whole Academy of France would have any right to look, and never uses a one-syllable word when he can "go two better," and never by any possible chance knows the meaning of any long word he uses, or ever gets it in the right place. Yet who will serenely venture an opinion on the most abstruse subject, and back it up complacently with quotations from authors who never existed, and finally when cornered will slide to the other side of the question, say he has been there all the time, and come back at you with your own spoken arguments, only with the big words all tangled, and play them in your very teeth as original with himself. He reads a chapter in the guide-books, mixes the facts all up, with his miserable memory, and then goes off to inflict the whole thing on somebody as stuff which has been festering in his brain for years, and which he gathered at college from erudite authors who are dead, now, and out of print. This morning at breakfast he pointed out the window and said:

"Do you see that there hill out there on that African coast?—it's one of them Pillows of Herkewls, I should say—and there's the ultimate one alongside of it."

"The ultimate one—that is a good word—but the Pillars are not both on the same side of the strait." (I saw he had been fooled by a carelessly-written sentence in the Guide Book.)

"Well, it ain't for you to say, nor for me. Some authors states it that way, and some states it different. Old Gibbons don't say nothing about it—just shirks it complete—Gibbons always done that when he got stuck—but there is Rolampton, what does *he* say? Why he says that they was both on the same side, and Trinculian, and Sobaster, and Syracus, and Langomarganbl—"

"Oh, that will do—that's enough. If you have got your hand in for inventing authors and testimony, I have got nothing more to say—let them *be* on the same side."

We don't mind the Oracle. We rather like him. Brown says Solomon was a fool to him. We can tolerate the Oracle very easily; but we have got a poet and a born ass on board, and they *do* worry the company. The one gives copies of his execrable verses to Consuls, commanders, hotel keepers, Arabs, Dutch, anybody and everybody, and passes himself off as the acknowledged successor of the late lamented Lord Byron! His poetry is all very well on shipboard, notwithstanding when he wrote an "Ode to the Ocean in a Storm" in one half hour, and an "Apostrophe to the Rŏoster in the Waist of the Ship" in the next, the transaction [transition] was considered to be rather abrupt; but when he sends a mess of rhymes to the Governor of Fayal and others in Gibraltar, with the compliments of the Laureate of the Ship, it is not popular with the passengers.

The other personage I have mentioned is young and green, and not bright, not learned and not wise. He will be, though, some day, if he recollects the answers to all his questions. He is known about the ship as the "Interrogation Point," and this by constant use has become shortened to "Interrogation." He has distinguished himself twice already. In Fayal they pointed out a hill and told him it was eight hundred feet high and eleven hundred feet long. And they told him there was a tunnel two thousand feet long and one thousand feet high running through the hill, from end to end. He believed it. He told it, discussed it, and read it from his notes. Brown said: "Well, yes, it *is* a little remarkable—curious tunnel altogether—stands up out of the top of the hill about two hundred feet, and one end of it sticks out of the hill about nine hundred!"

Here in Gibraltar he grabs these educated British officers and deluges them with buncombe braggadocio about America and the wonders she can perform. He told one of them a couple of our gunboats could come here and knock Gibraltar into the Mediterranean Sea! And he rode a mule all day and then was not forthcoming when the driver of it (the creature they called a "scorpion") came for his money. And he dickered and fussed over a few cents in a bargain with a poor devil Arab for some fruit in front of the hotel, in the presence of an audience of many nations, till some of the passengers snatched him away and threatened to hang him.

Such are two of our passengers—the rest will pass muster in Europe and elsewhere, never fear.

Mark Twain.

Mr. Brown's Report

Mr. Brown has exhausted Gibraltar and handed in his report. It is comprehensive. Its substance is to the effect that all nations of the earth are represented in its population, and an English shilling buys four drinks.

M. T.

This letter, numbered two by Twain, appeared in the *Daily Alta California* on August 27, 1867. In the book Twain revised the first sentence of this letter slightly, inserted other information to fill up a paragraph, and began the next paragraph with the second sentence of this letter. The rest of the letter follows, with revisions and interpolations here and there. He omitted the references to the forty years' wandering in the desert, Peter's walking on the water, and Joseph's mild treatment of his brothers. He omitted the last two sentences concerning the prophets' failure to inform their readers about the lands beyond the Pillars of Hercules. His revisions are usually improvements of diction. For instance, he changed "howsoever you look at it" to "from whatsoever point you contemplate it." In the book he used shorter paragraphs than in the letters, to make the reading easier. By repetition, he made the legend about the Queen's Chair more tiresome. He omitted the references to Othello and Shylock as well as the instruction to Brown to ask questions and find out everything. He softened a little the characterizations of the Oracle, the poet, and the Interrogation Point, the last becoming "a good-natured, enterprising idiot" rather than "a born ass," and he omitted the Interrogation's squabbles with the muleteer and the fruit vendor.

4. Tangier

Tangier, Africa, July 1st.

This is jolly! This is altogether the infernalest place I have ever come across yet. Let those who went up through Spain make much of it—these dominions of the Emperor of Morocco suit me well enough. We have had enough of Spain at Gibraltar for the present. Tangier is the spot we have been longing for all the time. Everywhere else one finds foreign-looking things and foreign-looking people, but always with things and people intermixed that we were familiar with before, and so the novelty of the situation lost a deal of its force. We wanted something thoroughly and uncompromisingly foreign—foreign from top to bottom—foreign from centre to circumference—foreign inside and outside and all around—nothing anywhere about it to dilute its foreignness—nothing to remind us of any other people or any other land under the sun. And lo! in Tangier we have found it. Here is not the slightest thing that ever we have seen save in pictures—and we always mistrusted the pictures before. We cannot any more. The pictures used to seem lies—they seemed too wierd [weird] and fanciful for reality. But behold, they were not wild enough—they were not fanciful enough—they have not told half the story. Tangier is a foreign land if ever there was one. And the true spirit of it can never be found in any book save the Arabian Nights. Here are no white men visible, yet swarms of humanity are all about me. Here is a packed and jammed city enclosed in a massive stone wall which is more than a thousand years old. All the houses nearly are one and two-story; made of thick walls of stone; plastered outside; square as a dry-goods box; flat as a floor on top; no cornices; whitewashed all over—a crowded city of snowy tombs! And the doors are arched with the peculiar arch we see in Moorish pictures; the floors are laid in vari-colored diamond-flags; in tasselated many-colored porcelain squares wrought in the furnaces of Fez; in red tiles and broad bricks that time cannot wear; there is no furniture in the rooms (of Jewish dwellings) save divans—what there is in Moorish ones no man may know; within their sacred walls no Christian dog can enter. And the streets are oriental—some of them three feet wide, some six, but only two that are over a dozen; a man can blockade the most of them by extending his body across them. Isn't it an oriental picture?

There are stalwart Bedouins of the desert here, and stately Moors, proud of a history that goes back to the night of time; and Jews, whose fathers fled hither centuries upon centuries ago; and swarthy Riffians from the mountains—born cutthroats—and original, genuine negroes, as black as Moses; and howling dervishes, and a hundred breeds of Arabs—all sorts and descriptions of people that are foreign and curious to look upon.

And their dresses are strange beyond all description. Here is a bronzed Moor in a prodigious white turban, curiously-embroidered jacket, gold and crimson sash, of many folds, wrapped round and round his waist, trowsers that only come a little below his knee, and yet have twenty yards of stuff in them, ornamented scimetar [scimitar], bare shins, bare feet, yellow slippers, and gun of preposterous length—a mere soldier—I thought he was the Emperor at least. And here are aged Moors with flowing white beards, and long white robes with vast cowls; and Bedouins with long, cowled, striped cloaks, and negroes and Riffians with heads clean-shaven, except a kinky scalp-lock back of the ear, or rather up on the after corner of the skull, and all sorts of barbarians in all sorts of wierd costumes, and all more or less ragged. And here are Moorish women who are enveloped from head to foot in coarse white robes, and whose sex can only be determined by the fact that they only leave one eye visible, and who never look at men of their own race, or are looked at by them in public. Here are five thousand Jews in blue gaberdines, sashes about their waists, slippers upon their feet, little skull-caps upon the backs of their heads, hair combed down on the forehead, and cut straight across the middle of it from side to side—the selfsame fashion their Tangier ancestors have worn for a thousand years. Their feet and ankles are bare. Their noses are all hooked, and hooked alike. They all resemble each other so much that one could almost believe they were of one family. Their women are plump and pretty, and do smile upon a Christian in a way which is in the last degree comforting.

A Cradle of Antiquity

What a funny old town it is! It seems like profanation to laugh, and jest, and bandy the frivolous chat of our day amid its hoary relics. Only the stately phraseology and the measured speech of the sons of the prophet are suited to a venerable antiquity like this. Here is a crumbling wall that was old when Columbus discovered America; was old when Peter the Hermit roused the knightly men of the Middle Ages to arm for the first Crusade; was old when Charlemagne and his paladins beleaguered enchanted castles and battled with giants and genii in the fabled days of the olden time; was old when Christ and his disciples walked the earth; stood where it stands to-day when the lips of Memnon were not silent, and men bought and sold in the streets of ancient Thebes!

The Phœnicians, the Carthagenians, the English, Moors, Romans, all have battled for Tangier—all have won it and lost it. Here is a ragged, Oriental-looking negro from some desert place in interior Africa, filling his goat-skin with water to sell in these streets from a ruined and battered fountain built by the Romans twelve hundred years ago. Yonder is a ruined arch of a bridge built by Julius Cæsar nineteen hundred years ago. Men who have seen the infant Savior in the Virgin's arms have stood upon it, may be.

Near it are the ruins of a dock-yard where Cæsar repaired his ships and loaded them with grain when he invaded Britain, fifty years before the Christian Era.

Here, under the quiet stars these old streets seem thronged with the phantoms of forgotten ages. My eyes are resting upon a spot where stood a monument which was seen and described by Roman historians less than two thousand years ago, whereon was inscribed:

"WE ARE THE CAANANITES. WE ARE THEY THAT HAVE BEEN DRIVEN OUT OF THE LAND OF CAANAN BY THE JEWISH ROBBER, JOSHUA."

Joshua drove them out and they came here. Not many leagues from here is a tribe of Jews whose ancestors fled thither after an unsuccessful revolt against King David, and these their descendants are still under a ban and keep to themselves.

Tangier has been mentioned in history for 3,000 years. And it was a town, though a queer one, when Hercules, clad in his lion-skin, landed here 4,000 years ago. In these streets he met Anitus, the King of the country, and caved his head in with his club. The people of Tangier (called Tingis, then,) lived in the rudest possible huts, and dressed in skins and carried clubs, and were as savage as the wild beasts they were constantly obliged to war with. But they were a gentlemanly race, and did no work. They lived on the natural products of the land. Their King's country residence was at the famous Garden of Hesperides, seventy miles down the coast from here. The garden with its golden apples (oranges) is gone, now—no vestige of it remains. Antiquarians concede that such a personage as Hercules did exist in ancient times, and agree that he was an enterprising and energetic man, but decline to believe him a good square out-and-out God.

Down here at Cape Spartel is the celebrated cave of Hercules, where that hero took refuge when he was vanquished and driven out of the Tangier country. It is full of inscriptions in the dead languages, which fact makes me think Hercules could not have travelled much, else he would not have kept a journal.

Five days' journey from here—say 200 miles—are the ruins of an ancient city, of whose history there is neither record nor tradition. And yet its arches, its columns and its statues proclaim it to have been built by an enlightened race.

Concerning Finance, etc.

The general size of a store in Tangier is about that of an ordinary shower-bath in a civilized land. The Mohammedan merchant, tinman, shoemaker, or vendor of trifles, sits cross-legged on the floor, and reaches after any article you may want to buy. You can rent a whole block of these pigeon-holes for fifty dollars a month. The market people crowd the market place with their baskets of figs, dates, melons, apricots, etc., and among them file trains of laden jackasses, not much larger, if any, than a Newfoundland dog. The scene is lively, is picturesque, and smells like the San Francisco Police Court. The Jewish money-changers have their dens close at hand, and all day long are counting bronze coins and transferring them from one bushel basket to another. They don't coin much money nowadays, I think. I saw none but what was dated four or five hundred years back, and was badly worn and battered. These coins are not very valuable. Brown went out to get a Napoleon changed, so as to have money suited to the general cheapness of things, and came back and said he had "cleaned out the bank; had bought eleven gallons of coin, and the head of the firm had gone on the street to negotiate for the balance of the change." I bought nearly half a pint of their money for a shilling myself.

The Moors have some small silver coins, and also some silver slugs worth a dollar each. The latter are exceedingly scarce—so much so that when poor ragged Arabs see one they beg to be allowed to kiss it.

They have also a small gold coin worth two dollars. And that reminds me of something. When Morocco is in a state of war, Arab couriers carry letters through the country and charge a liberal postage. Every now and then they fall into the hands of marauding bands and get robbed. Therefore, warned by experience, as soon as they have collected two dollars' worth of money, they exchange it for one of those little gold pieces, and when robbers come upon them, swallow it. The dodge was good while it was unsuspected, but after that the marauders simply gave the courier a dose of physic and sat down to wait.

Riches Have Their Little Drawbacks

The Emperor of Morocco is a soulless despot, and the great officers under him are despots on a smaller scale. There is no regular system of taxation, but when the Emperor or the Bashaw want money they levy on some rich man and he has to furnish the cash or go to prison. So, few men in Morocco dare to be rich. It is too dangerous a luxury. Vanity occasionally leads a man to display wealth, but sooner or later the Emperor trumps up a charge against him—any sort of one will do—and confiscates his property. Of course, there are many rich men in the Empire, but their money is buried and they dress in rags and counterfeit poverty. Every now and then the Emperor imprisons a man who is suspected of the crime of being rich, and makes things so uncomfortable for him that he is forced to discover where he has hidden his money.

Moors and Jews sometimes place themselves under the protection of the foreign Consuls, and then they can flout their riches in the Emperor's face with impunity.

This letter, numbered three by Twain, appeared in the *Daily Alta California* on August 31, 1867. With a few revisions, omissions, and interpolations, it was used as a chapter in the book (Volume I, Chapter VIII). In the first sentence, for instance, "jolly" became "royal," and the harsh second sentence was omitted. Farther down, "lies" became "exaggerations"; "smells like the San Francisco Police Court" became "smells like a police court"; "Brown" became "Jack"; "gallons of coin" became "quarts of coin"; "dodge" became "stratagem"; and "discover" became "disclose."

5. The Ways of the Moors

Tangier, Africa, July 1st, 1867.

About the first pass we made yesterday afternoon after landing here, came near passing in Mr. Brown's checks. We had just mounted some mules and asses, and started out under the guardianship of the stately, the princely, the magnificent Hadji Mohammed Lamarty, (may his tribe increase!) when we came upon a fine Moorish Mosque, with tall tower, rich with checker work of many-colored porcelain, and every part and portion of the edifice adorned with the quaint architecture of the Alhambra, and Brown started to ride into the open doorway. A startling "Hi-hi!" from our rusty camp-followers and a loud "Halt!" from an English gentleman in the party, checked the adventurer, and then we were informed that so dire a profanation is it for a Christian dog to set foot upon the sacred threshold of a Moorish mosque that no amount of purification can ever make it fit for the faithful to pray in again. Had Brown succeeded in entering the place he would no doubt have been chased through the town and stoned, and the time has been, and not many years ago either, when a Christian would have been ruthlessly slaughtered if captured in a mosque. We caught a glimpse of the handsome tesselated pavements within, and of the devotees performing their ablutions at the fountains, but even to take that glimpse was not relished by the Moorish bystanders.

Some years ago the clock in the tower of the mosque got out of order. The Moors of Tangier have so degenerated that it has been long since there was an artificer among them capable of curing so delicate a patient as a debilitated clock. The great men of the city met in solemn conclave to consider how the difficulty was to be met. They discussed the matter thoroughly, but arrived at no solution. Finally, a patriarch arose and said:

"Oh, children of the Prophet, it is known unto you that a Portughee dog of a Christian clock-mender pollutes the city of Tangier with his presence. Ye know, also, that when mosques are builded, asses bear the stones and the cement and cross the sacred threshold. Now, therefore, send the Christian dog on all fours and barefoot into the holy place to mend the clock, and let him go as an ass!"

And in that way it was done. Therefore if Brown ever sees the inside of a mosque he will have to cast aside his humanity and go in his natural character.

Moorish Customs

We visited the jail, and found Moorish prisoners making mats and baskets. This thing of utilizing crime savors of civilization. Murder is punished with death. A short time ago three murderers were taken beyond the city walls and shot. Moorish guns are not good and neither are Moorish marksmen. In this instance they set up the poor criminals at long range, like so many targets, and practiced on them—kept them hopping about and dodging bullets for half an hour before they managed to drive the centre.

When a man steals cattle, they cut off his right hand and left leg, and nail them up in the market-place, as a warning to everybody. Their surgery is not artistic. They slice around the bone a little, then break off the limb. Sometimes the patient gets well; but, as a general thing, he don't. But the Moorish heart is stout. The Moors were always brave. These criminals undergo the fearful operation without a wince, without a tremor of any kind, without a groan! No amount of suffering can bring down the pride of a Moor, or make him shame his dignity with a cry.

Here, marriage is contracted by the parents of the parties to it. There are no valentines, no stolen interviews, no riding out, no courting in dim parlors, no lovers' quarrels and reconciliations—no nothing that is proper to approaching matrimony. The young man takes the girl his father selects for him, marries her, and after that she is unveiled and he sees her for the first time. If after due acquaintance she suits him, he retains her; but if he suspects her purity he bundles her back to her father; if he finds her diseased, the same; or if, after just and reasonable time is allowed her, she neglects to bear children, back she goes to the home of her childhood.

Mohammedans here, who can afford it, keep a good many wives on hand. They are called wives, though I believe the Koran only allows four genuine wives—the rest are concubines. The Emperor of Morocco don't know how many wives he has got, but thinks he has five hundred. However, that is near enough—a dozen or so, one way or the other, don't matter.

Even the Jews in the interior have a plurality of wives.

I have caught a glimpse of the faces of several Moorish women (for they are only human, and will expose their faces for the admiration of a Christian dog when no he-Moor is by,) and I am full of veneration for the wisdom that leads them to cover up such atrocious ugliness. If I had a wife as ugly as some of those I have seen, I would go over her face with a nail-grab and see if I couldn't improve it.

They carry their children at their backs, in a sack, like other savages the world over.

Many of the negroes are held in slavery by the Moors. But the moment a female slave becomes her master's concubine her bonds are broken, and as soon as a male slave can read the first chapter of the Koran (which contains the creed) he can no longer be held in bondage. It would be a good idea to apply this educational test to his race in America.

They have three Sundays a week in Tangier. The Mohammedan's comes on Friday, the Jew's on Saturday, and that of the Christian Consuls on Sunday. The Jews are the most radical. The Moor goes to his mosque about noon on his Sabbath, as on any other day, removes his shoes at the door, performs his ablutions, makes his salaams, pressing his forehead to the pavement time and again, says his prayers and goes back to his work.

But the Jew shuts up shop; will not touch copper or bronze money at all; soils his fingers with nothing meaner than silver and gold; attends the Synagogue devoutly; will not cook or have anything to do with fire; and religiously refrains from embarking in any enterprise.

Now these fellows worship just as Moses did; their habits and customs are just as they were in Biblical times; they dress as they dressed in the buried and forgotten generations of the past—all of which is to say that they are an inconceivably rusty-looking set now and consequently must have been in the days of the Old Testament—and how they ever came to be the chosen people of the Lord is a mystery which will stagger me from this day forth till I perish.

The Moor who had made a pilgrimage to Mecca is entitled to high distinction. Men call him Hadji and he is thenceforward a great personage. Hundreds of Moors come to Tangier every year and embark for Mecca. They go part of the way in English steamers, and the ten or twelve dollars they pay for passage is about all the trip costs. They take with them a quantity of food, and when they run out they skirmish. From the time they leave till they get home again they never wash, either on land or sea. They are usually gone from five to seven months, and as they do not change their clothes during all that time, they are totally unfit for the drawing-room when they get back.

Many of them have to rake and scrape a long time to gather together the ten dollars their steamer passage costs, and when one of them gets back he is a bankrupt community forever after. Few Moors can ever build up their fortunes again in one short life-time, after so reckless an outlay. In order to confine the dignity of Hadji to gentlemen of patrician blood and possessions, the Emperor decreed that no man should make the pilgrimage save bloated aristocrats who were worth a hundred dollars in specie. But behold how iniquity can circumvent the law! For a consideration the Jewish money-changer lends the pilgrim $100 long enough for him to swear himself through, and then receives it back before the ship sails out of the harbor!

Spain and the Moors

Spain is the only nation the Moors fear. The reason is, that Spain sends her heaviest ships-of-war and her loudest guns to astonish these Moslems, while America and other nations send only a little contemptible trap of a gun-boat occasionally. The Moors, like other savages, learn by what they see—not what they hear or read. We have got great fleets in the Mediterranean, but they seldom touch at African ports. The Moors have a small opinion of England, France and America, and put their representatives to a deal of red-tape circumlocution before they grant them their common rights, let alone a favor. But the moment the Spanish Minister makes a demand, it is acceded to at once, whether it be just or not.

Spain threshed the Moors five or six years ago about a disputed piece of property opposite Gibraltar, and captured the city of Tetouan [Tetuán]. She compromised on an augmentation of her territory, $20,000,000 indemnity, in money, and peace. And then she gave up the city. But she never gave it up until the Spanish soldiers had eaten up all the cats. They would not compromise as long as the cats held out. Spaniards are very fond of cats. On the contrary, the Moors reverence cats as something sacred. So the Spaniards touched them on a tender point that time. Their unfeline conduct in eating up all the Tetouan cats aroused a hatred toward them in the breasts of the Moors to which even the driving them out of Spain was tame and passionless. Moors and Spaniards are foes forever now. France had a Minister here once who embittered the nation against him in the most innocent way. He killed a couple of battalions of cats (Tangier is full of them), and made a parlor-carpet out of their hides. He made his carpet in circles—first a circle of old grey tomcats, with their tails all pointing toward the centre; then a circle of yellow cats; next a circle of black cats and a circle of white ones; then a circle of all sorts of cats, and finally a centrepiece of assorted kittens. It was very beautiful, but the Moors curse his memory to this day.

Adieu

I find I cannot write up my notes, and so I will stop. When we went to call on our American Consul General, Mr. McMath, to-day, I noticed that all possible games for parlor amusement seemed to be represented on his centre-tables. I thought that hinted at lonesomeness. The notion was correct. His is the only American family in Tangier. There are many foreign Consuls in the place, but much visiting is not indulged in. Tangier is clear out of the world, and what is the use of visiting when people have nothing on earth to talk about? There is none. So each Consul's family stays at home chiefly and amuses itself as best it can. Tangier is full of interest for one day, but after that it is a weary prison. Mr. McMath has been here five years, and has got enough, and is going home shortly. His family seize upon their letters and papers when the mail arrives, read them over and over again for two days or three, talk them over and over again for two or three more till they wear them out, and after that, for days together, they eat and drink and sleep, and ride out over the same old road, and see the same old tiresome things that even decades of centuries have scarcely changed, and say never a single word! They have literally nothing whatever to talk about. The arrival of an American man-of-war is a God-send to them. "Oh, Solitude, where are the charms that sages have seen in thy face?" It is the completest exile I can conceive of. I would seriously recommend to the Government of the United States that when a man commits a crime so heinous that the law provides no adequate punishment for it, they make him Consul General to Tangier.

I am glad to have seen Tangier, the second oldest town in the world. But I am ready to bid it good-bye, I believe.

A Familiar Name

Looking over the register of the Royal Victoria Hotel a while ago, I came across the name of J. C. L. Wadsworth, of San Francisco, under date of April 27th. How came he to wander to this out-of-the-way place?

I forgot to say that the population of Tangier is about 20,000. Of these, 14,000 are Moors, Arabs and Bedouins; 5,000 are Jews; and 1,000 are Christians of many nations.

This letter, numbered four by Twain, appeared in the *Daily Alta California* on September 1, 1867. It was also used as a chapter in the book (Volume I, Chapter IX), but Twain tried to improve the diction: "the first pass we made" became "the first adventure we had"; "came near passing in Mr. Brown's checks" became "came near finishing that heedless Blucher"; "rusty camp-followers" became "camp followers"; "to take that glimpse" became "that we took that glimpse"; "he has got" became "he has"; "he-Moor" became "male Moor"; "when they run out they skirmish" became "when the commissary department fails they 'shirmish,' as Jack terms it in his sinful, slangy way"; "a bankrupt community" became "a bankrupt"; "trap of a gun-boat" became "tub of a gunboat"; "we have got" became "we have"; "threshed the Moors" became "chastised the Moors"; and "has got enough" became "has got enough of it to do him for a century." "He don't" and "the Emperor of Morocco don't" survive in the book. Twain omitted from the book the statement about what he would do if he had an ugly wife, the suggestion about educational tests for Negroes in the United States, the paragraph about Jews in Bible times, and the postscript of the letter. The book mentions the American consul general but does not give his name. I quote from a letter to me from the American consul general at Tangier, Mr. C. Vaughan Ferguson, Jr., under date of July 20, 1956: "From an old list of principal officers at this port . . . it appears that Jessie H. McNath (not McMath), of Cadiz, Ohio, was in charge of the office at Tangier from 1862 to 1869."

6. Versailles and Paris

Paris, July 12th, 1867

It is wonderfully beautiful! You gaze, and stare, and try to understand that it is real, that it is on the earth, that it is not the Garden of Eden—but your brain grows giddy, stupefied by the world of beauty around you, and you half believe you are the dupe of an exquisite dream. If I live a thousand years, I shall never see anything half so lovely. A noble palace, stretching its ornamented front block upon block away, till it seemed that it would never end; a grand promenade before it, whereon the armies of an empire might parade; all about it rainbows of flowers, and colossal statues that were almost numberless, and yet seemed only scattered over the ample space; broad flights of stone steps leading down from the promenade to lower grounds of the park—stairways that whole regiments might stand to arms upon and have room to spare; vast fountains whose great bronze effigies discharged rivers of sparkling water into the air and mingled a hundred curving jets together in forms of matchless beauty; wide grass-carpeted avenues that branched hither and thither in every direction and wandered to seemingly interminable distances, walled all the way on either side with compact ranks of leafy trees whose branches met above and formed arches as faultless and as symmetrical as ever were carved in stone; and here and there were glimpses of sylvan lakes with miniature ships glassed in their surfaces—and everywhere—on the palace steps, and the great promenade, around the fountains, among the trees, and far under the arches of the endless avenues—hundreds and hundreds of people in gay costumes walked or ran or danced, and gave to the fairy picture the life and animation which was all of perfection it could have lacked.

It was worth a pilgrimage to see. Everything is on so grand a scale. Nothing is small—nothing is cheap. The statues are all large; the promenade is vast; the palace is grand; the park covers a fair-sized county; the avenues are interminable. All the distances and all the dimensions about Versailles are vast. I used to think the pictures exaggerated these distances and these dimensions beyond all reason, and that they made Versailles more beautiful than it was possible for any place in the world to be. I know now that the pictures never came up to the subject in any respect, and that no painter could represent Versailles on canvas as beautiful as it is in reality. I used to abuse Louis XIV for spending two hundred millions of dollars in creating this marvelous park, when bread was so scarce with some of his subjects; but I have forgiven him now. He took a tract of land sixty miles in circumference and set to work to make this park and build this palace and a road to it from Paris. He kept 36,000 men employed daily on it, and the work was so unhealthy that they used to die and be hauled off by cart-loads every night. The wife of a nobleman of the time speaks of this as an "*inconvenience*," but naively remarks that "it does not seem worthy of attention in the happy state of tranquility we now enjoy."

I could not help thinking ill of people at home, who trimmed their shrubbery into pyramids, and squares, and spires, and all manner of unnatural shapes, and when I saw the same thing being practiced in this great Park I began to feel angry. But I soon saw the idea of the thing and the wisdom of it. They are after the general effect. We distort a dozen sickly trees into unaccustomed shapes in a little yard no bigger than a dining-room, and Heaven knows they look absurd enough. But here they take two hundred thousand tall forest trees and set them in a double row; allow no sign of leaf or branch to grow on the trunk lower down than six feet from the ground; from that point the boughs begin to project, and very gradually they extend outward further and further till they meet overhead, and a faultless tunnel of foliage is formed. The arch is mathematically precise. The effect is then very fine. They make trees take fifty different shapes, and so these quaint effects are infinitely varied and picturesque. The trees in no two avenues are shaped alike, and consequently the eye is not fatigued with anything in the nature of monotonous uniformity. I will drop this subject now, leaving it to others to cipher out how these people manage to make endless ranks of lofty forest trees grow to just a certain thickness of trunk (say a foot and two-thirds); how they make them grow to precisely the same height for miles; how they make them grow so close together; how they compel one huge limb to spring from the same identical spot on each tree and form the main sweep of the arch; and how all these things are kept just precisely in the same condition, and in the same exquisite shapeliness and symmetry month after month and year after—for I have tried to reason out the problem, and have failed.

I loitered through the great hall of sculpture and the one hundred and fifty galleries of paintings in the palace of Versailles, and felt that to be in such a place was useless unless one had a whole year at his disposal. I loitered, also, through the Grand Trianon and the Petit Trianon, those monuments of royal prodigality, and with histories so mournful—full of souvenirs of Napoleon the First, and three Kings and as many Queens. In one gorgeous bed they had all slept in succession, but no one occupies it now. In a large dining-room stood the table at which Louis XIV and his mistress, Madame Maintenon, and after them Louis XV, and Pompadour, had sat at their meals, naked and unattended—for the table stood upon a trap-door, which descended with it to regions below when it was necessary to replenish its dishes. In a room of the Petit Trianon stood the furniture, just as poor Marie Antoinette left it when the mob came and dragged her and the King to Paris, never to return. Near at hand, in the stables, were prodigious carriages that showed no color but gold—carriages used by former Kings of France on state occasions, and never used now save when a kingly head is to be crowned, or an imperial infant christened. And with them were some quaint sleighs, whose bodies were shaped like lions, swans, tigers, etc.—vehicles that had once been splendid with paint and fine workmanship, but were dusty and decaying now. They had their history. When Louis XIV had finished the Grand Trianon, he told Maintenon he had created a Paradise for her, and asked if she could think of anything now to wish for. He said he wished the Trianon to be perfection—nothing less. She said she could think of but one thing—it was summer, and it was balmy France—yet she would like well to sleigh-ride in the leafy avenues of Versailles! The next morning found miles and miles of grassy avenues spread thick with snowy salt and sugar, and a procession of those quaint sleighs waiting to receive the boss concubine of the gayest and most unprincipled court that France has ever seen!

The Contrast

From Imperial Versailles, with its palaces, its statues, its gardens and its fountains, I journeyed back to Paris and sought its antipodes—the Faubourg St. Antoine. Little, narrow streets; dirty children blockading them; greasy, slovenly women capturing and spanking them; filthy dens on first floors, with rag stores in them (the heaviest business in the Faubourg is the Chiffonier's;) other filthy dens where whole suits of second and third-hand clothing are sold at prices that would ruin any proprietor who did not steal his stock; still other filthy dens where they sold groceries—sold them by the halfpenny-worth—five dollars would buy the man out, good-will and all. Up these little crooked streets they will murder a man for seven dollars and dump the body in the Seine. I saw one of their customers at the Morgue—a man who had been stabbed and then thrown into the river—a horrid looking corpse exposed there to be claimed, but nobody would be likely to want it perhaps. And up some other of these streets—most of them, I should say—live lorettes.

All through this Faubourg St. Antoine, misery, poverty, vice and crime go hand in hand, and the evidences of it stare one in the face from every side. Here the people live who start the revolutions. Whenever there is anything of that kind to be done, they are always in. They take as much genuine pleasure in building a barricade as they do in cutting a throat or shoving a friend into the Seine. It is these savage-looking ruffians who storm the splendid halls of the Tuileries, occasionally, and swarm into Versailles when a King is to be called to account.

A Lost Opportunity

I never can have any luck. Something goes wrong every time a chance offers. We were driving in the Bois de Boulogne yesterday, along with some thirty thousand other parties, when a great body of gold-plastered men came dashing along on handsome horses, and the Frenchmen began to say *Vive l'Empereur,* gently. We stopped, and his Imperial Majesty Napoleon III, and his Serene Highness Abdul Azis, the Sultan of the Ottoman Empire, passed within six feet of us, and very properly took off their hats. Here was a chance for world-wide notoriety, and, with my usual infernal luck, I had left my derringer at home.

The Emperor Napoleon looks vastly older than his portraits, and has a keen, cunning, scheming look out of his almost closed eyes, that one does not find in the pictures, I believe. In his own proper person he looks a great, a very great man, but you know his pictures make him almost a nobody. That he is the greatest man in the world to-day, I suppose there is no question. Bismarck may be shrewder in some things, but there his greatness stops, while there is no element of true greatness which Napoleon does not possess. He has augmented the commercial prosperity of France, in ten years, to such a degree that figures can hardly compute it. He has rebuilt Paris, and has partly rebuilt every city in the State, and at no expense to commonwealth or city. But above all things, he has taken the sole control of the Empire of France into his hands, and made it the freest country in the world —perhaps—for people who will not attempt to go too far in meddling with government affairs. No country offers greater security to life and property than France does, and one has all the freedom he wants, but no license—no license to interfere with anybody, or make any one uncomfortable.

As for the Sultan, he is a very dark and a very common looking moustached and whiskered Mahommedan. I could set a trap anywhere and catch a dozen abler men in a night.

French Cars

French cars hold eight persons—four face four. They have no sleeping cars. At first, with your own party with you, you rather like them; but when you reflect that very disagreeable people might get in sometimes, and that you could never be permitted to change your car, and when you also recollect that there are no water-closets on the train and no place where you can get a drink, you soon begin to think less of them. There are plenty of water-closets at the stations, with signs on them, and this made trouble for Brown. He came to me and complained that there was a remarkable similarity between the names painted on all the French railway stations. Poor devil, he had them all down in his note-book: "*Cote des Hommes.*"

This letter, numbered five by Twain, appeared in the *Daily Alta California* on September 5, 1867. The information about French cars at the end of the letter was used in the book (Volume I, Chapter XII), but completely rewritten—and the reference to Brown's mistake was omitted.

The section on Versailles was followed closely in the book (Volume I, Chapter XVI). "The scene thrills one like military music!" was substituted for "If I live a thousand years, I shall never see anything half so lovely." Twain changed "I began to feel angry" to "I began to feel dissatisfied"; "Heaven knows they look absurd enough" to "then surely they look absurd enough"; "leaving it to others to cipher out" to "leaving it to others to determine"; "gorgeous bed" to "sumptuous bed"; "splendid with paint" to "handsome with pictured designs"; and "boss concubine" to "chief concubine." He inserted a passage about pictures of battle scenes and French victories which he had seen in the palace of Versailles.

The passage about the Faubourg St. Antoine follows immediately. The reference to the morgue was omitted, but in Chapter XIV he had given a detailed account of his visit to the morgue. The description of Napoleon III and Abdul Aziz was used at the end of Chapter XIII, but was almost completely rewritten. These rulers are also briefly mentioned near the end of Chapter XIV—and Napoleon III is mentioned a third time at the end of Chapter XVI. In the book Twain ridiculed Abdul Aziz much more vigorously than in the letter, and although he still admired Napoleon III for his abilities and his achievements, he stressed his cunning and no longer considered him the world's greatest man.

7. Genoa

Genoa, Italy, July 16th, 1867.

I WANT TO CAMP HERE. I had rather not go any further. There may be prettier women elsewhere, but I doubt it. They certainly cannot be so plenty anywhere else. The population of Genoa is 120,000: two-thirds of these are women, I think, and at least two-thirds of the women are beautiful. They are as dressy, and as tasteful and as graceful as they could possibly be without being angels. However, angels are not very dressy, I believe. At least the angels in pictures are not—they wear nothing but wings. But these Genoese women do look so charming. Most of the young demoiselles are robed in a cloud of white from head to foot, though many trick themselves out more elaborately. Nine-tenths of them wear nothing on their heads but a filmy sort of veil, which falls down their backs like a white mist. They are very fair, and many of them have blue eyes, but black and dreamy dark brown ones are met with oftenest.

The ladies and gentlemen of Genoa have a pleasant fashion of prowling around a large Park on the top of a hill in the centre of the city, from six till nine in the evening, and then eating ices in a neighboring garden an hour or two longer. We went to the Park on Sunday evening. Two thousand persons were present, chiefly young ladies and gentlemen. The gentlemen were dressed in the very latest Paris fashions, and the robes of the ladies glinted among the trees like so many snowflakes. The multitude moved round and round the Park in a great procession. The bands played, and so did the fountains; the moon and the gas lamps lit up the scene, and altogether it was a brilliant and an animated picture. I scanned every female face that passed, and it seemed to me that all were beautiful. I never saw such a perfect freshet of loveliness before. To be a belle in Genoa, a lady would have to be superhumanly beautiful. I do not see how a man of only ordinary decision of character could marry here, because, you know, before he could get his mind made up he would fall in love with somebody else. I fell in love with a hundred and eighty women myself, on Sunday evening, and yet I am not of a susceptible nature. Still, I would like to camp here. Brigham ought to come to Genoa. If he could only come here for one day, he would discharge those eighty-five miraculously ugly women who vegetate in his harem now. One of those girls I saw in the Park I can never forget. She was very beautiful, and she had a cold in the head. She blew her nose continually, and the more she blew it the more lovely she seemed to me. I would ask no other happiness on this earth could I always be with that girl and see her blow her nose. I followed her about the Park for an hour, trying to summon courage enough, but I could not do it. I wanted to ask her to let me blow her nose for her once. Only just once. If I could have blown her nose only just one time, I could have been contented and cheerful all the days of my life. But I was too modest. Modesty has always kept me down in the world, and always will, I suppose.

But speaking of fashion reminds me that one can see more real fashion, among gentlemen and ladies both, in one day in Genoa, than he can in three in Paris. I suppose there are fashionable people in Paris, but if they ever come on the street it must be in close[d] carriages.

Stub-Hunters

Never smoke any Italian tobacco. Never do it on any account. It makes me shudder to think what it must be made of. You cannot throw an old cigar "stub" down anywhere, but some seedy rascal will pounce upon it on the instant. I like to smoke a good deal, but it wounds my sensibilities to see one of these stub-hunters watching me out of the corners of his hungry eyes and calculating how long my cigar is going to last. It reminded me, too, painfully of that San Francisco undertaker who used to go to sick-beds with his watch in his hand and time the corpse. One of these infamous stub-hunters followed us all over the Park last night, and we never got a smoke that was worth a cent. We were always moved to appease him with the stub before the cigar was half gone, because he looked so viciously anxious. He regarded us as his own legitimate prey, by right of discovery, I think, because he drove off several other professionals who wanted to take stock in us.

Now, they must chew up those old stubs, and dry and sell them for smoking tobacco. Therefore, give your custom to other than Italian brands of the article.

Genoa, "The Superb"

"The Superb" and the "City of Palaces" are names which Genoa has held for centuries. She is full of palaces, certainly, and the palaces are sumptuous inside, but they are very rusty without, and make no pretensions to architectural magnificence. "Genoa, the Superb," must surely refer to the women.

We have visited several of the palaces—immense thick-walled piles, with great stone staircases, tesselated marble pavements on the floors, (sometimes they make a mosaic work, of intricate designs, wrought in pebbles, or little fragments of marble laid in cement), and grand saloons, hung with pictures by Rubens, Guido, Titian, Paul Veronese, and so on, and portraits of heads of the family, in plumed helmets and gallant coats of mail, and patrician ladies, in stunning costumes of centuries ago. But, of course, the folks were all out in the country for the summer, and might not have known enough to ask us to dinner if they had been at home, and so all the grand empty saloons, with their resounding pavements, their grim pictures of dead ancestors, and tattered banners with the dust of bygone centuries upon them, seemed to brood solemnly of death and the grave, and our spirits ebbed away, and our cheerfulness passed from us. We never went up to the eleventh story. We always began to suspect ghosts. There was always an undertaker-looking villain of a servant along, too, who handed us a programme, pointed to the picture that began the list of the saloon he was in, and then stood stiff and stark and unsmiling in his petrified livery till we were ready to move on to the next chamber, and then he marched sadly ahead and took up another malignantly respectful position as before. I took up so much time praying that the roof would fall in on these dispiriting flunkeys that I never had any left to bestow upon palace and pictures.

And besides, as in Paris, we had a guide. Perdition catch all the guides. This scoundrel said he was the most gifted linguist in Genoa, as far as English was concerned, and that only two persons in the city beside himself could talk the language at all. He showed us the birth-place of Christopher Columbus, and after we had reflected in silent awe before this inspiring shrine for fifteen minutes, he said it was not the birthplace of Columbus, but of Columbus's grandmother! When we demanded an explanation of his wretched conduct he only shrugged his shoulders and answered in barbarous Italian. He showed us three manuscript letters written by Columbus (they are kept in a marble pillar in the municipal palace under triple lock), and when I asked him if Columbus wrote them himself, he said "Oh, no." I said, "Then who the devil did write them?" and he said he didn't know.

I began to suspect that this fellow's English was shaky, and I thought I would test the matter. He showed us a fine bust of Columbus on a pedestal, and I said, "Is this the first time this person, this Columbus, was ever on a bust?" and he innocently answered, "Oh, no." I began to think, then, that when he didn't understand a question, he just answered, "Oh, no," at a risk and took the chances. So I said, "This Columbus you talk so much about—is he dead?" And the villain said quietly, "Oh, no!" I tested him further. I said, "This palace of the Dorias which you say is so old—is it fifty years old?" "Oh, no." "Is it five hundred?" "Oh, no." "It's a thousand, though, ain't it?" "Oh, yes." So his plan was to answer, "Oh, no," twice, always, and then, "Oh, yes," by way of a change. All the information we got out of that guide we shall be able to carry along with us, I think.

Church Magnificence

I haven't been to church so often in a century as I have in the last few weeks. The people in the old lands seem to make churches their best hold. Especially does this seem to be the case with the citizens of Genoa. I think there is a church every fifty yards all over town. The streets are sprinkled from end to end with shovel-hatted, long-robed, well-fed old priests, and the church bells by dozens are pealing all the day long, nearly. Every now and then one comes across a friar of orders gray, with shaven head, long, coarse robe, rope girdle and beads, and in sandals or entirely barefoot. These fellows suffer in the flesh, and do penance all their lives I suppose, but they look like consummate famine-breeders. They are all fat and greasy. They would try out well. The generality of them would yield oil like a whale.

The old Cathedral of San Lorenzo was about as notable a building as we have found to-day. It is vast, and has colonnades of noble pillars, and a great organ, and the customary pomp of gilded mouldings, pictures, frescoed ceilings, and so forth. I cannot describe it, of course—it would require a good many pages to do that. But it is a curious place. They said that half of it—from the front door half way down to the altar—was a Jewish Synagogue before the Savior was born, and that no alteration had been made in it since that time. I coppered the statement, but I did it reluctantly. I mentioned to the old church-guide that I doubted what he seemed so fully to believe, only because I couldn't help it—not because I wanted to. The place looked in too perfect repair to be so ancient. The main point of interest about the Cathedral is the little Chapel of St. John the Baptist. They only allow women to enter it on one day in the year, on account of the animosity they still cherish against the sex because of the murder of the Saint by Herodias. In this Chapel is a marble chest, in which, they told us, were the ashes of St. John; and around it was wound a chain, which, they said, had confined him when he was in prison. I did not desire to copper these statements, and yet I could not feel certain that they were correct—partly because I could have broken that chain, and so could St. John, and partly because I had seen St. John's ashes before, in another Church. I don't think St. John had two sets of ashes.

They also showed us a portrait of the Madonna which was painted by St. Luke, and it did not look half as old and rusty as some of the pictures by Rubens. I could not help admiring Luke's modesty in never once mentioning in his writings that he could paint. But isn't this relic business a little absurd? I find a piece of the true cross in every old church I go into, and some of the nails that held it together. I would not like to be positive, but I think I have seen as much as a keg of these nails. Then there is the crown of thorns; they have got one in Sainte Chapelle, in Paris, and I think they keep a couple in Notre Dame. And I have seen stacks of bones of St. Denis, enough to make four St. Denis's and have a bone or two to spare.

I started to write about the churches, but I keep shirking the subject. I could say that the Church of the Annunciation is a wilderness of beautiful columns, of statues, gilded mouldings, and pictures almost countless, but that would give no one an entirely perfect idea of the thing, and so where is the use? One family built the whole affair, and have got money left. There is where the mystery lies. I had an idea at first that a mint could not stand the expense.

How They Live

These people here live in the heaviest, highest, broadest, darkest, solidest houses one can imagine. Each one might "laugh a siege to scorn." Fifty feet front and a hundred high is about the style, and you go up three flights of stairs before you begin to come upon signs of occupancy. Everything is stone, and stone of the heaviest—floors, stairways, mantels, benches—everything. The walls are four to five feet thick. The streets generally are four or five to eight feet wide and as crooked as a corkscrew. You go along one of these gloomy cracks, and look up and behold the sky like a mere ribbon of light, far above your head, where the tops of the tall houses on either side of the street bend almost together. You feel as if you were at the bottom of some tremendous abyss, with all the world a mile above you. You wind in and out and here and there, in the most mysterious way, and have no more idea of the points of the compass than if you were a blind man. You can never persuade yourself that these are actually streets, and the frowning, dingy, monstrous houses dwellings, till you see one of these beautiful, exquisitely dressed women emerge from them—see her emerge from a dark, dreary-looking den that looks dungeon all over, from the ground away half-way up to heaven. And then you wonder that such a charming moth could come from such a forbidding shell as that. The streets are wisely made narrow and the houses heavy and thick and stony, in order that the people may be cool in this roasting climate. And they are cool, and stay so. And while I think of it—the men wear hats and have very dark complexions, but the women wear no head-gear but a flimsy veil like a gossamer's web, and yet are exceedingly fair as a general thing. Singular, isn't it?

The wonderful Pallavicini Garden is—but the mail is closing.

This letter, numbered six by Twain, appeared in the *Daily Alta California* on September 8, 1867. It was used, with many improvements in diction, in Chapter XVII. In the third sentence, "elsewhere" was changed to "Europe," and the fourth sentence was omitted—Twain had already said that the most beautiful women he had seen in Paris were American. The second half of the second paragraph was omitted (beginning with "I fell in love with a hundred and eighty women myself"), and the short third paragraph was omitted also.

In the passage on Italian tobacco, "seedy rascal" became "vagabond" and "infamous stub-hunters" lost the adjective. In the account of his visit to the palaces, "villain of a" was dropped from "undertaker-looking villain of a servant," and "I never had any left" was changed to "I had but little left."

In the account of the guide, "this scoundrel" and "his wretched conduct" became "this one" and "his conduct." Of the two paragraphs devoted to the guide, the last two sentences of the first and all of the second except the last sentence were omitted at this point, but Twain wrote: "I shall speak further of this guide in a future chapter." He kept his word many chapters later. The Columbus manuscript, bust, and pedestal and the question "Is he dead?" were utilized with great effect in his celebrated comment on European guides in Chapter XXVII. This is an excellent example of Twain's ability to build largely with few materials—and imagination.

The remainder of the letter follows (Volume I, Chapter XVII), but with a good many rephrasings. "I haven't been to church so often in a century" became "I have not been to church so often in a long time"; "their best hold" became "their specialty"; "every fifty yards" became "every three or four hundred yards"; "They are all fat and greasy" became "They are all fat and serene"; "I coppered the statement" became "I doubted the statement"; the following sentence became "We would much rather have believed it"; "the murder of the Saint by Herodias" became "the murder of the Saint to gratify a caprice of Herodias"; "old and rusty" became "old and smoky"; "enough to make four St. Denis's, and have a bone or two to spare" became "enough of them to duplicate him, if necessary"; "the whole affair" became "the whole edifice"; "a mile above you" became "far above you"; and "exquisitely dressed women" became "prettily dressed women." The "wonderful Pallavicini Garden" was described in a much later letter—one telling of travel in the Holy Land (Letter 44).

8. Milan

Milan, Italy, July, 1867.

What a wonder it is! So grand, so solemn, so vast! And yet so delicate, so airy, so graceful! A very world of solid weight, and yet it seems in the soft moonlight only a fairy delusion of frost-work that might vanish with a breath! How sharply its pinnacled angles and its wilderness of spires were cut against the sky, and how richly their shadows fell upon its snowy roof! It was a vision!—a miracle!—an anthem sung in stone, a poem wrought in marble!

Howsoever you look at the great Cathedral, it is noble, it is beautiful! Wherever you stand in Milan, or within seven miles of Milan, it is visible—and when it is visible, no other object can chain your whole attention. Leave your eyes unfettered by your will but a single instant and they will surely turn to seek it. It is the first thing you look for when you rise in the morning, and the last your lingering gaze rests upon at night. Surely, it must be the princeliest creation that ever brain of man conceived.

This morning at 9 o'clock we went and stood before this marble colossus. The central one of its five great doors is bordered with a bas-relief of birds and fruits and beasts and insects, which have been so exquisitely carved out of the marble that they seem like living creatures—and the figures are so numerous and the design so complex, that one might study it a week without exhausting its interest. On the great steeple—surmounting the myriad of spires—inside of the spires—over the doors, the windows—everywhere that a nook or a corner can be found about the enormous building, from roof to base, there is a marble statue, and every statue is a study in itself! Raphael, Angelo, Canova—giants like these gave birth to the designs, and their own pupils carved them. Every face is eloquent with expression, and every attitude is full of grace. Away above, on the lofty roof, rank on rank of carved and fretted spires spring high in the air, and through their rich tracery one sees the sky beyond. In their midst the central steeple towers proudly up like the mainmast of some great Indiaman among a fleet of coasters.

Within the church, long rows of fluted columns, like huge monuments, divided the building into broad aisles, and on the figured pavement fell many a soft blush from the painted windows above. I knew the church was very large, but I could not perceive its great size until I noticed that the men standing far down by the altar looked like half-grown boys, and seemed to glide, rather than walk.

We wanted to go aloft. The Sacristan showed us a marble stairway (of course it was marble, and of the purest and whitest—there is no other stone, and no brick, no wood, and no iron, among its building materials), and told us to go up 182 steps and stop till he came. It was not necessary to say stop—we should have done that anyhow. We were tired by the time we got there. This was the roof. Here, springing from its broad marble flagstones, were the long files of spires, looking very tall close at hand, but diminishing in the distance like the pipes of an organ. We could see, now, that the statue on the top of each was the size of a large man, though they all looked like dolls from the street. We could see, also, that from the inside of these hollow spires, from sixteen to thirty-one beautiful marble statues looked out upon the world below.

From the eaves to the comb of the roof stretched in endless succession great curved marble beams, like the fore-and-aft braces of a steamship, and along each beam from end to end stood up a row of richly carved flowers and fruits—each separate and distinct, and over 15,000 species represented. At a little distance these rows seem to close together like the ties of a railroad track, and then the mingling together of the buds and blossoms of this marble garden forms a picture that is exquisitely beautiful.

We climbed about two hundred and fifty steps higher, and stood not far below the gilded Madonna that keeps eternal watch and ward on the central steeple, and all Italy lay spread out before us! As far as the eye could reach were groves and gardens, highways and villages, and tiny white specks that stood for houses—and far below clustered the forest of pinnacles; and yet further down pigmy men and women moved busily about the streets, like processions of creeping insects. We were filled with the sublimity of the scene.

We then took a drink. The Sacristan—I think that is what they call him, though maybe it was Christian, for he had excellent beer—the Sacristan got out his bottles, and when we found we were not just quite exactly full of sublimity, we went to work and filled up with beer. And we kept on, you know, until the beer had rather the advantage of the sublimity. I did not mind that, though, because you can get sublimity at any great altitude, but you can't always get beer above the snow belt. But mixed liquors are bad, and mixed magnificence is worse. When you come to mix beer and sublimity it is bound to fetch you. It would have been too many for us but for a most fortunate circumstance. Some people came up into that steeple, and we judged it best to assist them down. Each one of us got between two of these parties and let them take hold of our arms, and then we helped them down. This kept our minds employed, and so the beer had no chance to affect us.

The Side-shows

I did intend to write about some other wonders connected with the Cathedral, but I have overheard Brown describing them to the chambermaid, (who does not understand English,) and have taken down his words in short-hand. I can give his account, and that will save trouble. I am only sorry his language is not more refined. He said:

"You understand, Susan, that this church used to be bossed by a gorgeous old brick that was an Archbishop—San Carlo Borromeo—he had rich parents, and they made him a saint. He has been dead nearly three hundred years, but they've dried him, and stowed him away in the hold of the church, and one of them priests took us down to see him for five francs. It's not part of the regular circus, you know, and so you have to pay extra, like it is when you go to see the foreigner swallow butcher-knives outside the menagerie. Well, this rooster lit a tall candle, like a broomstick, and convoyed us through the cellar till he got to a place the size of a single bed-room for a student that don't keep a trunk, which had a solid silver coffin in it as large as a bath-tub, and had a fresco all around the upper part of the walls made of solid silver, worth 2,000,000 francs, by weight, and representing deceased when he was born, and when he borrowed money and gave it to the poor, and when a highwayman tried to shoot him, but a miracle made the pistol hang fire, because the powder was wet, and how he was Marshal of the Day in a procession to stop the plague, but it didn't work—and I don't remember the others. And then this old sport lit some more candles and began to grind a crank in the end of the coffin like a hand-organ, and it all sunk away from the lid, and went down out of sight, and showed a pure crystal coffin, clearer than any glass, with the defendant inside of it. He was wrapped up, from his chin to his heels, in cloth made of gold, and covered all over with diamonds and such things, and you couldn't see anything of him but his head—and when I saw that, I just antied up and left."

And so I must finish the subject myself. The head was black with age, the dry skin was drawn tight to the bones, the eyes were gone, there was a hole in the temple and another in the cheek, and the skinny lips were parted as in a ghastly smile! Over this dreadful face, its dust and decay, and its mocking grin, hung a crown sown thick with splendid gems, and crosses and croziers that flamed with emeralds and diamonds, and the furniture of the narrow chambers of death weighed six millions of francs in ounces and carats alone, without a cent thrown into the account for the costly workmanship bestowed upon them. What a sermon was here upon poor human vanity!

As we came out upon the floor of the church again, another smiling, curtsying, long-robed priest besought us to take a chance in his little side-show for two and a half francs, and we followed him into a large room filled with tall wardrobes—at least so they looked. Three other smiling, bowing priests opened the doors of the wardrobes, and I never felt so out of funds in my life before. They had old bishops there, above their natural size, wrought in solid silver, each worth, by weight, from eight hundred thousand to two millions of francs, and bearing gemmed books in their hands worth eighty thousand; and bas-reliefs that weighed six hundred pounds, carved in solid silver; and croziers and crosses, and candlesticks six and eight feet high, all of virgin gold, and brilliant with precious stones; and besides these were all manner of cups and vases, and such things, rich in proportion. It was an Aladdin's palace. The treasures here, by simple weight, without counting workmanship, were valued at fifty millions of francs! If I could get the custody of them for a while, I would start a mint.

The priests showed us two of St. Paul's fingers, and one of St. Peter's; a bone of Judas Iscariot, (it was very black,) and also bones of all the other disciples; a handkerchief in which the Savior had left the impression of his face; and among the most precious of the relics were a stone from the Holy Sepulchre, part of the crown of thorns, (they have got a whole one at Notre Dame,) a fragment of the purple robe worn by the Savior, a nail from the Cross, and a picture of the Virgin and Child painted by the veritable hand of St. Luke. This is the second of St. Luke's Virgins I have seen (they have the other in Genoa), and so I begin to think he was an artist by profession. Once a year all these holy relics are paraded in a priestly procession through the streets of Milan.

A Few Details

I like to revel in the dryest details of the great cathedral. The building is 500 feet long by 180 wide, and the principal steeple is in the neighborhood of 400 feet high. It has 7,148 marble statues, and will have upwards of 3,000 more when it is finished. In addition, it has 1,500 bas-reliefs. It has 136 spires—21 more are to be added. Each spire is surmounted by a statue six and a half feet high. Everything about the church is marble, and all from the same quarry; it was bequeathed to the Archbishopric for this purpose centuries ago. So nothing but the mere workmanship costs; still that is expensive—the bill foots up six hundred and eighty-four millions of francs, thus far (considerably over a hundred millions of dollars), and it is estimated that it will take a hundred and twenty years yet to finish the cathedral. It looks complete, but is far from being so. We saw a new statue put in its niche yesterday alongside of one which had been standing there four hundred years. There are four staircases leading up to the main steeple, each of which cost a hundred thousand dollars, with the 408 statues which adorn them. Marco Campioni was the architect who designed the wonderful structure more than five hundred years ago, and it took him forty-sixty years to work out the plan and get it ready to hand over to the builders. He is dead now. The building was begun a little less than five hundred years ago, and the third generation hence will not see it completed.

That is all I wished to say, I believe, except that the vast windows which I called "painted," are not painted at all, but every one of the beautiful pictures is a mosaic, formed of countless fragments patiently and laboriously pieced together, and with such exquisite art that no oil painting could be more soft, or rich, or more delicately shaded or more beautiful. In some of the windows there are sixty-four of these pictures, and each of them is capable of feasting your eyes with pleasure for many a day.

They say this Cathedral is second to St. Peter's at Rome. I cannot understand how it can be second to anything made by human hands.

This letter, numbered seven by Twain, appeared in the *Daily Alta California* on September 15, 1867. It was used in Chapter XVIII. Omitted were the second half of the paragraph beginning "Within the church" (the first half was moved to a later position) and the paragraphs beginning "We climbed about two hundred and fifty steps higher" and "We then took a drink." The first four paragraphs under the heading

"The Side-Shows" were rewritten and mixed with other material. The remainder of the letter (except the second paragraph from the end)) was followed rather closely, but with some revisions.

9. Lake Como

Lake of Como, July, 1867.

I DID NOT LIKE it yesterday. I thought Lake Tahoe was much finer. I have to confess now, however, that I was too hasty. I always had an idea that Como was a vast basin of water, like Tahoe, shut in by great mountains. Well, the border of huge mountains is here, but the lake itself is not a basin. It is as crooked as the Sacramento River, and not much wider. There is not a yard of low ground on either side of it —nothing but endless chains of mountains that spring abruptly from the water's edge, and tower to altitudes varying from a thousand to two thousand feet. Their craggy sides are clothed with greenest vegetation, and white specks of houses peep out from the luxuriant foliage everywhere—even perched upon jutting and picturesque pinnacles a thousand feet above your head.

Again, for miles along the shores, handsome country seats, surrounded by gardens and groves, sit fairly in the water, sometimes in nooks carved by Nature out of the vine-hung precipices, and with no ingress or egress save by boats. Some have great broad stone staircases leading down to the water, with heavy stone balustrades ornamented with statuary and fancifully adorned with creeping vines and bright-colored flowers—for all the world like a drop-curtain in a theatre, and lacking nothing but long-waisted, high-heeled women and plumed gallants in silken tights coming down to go serenading in the splendid gondola in waiting.

A great feature of Como's attractiveness is the multitude of pretty houses and gardens that cluster upon its shores and on its mountain sides. They look so snug and so homelike, and at eventide when everything seems to slumber, and the music of the vesper bells comes stealing over the water, one half believes that nowhere else than on the Lake of Como can there be found such a paradise of peacefulness and repose.

From my window here in Bellaggio, I have a view of the other side of the lake now, which is as beautiful as a picture. A scarred and wrinkled precipice rises to a height of eighteen hundred feet; on a tiny bench half way up its vast wall, sits a little snow-flake of a church, no bigger than a marten-box, apparently; skirting the base of the cliff are a hundred orange groves and gardens, flecked with glimpses of the white dwellings that are buried in them; in front, three or four gondolas lie idle upon the water—and in the burnished mirror of the lake, mountain, chapel, houses, groves and boats are counterfeited so brightly and so clearly that one scarce knows where the reality leaves off and the reflection begins!

The surroundings of this picture are fine. A mile away, a grove-plumed promontory juts far into the lake and glasses its palace in the blue depths; in midstream a boat is cutting the shining surface and leaving a long track behind, like a ray of light; the mountains beyond are veiled in a dreamy purple haze that is unspeakably beautiful; far in the opposite direction a tumbled mass of domes and verdant slopes and valleys bars the lake, and here indeed does distance lend enchantment to the view—for on this broad canvas, sun and clouds and the richest of atmospheres have blended a thousand tints together, and over its surface the filmy lights and shadows drift, hour after hour, and glorify it with a beauty that seems reflected out of Heaven itself. Beyond all question, this is the richest, softest, dreamiest picture I have ever looked upon.

Last night the scenery was striking and picturesque. On the other side crags and trees, and snowy houses were pictured in the glassy lake with a wonderful distinctness, and streams of light from many a distant window shot far abroad over the still waters. On this side, near at hand, great white palaces, splendid with moonlight, glared out from the midst of dense masses of foliage, robed in the gloomiest of shadows, cast from the beetling cliff above—and down in the margin of the lake every feature of the weird picture was faithfully repeated.

Today we have idled through a wonder of a garden attached to a ducal estate—but enough of description is sufficient, I judge. I suspect it is the same place that the gardener's son roped in the Lady of Lyons with, but I do not know. You know the passage:

A deep vale,
Shut out by Alpine hills from the rude world,
Near a clear lake margined by fruits of gold
And whispering myrtles;
Glossing softest skies, cloudless,

Save with rare and roseate shadows;
A palace lifting to eternal heaven its marbled walls,
From out a glossy bower of coolest foliage musical with birds.

That is all very well, except the "clear" part of the lake. It certainly is clearer than a great many lakes, but how dull its waters are compared with the wonderful translucence of our Lake Tahoe! I speak of the north shore of Tahoe, where one can count the scales on a trout at a depth of a hundred and eighty feet. I have tried to get this statement off at par here, but with no success; so I have been obliged to negotiate it at fifty per cent. discount. At this rate I find some takers, perhaps you may as well receive it on the same terms—ninety feet instead of a hundred and eighty.

This lake is a little deeper than Tahoe, if people here tell the truth. They say it is eighteen hundred feet at this point, but it don't look a dead enough blue for that. Tahoe is 1,525 feet deep in the centre, by the State Geologist's measurement. They say the great peak opposite this town is 5,000 feet high; but I feel sure that three thousand feet of that statement is a good honest lie. The lake is a mile wide, here, and hence to its northern extremity—sixteen miles; hence to its southern extremity—fifteen miles—it is not over half a mile wide in any place, I should think—but it is excessively crooked and very picturesque. Its snow-clad mountains one hears so much about are only seen occasionally, and then, far in the distance, the Alps. Tahoe is ten to eighteen miles wide and its snow-clad peaks enclose it at all seasons like a wall.

I am losing faith in all our pet traditions. Both here and in Lyons I have inquired around and around for the Lady of Lyons, but never a rascally citizen has ever heard of her. I am satisfied now that she is a swindle. After a good deal of worry and tramping under a roasting Spanish sun, I managed to tree the Barber of Seville, and I was sorry for it afterwards. With all that fellow's reputation, he was the worst barber on earth. If I am not pleased with the Two Gentlemen of Verona when I get there next week, I shall not hunt for any more lions.

Speaking of barbers reminds me that in Europe they do not have any barber-shops. The barbers come to your room and skin you. (I use that term because it is more correctly descriptive than shave.) They have a few trifling barber-shops in Paris, but the heaviest establishment of the kind we could find only boasted three barbers. There, as everywhere else in Europe, as far as our experience goes, they put a bowl under your chin and slop your face with water, and then rub it with a cake of soap, (except at Gibraltar, where they spit on the soap and use no bowl, because it is handier;) then they begin to shave, and you begin to swear; if you have got a good head of profanity on, you see the infliction through; but if you run out of blasphemy, there is nothing for it but to shut down on the operation till you recuperate. The further I go, the worse the barbers get. Along, at first, it answered well enough to swear in English, but I do not think I could worry with another Italian shave unless I knew how to swear in seven different languages. My beard must grow now till I see America again.

I think they don't use soap, much, in these countries. They never put any in your room, and when you order it they put it in the bill. They don't even keep soap in the public bath-houses. This reminds me of Brown's note to the landlord in Paris. I thought it rather a gem of French composition:

Paris, le 7 Juillet.

Monsieur le Landlord—Sir: *Pourquoi* don't you *mettez* some *savon* in your dang bed-chambers? *Est-ce que vous pensez* I am going to steal it? *La nuit passée* you charged me *pour deux chandelles* when I only had one; *hier vous avez* charged me *avec glace* when I hadn't any at all; *tous les jours* you are coming some fresh game or other on me *mais* you *ne pouvez pas* play this *savon* dodge on me twice. *Savon* is a necessary *de la vie* to anybody but a Frenchman, *et je l'aurai hors de cet hôtel* or bust. You hear *me. Après cet avis, vous trouverez à votre intérêt* to go slow, anyways *sur le savon* question. *Allons,*

Brown.

I remonstrated against the sending of this note, because it was so mixed up that the landlord would never to be able to make head or tail out of it; but Brown said he guessed the old man could read the French of it and average the rest.

Brown's French is bad enough, but it isn't much worse than the English one finds in advertisements all over Italy every day. For instance, observe the pointed [printed] card of this hotel where we tarry at present:

This hotel which the best it is in Italy and most suberb, is handsome locate on the best situation of the lake, with the most splendid view near the Villas Melzy, to the

King of Belgian, and Serbelloni. This hotel have recently enlarged, do offer all commodities on moderate price, at the strangers gentlemen who whish spent the seasons on the Lake Como.

How is that, for a specimen? In the hotel is a handsome little chapel where an English clergyman is employed to preach to such of the guests of the house as hail from England and America, and this fact is also set forth in barbarous English in the same advertisement. Wouldn't you have supposed that the adventurous linguist who framed the card would have known enough to submit it to that clergyman before he sent it to the printer?

In Milan, an ancient tumble-down old ruin of a church, is the mournful wreck of the most celebrated painting in the world—"The Last Supper," by Leonardo da Vinci. We don't know any more about pictures than a kangaroo does about metaphysics, but of course we went there to see the wonderful fresco, once so beautiful, always so worshipped by masters in art, and forever to be famous in song and story. And the first thing that occurred was the infliction on us of a placard fairly reeking with rotten English. Take a morsel of it:

"Bartholomew (that is the first figure on the left hand side at the spectator,) uncertain and doubtful about what he thinks to have heard, and upon which he wants to be assured by himself at Christ and by no others."

Good, isn't it? And then Peter is described as "argumenting in a threatening and angrily condition at Judas Iscariot."

This paragraph recalls the picture. And now forevermore I am down on the old masters. "The Last Supper" is painted on the dilapidated wall of what was a little chapel attached to the main church in ancient times, I suppose. It is battered and scarred in every direction, and stained and discolored by time, and Napoleon's horses kicked the legs off most of the disciples when they were stabled there more than half a century ago. So, what is left of the once miraculous picture? Simon looks seedy; John looks sick, and half of the other blurred and damaged apostles have a general expression of discouragement about them. To us, the great uncultivated, it is the last thing in the world to call a picture. Brown said it looked like an old fire-board. The language was vulgar and irreverent, but it was wonderfully accurate in description. He seemed to regard the guide with an evil eye, and doubtless considered him a sort of imposter for bringing us to such a place. At last he said:

"Is this fellow dead?"

"Who?"

"That dobbed this."

"Da Vinci? Oh, yes, Monsieur—three hundred year."

This information seemed to give Brown great satisfaction, and the gloom passed away from his countenance.

I recognized the old picture in a moment—the Saviour with bowed head seated at the centre of a long, rough table with scattering fruits and dishes upon it, and six disciples on either side in their long robes, talking to each other—the picture from which all engravings and all copies have been made for three centuries. I have never known an attempt to paint the Lord's Supper differently. The world seems to have become settled in the belief, long ago, that it is not possible for human genius to outdo this creation of Da Vinci's. I suppose painters will go on copying it as long as any of the original is left visible to the eye. There were a dozen easels in the room, and as many artists transferring the great picture to their canvases. Fifty proofs of steel engravings and lithographs were scattered around, too. And as usual, I could not help noticing how superior the copies were to the original, that is, to my uneducated eye. Wherever you find a Raphael, a Rubens, a Michael Angelo, a Caracci, or a Da Vinci (and we see them every day), you find artists copying them, and the copies are always the handsomest. Maybe the originals were handsome when they were new, but they have got over it now.

I have got enough of the old masters! Brown says he has "shook" them, and I think I will shake them, too. You wander through a mile of picture galleries and stare stupidly at ghastly old nightmares done in lampblack and lightning, and listen to the ecstatic encomiums of the guides, and try to get up some enthusiasm, but it won't come—you merely feel a gentle thrill when the grand names of the old kings of art fall upon your ears—nothing more. Stowed away among the treasures of the Milan Cathedral they showed us a precious little Titian a foot square—value, 30,000 francs. Brown did not try to conceal his contempt for this thing. He told the priest there was a man in San Francisco who could paint pictures infinitely greater than that—some as much as forty feet long—dash them off in two weeks and sell them for a hundred and fifty dollars.

Well, Dan and the Doctor are going out in the lake to take a swim, and I suppose we may as well go along also. Boats were abroad in every direction, last night, filled with ladies and gentlemen who enlivened the tranquil scene with music, and to-night we propose to do some serenading on our own account. We have got an accordeon. She is a little shaky on her upper notes and has lost a tooth or so on her bass ones; but I reckon she will do.

This letter, numbered eight by Twain, appeared in the *Daily Alta California* on September 22, 1867. The first nine paragraphs were used in Chapter XX, a paragraph of new material being inserted. "The Sacramento River, and not much wider" became "any brook, and only from one-quarter to two-thirds as wide as the Mississippi." The last four words were dropped from "the mountains beyond are veiled in a dreamy purple haze that is unspeakably beautiful." "This is the richest, softest, dreamiest picture I have ever looked upon" became "this is the most voluptuous scene we have yet looked upon"; "roped in the Lady of Lyons with" became "deceived the Lady of Lyons with"; and "it don't look" became "it does not look." (Apparently it was while writing *The Innocents Abroad* that Twain decided that "it don't" and "he don't" should be avoided, although a few examples survive in the book.)

The Lady of Lyons, or Love and Pride (originally called *The Adventurer)*, a romantic comedy by Bulwer-Lytton, was first produced in 1838. Pauline Deschapelles, the proud daughter of a merchant of Lyons, married Claude Melnotte, son of the Deschapelles old gardener.

In the book Twain greatly lengthened the discussion of Lake Tahoe. The paragraph beginning "I am losing faith in all our pet traditions" was omitted. The account of the barbers was not used with the rest of the letter but appeared in revised form in Chapter XII. A somewhat similar passage is found in Chapter XXIII. The passages on soap, Brown's (changed to Blucher's) note to the landlord in Paris, the English used in advertisements in Italy, and *The Last Supper* and the Old Masters were used in Chapter XIX—with much rewriting and a good many deletions and additions. The last paragraph of the letter was not used.

10. Venice

Venice, July 29th, 1867.

What a funny old city this Queen of the Adriatic is! Narrow streets, vast, gloomy marble palaces, black with the corroding damps of centuries, and all partly submerged; no dry land visible anywhere, and no sidewalks worth mentioning; if you want to go to church, to the theatre, or to the restaurant, you must call a gondola. It must be a paradise for cripples, for verily a man has no use for legs here.

For a day or two the place looked so like an overflowed Sacramento, with its currentless waters laving the very doorsteps of all the houses, and the cluster of gondolas made fast under the windows, or skimming in and out of the alleys and by-ways, that I could not get rid of the impression that there was nothing the matter here but a spring freshet, and that the river would fall in a few weeks and leave a dirty high-water mark on the houses, and the streets full of mud and rubbish.

In the glare of day, there is little poetry about Venice, but under the charitable moon its stained palaces are white again, their battered sculptures are hidden in shadows, and the old city seems crowned again with the grandeur that was hers three hundred years ago. It is easy, then, in fancy, to people these silent canals with plumed gallants and fair ladies—with Shylocks in gaberdine and sandals, venturing loans upon the rich argosies of Venetian commerce—with Othellos and Desdemonas, with Iagos and Rod[e]rigos—with noble fleets and victorious legions returning from the wars. In the treacherous sunlight we see Venice decayed, forlorn, poverty-stricken, and commerceless—forgotten and utterly insignificant. But in the moonlight, her fourteen centuries of greatness fling their glories about her, and once more is she the princeliest among the nations of the earth.

There is a glorious city in the sea;
The sea is in the broad, the narrow streets,
Ebbing and flowing; and the salt-sea weed
Clings to the marble of her palaces.
No track of men, no footsteps to and fro,
Lead to her gates! The path lies o'er the sea,
Invisible; and from the land we went,
As to a floating city—steering in,
And gliding up her streets, as in a dream,
So smoothly, silently—by many a dome,
Mosque-like, and many a stately portico,
The statues ranged along an azure sky;
By many a pile, in more than Eastern pride,
Of old the residence of merchant kings;
The fronts of some, tho' time had shatter'd them,
Still glowing with the richest hues of art,
As tho' the wealth within them had run o'er.

The Palace of the Doges

What would one naturally want to see first in Venice? The Bridge of Sighs, of course—and next the Church and the Great Square of St.

Mark, the Bronze Horses, and the famous Lion of St. Mark.

We started to go to the Bridge of Sighs, but happened into the Ducal Palace first—a building which necessarily figures largely in Venetian poetry and tradition. In the Senate Chamber of the ancient Republic we wearied our eyes with staring at acres of historical paintings by Tintoretto and Paul Veronese, but nothing struck me forcibly except one black square with no picture in it. In one long row, around the great hall, were painted the portraits of the Doges of Venice (venerable fellows, with flowing white beards, for of the three hundred Senators eligible to the office, the oldest was always chosen Doge,) and each had its complimentary inscription attached—till you came to the place that should have had Marino Faliero's picture in it, and that was blank and black—blank, except that it bore a terse inscription, saying that the conspirator had died for his crime. It seemed cruel to keep that pitiless inscription still staring from the walls after the unhappy wretch had been in his grave five hundred years.

The Lion's Mouth—Council of Three

At the head of the Giant's Staircase, where Marino Faliero was beheaded, and where the Doges were crowned in ancient times, two small slits in the stone wall were pointed out—two harmless, insignificant orifices that would never attract a stranger's attention—yet these were the terrible Lion's Mouths! The heads were gone (knocked off by the French during their occupation of Venice), but these were the throats, down which went the anonymous accusation, thrust in secretly at dead of night by an enemy, that doomed many an innocent man to walk the Bridge of Sighs and descend into the dungeon which none entered and hoped to see the sun again. This was in the old days of the Council of Ten and the Council of Three. The Patricians alone governed Venice—the common herd had no vote and no voice. There were 1,500 Patricians; from these, 300 Senators were chosen; from the Senators a Doge and a Council of Ten were selected, and by secret ballot the Ten chose from their own number a Council of Three. All these were Government spies, then, and every spy was under surveillance himself—men spoke in whispers in Venice, and no man trusted his neighbor—not always his own brother. No man knew who the Council of Three were—not even the Senate, not even the Doge; the members of that terrific tribunal met at night in a chamber to themselves, masked, and robed from head to foot in scarlet cloaks, and did not even know each other, unless by voice. It was their duty to judge heinous political crimes, and from their sentence there was no appeal. A nod to the executioner was sufficient. The doomed man was marched down a hall and out at a door-way into the covered Bridge of Sighs, through it and into the dungeon and unto his death. At no time in his transit was he visible to any save his conductor. If a man had an enemy in those old days, the neatest thing he could do was to slip a note for the Council of Three into the Lion's mouth, saying "This man is plotting against the Government." If the awful Three found no proof, ten to one they would drown him anyhow, because he was a deep rascal, since his plots were unsolvable. Masked judges and masked executioners, with unlimited power, and no appeal from their judgments, in that hard, cruel age, were not likely to be lenient with men they suspected yet could not convict.

I walked through the hall of the Council of Ten, and presently entered the infernal den of the Council of Three.

The table around which they sat was there still, and the places where the masked inquisitors and executioners stood, frozen, upright and silent, till they received a bloody order, and then, without a word, moved off, like the inexorable machines they were, to carry it out. The frescoes on the walls were startlingly suited to the place. In all the other saloons, the halls, the great state chambers of the palace, the walls and ceilings were bright with gilding, rich with elaborate carving, and splendid with gallant pictures of Venetian victories in war, and Venetian display in foreign courts, and hallowed with portraits of the Virgin, the Saviour of men, and the holy saints that preached the Gospel of Peace upon earth—but here, in dismal contrast, were none but pictures of death and dreadful suffering!—not a living figure but was writhing in torture, not a dead one but was smeared with blood, gashed with wounds, and distorted with the agonies that had taken away its life!

The Dungeons and the Bridge of Sighs

From the palace to the gloomy prison is but a step—one might spit across the narrow canal that intervenes. The ponderous stone Bridge of Sighs crosses it at the second story—a bridge that is a covered tunnel—you cannot be seen when you walk in it. It is partitioned lengthwise, and through one compartment walked such as bore light sentences in ancient times, and through the other marched sadly the wretches whom the Three had doomed to lingering misery and utter oblivion in the dungeons, or to sudden and mysterious death. Down below the level of the water, by the light of smoking torches, we were shown the damp, thick-walled cells where many a proud patrician's life was eaten away by the long-drawn miseries of solitary imprisonment—without light, air, books; naked, unshaven, uncombed, covered with vermin; his useless tongue forgetting its office, with none to speak to; the days and nights of his life no longer marked, but merged into one eternal eventless night; far away from all cheerful sounds, buried in the silence of a tomb; forgotten by his helpless friends, and his fate a dark mystery to them forever; losing his own memory at last, and knowing no more who he was or how he came there; devouring the loaf of bread and drinking the water that was thrust into the cell by unseen hands, and troubling his worn spirit no more with hopes and fears and doubts and longings to be free; ceasing to scratch vain prayers and complainings on walls where none, not even himself, could see them, and resigning himself to hopeless apathy, driveling childishness, lunacy! Many and many a sorrowful story like this these stony walls could tell if they could but speak.

In a little narrow corridor, near by, they showed us where many a prisoner, after lying in the dungeons until he was forgotten by all save his persecutors, was brought by masked executioners and garroted, or sewed up in a sack, passed through a little window to a boat, at dead of night, and taken to some remote spot and drowned.

They used to show to visitors the implements of torture wherewith the three used to worm secrets out of the accused—villainous machines for crushing thumbs; the stocks where a prisoner sat immovable while water fell drop by drop upon his head till the torture was more than humanity could bear; and a devilish contrivance of steel, which enclosed a prisoner's head like a shell, and crushed it slowly by means of a screw. It bore the stains of blood that had trickled through its joints long ago, and on one side it had a projection whereon the torturer rested his elbow comfortably and bent down his ear to catch the moanings of the sufferer perishing within.

Basilica of St. Mark's

Of course we went to see this venerable relic of the ancient glory of Venice, with its pavements worn and broken by the passing feet of a thousand years of plebeians and patricians. It is built entirely of precious marbles, brought from the Orient—nothing in its composition is domestic. Its hoary traditions make it an object of absorbing interest to even the most careless stranger, and thus far it had interest for me; but no further. I could not go into ecstasies over its coarse mosaics, its unlovely Byzantine architecture, or its five hundred curious interior columns from as many distant quarries. Everything was worn out—every block of stone was smooth and almost shapeless with the polishing hands and shoulders of loungers who devoutly idled here in bygone centuries and have died and gone to the dev—no, simply died, I mean.

A Dead Saint

Under the altar reposes the ashes of St. Mark—and Matthew, Luke and John, too, for all I know. Venice reverences those relics above all things earthly. She bets her all on St. Mark. For fourteen hundred years he has been her patron saint. Everything about the city seems to be named after him or so named as to refer to him in some way—so named, or some purchased [purchase] rigged in some way to scrape a sort of hurrahing acquaintance with him. That seems to be the idea. To be on good terms with St. Mark, and have him beg for you, seems to be the very summit of Venetian ambition. They say St. Mark had a tame lion, and used to travel with him—and everywhere that St. Mark went, the lion was sure to go. It was his book-keeper. And so the Winged Lion of St. Mark, with the open Bible under his paw, is a favorite emblem in Venice. It casts its shadow from the most ancient pillar in Venice, in the Grand Square of St. Mark, upon the throngs of free citizens below, and has so done for many a long century. The winged lion is found everywhere—and doubtless here, where the winged lion is, no harm can come.

St. Mark died at Alexandria, in Egypt. I do not know whether he died a natural death or was martyred. However, that has nothing to do with my legend. About the founding of the city of Venice—say 450 years after Christ—(for Venice is much younger than any other Italian city,) a priest ate something which did not agree with him, and so he got the nightmare and dreamed that an angel told him that until the remains of St. Mark were brought to Venice, the city could never rise to high distinction among the nations; that the body must be captured, brought to the city, and a magnificent church built over it; and that if ever the Venetians allowed the Saint to be removed from its new resting-place, in that day Venice would perish from off the face of the earth. The dyspeptic priest proclaimed his dream, and forthwith Venice set about procuring the corpse of St. Mark. One expedition after another tried and failed, but the project was never abandoned during four hundred years. At last it was secured by stratagem, in the year eight hundred and something. The commander of a Venetian expedition disguised himself, stole the bones, separated them, and packed them in vessels filled with lard. The religion of Mahomet causes its devotees to abhor anything that is in the nature of pork, and so when the Christian was stopped by the officers at the gates of the city, they only glanced into his precious baskets, then turned up their noses at the unholy lard, and let him go. The bones were buried in the vaults of the grand cathedral, which had been waiting for ages to receive them, and the safety and the greatness of Venice secured. And to this day there be those in Venice who believe that if those holy ashes were stolen away, the ancient city would vanish like a dream, and its foundations be buried forever by the unremembering sea.

This letter, numbered fourteen by Twain, appeared in the *Daily Alta California* on October 13, 1867. It was also used in Chapter XXII, immediately following the passage on Venice from Letter 17. Despite the heading, the letter may have been written in Naples early in August, for it was published in the newspaper later than Letter 17, and Twain's numbering indicated that this letter immediately followed it. Moreover, since he was in Naples at least as early as August 2—when he wrote a local newspaper protesting against the quarantine of the *Quaker City*—and since he had visited Florence, Pisa, Leghorn, Civita Vecchia, and Rome after he left Venice, it does not seem likely that he was still in Venice on July 29, unless his eagerness to rejoin the ship at Naples had caused him to cut his visits short. Of course, it may be that that is exactly what he did. (The *Quaker City* sailed from Naples at 6 A.M. on August 11. See *Mark Twain's Notebook*, 70.)

"An overflowed Sacramento, with" became "an overflowed Arkansas town, because of"; "three hundred years ago" became "five hundred years ago"; "nothing struck me forcibly except one black square with no picture in it" became "nothing struck us forcibly except the one thing that strikes *all* strangers forcibly—a black square in the midst of a gallery of portraits"; "that terrific tribunal" became "that dread tribunal"; "neatest thing" became "cleverest thing"; "saloon" became "salon"; and "spit across" became "almost jump across." "She bets her all on St. Mark" was omitted; "purchased rigged" became "purchase rigged"; "And have him beg for you" was omitted. "It was his book-keeper" became "It was his protector, his friend, his librarian"; "emblem in Venice" became "emblem in the grand old city"; "a priest ate something which did not agree with him, and so he got the nightmare and dreamed" became "a priest dreamed"; "dyspeptic priest" became "priest"; "Mahomet" became "Mohammed"; "secured" became "were secured"; and "by the unremembering sea" became "in the unremembering sea."

11. Florence

Abroad in Italy, July, 1867.

THERE ARE a good many things about this Italy that I don't understand—and more especially I cannot understand how a bankrupt Government can have such palatial railroad depots and such marvels of turnpikes. Why, these latter are as hard as adamant, as straight as a line, as smooth as a floor, and as white as snow. When it is too dark to see any other object, one can still see the white turnpikes of France and Italy; and they are clean enough to eat from, without a tablecloth. And yet no tolls are charged.

As for the railways—we have none like them. The cars slide as smoothly along as if they were on runners. The depots are vast palaces of cut marble, with stately colonnades of the same royal stone traversing them from end to end, and with ample walls and ceilings richly decorated with frescoes. The lofty gateways are graced with statues, and the broad floors are all laid in polished flags of marble.

These things win me more than Italy's hundred galleries of priceless art treasures, because I can understand the one and am not competent to appreciate the other. In the turnpikes, the railways, the depots and the new boulevards of uniform houses in Florence and other cities here, I see the genius of Louis Napoleon, or rather, I see the works of that giant imitated. But Louis has taken care that in France there shall be a foundation for these improvements—money. He has always the wherewithal to back up his projects; they strengthen France and never weaken her. Her prosperity is genuine. But here the case is different. This country is bankrupt. There is no real foundation for these great works. The prosperity they would seem to indicate is a pretence. There is no money in the Treasury, and so they enfeeble her instead of strengthening. Italy has achieved the dearest wish of her heart and become an independent State—and in so doing she has drawn an elephant. She has got nothing to feed it on. Green in government, she plunged into all manner of useless expenditure, and irretrievably swamped her treasury almost in a day. She squandered millions of francs on a navy which she did not need, and the first time she took her new toy into action she got it knocked higher than Gilderoy's kite.

How to Fill an Empty Treasury

But it is an ill-wind that blows nobody good. A year ago, when Italy saw utter ruin staring her in the face and her greenbacks hardly worth the paper they were printed on, her Parliament ventured upon a *coup de main* that would have appalled the stoutest of her statesmen under less desperate circumstances. They, in a manner, confiscated the domains of the Church! This in priest-ridden Italy! This in a land which has groped in the midnight of priestly superstition for sixteen hundred years! It was a rare good fortune for Italy, the stress of weather that drove her to break from this prison-house.

They do not call it *confiscating* the church property. That would sound too harshly yet. But it amounts to that. There are thousands of churches in Italy, each with untold millions of treasure stored away in its closets, and each with its forty-horse teams of lazy priests to be supported. And then there are the estates of the Church—league on league of the richest lands and the noblest forests in all Italy—all yielding immense revenues to the Church, and none paying a cent of taxes. Why, bless me, in some great districts the Church owns *all* the property—lands, watercourses, woods, mills and factories. They buy, they sell, they manufacture, and since they pay no taxes, who can hope to compete with them?

Well, in effect, the Government has just gobbled all this, and will yet gobble it in rigid and unpoetical reality, no doubt. Something has got to be done to feed a starving treasury, and there is no other resource in all Italy—none but the riches of the Church. So the Government is going to seize a great portion of the revenues arising from priestly farms, factories, etc., and is also going to take possession of the churches and run them itself. In a few instances it will leave the establishments of great pet churches undisturbed, but in all others only a handful of priests will be retained to preach and pray, a few will be pensioned, and the balance turned adrift. As concerns the latter, it is said that God will take care of them—but of course that is only a matter of opinion.

Ecclesiastical Splendor

Now suppose you glance at some of these churches and their embellishments, and see whether you think the Government is doing a righteous thing or not. In Venice, to-day, a city of a hundred thousand inhabitants, there are twelve hundred priests. Heaven only knows how many there were before the Parliament got after them. Now there was the great Jesuit Church. Under the old regime it required sixty priests to run it—the Government runs it with five, now, and the others are discharged from service. All about that church wretchedness and poverty abound. At its door a dozen hats and bonnets were doffed to us, as many heads were humbly bowed, and as many hands extended, appealing for pennies—appealing with foreign words we could not understand, but appealing mutely, with sad eyes, and sunken cheeks and ragged raiment, that needed no words to translate. Then we passed within the great doors, and it seemed that the riches of the world were before us. Tall, huge columns carved out of single masses of marble, and inlaid from top to bottom with a hundred intricate figures wrought in costliest verde antique; pulpits of the same rich materials, whose draperies hung down in many a pictured fold, the stony fabric counterfeiting the delicate work of the loom; the grand altar brilliant with polished facings and balustrades of oriental agate, jasper, porphyry, verde antique, and other rare marbles and precious stones, whose names, even, we seldom hear, and never see, save in jewels and the sumptuous ornaments of patrician drawing-rooms—and slabs of priceless lapis lazuli lavished everywhere as recklessly as if the church owned a quarry of it. In the midst of all this magnificence, the solid gold and silver furniture of the altar seemed cheap and trivial. Even the floors and ceilings were worth the price of a dukedom. To estimate the moneyed value of all the splendor around us there, would have annihilated my arithmetic beyond redemption.

Now, where is the use of allowing all that cash to be gouged out of a community by the ten thousand stratagems so deftly played by those priests, while half of that community hardly know, from day to day, how they are going to keep body and soul together? And, where is the sense in permitting hundreds upon hundreds of millions of francs to be locked up in the useless trumpery of churches all over Italy, and the people ground to death with taxation to uphold a perishing Government?

As far as I can see, Italy, for fifteen hundred years, has turned all her energies, all her finances, and all her industry to the building up of a vast array of wonderful monuments of human folly, and starving half her citizens to accomplish it. She is to-day one vast museum of magnificence and misery. All the churches in San Francisco put together could not buy the jewelled trumpery in one of her hundred cathedrals. And for every beggar in San Francisco, Italy can show you ten thousand—and rags and vermin to match. It is the lousiest, princeliest land on the face of the earth.

Look at the grand Duomo of Florence—a vast pile that has been sapping the purses of her citizens for five hundred years, and is not nearly finished yet. Like all other men, I fell down and worshipped it, but I had it in me to burn it down if I had a chance. When the filthy beggars swarmed around me I grew savage, and said, "Curse your indolent worthlessness, why don't you rob your church?"

It takes three hundred flabby, greasy vagabonds in holy orders to run this awful ecclesiastical swindle. And they don't stand a watch worth twenty dollars a month. They begin dinner at noon and gorge till 3; then they smoke, and swill, and sleep till 5, and then they come on watch for just two hours.

I saw one of their performances. Sixty of them singing and talking Latin at once. And I say in all seriousness that the majority of them looked stupid, and brainless, and sensual beyond anything I have seen for many a day. Those fat-cheeked, sleepy-eyed, bull-necked fellows, may have been good men—of course I cannot say they were not—but their general build was better suited to a butcher shop than a cathedral. Whenever you see a Catholic priest in America, you can pretty safely set him down as a man of brains—as a man of ability and intelligence, away above the average of men, but when you see one in Italy you can as safely set him down as altogether the reverse. It seems so to me at any rate, and I certainly could not conveniently jump out of a third-story window without mashing a priest or a soldier, one or the other. Both are plenty enough.

A Blast on General Principles

And now that I have got my temper up, I might as well go on and abuse everybody I can think of. They have got a grand mausoleum in Florence, which they built to bury our Lord and Saviour and the Medici family in. It sounds blasphemous, but it is true, and here in this godly country they *act* blasphemy. The dead and damned Medici villains, who cruelly tyrannized over Florence and were her curse for over two hundred years, are stowed away in a circle of princely vaults, and in their midst the Holy Sepulchre was to have been set up. The expedition sent to Jerusalem to steal the Sepulchre missed fire and got into trouble and could not accomplish the burglary, and so the centre of the mausoleum is vacant now. They say the entire mausoleum was intended for the Holy Sepulchre, and was only turned into a family burying ground after the Jerusalem expedition failed—but you will excuse me. They would have roped in some of those Medicis, sure. What they hadn't the cheek to do was not worth doing. And they wouldn't even have been content to sleep around the outside of the Sepulchre, those dead Medicis—they would have got up and climbed in. Say nothing about cheek when you are talking about that family. Why, they had their trivial, forgotten exploits on land and sea pictured out in grand frescoes (as did the ancient Doges of Venice) with the Saviour and the Virgin Mary throwing bouquets to them out of the clouds, and the Deity himself applauding from his throne in Heaven! And who painted these things? Why, Titian, Tintoretto, Paul Veronese, Raphael—none other than the world's idols, the "old masters."

Andrea del Sarto glorified his princes in pictures that must save them forever from the oblivion they merited, and they let him starve. Served him right. Raphael pictured such infernal villains as Catherine and Marie de Medicis loafing around in Paradise and hobnobbing familiarly with the Virgin Mary and the angels, (to say nothing of higher personages,) and people abuse me because I am so bitterly prejudiced against the old masters that I cannot see any beauty in their productions. It makes me perfectly savage to look at one of those pictures. I cannot help but see beauty in one of their pictures now and then, but I keep on despising the groveling spirit that could persaude those masters to prostitute their grand talents to the disgusting adulation of such monsters as the French, Venetian and Florentine Princes of two and three hundred years ago, all the same.

More Magnificence

But somehow, I cannot keep that gorgeous Medici mausoleum out of my head. It is as large as a church; its pavement is rich enough for the pavement of a King's palace; its great dome is splendid with frescoes; its walls are made of—what? Marble?—plaster?—wood?—paper? No. Red porphyry—verde antique—jasper—oriental agate—alabaster—mother of pearl—chalcedony—red coral—lapis lazuli! All the vast walls made wholly of these precious stones, worked in, and in and in together in elaborate patterns and figures, and polished till they glow like great mirrors with the pictured splendors reflected from the dome overhead. And before a statue of a dead Medici reposed a royal crown that blazed with diamonds and emeralds enough to buy a city, almost. These are the things the Government has its evil eye upon, and a happy thing it will be for Italy when they melt away in the public treasury.

And now———. However, another beggar approaches. I will go out and destroy him, and then come back and write another column of vituperation.

MARK TWAIN.

This letter, numbered nine by Twain, appeared in the *Daily Alta California* on September 26, 1867. It was used in Chapter XXV. "Giant" became "statesman"; "green" became "inexperienced"; "forty-horse teams of lazy priests" became "battalion of priests"; and "has got to be" became "must be." The last sentence in the sixth paragraph was omitted. "Got after them" became "reduced their numbers"; "that needed no words to translate" became "that no words were needed to translate"; "that cash to be gouged out of a community by the ten thousand stratagems so deftly played by those priests" became "those riches to lie idle"; "monuments of human folly" became "church edifices"; "churches in San Francisco" became "churches in an ordinary American city"; "beggar in San Francisco" became "beggar in America"; "Italy can show you ten thousand" became "Italy can show a hundred"; and "lousiest" became "wretchedest." "I had it in me to burn it down if I had a chance" was omitted. "It takes three hundred flabby, greasy vagabonds in holy orders to run this awful ecclesiastical swindle" became "Three hundred happy, comfortable priests are employed in that cathedral"—and all the remainder of the paragraph and the following paragraph were omitted.

"The dead and damned Medici villains" became "the dead and damned Medici." "They would have roped in some of those Medicis, sure. What they hadn't the cheek to do was not worth doing" became "Some of those Medicis would have smuggled themselves in sure. What *they* had not the effrontery to do, was not worth doing"—and the next two sentences were omitted. "Loafing around in Paradise and hobnobbing" became "seated in heaven and conversing," and "so bitterly prejudiced" became "a little prejudiced." "It makes me perfectly savage to look at one of those pictures" was omitted. "Despising" became "protesting against," and "disgusting adulation" became "adulation." A paragraph was inserted before the last two paragraphs of the letter. "Gorgeous Medici mausoleum" became "Medici mausoleum," and "city" became "ship of the line."

Traveling with the Innocents Abroad

12. Civita Vecchia

At Large in Italy, July, 1867.

This is the vilest nest of dirt, vermin, and ignorance we have got into yet, except that African perdition they call Tangier, which is just like it. The people here live in alleys two yards wide. It is lucky the alleys are not wide, because they hold as much smell now as a person can stand, and of course, if they were wider, they would hold more, and then the people would die. These alleys are paved with stone, and carpeted with slush, and decayed rags, and decomposed vegetable tops, and remnants of old boots, all soaked with dishwater, and the people sit around on stools and enjoy it. They are indolent, as a general thing, and yet have few pastimes. They work two or three hours at a time, but not hard, and then they knock off and catch fleas. This does not require talent, because they only have to grab—if they don't get the one they are after, they get another. It is all the same to them. They are not particular. They have no partialities. Whichever one they get is the one they want. They have other kinds of insects, but it does not make them arrogant. They are very quiet, unpretending people. They have more of this kind of things than other communities, but they do not brag.

They are very uncleanly, these people, in face, in person, and dress. When they see anybody with a clean shirt on, it arouses their scorn. The women wash clothes half the day at the public fountains, but they are probably somebody else's; or, maybe, they keep one suit to wear and another to wash, because they never wear any that have ever been washed. When they get done washing, they sit in the alleys and nurse their cubs. All the women in Civita Vecchia have large families. They nurse one at a time, and the others scratch their backs against the door-posts and are happy. All the people scratch. It is their delight. There is a rusty shrine here and there along the streets, where the people can watch and pray; but they don't do that; they scratch and pray. They like it better.

All this country is presided over by the Pope. They do not appear to have any schools here, and only one billiard table. Their education is at a very low stage. One portion of the men go into the military, another into the priesthood, a third into the shoemaking business, and the balance "lay around."

They keep up the passport system here yet, but so they do in Turkey. This shows that Turkey is not a whit more enlightened than the Papacy, whatever malignant villains may say to the contrary. I had to get my passport viséd in Florence, and then they would not let me come ashore here from Leghorn till a degraded policeman had examined it on the wharf and sent me a permit. They did not even dare to let me take my passport in my hands for 12 hours, I looked so formidable. They judged it best to let me cool down. They thought I wanted to take the town, likely. But such was not my desire—not if I had a chance to swap off and take the small-pox, any how. They examined my baggage at the depot a while ago. They passed my shirts, but they held on to my tooth-brush, so as to lay it before the Board of Commissioners and let them find out what it is for, and whether there is any harm in it or not. This was unfortunate, because I borrowed it from my shipmate, who is particular about his teeth to an extent which is ridiculous. And they took one of my ablest jokes (it was one of those extraordinary conundrums which I get up sometimes), and read it over carefully, and then read it again; and finally turned it around, and read it the wrong way. But it was too deep for them. They handed it around, and everybody ciphered at it a while, but it was no use. They all had to pass. It was no common joke. At last one of the oldest of the officers, apparently, and certainly one of the most abandoned and ignorant men I have ever looked upon, spelled it over very slowly and laboriously, and then shook his head three or four times, and said that in his opinion it was seditious. That was the first time I was alarmed. I immediately said I would explain the document, and they crowded around. And so in that sweltering place I explained, and perspired and perspired, and explained, with my coat off, and they took notes of all I said, but the more I explained the more they couldn't understand, and when they desisted at last, and summed up their notes, I couldn't understand it myself. They said they believed it was an incendiary document, leveled at the Government. I declared it was not, but they only shook their heads, and would not be satisfied. And then they consulted, and consulted, and consulted, a good while, and finally they confiscated it. I cannot tell how much I was grieved; because I had worked a long time on that joke, and took a good deal of pride in it, and now I shall never see it any more. I suppose it will be sent up and stowed away among the criminal archives of Rome, and will always be regarded as a mysterious infernal machine which would have blown up like a mine, and scattered the good Pope all around, but for a miraculous Providential interference. And I suppose that all the time I am in Rome the police will dog me about from place to place because they think I am a dangerous character.

It is fearfully hot in Civita Vecchia. The streets are made very narrow, and the houses built very solid, and heavy, and high, as a protection against the heat. This is the first Italian town I have seen which does not seem to have a patron saint. I suppose no saint but the one that went up in the fiery chariot could stand the climate. This is a miserable town. They haven't any wonders here at all to exhibit to strangers. They haven't even a cathedral, with eleven tuns [tons] of solid silver archbishops in the back-room, and a petrified saint in the cellar; and they don't show you any rusty buildings that are seven thousand years old, nor any ratty, smoke-dried, old fire-screens, which are splendid *chef d'oeuvres* of Titian, or Simpson, or Reubens, or Ferguson, or any of those parties. I am going to Rome—there's nothing to see here. This town is the worst swindle yet.

This letter, which appeared in the *New York Tribune* on September 6, 1867, was also used in Chapter XXV, but with revisions, some of which are indicated below. "Vilest nest of dirt" became "finest nest of dirt," and the last sixty-six words of the second paragraph were reduced to nineteen. "This shows that Turkey is not a whit more enlightened than the Papacy, whatever malignant villains may say to the contrary" became "This shows that the Papal States are as far advanced as Turkey. This fact will be alone sufficient to silence the tongues of malignant calumniators." "A degraded policeman" became "a policeman." The reference to the toothbrush was omitted, and "at last one of the oldest of the officers, apparently, and certainly one of the most abandoned and ignorant men I have ever looked upon" became "at length a veteran officer."

13. Quarantined in Naples Harbor

(Editor's note: We were informed by the cable, some weeks since, that the *Quaker City*, on board of which is "Mark Twain," our chronicler of the Holy Land Excursion, had been quarantined at Naples. We have received a copy of the Naples *Observer*, of August 3d, in which appears the following characteristic protest:)

Harbor of Naples, August 2d, 1867.

Mr. Editor: I must mildly, but firmly, protest against the quarantining of our excursion vessel, the *Quaker City*, in the harbor of Naples.

You need not be afraid of catching the cholera from us. We have been fumigated—not once only, but several times—at the Lake of Como, at Lecco, and most infernally at Venice. We have been fumigated until we smell of all the vile stenches that can be compounded or imagined. Each and every passenger has acquired a distinct and individual odor, and made it his own, and you can recognize any one of them by it in the dark as far as you can smell him. Now there is no possible danger in us. We do not smell like anything on earth, or like anything in any other place, except it be perdition itself. Therefore why not let us go at large? Your people can easily tell when any of us are around, if we get to windward of them, and save themselves by flight. You need not be afraid they will take other smells from ours. They may imagine they smell us sometimes, when they do not, but whenever they do smell us in reality they will not be in doubt any more. Now, do not leave us here to "waste our sweetness on the desert air," but set us at large in your magnificent city, and let us give a pleasing variety to the fragrance that dwells in its atmosphere. Do it. We can make you sing "Hark from the Tombs." You would think we were right from there.

But seriously now, it is a great hardship to be cooped up here day after day, when we have done no harm. Honestly, we have not brought any cholera with us from Leghorn. They would not have let us take it out of the country without paying duty on it. You know that yourself. If we had had any cholera with us we would have given it to the people at Civita Vecchia. We wanted to give them something for inflicting such hot weather on us, but we had not any cholera or anything they would be likely to care about, and so they had to go without, which was shameful.

They never interfered with us at Fayal (Azore Islands) nor at Gibraltar, Marseilles, Genoa or Leghorn—except at the latter place they mistook us for a piratical revolutionary expedition of some sort or other, with designs against the Government, and therefore sent a gunboat to watch us day and night—but here you have gone and done a thing which will give us a reputation for peddling cholera around the world, and we may never get rid of it. We want to go to Athens, Constantinople, Thebes, the Pyramids and the Holy Land, and we want to go with a good name. How can we go even at all, if the people in these countries gather the impression that we are a gigantic exterminating expedition, whose mission it is to kill all we can with cholera, and finish the rest with a stench so atrocious that only such as are educated to it can hope to smell and survive?

Come let us out of this, and behold we will bless you.

I am yours obediently,

MARK TWAIN

P. S. If you cannot let us out I wish you would at least suspend the rule that forbids profanity here. Let us have some little comfort anyhow.

This letter appeared in the *Daily Alta California* on September 16, 1867. In the book Twain wrote that it had been said that the *Quaker City* would probably be quarantined at Naples, and for this reason he left the *Quaker City* at Leghorn, took a French steamer to Civita Vecchia, visited Rome, and went by train to Naples. Probably he remained ashore until the quarantine of the ship had been lifted. In Chapter XX Twain described the fumigation of his party at Bellagio. In Chapter XXIV he told of the gunboat set to watch the *Quaker City* at Leghorn.

14. The Buried City of Pompeii

Naples, Italy, August, 1867.

THEY PRONOUNCE IT Pom-*pay*-e. I always had an idea that you went into Pompeii with torches, by the way of damp, dark stairways, just as you do in silver mines, and traversed gloomy tunnels with lava overhead and something on either hand like dilapidated prisons, gouged out of the solid earth, that faintly resembled houses. But you do nothing of the kind. Fully one-half of the buried city, perhaps, is completely exhumed and thrown open freely to the light of day; and there stands the long rows of solidly-built brick houses (roofless) just as they stood eighteen hundred years ago, hot with the flaming sun; and there lie their floors, clean-swept, and not a bright fragment tarnished or wanting of the labored mosaics that pictured them with the beasts, and birds, and flowers which we copy in perishable carpets today; and there are the Venuses, and Bacchuses, and Adonises, making love and getting drunk in many-hued frescoes on the walls of saloon and bed-chamber; and there are the narrow streets and narrower sidewalks, paved with flags of good hard lava, the one deeply rutted with the chariot-wheels, and the other with the passing feet of the Pompeiians of by-gone centuries; and there are the bake-shops, the temples, the halls of justice, the baths, the theatres—all clean-scraped and neat, and suggesting nothing of the nature of a silver mine away down in the bowels of the earth. The broken pillars lying about, the doorless doorways and the crumbled tops of the wilderness of walls was wonderfully suggestive of the "burnt district" in one of our cities, and if there had been any charred timbers, shattered windows, heaps of debris, and general blackness and smokiness about the place, the resemblance would have been perfect. But no—the sun shines as brightly down on old Pompeii to-day as it did when Christ was born in Bethlehem, and its streets are cleaner a hundred times than ever Pompeiian saw them in her prime. I know whereof I speak—for in the great, chief thoroughfares (Merchant street and the Street of Fortune) have I not seen with my own eyes how for two hundred years at least the pavements were not repaired?—how ruts five and even ten inches deep were worn into the thick flag-stones by the chariot-wheels of generations of swindled tax-payers? And don't I know by these signs that the Street Commissioners of Pompeii never attended to their business, and that if they never mended the pavements they never cleaned them? And, besides, isn't it the inborn nature of Street Commissioners to shirk their duty whenever they get a chance? I only wish I knew the name of the last one that held office in Pompeii so that I could give him a blast. I speak with feeling on this subject, because I caught my foot in one of those ruts, and the sadness that came over me when I saw the first skeleton, with ashes and lava sticking to it, was tempered by the reflection that maybe that party was the Street Commissioner.

No—Pompeii is no longer a buried city. It is a city of hundreds and hundreds of roofless houses, and a tangled maze of streets where one could easily get lost, without a guide, and have to sleep in some ghostly palace that had known no living tenant since that awful November night of eighteen centuries ago.

The Judgment Seat

We passed through the gate which faces the Mediterranean (called the "Marine Gate"), and by the rusty, broken image of Minerva, still keeping tireless watch and ward over the possessions it was powerless to save, and went up a long street and stood in the broad court of the Forum of Justice. The floor was level and clean, and up and down either side was a noble colonnade of broken pillars, with their beautiful Ionic and Corinthian columns scattered about them. At the upper end were the vacant seats of the Judges, and behind them we descended into a dungeon where the ashes and cinders had found two prisoners chained on that memorable November night, and tortured them to death. How they must have tugged at the pitiless fetters as the fierce fires surged around them!

The Desolate Dwellings

Then we lounged through many and many a sumptuous private mansion which we could not have entered without a formal invitation in incomprehensible Latin, in the olden time, when the owners lived there—and we probably wouldn't have got it. These people built their houses a good deal alike. The floors were laid in fancifiul figures wrought in mosaics of many-colored marbles. At the threshold your eyes fall upon a Latin sentence of welcome, sometimes, or a picture of a dog, with the legend "Beware of the Dog," and sometimes a picture of a bear or a faun with no inscription at all. Then you enter a sort of vestibule, where they used to keep the hat-rack, I suppose; next a room with a large marble basin in the midst (to catch the rain water), and the pipes of a fountain; on either side are bed-rooms; beyond the fountain are a reception-room, then a little garden, dining-room, and so forth and so on. The floors were all mosaic, the walls were stuccoed, or frescoed, or ornamented with bas-reliefs, and here and there were statues, large and small, and little fish-pools, and cascades of sparkling water that sprang from secret places in the colonnade of handsome pillars that surrounded the court, and kept the flower-beds fresh and the air cool. Those Pompeiians were very luxurious in their tastes and habits. The most exquisite bronzes we have seen in Europe, by far, came from the exhumed cities of Herculaneum and Pompeii, and also the finest cameos and the most delicate engravings on precious stones; their pictures, eighteen or nineteen centuries old, are often much more pleasing than the celebrated rubbish of the old masters of three centuries ago. They were high up in art. From these works of the first up to the eleventh century, art seems hardly to have existed at all—at least no remnants of it are left—and it was curious to see how far these old time pagans excelled the remote generations of masters that came after them in these matters. The pride of the world in sculptures are the Laocoon and the Dying Gladiator, in Rome. They are as old as Pompeii, were dug from the earth like Pompeii; but their exact age or who made them can only be conjectured. But worn, and cracked, without a history, and with the blemishing stains of numberless centuries upon them, they still mutely mock at all efforts to rival their perfections.

Footprints of the Departed

It was a quaint and curious pastime, wandering through this old silent city of the dead—lounging through utterly deserted streets where a hundred thousand human beings once bought and sold, and walked and rode, and made the place resound with the noise and confusion of traffic and pleasure. They were not lazy. They hurried in those days. I had evidence of that. There was a temple on one corner, and it was a shorter cut to go between the columns of that temple from one street to the other than to go around—and behold that pathway had been worn deep into the heavy flag-stone floor of the building by generations of time-saving feet! They wouldn't go around when it was quicker to go through. We do that way in our cities.

Everywhere you see things that make you wonder how old these old houses were before the night of destruction came—things, too, which bring back those long dead inhabitants and place them living before your eyes. For instance: The steps (two feet thick—lava blocks) that lead up out of the school, and the same kind of steps that lead up into the dress circle of the principal theatre, are almost worn through! For ages the boys hurried out of that school, and for ages their parents hurried into that theatre, and the nervous feet that have been dust and ashes for eighteen centuries have left their record for us to read to-day. I imagined I could see crowds of gentlemen and ladies thronging into the theatre, with tickets for secured seats in their hands, and on the wall, as plainly as ever I read anything in my life, I read the imaginary placard, in infamous grammar, "POSITIVELY NO FREE LIST, EXCEPT MEMBERS OF THE PRESS!" Hanging about the doorway were slouchy Pompeiian street-boys uttering slang and profanity, and keeping an eye out for checks. I entered the theatre, and sat down in one of the long rows of stone benches in the dress circle, and looked at the place for the orchestra, and the ruined stage, and around at the wide sweep of empty boxes, and thought to myself, "This house won't pay." I tried to imagine the music in full blast, the leader of the orchestra beating time, and the "versatile" So-and-So (who had "just returned from a most successful tour in the provinces to play his last and farewell engagement of positively six nights only, in Pompeii, previous to his departure for Herculaneum,") cavorting around the stage and piling the agony mountains high—but I couldn't do it with such a "house" as that; those empty benches tied my fancy down to dull reality. I said, these people that ought to be here have been dead, and still, and mouldering to dust for ages and ages, and will never care for the trifles and follies of life any more forever—"Owing to circumstances, etc., etc., there will not be any performance to-night."

And so I turned away and went through shop after shop and store after store, far down the long street of the merchants, and called for the wares of Rome and the East, but the tradesmen were gone, the marts were silent, and nothing was left but the broken jars all set in cement of cinders and ashes; the wine and the oil that once had filled them were gone with their owners.

In a bake-shop was a mill for grinding the grain, and the furnaces for baking the bread; and they say that here, in the same furnaces, the exhumers of Pompeii found nice, well baked loaves which the baker had not found time to remove from the ovens the last time he left his shop, because circumstances compelled him to leave in such a hurry.

In the bawdy-house (the only building in Pompeii which no woman is now allowed to enter,) were the small rooms and short beds of solid masonry, just as they were in the old times, and on the walls were pictures which looked almost as fresh as if they were painted yesterday, but which no pen could have the hardihood to describe; and here and there were Latin inscriptions—vulgar, obscene scintillations of wit, scratched by hands that possibly were uplifted to Heaven for succor in the midst of a driving storm of fire before the night was done.

In one of the principal streets was a ponderous stone tank, and a water-spout that supplied it, and where the tired, heated toilers from the Campagna used to rest their right hands when they bent over to put their lips to the spout, the thick stone was worn down to a broad groove an inch or two deep. Think of the countless thousands of hands that had pressed that spot in the ages that are gone, to so reduce a stone that is as hard as iron!

They had a great public bulletin board in Pompeii—a place where announcements for gladiatorial combats, elections, and such things, were pasted—not on perishable paper, but carved in enduring stone. One lady, who, I take it, was rich and well raised, advertised a dwelling or so to rent, with baths and all the modern improvements, and several hundred shops, stipulating that the dwellings should not be put to immoral purposes. You can find out who lived in many a house in Pompeii by the carved stone door-plates affixed to them; and in the same way you can tell who they were that occupy the tombs. Everywhere around are things that reveal to you something of the customs and history of this forgotten people. But what would a volcano leave of an American city, if it once got after it? Not a sign or a symbol to tell its story.

In one of these long Pompeiian halls the skeleton of a man was found, with ten pieces of gold in one hand and a large key in the other. He had seized his money and started for the door, but the fiery tempest caught him at the very threshold, and he sank down and died. One more minute of precious time would have saved him. I saw the skeletons of a man, a woman, and two young girls. The woman had her hands spread wide apart, as if in mortal terror, and I imagined I could still trace upon her face the expression of wild despair that distorted it when the heavens rained fire in these streets, so many years ago. The girls and the man lay with their faces upon their arms, as if they had tried to shield them from the enveloping cinders. In one apartment eighteen skeletons were found, all in sitting postures, and blackened places on the walls still mark their shapes and show their attitudes, like shadows. One of them, a woman, still wore upon her skeleton throat a necklace, with her name engraved upon it—Julie di Diomede. In a stone sentry-box, just outside the city wall, we saw where the gallant mail-clad soldier stood his fearful watch that dreadful night, till he died, scorning to desert his post till he heard the relief call which was never more to sound.

Half the interest of Pompeii is lost by the removal to the Museum at Naples of half the great pictures, and the numberless pieces of statuary and other ornamental furniture that used to adorn her ruined temples and palaces. It looks a good deal like Vandalism to me. It leaves Pompeii nothing much but a wreck of battered walls, whereas it could be made to look almost exactly as it did when its citizens moved about its streets in the flesh. Now you are shown two or three palaces, with all their elegant apurtenances untouched, and kept under lock and key, and from these you must refurnish the rest of Pompeii from your own imagination.

There are not half a dozen flights of stairs in Pompeii, and no other evidences that the houses were more than one story high. They did not live in the clouds, as do the Venitians, the Genoese and Neapolitans of to-day.

Rip Van Winkle

We came out from under the solemn mysteries of this city of the Venerable Past—this city which perished, with all its old ways and its quaint old fashions about it, remote centuries ago, when the Disciples were preaching the new religion, which is as old as the hills to us now—and went dreaming among the trees that grow over acres and acres of its still buried streets and squares, till a shrill whistle and the cry of "All aboard—last train for Naples!" woke me up and reminded me that I belonged in the nineteenth century, and wasn't a rusty mummy, caked with ashes and cinders, eighteen hundred years old. The transition was startling. The idea of a railroad train actually running to the old dead Pompeii, and whistling irreverently, and calling for passengers in the most bustling and business-like way, was as strange a thing as one could imagine, and as unpoetical and disagreeable as it was strange.

Compare the cheerful life and the sunshine of this day with the horrors the younger Pliny saw here, the 9th of November, A.D. 79, when he was so bravely striving to remove his mother out of reach of harm, while she begged him, with all a mother's unselfishness, to leave her to perish and save himself:

> By this time the murky darkness had so increased that one might have believed himself abroad in a black and moonless night, or in a chamber where all the lights had been extinguished. On every hand was heard the complaints of women, the wailing of children and the cries of men. One called his father, another his son and another his wife, and only by their voices could they know each other. Many in their despair begged that death would come and end their distress.
>
> Some implored the gods to succor them, and some believed that this night was the last, the eternal night which should engulf the universe!

Even so it seemed to me—and I consoled myself for the coming death with the reflection: BEHOLD, THE WORLD IS PASSING AWAY!

This letter, numbered ten by Twain, appeared in the *Daily Alta California* on September 29, 1867. In the book, it became Chapter IV of Volume II. "Don't I" became "do I not," and "shirk their duty" became "avoid their duty." "Beyond the fountain are a reception-room, then a little garden, dining-room, and so forth and so on" became "beyond the fountain is a reception-room, then a little garden dining-room, and so forth and so on." "The pride of the world in sculptures are the Laocoon and the Dying Gladiator" became "The pride of the world in sculptures seem to be the Loacoön and the Dying Gladiator"—which was no improvement in the grammar.

"A hundred thousand" became "thousands and thousands"; "wouldn't" became "would not"; "were slouchy Pompeiian street-boys" became "(I fancied) were slouchy Pompeiian street-boys"; and "cavorting around" became "charging around." After "there will not be any performance tonight," Twain added, "Close down the curtain. Put out the lights." "In the bawdy-house" became "in one house"; "vulgar, obscene" became "obscene"; "well raised" became "well brought up"; and "got after it" became "rained its cinders on it."

The short passage about the Roman soldier who would not desert his post was rewritten in a grandiloquent style, nearly doubled in length, and set off in a paragraph to itself. For the next paragraph in the letter he substituted a paragraph humorously contrasting the soldier with a policeman. Twain should have kept the original sentence about the Roman soldier and omitted the joke. (See footnote 3 in my introduction.)

Twain followed the remainder of the letter almost verbatim ("wasn't" became "was not," and "rusty mummy" became "dusty mummy"). He added a passage about "the unsubstantial, unlasting character of fame"; otherwise, the letter fills the chapter.

15. Ascent of Mount Vesuvius

Naples, August, 1867.

Editors Alta: I shall remember our trip to Vesuvius for many a day—partly because of its sight-seeing experiences, but chiefly on account of the fatigue of the journey. Two or three of us had been resting ourselves among the tranquil and beautiful scenery of the island of Ischia, eighteen miles out in the harbor, for two days; we called it "resting," but I do not remember now what the resting consisted of, for when we got back to Naples we had not slept for forty-eight hours, and all the pleasant memories we had of Ischia were that it was a place where there were no antiquities seven thousand years old, and no paintings by the old masters.

Never mind what the trouble was.

(I am not aware that I know what I am trying to write about; this is the first time I have been on board the ship for six weeks, and this morning I was pluming myself upon the quiet day I was going to have, but now I have only written a dozen lines here in the cabin and already all those anticipations of quiet are blighted; there is one party of Italian thieves fiddling and singing for pennies on one side of the ship, and a bagpiper, who only knows one tune, on the other; I am expecting to go crazy every minute, and if I do, I hope I will be driven to massacre those parties before I come to my senses again.) Very well; we came back from Ischia and were just about to go to bed early in the evening, and catch up on some of the sleep we had lost, when we heard of this Vesuvius expedition. There were to be eight of us in the party, and were to leave Naples at midnight. One more night and one more day without sleep—pleasant prospect. However, we laid in some provisions for the trip, engaged carriages to take us to Annunciation, and then poked about the city to keep awake till 12. We got away punctually, and in the course of an hour and a half arrived at that town of Annunciation. This Annunciation is the very last place under the sun. In other towns in Italy they lay around quietly and wait for you to ask them a question or do some overt act that can be charged for—but in Anunciation they have lost even that fragment of delicacy; they seize a lady's shawl from a chair and hand it to her and charge a penny; they open a carriage door, and charge for it—shut it when you get out, and charge for it; they help you take off a duster—two cents; brush your clothes and make them worse than they were before—two cents; smile upon you—two cents; bow, with a lick-spittle smirk, hat in hand—two cents; they volunteer all information, such as that the mules will arrive presently—two cents—warm day, sir—two cents—take you four hours to make the ascent—two cents. And so they go. They crowd you—infest you—swarm about you, and sweat and stink, and lie, and look sneaking, and mean, and obsequious—the concentrated essence of the soulless, dust-licking scum of the earth the lower classes of the whole nation are! There is no office too degrading or too disgusting for them to perform, for money. I have had no chance to find out anything about the upper classes by my own observation, but from what I hear said about them I judge that what they lack in one or two of the vile traits the *canaille* have, they make up in one or two others that are infinitely meaner. How the people beg!—many of them very well dressed, too.

But I said I knew nothing against the upper classes by personal observation. I recall it! I had forgotten. What I saw their bravest and their fairest do last night, the lowest and meanest multitude that could be scraped up out of the purlieus of Christendom would blush to do, I think. They assembled by hundreds, and even thousands, in the great Theatre of San Carlo, to do—what? Why, simply, to make fun of an old woman—to deride, to hiss, to jeer at an actress they once worshipped, but whose beauty is faded now and whose voice has lost its former richness. Everybody spoke of the rare sport there was going to be. They said the theatre would be crammed, because Frezzolini was going to sing. It was said she could not sing well, now, but then the people liked to see her, anyhow. And so we went. And every time the woman sang they hissed and laughed—the whole magnificent house—and as soon as she left the stage they called her on again with applause. Once or twice she was encored five and six times in succession, and received with hisses when she appeared, and discharged with hisses and laughter when she had finished—then instantly encored and insulted again. And how the brutal, high-born knaves enjoyed it. White-kidded gentlemen and ladies laughed till the tears came, and clapped their hands in wild ecstacy when that unhappy old woman would come meekly out for the sixth time, with uncomplaining patience, to meet a storm of hisses. It was the cruelest exhibition I ever looked upon—the most wanton, the most heartless, the most unfeeling. The singer would have conquered an audience of American rowdies by her brave, unflinching tranquility (for she answered encore after encore, and smiled and bowed pleasantly, and sang the best she possibly could, and went bowing off, through all the jeers and hisses, without ever losing countenance or temper;) and surely in any other land than Italy her sex and her helplessness must have been an ample protection to her—she could have needed no other. Think what a multitude of small souls were crowded into that theatre last night—and a fair sample of Neapolitan souls they must have been, too. If the manager could have filled his theatre with Neapolitan souls alone, without the bodies, he could not have cleared less than ninety millions of dollars. What traits of character does a man have to have to enable him to help three thousand brutes to hiss, and jeer, and laugh at one friendless old woman, and shamefully humiliate her? He has to be heartless, soulless, groveling, mean-spirited, cruel and cowardly. My observation teaches me (I do not like to venture beyond my own personal observation,) that the upper classes of Naples possess those traits of character. Otherwise, they may be very good people; I cannot say.

Ascent of Vesuvius—Continued

And while I am about it, now, confound them, I will mention that in this city of Naples they believe in and support one of the wretchedest of all the wretched religious humbugs you can find in Italy—the miraculous liquifaction of the blood of St. Januarius. Twice a year the priests corral all the people at the Cathedral, and get out this old vial of clotted blood and let them see it slowly dissolve and become liquid—and every day for eight days, this dismal farce is repeated, while the priests browse around among the crowd of staring asses and collect toll for the exhibition. The first day, the blood liquifies in forty-seven minutes—the church is crammed, then, and time must be allowed the cash-collectors to get around; after that it liquifies a little quicker and a little quicker, every day, as the houses grow smaller, till on the eighth day, with only a few dozen present to see the miraculous swindle, it liquifies in four minutes.

And here, also, they used to have a grand procession, of priests, citizens, soldiers, sailors, and the high dignitaries of the City Government, once a year, to shave the head of a made-up Holy Virgin—a stuffed and painted thing, you know, like a milliner's dummy—whose hair miraculously grew and restored itself every twelve months. They were in the habit of running this shaving procession as late as four or five years ago. It was a source of great profit to the church that possessed the remarkable dummy, and the ceremony of the public barbering of her was always carried out with the greatest possible eclat and display—the more the better, because the more tom-foolery there was about it the bigger the crowds it drew and the better the circus paid—but at last a day came when the Pope and his servants were unpopular in Naples, and the City Government stopped the Virgin's annual show. They intimated that if her hair must and would grow, and if it was so uncomfortable that she could not wear it after it did grow, she must get some friend to cut it in private, or else go to the barber-shop like anybody else. She couldn't have her head shingled in the public streets any more—that was a settled thing. But there you have two specimens of these Neapolitans—two of the silliest possible church swindles, which half the population religiously and faithfully believed, and the other half either believed also or else said nothing about, and thus lent themselves to the support of the swindle. I am willing to think the whole population believed in those poor, cheap miracles—a people who want two cents every time they bow to you, and who abuse a woman in public, are capable of anything, I think.

Ascent of Vesuvius—Continued

These Neapolitans are a bad lot. There is no question in my mind about that. They cheat everybody they can, and they always are expecting to get cheated themselves. They always ask four times as much money as they intend to take, but if you give them what they first demand, they feel ashamed of themselves for aiming so low, and immediately ask more. When money is to be paid and received, there is always and invariably a lot of vehement jawing and gesticulating. You cannot buy and pay for two cents worth of clams without trouble and a quarrel. One "course," in a two-horse carriage, costs a franc—that is law—but the hackman always demands more, on some pretence or other, and if you give it he makes a new demand. A friend of mine took a one-horse carriage for a course—tariff, half a franc. He gave the man five francs, by way of experiment. He demanded more, and received another franc. Again he demanded more, and received another franc. Again he demanded more, and got a franc—demanded more, and it was refused. He grew vehement—was again refused, and got noisy. The man said, "Well, give me the seven francs again, and I will see what I can do"—and when he got them, he handed the hackman half a franc, and he immediately asked for two cents to buy a drink with.

Ascent of Vesuvius—Continued

Well, as I was saying, we got our mules and horses, after an hour and a half of bargaining with the mangy population of Annunciation, and started sleepily up the mountain, with a scoundrel at each mule's tail who pretended to be driving the brute along, but was really holding on and getting himself dragged up instead. I made slow headway at first, but I began to get mad at the idea of paying my minion five francs to hold my mule back by the tail and keep him from going up the hill, and so I discharged him. I got along faster then.

We had one magnificent picture of Naples from a high point on the mountain side. We saw nothing but the gas lamps, of course—two-thirds of a circle, skirting the great Bay—a necklace of diamonds glinting up through the darkness from the remote distance—less brilliant than the stars overhead, but more softly, richly beautiful—and over all the great city the lights crossed and recrossed each other in many and many a sparkling line and curve. And back of the town, far around and abroad over the miles of level campagna, were scattered rows, and circles, and clusters of lights, all glowing like so many gems, and marking where a hundred villages were sleeping. About this time, the fellow who was hanging on to the tail of the horse in front of me and practising all sorts of unnecessary cruelty upon the animal, got kicked some fourteen rods, and this incident, together with the fairy spectacle of the lights far away in the distance, made me perfectly happy, and I was glad I started to Vesuvius.

Ascent of Mount Vesuvius

This subject will be excellent matter for a paragraph, and to-morrow or next day I think I will write it.

MARK TWAIN

This letter, numbered eleven by Twain, appeared in the *Daily Alta California* on October 1, 1867. It became Chapter II in Volume II. Twain provided an introductory paragraph about the quarantine of the ship and those passengers who had escaped it by coming on the train from Rome to Naples. That part of the letter following "we had not slept for forty-eight hours" (near the end of the first paragraph) down through the passage enclosed in parentheses was omitted. "One more night and one more day without sleep—pleasant prospect" was also omitted. "Poked about the city" became "moved about the city"; "they lay around" became "the people lie around"; and "stink" became "smell offensively." "The concentrated essence of the soulless, dust-licking scum of the earth the lower classes of the whole nation are" was omitted.

"Too degrading or too disgusting" became "too degrading"; "chance" became "opportunity"; "vile traits" became "bad traits"; "infinitely meaner" became "worse"; "the lowest and meanest" became "the lowest," and "there was going to be" became "there was to be." "Brutal" was dropped from "brutal, high-born knaves," and "and a fair sample of Neapolitan souls they must have been, too" was omitted. "Brutes" became "miscreants"; "he has to be heartless, soulless, groveling, mean-spirited, cruel and cowardly" became "he must have *all* the vile, mean traits there are"; and "teaches me" became "persuades me."

"And while I am about it, now, confound them, I will mention that" was omitted. "Wretched religious humbugs" became "religious impostures"; "corral all the people" became "assemble all the people"; "this old vial" became "this vial"; "browse around among" became "go among"; "the crowd of staring asses" became "the crowd"; "collect toll" became "collect money"; "cash-collectors" became "collectors"; "the miraculous swindle" became "the miracle"; "a stuffed and painted thing, you know" became "a stuffed and painted image"; "dummy" became "effigy"; "tom-foolery" became "excitement"; and "the better the circus paid" became "the heavier the revenues it produced."

The sentence beginning "They intimated that if her hair" and the following sentence were omitted. "Church swindles" became "frauds," and "support of the swindle" became "support of the imposture." "These Neapolitans are a bad lot. There is no question in my mind about that. They cheat everybody they can, and they always are expecting to get cheated themselves. "They always ask" became "These Neapolitans always ask." "A lot of" became "some." After "to buy a drink with" Twain added "It may be thought that I am prejudiced. Perhaps I am. I would be ashamed of myself if I were not." "Mangy population" became "population"; "scoundrel" became "vagrant"; "get mad" became "get dissatisfied"; "hundred villages" became "score of villages"; and "perfectly happy" became "serenely happy."

16. More on Ascent of Mount Vesuvius

Naples, August, 1867.

"See Naples and die." Well, I don't know that one would necessarily die after merely seeing it, but to start in to try to live there might turn out a little differently. To see Naples as we saw it in the early dawn from far up on the side of Vesuvius, is to see a picture of wonderful beauty. At that distance its dingy buildings looked white—and so, rank on rank of balconies, windows and roofs, they piled themselves up from the blue ocean till the colossal castle of St. Elmo topped the grand white pyramid and gave the picture symmetry, emphasis and completeness. And when its lilies turned to roses—when it blushed under the sun's first kiss—it was beautiful beyond all description. One might well say, then, "See Naples and die." The frame of the picture was charming itself. In front, the smooth sea—a vast mosaic of many colors; the lofty islands swimming in a dreamy haze in the distance; at our end of the city the stately double peak of Vesuvius, and its strong black ribs and seams of lava stretching down to the limitless level campagna—a green carpet that enchants the eye and leads it on and on, past clusters of trees, and isolated houses, and snowy villages, until it shreds out in a fringe of mist and general vagueness far away. It is from the Hermitage, there on the side of Vesuvius, that one should "see Naples and die."

But don't go within the walls and look at it in detail. That takes away some of the romance of the thing. You see, the people are filthy in their habits, and this makes filthy streets and breeds disagreeable sights and smells. (N.B.—You never saw a community so prejudiced against the cholera as these Neapolitans are. But they have good reason to be. The cholera generally fetches a Neapolitan when it gets hold of him, because, you understand, before the doctor can dig through the dirt and get at the disease the man dies. The upper classes take a sea bath every day, and are pretty decent.)

The streets are generally about wide enough for one wagon, and how they do swarm with people! It is Broadway repeated in every street, in every court, in every alley! Such masses, such throngs, such multitudes of hurrying, bustling, struggling humanity! I never saw the like of it, hardly even in New [York], I think. There are seldom any sidewalks, and when there are, they are not often wide enough to pass a man on without caroming on him. So everybody walks in the street—and where the street is wide enough, carriages are forever dashing along. Why a thousand people are not run over and crippled every day is a mystery that no man can solve.

But if there is a ninth wonder in the world, it must be the dwelling-houses of Naples. I honestly believe a good square majority of them are a hundred feet high! And the solid brick walls are seven feet through. You go up nine flights of stairs before you get to the "first" floor. No, not nine, but there or thereabouts. There is a little birdcage of an iron railing in front of every window clear away up, up, up, among the eternal clouds, where the roof is, and there is always somebody looking out of every window—people of ordinary size looking out from the first floor, people a shade smaller from the second, people that look a little smaller yet from the third—and from thence upward they grow smaller and smaller by a regularly graduated diminution, till the folks in the topmost windows seem more like birds in an uncommonly tall marten-box than anything else! The perspective of one of these narrow cracks of streets, with its rows of tall houses stretching away till they come together in the distance; its clothes-lines crossing over at all altitudes and waving their bannered raggedness over the swarms of people below; and the whitedressed women perched in balcony railings all the way from the pavement up to the heavens—a perspective like that is really worth going into Neapolitan details to see.

Ascent of Vesuvius—Continued

Naples, with its immediate suburbs, contains 625,000 inhabitants, but I am satisfied it covers no more ground than San Francisco. It reaches up into the air infinitely higher than three San Franciscos, though, and there is where the secret of it lies. I will observe here, in passing, that the contrasts between opulence and poverty, and magnificence and misery, are more frequent and more striking in Naples than in Paris even. You must go to the Bois de Boulogne to see fashionable dressing, splendid equipages and stunning liveries, and to the Faubourg St. Antoine to see vice, misery, hunger, rags, dirt—but in the thoroughfares of Naples these things are all mixed together. Naked boys of nine years and the pampered children of luxury; shreds and tatters, and brilliant uniforms; jackass carts and state carriages; beggars, Princes and Bishops, jostle each other in every street. At 6 o'clock every evening, all Naples turns out to drive on the *Riviere di Chiaja*, (whatever that may mean;) and for two hours one may stand there and see the motliest and the worst mixed procession go by that ever eyes beheld. Princes (there are more Princes than policemen in Naples —the city is infested with them)—Princes who live up seven flights of stairs and don't own any principalities, will keep a carriage and go hungry; and clerks, mechanics, milliners and strumpets will go without their dinners and squander the money on a hack-ride in the Chiaja; the rag-tag and bob-tail of the city stack themselves up, to the number of twenty or thirty, on a ricketty little go-cart hauled by a donkey not much bigger than a tom-cat, and *they* drive in the Chiaja; Dukes and bankers, in sumptuous carriages and with gorgeous drivers and footmen, turn out, also, and so the furious procession goes. For two hours rank and wealth, and obscurity and poverty clatter along side by side in the wild procession, and then go home serene, happy, covered with glory!

I was looking at a magnificent marble staircase in the King's palace, the other day, which, it was said, cost five million francs, and I suppose it did cost half a million, maybe. I felt as if it must be a fine thing to live in a country where there was such comfort and such luxury as this. And then I stepped out musing, and almost walked over a rusty-looking wretch who was eating his dinner on the curbstone—a piece of bread and a bunch of grapes. When I found that this fellow was clerking in a fruit establishment (he had the establishment along with him in a basket), at two cents a day, and that he had no palace at home where he lived, I lost some of my enthusiasm concerning the happiness of living in Italy.

This naturally suggests to me a thought about wages here. Lieutenants in the army get about a dollar a day, and common soldiers a couple of cents. I only know one clerk—he gets four dollars a month. Printers get six dollars and a half a month, but I have heard of a foreman who gets thirteen. To be growing suddenly and violently rich, as this man is, naturally makes him a bloated aristocrat. The airs he puts on are insufferable.

And, speaking of wages, reminds me of prices of merchandise. In Paris you pay twelve dollars a dozen for Jouvin's best kid gloves; gloves of about as good quality sell here at three or four dollars a dozen. You pay five and six dollars apiece for fine linen shirts in Paris; here and in Leghorn you pay two and a half. In Marseilles you pay forty dollars for a first class dress coat, made by a good tailor, but in Leghorn you can get a full dress suit for the same money. Here you get handsome business suits at from ten to twenty dollars, and in Leghorn you can get an overcoat for fifteen dollars that would cost you seventy in New York. Fine kid boots are worth eight dollars in Marseilles and four dollars here. Lyons velvets rank higher in America than those of Genoa. Yet the bulk of Lyons you buy in the States are made in Genoa and imported into Lyons, where they receive the Lyons stamp and are then exported to America. You can buy enough velvet in Genoa for $25 to make a five hundred dollar cloak in New York. Of course these things bring me back, by a natural and easy transition, to the

Ascent of Vesuvius—Continued

And the wonderful Blue Grotto is thus suggested to me. It is situated on the Island of Capri, 22 miles from Naples. We chartered a little steamer and went out there. Of course, the police boarded us and put us through a health examination, and inquired into our politics before they would let us land. The frills these little one-horse Governments put on are in the last degree ridiculous. They even put a policeman on board of our boat to keep an eye on us as long as we were in the Capri dominions. They thought we wanted to steal that grotto, I suppose. Well, it was worth stealing. The entrance to the cave is four feet high and four feet wide, and is in the face of a lofty perpendicular cliff—the sea-wall. You enter in small boats—and a tight squeeze it is, too. You cannot go in at all when the tide is up. Once within, you find yourself in an arched cavern about one hundred and sixty feet long, one hundred and twenty wide, and about seventy high. How deep it is no man knows. It goes down to the bottom of the ocean. The waters of this placid subterranean lake are the brightest, loveliest blue that can be imagined. They are as transparent as plate glass, and their coloring would shame the richest sky that ever bent over Italy. No tint could be more ravishing, no lustre more superb. Throw a stone into the water, and the myriad of tiny bubbles that are created flash out a brilliant glare like blue theatrical fires. Dip an oar, and its blade turns to splendid frosted silver, tinted with blue. Let a man jump in, and instantly he is cased in an armor more gorgeous than ever a kingly Crusader wore.

Then we went to Ischia, but I had already been to that island and tired myself to death "resting" a couple of days and studying human villainy, with the landlord of the Gaude [Grande] Sentinelle for a model. So we went to Procida, and from thence to Pozzuoli, where Saint Paul landed after he sailed from Samos. I landed at precisely the same spot where Paul landed, and so did Dan and the others. It was a remarkable coincidence. St. Paul preached to these people seven days before he started to Rome.

Nero's Baths, the ruins of Baia [Baiae], the Temple of Serapis; Cumae, where the Cumæn [Cumæan] Sybil interpreted the oracles, the Lake Agnano, with its ancient submerged city still visible far down in its depths—these and a hundred other points of interest we poked around and examined with critical imbecility, but the Grotto of the Dog claimed my chief attention, because I had heard and read so much about it. Everybody has written about the Grotto del Cane and its poisonous vapors, from Pliny down to Smith, and every tourist has held a dog over its floor by the legs to test the capabilities of the place. The dog dies in a minute and a half—a chicken instantly. As a general thing, strangers who crawl in there to sleep do not get up until they are called. And then they don't either. The stranger that ventures to sleep there takes a permanent contract. I wanted to see this grotto. I resolved to take a dog and hold him myself; suffocate him a little, and time him; suffocate him some more and then finish him. We reached the grotto at about three in the afternoon, and proceeded at once to make the experiments. But now, an important difficulty presented itself. After I had taken off my coat and bathed a handkerchief with cologne, and tied it over my face, and got all ready, and was wrought up to the highest pitch of enthusiasm, I recollected that we hadn't any dog. This toned me down some. Well, I thought the matter over, and concluded to go back to a house, about half a mile away, where I had seen a dog, and see if I could borrow it. Brown grumbled a good deal, for the day was hot, but my interest was hot, too, and we started. And so we tramped, tramped, tramped, till I thought we had walked ten miles, and at last we reached the house, almost fagged out. We sat there and chatted awhile, and dropped gently into the subject of the dog, and found that the woman who owned him was prejudiced against loaning him out to be experimented on with poisoned air. It was singular, but we had no time to discuss the foolish prejudices of "them pheasants," as Brown calls the peasantry, and so we just bought the dog, out and out, and started back. It was a long pull, and a weary one. Pull is the correct word, because the dog didn't want to come, and so we had to haul him, turn about, by a long rope he had around his neck. Sometimes that dog would sit down and brace his fore-paws, and it took both of us to start him; and when he did come he would come with a yelp, a skip and a jump, and then he would prance twenty steps to the right and twenty to the left with his paws in the air and his collar half over his ears, and cavort around and carry on like a lunatic. And Brown would "rair back" on the rope and sweat and swear. He swore at me, too, for wanting to take so much trouble just to try some foolish experiments. This person has no appreciation of science.

Well, toward sunset we got the dog to the place, and I took off my coat in a fever of excitement, and rolled up my sleeves, and saturated my handkerchief again and tied it over my nose. And then—just then, after all my trouble and vexation, the dog went up and smelt Brown's breath and laid down and died.

Ascent of Vesuvius—Continued

This subject will keep till my next, I suppose.

This letter, numbered twelve by Twain, appeared in the *Daily Alta California* on October 6, 1867. Chapter III of Volume II begins with this letter, which Twain followed rather closely until near the end. "Fetches" became "vanquishes"; "gets hold of" became "seizes"; "ninth wonder" became "eighth wonder"; "than San Francisco" became "than an American city of one hundred and fifty thousand"; "three San Franciscos" became "three American cities"; "fancy-dressed" became "pampered"; "bobtail" became "rubbish"; "tomcat" became "cat"; "rusty-looking wretch" became "vagabond"; "fellow" became "mustang"; "frills" became "airs"; "one-horse" became "insect"; and "poked around and examined" became "examined." The episode concerning the purchase and the death of the dog was omitted. Twain followed the letter through the sentence "But now, an important difficulty presented itself." He then added "We had no dog"—and omitted the remainder of the letter.

17. Descent of Mount Vesuvius

Naples, August, 1867

At the hermitage we were about fifteen or eighteen hundred feet above the sea, and thus far a portion of the ascent had been pretty abrupt. For the next two miles the road was a mixture—sometimes the ascent was abrupt and sometimes it was not; but one characteristic it possessed all the time, without failure—without modification—it was all uncompromisingly and unspeakably infernal. It was a rough, narrow trail, and led over an old lava flow—a black ocean which was tumbled into a thousand fantastic shapes—a wild chaos of ruin, desolation and barrenness—a wilderness of billowy upheavals, of furious whirlpools, of miniature mountains rent assunder—of gnarled and knotted, wrinkled and twisted masses of blackness that mimicked branching roots, great vines, trunks of trees, all interlaced and mingled together:—and all these wierd shapes, all this turbulent panorama, all this stormy, far-stretching waste of blackness, with its thrilling suggestiveness of life, of action, of boiling, surging, furious motion, was petrified!—all stricken dead and cold in the instant of its maddest rioting!—fettered, paralyzed, and left to glower at heaven in impotent rage forever more!

Finally we stood in a level, narrow valley (a valley that had been created by the terrific march of some old-time irruption [eruption]) and on either hand towered the two steep peaks of Vesuvius. The one we had to climb—the one that contains the active volcano—seemed about 800 or 1,000 feet high, and looked almost too straight-up-and-down for any man to climb, and certainly no mule could climb it with a man on his back. Four of these native pirates will lug you to the top in a sedan chair, if you wish it, but suppose they were to slip and let you fall,—is it likely that you would ever stop rolling? Not this side of eternity, perhaps. We left the mules, sharpened our finger-nails, and began the ascent I have been writing about so long, at 20 minutes to 6 in the morning. The path led straight up a rugged sweep of loose chunks of pumice stone, and for about every two steps forward we took, we slid back one. It was so excessively steep that we had to stop, every fifty or sixty steps, and rest a moment. To see our comrades, we had to look very nearly straight up at those above us, and very nearly straight down at those below. The ladies wore no hoops, which was well. They would have looked like so many umbrellas. We stood on the summit at last—it had taken an hour and fifteen minutes to make the trip.

What we saw there was simply a circular crater—a circular ditch, if you please—about two hundred feet deep, four or five hundred feet wide, and half a mile in circumference. In the centre was a torn and ragged upheaval a hundred feet high, all snowed over with a sulphur crust of many and many a brilliant and beautiful color, and the ditch enclosed this like the moat of a castle, or surrounded it as a little river does a little island, if you like the simile better. The sulphur coating of that island was gaudy in the extreme—all mingled together in the richest confusion were red, blue, brown, black, yellow, white—I do not know that there was a color, or shade of a color, or combination of colors unrepresented—and when the sun burst through the morning mists and fired this tinted magnificence, it topped imperial Vesuvius like a jewelled crown!

The crater itself—the ditch—was not so variegated in coloring, but yet, in its softness, richness, and unpretentious elegance it was more charming, more fascinating to the eye. There was nothing "loud" about its wellbred and well-dressed look. Talk of beauty!—why one could stand and look down upon it for a week without getting tired of it. It had the semblance of a pleasant meadow, whose slender grasses and whose velvety mosses were frosted with a shining dust, and tinted with palest green that deepened gradually to the darkest hue of the orange leaf, and deepened yet again into gravest brown, then faded into orange, then into brightest gold, and culminated in the delicate pink of a new-blown rose. Where portions of the meadow had sunk, and where other portions had been broken up like an ice-floe, the cavernous openings of the one, and the ragged upturned edges exposed by the other, were hung with a lace-work of soft-tinted crystals of sulphur that changed their deformities into quaint shapes and figures that were full of grace and beauty.

The walls of the ditch were brilliant with yellow banks of sulphur and with lava and pumice stone of many colors. No fire was visible anywhere, but gusts of sulphurous steam issued silently and invisibly from a thousand little cracks and fissures in the crater, and were wafted to our noses with every breeze. But so long as we kept our snouts buried in our handkerchiefs, there was small danger of suffocation.

Some of the boys poked long slips of paper into holes and set them on fire, and so achieved the glory of lighting their cigars by the flames of Vesuvius, and others cooked eggs over fissures in the rocks and were happy.

The view from the summit would have been superb but for the fact that the sun could only pierce the mists at long intervals. Thus the glimpses we had of the grand panorama below were only fitful and unsatisfactory.

The Descent

The descent of the mountain was a labor of only four minutes. Instead of stalking down the rugged path we ascended we chose one which was bedded knee-deep in loose ashes, and ploughed our way with prodigious strides, that would have shamed the performances of him of the seven-league boots.

The Vesuvius of to-day is a very slow affair compared to the mighty volcano of Kilauea, in the Sandwich Islands, but I am glad I visited it, partly because it was well worth it, and chiefly because I shall never have to do it again.

It is said that during one of the grand eruptions of Vesuvius it discharged massy rocks weighing many tons a thousand feet into the air, its vast jets of smoke and steam ascended thirty miles toward the firmament, and clouds of its ashes were wafted abroad and fell upon the decks of ships seven hundred and fifty miles at sea! I will take the ashes at a moderate discount, if any one will take the thirty miles of smoke, but I do not feel able to take a commanding interest in the whole story by myself.

Descent of Vesuvius—Continued

But what has this got to do with Venice? We reached Venice at eight in the evening, three weeks ago, and entered a hearse belonging to the Grand Hotel d'Europe. At any rate, it was more like a hearse than anything else, though to speak by the card, it was a gondola. And this was the storied gondola of Venice!—the fairy boat in which the princely cavaliers of the olden time were wont to cleave the waters of the moonlit canals and look the eloquence of love into the soft eyes of patrician beauties, while the gay gondolier in silken doublet touched his guitar and sang as only gondoliers can sing! This the famed gondola and this the gorgeous gondolier!—the one an inky, rusty old canoe with a sable hearse-body clapped onto the middle of it, and the other a mangy, barefooted guttersnipe with his shirt-tail out! Presently, as he turned a corner and shot his hearse into a dismal ditch between two long rows of towering, frowning, untenanted buildings, the gay gondolier began to sing, true to the traditions of his race. I stood it about four minutes. Then I said:

"Now, here, Roderigo Gonzales Michael Angelo, I'm a pilgrim, and I'm a stranger, but I'm not going to have my feelings lacerated by any such caterwauling as that. If that goes on, one of us has got to take water. It is enough that my cherished dreams of Venice have been blighted forever as to the romantic gondola and the gorgeous gondolier; this system of destruction shall go no farther; I will accept the hearse, under protest, and you may fly your flag of truce in peace, but here I register a dark and bloody oath that you shan't sing."

I began to feel that the old Venice of song and story had departed forever. But I was too hasty. In a few minutes we swept gracefully out into the Grand Canal, and under the mellow moonlight the Venice of poetry and romance stood revealed. Right from the water's edge rose lines of stately palaces of marble; gondolas were gliding swiftly hither and thither and disappearing suddenly through unsuspected gates and alleys; ponderous stone bridges threw their shadows athwart the glittering waves. There was life and motion everywhere, and yet everywhere there was a hush, a stealthy sort of stillness, that was suggestive of secret enterprises of bravoes and of lovers; and clad half in moonbeams and half in mysterious shadows, the grim old mansions of the Republic seemed to have an expression about them of having an eye out for just such enterprises as these at that same moment. Music came stealing over the waters—Venice was complete. It was a beautiful picture—very soft and dreamy and beautiful. But what was this Venice to compare with the Venice of midnight? Nothing. There was a fête —a grand fête in honor of some saint who had been instrumental in getting the cholera choked off three hundred years ago, and all Venice was abroad on the water. It was no common affair, for the Venetians did not know how soon they might need the saint's services again, now that the cholera was spreading everywhere. So in one vast space—say a third of a mile wide and two miles long—were collected two thousand gondolas, and every one of them had from two to ten, twenty and even thirty colored lanterns suspended about it, and from four to a dozen occupants. Just as far as the eye could reach, these painted lights were massed together—like a vast garden of many-colored flowers, except that these blossoms were never still; they were ceaselessly gliding in and out, and mingling together, and seducing you into bewildering attempts to follow their mazy evolutions. Here and there a strong red, green, or blue glare from a rocket that was struggling to get away, splendidly illuminated all the boats around it. Every gondola that swam by us, with its crescents and pyramids and circles of colored lamps hung aloft, and lighting up the faces of the young and sweet-scented and lovely below, was a picture; and the reflections of those lights, so long, so slender, so numberless, so many-colored and so distorted and wrinkled by the waves, was a picture likewise, and one that was wonderfully beautiful. Many and many a party of young ladies and gentlemen had their state gondolas handsomely decorated and ate supper on board, bringing their swallow-tailed, white-cravatted varlets to wait upon them, and having their tables tricked out as if for a bridal supper. They had brought along the costly globe lamps from their drawing-rooms, and the lace and silken curtains from the same places, I suppose. And they had also brought pianos and guitars, and they played and sang operas, while the plebeian paper-lanterned gondolas from the suburbs and the back alleys crowded around to stare and listen.

There was music everywhere—choruses, string bands, brass bands, flutes, everything. Why, I was so surrounded, walled in, with music, magnificence and loveliness, that I got inspired with the spirit of the scene, and sang one tune myself. However, when I had finished the third verse and observed that the other gondolas had sailed away, and my gutter-snipe was preparing to go overboard, I stopped.

That fête was magnificent—there is no question about that. They kept it up the whole night long, and I never enjoyed myself better than I did while it lasted; which brings me, by a natural and easy transition, back to the legitimate subject of this letter, which is—

Descent of Vesuvius—Continued

I will speak of this in my next.

This letter, numbered thirteen by Twain, appeared in the *Daily Alta California* of October 10, 1867. With the exception of the part on Venice, it was also used in Chapter

III. "Infernal" became "infamous," and "lug" became "carry." Twain omitted "The ladies wore no hoops, which was well. They would have looked like so many umbrellas." "Snouts" became "nostrils," and "poked" became "thrust." "Partly because it was well worth it, and chiefly because I shall never have to do it again" became "It was well worth it."

After Twain visited Venice (near the middle of July), he visited Florence, Pisa, Leghorn, Civita Vecchia, Rome, and Naples, but apparently he did not send his reports on Venice to the newspaper until after he had reached Naples. Probably he had taken notes but had not had time to write them up.

The passage on Venice was used in Chapter XXII of Volume I, beginning with the third paragraph of the chapter. Of course Twain omitted the first sentence of the letter and "three weeks ago" from the second sentence. "With his shirt-tail out" became "with a portion of his raiment on exhibition which should have been sacred from public scrutiny" (Twain's revisions were usually good, but this is an exception). "Another yelp, and overboard you go" was omitted. "Music came stealing" became "music came floating"; "getting the cholera choked off" became "checking the cholera"; "I got inspired" became "I became inspired"; and "my gutter-snipe" became "my gondolier." "There is no question about that" was omitted—and also, of course, the reference to Vesuvius.

18. Ancient Athens

Grecian Archipelago, At Sea,
August 15th, 1867.

We arrived and entered the ancient harbor of the Piræus yesterday morning. We dropped anchor within half a mile of the village. Away off, across the undulating Plain of Attica, could be seen a little square-topped hill with a something on it, which our glasses soon discovered to be the ruined edifices of the ancient citadel of the Athenians, and most prominent among them loomed the famous Parthenon. So exquisitely clear and pure is this wonderful atmosphere that every column of this noble structure was discernible through the telescope, and even the smaller ruins about it assumed some semblance of shape. This at a distance of five or six miles. In the valley, near the Acropolis, (the square-topped hill before spoken of,) Athens itself could be vaguely made out with an ordinary lorgnette. Everybody was anxious to get ashore and visit these classic localities as quickly as possible. No land we have yet seen has aroused such universal interest among the passengers.

But bad news came. The commandant of the Piræus came in his boat, and said we must either depart or else get outside the harbor and remain imprisoned on our ship, under rigid quarantine, for eleven days! So we took up the anchor and moved outside, to lay a dozen hours or so, taking in supplies, and then sail for Constantinople. It was the bitterest disappointment we had yet experienced. To lie a whole day right in sight of the Acropolis, and yet be obliged to go away without visiting Athens! Disappointment was hardly a strong enough word to describe the circumstances.

All hands were on deck, all the afternoon, with books and maps and glasses, trying to cipher out which "narrow rocky ridge" was the Areopagus, which sloping hill the Pnyx, which elevation the Museum Hill, and so on. And we got things mixed. Discussion became heated and party spirit ran high. Church members were gazing with emotion upon a hill which they said was the one St. Paul preached from, and another faction claimed that that hill was Hymettus, and another that it was Pentelicon! After all the trouble, we could be certain of only one thing—the square-topped hill was the Acropolis, and the noble ruin that crowned it was the Parthenon, whose picture we knew in infancy in the school books.

We inquired of everybody who came near the ship, whether there were guards in the Piræus, whether they were strict, what the chances were of capture should any of us slip ashore, and in case any of us ventured on land and were caught, what would be probably done to us? The answers were discouraging: There was a large guard or police force; the Piræus was a small town, and any stranger seen in it would surely attract attention—capture would be certain. The Commandant said the punishment would be "heavy"; when asked "how heavy?" he said it would be "very severe"—that was all we could get out of him.

Running the Blockade

At eleven o'clock at night, when most of the ship's company were abed, four of us (Dr. Jackson, surgeon of the ship; Dr. Birch, Colonel Denny and myself,) stole softly ashore in a small boat, a clouded moon favoring the enterprise, and started two and two, and far apart, over a low hill, intending to go clear around the Piræus, out of the range of its police. Picking our way so stealthily over that rocky, nettle-grown eminence, made me feel a good deal as if I were on my way somewhere to steal something. My immediate comrade and I talked in an undertone about quarantine laws and their penalties, but we found nothing cheering in the subject. I was posted. Only a few days before I was talking with our Captain, and he mentioned the case of a man who swam ashore from a quarantined ship somewhere, and got imprisoned six months for it; and when he was in Genoa a few years ago, a Captain of a quarantined ship went in his boat to a departing ship, which was already outside of the harbor, and put a letter on board to be taken to his family, and the authorities imprisoned him three months for it, and then conducted him and his ship fairly to sea, and warned him never to show himself in that port again while he lived. This kind of conversation did no good, further than to give a sort of dismal interest to our quarantine-breaking expedition, and so we dropped it. We made the entire circuit of that town without seeing anybody but one man, who stared at us curiously, but said nothing, and a dozen persons asleep on the ground before their doors, whom we walked among and never woke—but we woke up dogs enough, in all conscience—we always had one or two barking at our heels, and several times we had as many as ten and twelve at once. They made such an infernal din that persons aboard our ship said they could tell how we were progressing for a long time, and where we were, by the barking of the dogs. The clouded moon still favored us. When we had made the whole circuit, and were passing among the houses on the further side of the town, the moon came out splendidly, but we no longer feared the light. As we approached a well, near a house, to get a drink, the owner merely glanced at us and went within. He left the quiet, slumbering town at our mercy. I record it here proudly, that we didn't do anything to it.

Seeing no road, we took a tall hill to the left of the distant Acropolis for a mark, and steered straight for it over all obstructions, and over a little rougher piece of country than exists anywhere else outside of the State of Nevada, perhaps. Part of the way it was covered with small, loose stones—you trod on six at a time, and they all rolled. Another part of it was dry, loose, newly-ploughed ground. Still another part of it was a long stretch of low grapevines, which were tanglesome and troublesome, and which we took to be weeds. The Attic Plain, barring the grapevines, was a barren, desolate, unpoetical waste—I wonder what it was in Greece's Age of Glory, five hundred years before Christ?

Refreshments

In the neighborhood of 1 o'clock in the morning, when we were heated with fast walking and parched with thirst, Col. Denny exclaimed, "Why these weeds are grapevines!" and in five minutes we had a score of bunches of large, white, delicious grapes, and were reaching down for more when a dark shape rose mysteriously up out of the shadows beside us and said "Ho!" And so we left.

On the Road

In ten minutes more we struck into a beautiful road, and unlike some others we had stumbled upon at intervals, it led in the right direction. We followed it. It was broad, and smooth and white—handsome and in perfect repair, and shaded on both sides for a mile or so with single ranks of trees, and also with luxuriant vineyards. Twice we entered and stole grapes, and the second time somebody shouted at us from some invisible place. Whereupon we left again. We speculated in grapes no more on that side of Athens.

Shortly we came upon an ancient stone aqueduct, built upon arches, and from that time forth we had ruins all about us—we were approaching our journey's end. We could not see the Acropolis now or the high hill, either, and I wanted to follow the road till we were abreast of them, but the others overruled me, and we toiled laboriously up the stony hill immediately in our front—and from its summit saw another—climbed it and saw another! It was an hour of exhausting work. Soon we came upon a row of open graves, cut in the solid rock —(for a while one of them served Socrates for a prison)—we passed around the shoulder of the hill, and the citadel, in all its ruined magnificence, burst upon us! We hurried across the ravine and up a winding road, and stood on the old Acropolis, with the prodigious walls of the citadel towering high above our heads. We did not stop to inspect their massive blocks of marble, or measure their height, or guess at their extraordinary thickness, but passed at once through a great arched passage like a railway tunnel, and went straight to the gate that leads to the ancient temples. It was locked! So, after all, it seemed that we were not to see the great Parthenon face to face. We sat down and held a council of war. Result: the gate was only a flimsy structure of wood—we would break it down. It seemed like desecration, but then we had travelled far, and our necessities were urgent. We could not hunt up guides and keepers—we must be on the ship before daylight. So we argued. This was all very fine, but when we came to break the gate, we couldn't do it. We moved around an angle of the wall and found a low bastion—eight feet high without—ten or twelve within. Denny prepared to scale it, and we got ready to follow. By dint of hard scrambling he finally straddled the top, but some loose stones crumbled away and fell with a crash into the court within. There was instantly a banging of doors and a shout, Denny dropped from the wall in a twinkling, and we retreated in disorder to the gate. Xerxes took that mighty citadel 480 years before Christ, when his five million of soldiers and camp-followers followed him to Greece, and if we four Americans could have remained unmolested five minutes longer we would have done so, too.

Among the Glories of the Past

The garrison had turned out—four Greeks. We clamored at the gate and they admitted us.

We crossed a large court, entered a great door, and stood upon a pavement of purest white marble, deeply worn by foot-prints. Before us, in the flooding moonlight, rose the noblest ruins we ever looked upon—the Propylæ [Propylæa]; a small Temple of Minerva; the Temple of Hercules, and the grand Parthenon. (We got these names from the Greek guide, who didn't seem to know more than seven men ought to know.) These edifices were all built of the whitest Pentelican marble, but have a pinkish stain upon them now. Where any part is broken, though, the fracture looks like fine loaf sugar. Six caryatides, or marble women, clad in flowing robes, support the portico of the Temple of Hercules, but the porticos and colonnades of the other structures are formed of massive Doric and Ionic pillars, whose flutings and capitals are still measurably perfect, notwithstanding the centuries that have gone over them and the sieges they have suffered. The Parthenon, originally, was 226 feet long, 100 wide and 70 high, and had two rows of great columns, eight in each, at either end, and single rows of seventeen each down the sides, and was one of the most graceful and beautiful edifices ever erected. How tame, how unimpressive, are the vaunted monuments of ancient Rome beside it.

Most of the Parthenon's imposing columns are still standing, but the roof is gone. (It was a perfect building two hundred and fifty years ago, when a shell dropped into the Venetian magazine stored here, and the explosion which followed wrecked and unroofed it.)

As we wandered thoughtfully down the length of this stately temple, the scene about us was strangely impressive. Here were floors of vast flags of cut marble, neatly fitted together and perfectly level; cut into this floor were two semi-circular grooves which the casters of the great doors used to traverse; here and there, in lavish profusion, were gleaming white statues of men and women, propped against blocks of marble, some of them armless, some without legs, others headless—but all looking mournful and sentient, and startlingly human! They rose up and confronted the midnight intruder on every side—they stared at him with stony eyes from unlooked-for nooks and recesses; they peered at him over fragmentary heaps far down the desolate corridors; they barred his way in the midst of the broad forum, and solemnly pointed with handless arms the way from the sacred fane; and through the roofless temple the moon looked down, and banded its floor and darkened its scattered fragments and its broken statues with the slanting shadows of its columns.

What a world of ruined sculpture was about us! Stood up in rows—stacked up in piles—scattered broadcast over the wide area of the Acropolis—were hundreds of crippled statues of all sizes and of the most exquisite workmanship; and vast fragments of marble that once belonged to the entablatures, covered with bas-reliefs representing battles and sieges, ships of war with three and four tiers of oars, pageants and processions—everything you could think of. History says that the temples of the Acropolis were filled with the noblest works of Praxiteles and Phidias, and of many a great master in sculpture besides—and surely these elegant fragments attest it.

We walked out into the grass-grown, fragment-strewn court beyond the Parthenon. It startled me, every now and then, to see a stony white face stare suddenly up at me out of the grass with its dead eyes. The place seemed alive with ghosts. I half expected to see the Athenian heroes of twenty centuries ago glide out of the shadows and steal into the old temple they knew so well and regarded with such boundless pride.

A Vision

The full moon was riding high in the cloudless heavens, now. We sauntered carelessly and unthinkingly to the edge of the lofty battlements of the citadel, and looked down—a vision! And such a vision! All the beauty in all the world combined could not rival it!—Athens by moonlight! The prophet that thought the splendors of the New Jerusalem were revealed to him, surely saw this instead! It lay in the level plain right under our feet—all spread abroad like a picture—and we looked down upon it as we might have looked from a balloon. We saw no semblance of a street, but every house, every window, every clinging vine, every projection, was as distinct and sharply marked as if the time were noonday; and yet there was no glare, no glitter, nothing harsh or repulsive—the noiseless city was flooded with the mellowest light that ever streamed from the moon, and seemed like some living creature wrapped in peaceful slumber. On its further side was a little temple, whose delicate pillars and ornamented front glowed with a rich lustre that chained the eye like a spell; and nearer by, the palace of the King reared its creamy walls out of the midst of a great garden of shrubbery that was flecked all over with a random shower of amber lights—a spray of golden sparks that lost their brightness in the glory of the moon, and glinted softly upon the sea of dark foliage like the pallid stars of the milky-way. Overhead the stately columns, majestic still in their ruin—under foot the dreaming city—in the distance the silver sea—not on the broad earth is there another picture half so beautiful!

As we turned and moved again through the temple, I wished that the illustrious men who had sat in it in the remote ages could visit it again and reveal themselves to our curious eyes—Plato, Aristotle, Demosthenes, Socrates, Phocion, Pythagoras, Euclid, Pinder [Pindar], Xenophon, Herodotus the historian, Praxiteles and Phidias the sculptors, and Zeuxis the painter. What a constellation of celebrated names! But more than all, I wished that old Diogenes, groping so patiently with his lantern, searching so zealously for one solitary honest man in all the world, might meander along and strike our crowd. I ought not to say it, may be, but still I reckon he would have put out his light.

Famous Localities

We left the Parthenon to keep its watch over old Athens, as it had kept it for twenty-three hundred years, and went and stood outside the walls of the citadel. In the distance was the ancient, but still almost perfect Temple of Theseus, and close by, looking to the west, was the Bema, from whence Demosthenes thundered his Phillippics and fired the wavering patriotism of his countrymen. To the right was Mars

Hill, where the Areopagus sat in ancient times, and where St. Paul defined his position, and below was the market place where he "disputed daily" with the gossip-loving Athenians. We climbed the stone steps St. Paul ascended, and stood in the square-cut place he stood in, and tried to recollect the Bible account of the matter—but for certain reasons I could not recall the words. But I have found them since:

> Now while Paul waited for them at Athens, his spirit was stirred in him when he saw the city wholly given up to idolatry.
>
> Therefore disputed he in the synagogue with the Jews, and with the devout persons, and in the market daily with them that met with him.
>
> . . . .
>
> And they took him and brought him unto Areopagus, saying, may we know what this new doctrine whereof thou speakest is?
>
> . . . .
>
> Then Paul stood in the midst of Mars-hill, and said, Ye men of Athens, I perceive that in all things ye are too superstitious:
>
> For as I passed by and beheld your devotions, I found an altar with this inscription: TO THE UNKNOWN GOD. Whom, therefore, ye ignorantly worship, him declare I unto you.—Acts, ch. xvii.

Homeward Bound

It occurred to us, after a while, that if we wanted to get home before daylight betrayed us, we had better be travelling. So we hurried away. When far on our road, we had a parting view of the Parthenon, with the moonlight streaming through its open colonnades and touching its capitals with silver. As it looked then, solemn, grand and beautiful, it will always remain in my memory.

As we marched along, we began to get over our fears, and ceased to care much about quarantine scouts or anybody else. We got bold and reckless; and once, in a sudden burst of courage, I even threw a rock at a dog. It was a pleasant reflection, though, that I didn't hit him, because his master might just possibly have been a policeman, you know. Inspired by this happy failure, my valor became utterly uncontrollable, and at intervals I absolutely whistled, though on a moderate key. But boldness breeds boldness, and shortly I plunged into a vineyard, in the full light of the moon, and captured a gallon of superb grapes, not even minding the presence of a peasant who rode by on a mule. Denny and Birch followed my example. Now I had grapes enough for a dozen, but then Jackson was all swollen up with courage, too, and he was obliged to enter a vineyard presently. The first bunch he seized brought trouble. A frowsy, bearded brigand sprang into the road with a shout, and flourished a musket in the light of the moon! We sidled toward the Piræus—not running, you understand, but only advancing with celerity. The brigand shouted again, but still we advanced. It was getting late, and we had no time to fool away on every ass that wanted to drivel Greek platitudes to us. We would just as soon have talked to him as not if we hadn't been in a hurry. Presently Denny said, "Those fellows are following us!"

We turned, and, sure enough, there they were—three lubberly pirates armed with guns. We slackened our pace to let them come up, and in the meantime I got out my cargo of grapes and dropped them firmly but reluctantly into the shadows by the wayside. But I was not afraid. I only felt that it was dishonest to steal grapes. And all the more so when the owner was around—and not only around, but with his friends around also. The villains came up and searched a bundle Dr. Birch had in his hand, and scowled upon him when they found it had nothing in it but some rocks from Mars Hill, and these were not contraband. They evidently suspected him of playing some wretched swindle upon them, and seemed half inclined to scalp the party. But finally they dismissed us with a warning, couched in excellent Greek, I suppose, and dropped tranquilly in our wake. When they had gone three hundred yards they stopped, and we went on rejoiced. But behold, another armed rascal came out of the shadows and took their place, and followed us two hundred yards. Then he delivered us over to another miscreant, who emerged from some mysterious place, and he in turn to another! For a mile and a half our rear was guarded all the while by armed men. I never travelled in so much state before in all my life.

It was a good while after that before we ventured to steal any more grapes, and when we did we stirred up another disgusting brigand, and then we ceased all further speculation in that line. I suppose that fellow that rode by on the mule posted all the sentinels, from Athens to the Piræus, about us.

Every field on that long route was watched by an armed sentinel, some of whom had fallen asleep, no doubt, but were on hand, nevertheless. This shows what sort of a country modern Attica is—a community of thieves. These men were not there to guard their possessions against strangers, but against each other; for strangers seldom visit Athens and the Piræus, and when they do, they go in daylight, and can buy all the grapes they want for a trifle. The modern inhabitants are thieves and liars of high repute, if gossip speaks truly concerning them, and I freely believe it does.

Home Again

Just as the earliest tinges of the dawn flushed the eastern horizon, we closed our thirteenth mile of weary, round-about marching, and emerged upon the sea-shore abreast the ships, with our usual escort of fifteen hundred Piræan dogs howling at our heels. I hailed a boat that was too or three hundred yards from shore, and discovered in a moment that it was a police-boat on the lookout for any quarantine-breakers that might chance to be abroad. So we dodged—we were used to that by this time—and when the scouts reached the spot we had so lately occupied, we were absent. They cruised along the shore, but in the wrong direction, and shortly our own boat issued from the gloom and took us aboard. They had heard my signal on the ship. We rowed noiselessly away, and before the police-boat came in sight again we were safe at home once more.

Four more of our passengers were anxious to visit Athens, and started half an hour after we returned; but they had not been ashore five minutes till the police got after them and chased them so hotly that they barely escaped to their boat again, and that was all. They pursued the enterprise no further.

We set sail for Constantinople to-day, but some of us don't care a fig for that. We have seen all that there was to see in the old city that had its birth sixteen hundred years before Christ was born, and was an old town before the foundations of Troy were laid—and saw it in its most attractive aspect. Wherefore, why should *we* worry.

Two others, Rev. Mr. Bullard, and Mr. Beach, of the New York *Sun,* ran the blockade successfully last night.

This letter, numbered fifteen by Twain, appeared in the *Daily Alta California* of October 18, 1867. It was used in Volume II, Chapter V. "Famous Parthenon" became "venerable Parthenon"; "to lay a dozen hours" became "to lie a dozen hours"; "to cipher out" became "to determine"; "noble ruin" became "grand ruin"; "infernal" became "preposterous"; and "we ever looked upon" became "we had ever looked upon." "How tame, how unimpressive, are the vaunted monuments of ancient Rome beside it" was omitted. Twain inserted acknowledgments of his debt to a guidebook for some facts about the Parthenon and added a few descriptive details. "All the beauty in all the world combined could not rival it" was omitted. "Strike our crowd" became "stumble on our party"; "I reckon" became "I suppose"; "got bold" became "grew bold"; "lubberly" became "fantastic"; "dishonest" became "not right"; "swindle" became "fraud"; "disgusting" became "troublesome"; "thieves" became "questionable characters"; "thieves and liars" became "confiscators and falsifiers"; "flushed the eastern horizon" became "flushed the eastern sky and turned the pillared Parthenon to a broken harp hung in the pearly horizon"; "got after them and chased them" became "discovered and chased them"; "don't care a fig" became "little care"; and "Two others, Rev. Mr. Bullard, and Mr. Beach, of the New York *Sun*" became "two other passengers."

19. Arrival at Constantinople

Constantinople, August 20th, 1867.

From Athens all through the islands of the Grecian Archipelago, we saw nothing but forbidding sea-walls and barren hills, sometimes surmounted by three or four graceful columns of some ancient temple, lonely and deserted—a fitting symbol of the desolation that has come upon all Greece in these latter ages. We saw no ploughed fields, very few villages, no trees or grass or vegetation of any kind, and hardly ever an isolated house. Greece is a bleak, unsmiling desert, without agriculture, manufactures or commerce. What supports its poverty-stricken people or its Government, is a mystery to me.

I suppose that ancient Greece and modern Greece compared, furnish the most extravagant contrast to be found in history. George I, an infant of eighteen, and a scraggy lot of foreign office-holders, sit in the places of Themistocles, Pericles, and the illustrious scholars and generals of the Golden Age of Greece. The fleets that were the wonder of the world when the Parthenon was new, are a beggarly handful of fishing-smacks now, and the manly people that performed such miracles of valor at Marathon are only a tribe of degraded thieves and liars to-day. The classic Illyssus [Ilissus] has gone dry, and so have all the sources of Grecian wealth and greatness. The nation numbers only eight hundred thousand souls, and there is poverty and misery and rascality enough among them to furnish forty millions and be liberal about it. Under King Otho the revenues of the State were five millions of dollars—raised from a tax of *one-tenth* of all the agricultural products of the land (which tenth the farmer had to bring to the royal granaries on pack-mules any distance not exceeding six leagues) and terrific taxes on trade and commerce. Out of that five millions the little tyrant tried to keep an army of ten thousand men, pay all the hundreds of useless Grand Equerries in Waiting, First Grooms of the Bedchamber, Lord High Chancellors of the Busted Exchequer, and all the other absurdities which these puppy kingdoms indulge in, in imitation of the great monarchies; and in addition he set about building a white marble palace to cost about five millions itself. Well, the result was, simply: ten into five goes no times and none over. All these things couldn't be done with five millions, and Otho got into trouble.

The Greek throne with its unpromising adjuncts of a mangy, ragged population of thieves, who were out of employment eight months in the year because there wasn't anything for them to steal; its barren hills and its weed-grown deserts, went begging for a good while. It was offered to one of Victoria's boys, and afterwards to various other younger sons of royalty who had no thrones and were out of business, but they all had the charity to decline the dreary honor, and veneration enough for Greece's ancient greatness to refuse to mock her sorrowful rags and dirt with a tinsel throne in this day of her humiliation—till they came to this young Danish George (I believe he is a Dane), and he took it. He has finished the splendid palace I saw in the radiant moonlight the other night, and is doing many other things for the salvation of Greece, they say.

Footprints of History

We sailed through the barren archipelago, and into the narrow channel they sometimes call the Dardanelles and sometimes the Hellespont. This part of the country is rich in historic reminiscences, and poor as Sahara in everything else. For instance, as we approached the Dardanelles, we coasted along the Plains of Troy and past the mouth of the Scamander; saw where Troy had stood (in the distance), and where it does not stand now—a city that perished fourteen hundred years before the birth of Christ, and yet Athens was two hundred and fifty years old when its foundations were laid. We saw where Agamemnon's fleets rendezvoused, and away inland a mountain which the map said was Mount Ida. Within the Hellespont we saw where the old original first shoddy contract mentioned in history was carried out, and the "parties of the second part" gently rebuked by Xerxes. I speak of the famous bridge of boats which Xerxes ordered to be built over the narrowest part of the Hellespont (where it is only two or three miles wide). A moderate gale destroyed the flimsy structure, and the King, thinking that to publicly rebuke the contractors might have a good effect on the next set, called them out before the army and had them beheaded. In the next ten minutes he let a new contract for the bridge. It has been observed by ancient writers that the second bridge was a very good bridge. Xerxes crossed his host of five millions of men on it, and if it had not been purposely destroyed, it would probably have been there yet. If our Government would rebuke some of our shoddy contractors occasionally, it might work much good. Well, in the Hellespont we saw where Leander and Lord Byron swam across, the one to see her upon whom his soul's affections were fixed with a devotion that only death could impair, and the other merely for a flyer, as you may say. We had two noted tombs about us, too. On one shore slept Ajax, and on the other Hecuba.

We had water batteries and forts on both sides of the Hellespont, and the crimson flag of Turkey, with its white crescent, and occasionally a village, and sometimes a train of camels; we had all these to look at till we entered the broad sea of Marmora, and then the land soon fading from view, we resumed euchre and seven-up once more.

Constantinople

We dropped anchor in the mouth of the Golden Horn early in the morning. This is a narrow arm of the sea which branches from the Bosphorus (a sort of broad river which connects the Marmora and Black Seas), and, curving around, divides the city in the middle. Galata and Pera are on one side of the Bosphorus, and the Golden Horn; Stamboul (ancient Byzantium) is upon the other. On the other bank of the Bosphorus is Scutari and other suburbs of Constantinople. This great city contains a million inhabitants, but so narrow are its streets, and so crowded together are its houses, that it does not cover much more than half as much ground as New York City. Seen from the anchorage or from a mile or so up the Bosphorus, it is by far the handsomest city we have seen. Its dense array of houses swells upward from the water's edge, and spreads over the domes of many hills; and the gardens that peep out here and there, the great globes of the mosque[s], and the countless minarets that meet the eye everywhere, invest the metropolis with the quaint Oriental aspect that one dreams of when he reads books of eastern travel. Constantinople makes a noble picture.

But its attractiveness begins and ends with its picturesqueness. From the time you start ashore till you get back again, you damn it. The boat you go in is admirably miscalculated for the service it is built for. It is handsome and neatly fitted up, but no man could handle it in the turbulent currents that sweep down the Bosphorus from the Black Sea, and few men could row it satisfactorily even in still water. It is a long, light canoe (caique), large at one end and tapering to a knife-blade at the other. They make that long sharp end the bow, and you can imagine how these boiling currents spin it about. It has two oars, and sometimes four, and no rudder. You start to go to a given point and you run in fifty different directions before you get there. First one oar is backing water, and then the other; it is seldom that both are going ahead at once. This kind of boating is calculated to drive a nervous man crazy in a week. The boatmen are the awkwardest, the stupidest, and the most unscientific on earth, I think.

The Fashions

Ashore, it was—well, it was an eternal circus. People were thicker than bees, in those narrow, crowded streets, and the men were dressed in all the outrageous, outlandish, idolatrous, extravagant, infernal costumes that ever a tailor with the delirium tremens and seven devils could conceive of. There was no freak in dress too crazy to be indulged in; no absurdity too absurd to be tolerated; no frenzy in ragged diabolism too fantastic to be attempted. No two men were dressed alike. It was a wild masquerade of all imaginable costume—every struggling throng in every street was a dissolving view of stunning contrasts. Some patriarchs wore awful turbans, but the grand mass of the infidel horde wore the skull-cap they call a fez. All the remainder of the raiment they indulged in was utterly indescribable.

Street Life

The shops here are mere coops, mere boxes, bathrooms, closets—anything you please to call them—on the first floor. The Turks sit cross-legged in them, and work and trade and smoke long pipes, and smell like a slaughter-house in summer. Crowding the narrow street in front of them are beggars, who beg eternally yet never collect anything; and wonderful cripples, distorted out of all semblance of humanity, almost; vagabonds driving laden asses; porters carrying dry-goods boxes as big as cottages on their backs; pedlars of grapes, hot corn, pumpkin seeds, and a hundred other things, yelling like fiends; and sleeping placidly among the hurrying feet are the famed dogs of Constantinople; drifting noiselessly about are squads of Turkish women, draped from chin to feet in flowing robes, and with snowy veils bound about their heads, that disclose only the eyes and a vague, shadowy notion of their features. Seen moving about, far away in the dim, arched aisles of the Great Bazaar, they look as the shrouded dead must have looked when they walked forth from their graves amid the storms and thunders and earthquakes that burst upon Calvary that awful night of the Crucifixion. A street in Constantinople is a picture which one ought to see once—not oftener.

And then there was the goose-rancher—a fellow who drove a hundred geese before him about the city, and tried to sell them. He had a pole ten feet long, with a crook in the end of it, and occasionally a goose would branch out from the flock and make a lively break around a corner, with wings half lifted and neck stretched to its utmost. Did the goose-merchant get excited? No. He took his pole and reached after that goose with unspeakable *sang froid*—took a hitch round his neck, and yanked him back to his place in the flock without an effort. He steered his geese with that stick as comfortably as another man would steer a yawl. A few hours afterward we saw him sitting on a stone at a corner, in the midst of the turmoil, sound asleep in the sun, with his geese squatting around him, or dodging out of the way of asses and men. We came by again, within the hour, and he was taking account of stock, to see whether any of his flock had strayed or been stolen. The way he did it was unique. He put the end of his stick within six or eight inches of a stone wall, and made the geese march in single file between it and the wall. He counted them as they went by. There was no shirking that arrangement.

This letter, numbered sixteen by Twain, appeared in the *Daily Alta California* on October 20, 1867. It was used in Chapter VI of Volume II. "Nothing but" became "little but"; "not of" became "nest of"; "degraded thieves and liars" became "unconsidered slaves"; "rascality" became "mendacity"; "terrific taxes" became "extravagant taxes"; "Busted Exchequer" became "Exploded Exchequer"; "got into trouble" became "fell into trouble"; "mangy, ragged population of thieves" became "ragged population of ingenious rascals"; "there wasn't anything for them to steal" became "there was little for them to borrow and less to confiscate"; and "Victoria's boys" became "Victoria's sons." The reference to Troy was revised. "As you may say" became "as Jack says," and "seven-up" became "whist." Twain inserted four sentences about their arrival at the mouth of the Golden Horn. "You" became "one"; "you damn it" became "he execrates it"; "a nervous man crazy" became "an impatient man mad"; "infernal costumes" became "thunder-and-lightning costumes"; "smell like a slaughter-house in summer" became "smell like—like Turks. That covers the ground"; "sleeping placidly" became "sleeping happily, comfortable, serenely."

20. The Cripples of Constantinople

Constantinople, August 23d, 1867.

If you want dwarfs—I mean just a few dwarfs for a curiosity—go to Genoa. If you want to buy them by the gross, for retail, go to Milan. There are plenty of dwarfs all over Italy, but it did seem to me that in Milan the crop was luxuriant. If you would see a fair average style of assorted cripples, go to Naples, or travel through the Roman States. But if you would see the very heart and home of cripples and human monsters, both, go straight to Constantinople. A beggar in Naples who can show a foot which has all run into one horrible toe, with one shapeless nail on it, has got a good thing—but such an exhibition as that wouldn't stand any show in Constantinople. The man would starve. Who would pay any attention to attractions like his among the rare monsters that throng the bridges of the Golden Horn and display their deformities in the gutters of Stamboul? O, wretched imposter! How could he stand against the three-legged woman, and the man with his eye in his cheek? How he would blush in presence of the man with fingers on his elbow? Where would he hide himself when the dwarf with seven fingers on each hand, no upper lip, and his under-jaw gone, came down in his majesty? Bismillah! The cripples of Europe are a delusion and a fraud. The truly gifted flourish only in the by-ways of Pera and Stamboul.

That three-legged woman lay on the bridge, with her stock in trade so disposed of as to command the most striking effect—one natural leg, and two long, slender, twisted ones with feet on them, like somebody else's fore-arm. Then there was a man further along who had no eyes, and whose face was the color of a fly-blown beefsteak, and wrinkled and twisted like a lava-flow—and verily so tumbled and distorted were his features that no man could tell the wart that served him for a nose from his cheek bones. In Stamboul was a man with a prodigious head, an uncommonly long body, legs eight inches long and feet like cradle-rockers. He travelled on those feet and his hands, and was as sway-backed as if the Colossus of Rhodes had been riding him. Ah, I tell you, a beggar has to have exceedingly good points to make a living in Constantinople. A blue-faced man, that had nothing to offer except that he had been blown up in a mine, would be regarded as a rank imposter, and a mere damaged soldier on crutches would never make a cent. It would pay him to get a piece of his head taken off, and cultivate a wen like a carpet sack.

St. Sophia

The Mosque of St. Sophia is the chief lion of Constantinople. You must get a firman and rush there the first thing. We did that. We did not get a firman, but we took along five francs apiece, which is much the same thing.

I don't think much of the Mosque of St. Sophia. I suppose I lack appreciation. Well, let it go at that. It is the rustiest old barn in heathendom. I believe all the interest that attaches to it comes from the fact that it was built for a Christian church and then turned into a mosque, without much alteration, by the Mohammedan conquerors of the land. They made me take off my boots and travel into the place in my sock-feet. I caught cold, and got myself so stuck up with a complication of gums, slime and general corruption, that I wore out two pairs of boot-jacks getting my boots off that night, and even then some Christian hide peeled off with them.

St. Sophia is a colossal church, thirteen or fourteen hundred years old, and ratty enough to be a million. Its immense dome is said to be more wonderful than St. Peter's, but its dirt is much more wonderful than its dome, though they never mention it. The church has a hundred and seventy pillars in it, each a single piece, and all of costly marbles of various kinds, but they came from ancient temples at Baalbec, Heliopolis, Athens and Ephesus, and are battered, ugly and repulsive. They were a thousand years old when this church was new, and then the contrast must have been ghastly—if Justinian's architects did not trim them any. The inside of the dome is figured all over with a monstrous inscription in Turkish characters, wrought in gold mosaic, that looks as glaring as a circus bill; the pavements and the marble balustrades are all battered and dirty; the perspective is marred everywhere by a web of ropes that depend from the dizzy height of the dome, and suspend countless dingy, coarse oil lamps, six or seven feet above the floor. Squatting and sitting in groups, here and there and far and near, were ragged Turks reading books, hearing sermons, or receiving lessons like children, and in fifty places were more of the same sort bowing and straightening up, bowing again and getting down to kiss the earth, muttering prayers the while, and keeping up their gymnastics till they ought to have been tired, if they were not.

Everywhere was dirt, and dust, and dinginess, and gloom; everywhere were signs of hoary antiquity, but with nothing touching or beautiful about them; everywhere were those groups of fantastic pagans; overhead the gaudy mosaics and the web of lamp-ropes—nowhere was there anything to win one's love or challenge his admiration.

I understand it, I think. The people who go into ecstacies over St. Sophia get them out of the guide book (where every church is spoken of as being "considered by good judges to be the most marvelous structure, in many respects, that the world has ever seen.") Or else they are these old-master worshippers from the wilds of New Jersey, who can't tell a fresco from lath-and-plaster, and don't know any more about pictures than a kangaroo does about astronomy. And so you always hear them carrying on about wonderful pictures, wonderful statuary and wonderful architecture, the shameless lunatics! as if they had always been used to palaces and studios, extensive travel and the company of the elegant and accomplished, instead of being raised in a cow-lot, educated in a saw-mill, and their minds enlarged and stored with precious knowledge by travel down a creek on a shingle raft.

Now there was that wretched woman in the Vatican in Rome. She overheard Brown say something outrageous about the old masters, and she permitted him to overhear her say something rather savage about "people who had no appreciation of the divine works of the great masters." It was not a gentlemanly thing for a lady to do, but she did not know that, perhaps. However, she went into hysterics, pretty soon, over a picture marked "Angelo," and called it a miracle of art, and a heavenly conception and a work such as none but inspired hands could have wrought, and a lot more of sickening nonsense like that, but finally an officer of the institution came along and set her back. He said that that particular "Angelo" was *not* Mike, but a certain other Angelo who used to be a butcher in Pisa—and that after painting until he found out it was not his best hold, he went back into the butchering business again. I just had an idea that may be that woman had had more experience in tending babies on a salary than in setting in judgment on the inspired fire-screens of the old masters.

The Dancing Dervishes

There were twenty-one of them. They wore a long, light-colored loose robe that hung to their heels. Each in his turn went up to the priest (they were all within a large circular railing) and bowed profoundly and then went spinning away like a grand-daddy-long-legs, with one foot fast in a candle and took his appointed place in the circle, and continued to spin. When all had spun themselves to their places, they were about five or six feet apart, and remained spinning where they were during the remainder of the service—twenty-five minutes. They spun on the left foot, and kept themselves going passing the right rapidly before it and digging it against the waxed floor. Some of them made incredible "time." Most of them spun around forty times in a minute, and one artist averaged about sixty-one times a minute, and kept it up during the whole twenty-five. His robe filled with air and stood out all around him like a balloon.

They made no noise of any kind, and most of them tilted their heads back and closed their eyes, entranced with a sort of devotional ecstacy. There was a rude kind of music, part of the time, but the musicians were not visible. None but spinners were allowed within the circle. A man had to either spin or stay outside. It was about as borborous [barbarous] an exhibition as I have ever witnessed.

Other Lions

We visited the Thousand and One Columns. I do not know what it was originally intended for, but they said it was built for a reservoir. It is situated in the centre of Constantinople. You go down a flight of stone steps in the middle of a barren place, and there you are. You are forty feet under ground, and in the midst of a perfect wilderness of tall, slender, granite columns of the Byzantine order of architecture. Stand where you would, or change your position as often as you pleased, you were always a centre from which radiated a dozen long archways and colonnades that lost themselves in distance and the sombre twilight of the place. This old dried-up reservoir is occupied by a few ghostly silk-spinners now, and one of them showed me a cross cut high up in one of the pillars. I suppose he meant me to understand that the institution was there before the Turkish occupation, and I thought he made a remark to that effect; but he must have had an impediment in his speech, for I did not understand him.

We took off our shoes and went into the marble mausoleum of the Sultan Mahmoud, the neatest piece of architecture, inside, that I have seen lately. Mahmoud's tomb was covered with a black velvet pall, which was elaborately embroidered with silver: it stood within a fancy silver railing; at the sides and corners were silver candlesticks that would weigh more than a hundred pounds, and they supported candles as large as the calf of a man's leg; on the top of the sarcophagus was a fez, with a handsome diamond ornament upon it, which an attendant said cost a hundred thousand pounds, and lied like a Turk when he said it. Mahmoud's whole family were comfortably planted around him.

We went to the great Bazaar in Stamboul, of course, and I shall not describe it further than to say it is a monstrous hive of little shops—thousands, I should say—all under one roof, and cut up into innumerable little blocks by narrow streets which are arched overhead. One street is devoted to a particular kind of merchandise, another to another, and so on. When you want to buy a pair of shoes you have got the swing of the whole street—you don't have to walk yourself down hunting stores in different localities. It is the same with silks, antiquities, shawls, etc. The place is crowded with people all the time, and as the gay-colored Eastern fabrics are lavishly displayed before every shop, the great Bazaar of Stamboul is one of the sights that are worth seeing. It is full of life, and stir, and business.

This letter, numbered seventeen by Twain, appeared in the *Daily Alta California* of October 23, 1867. It was also used in Chapter VI of Volume II. "Has got a good thing" became "has a fortune"; "stand any show" became "provoke any notice"; "cradle-rockers" became "snow-shoes"; "travel into the place in my sock-feet" became "walk into the place in my stocking feet"; "two pair of boot-jacks" became "more than two thousand pair of boot-jacks"—and Twain added "I abate not a single boot-jack." "Ratty enough to be a million" became "unslightly enough to be very, very much older"; "these old-master worshippers from the wilds of New Jersey" became "those old connoisseurs from the wilds of New Jersey"—and for the remainder of the paragraph Twain substituted: "who laboriously learn the difference between a fresco and a fire-plug, and from that day forward feel privileged to void their critical bathos on painting, sculpture, and architecture forevermore." Twain omitted the following paragraph (about the woman in the Vatican). "Spinning away like a grand-daddy-long-legs, with one foot fast in a candle" became "spinning away deliriously"—and the following sentence was rewritten in two sentences. "As I have ever witnessed" became "as we have witnessed yet"—and then Twain added a passage of about one hundred words. "You have got" became "you have." To the last sentence in the letter, "It is full of life, and stir, and business," Twain added: "dirt, beggars, asses, yelling peddlers, porters, dervishes, high-born Turkish female shoppers, Greeks, and weird-looking and weirdly dressed Mohammedans from the mountains and the far provinces—and the only solitary thing one does not smell when he is in the Great Bazar, is something which smells good."

21. Morals of the Mohammedans

Constantinople, August, 1867.

Mosques are plenty, churches are plenty, graveyards are plenty, but morals and whiskey are scarce. The Koran does not permit Mohammedans to drink. Their general principles do not permit them to be moral. They say the Sultan has eight hundred wives. This almost amounts to bigamy. It makes our cheeks burn with shame to see such a thing permitted here in Turkey. We don't mind it so much in Salt Lake, however.

Circassian and Georgian girls are still sold in Constantinople by their parents, but not publicly. The great slave marts we have all read so much about—where tender young girls were stripped for inspection, and their points discussed just as if they were horses at an agricultural fair—no longer exist. The exhibition and the sales are private now. Stocks are up just at present, partly because of a brisk demand created by the recent return of the Sultan's suite from the inhospitable Courts of Europe; partly on account of an unusual abundance of breadstuffs, which leaves holders untortured by hunger and enables them to hold back for high prices; and partly because buyers are too weak to bear the market, while sellers are amply prepared to bull it. Under these circumstances, if the *Alta* were published here in Constantinople, your next commercial report would read about as follows, I suppose:

Slave-Girl Market Report

Best brands Circassians, crop of 1850, £200; 1852, £250; 1854, £300. Best brands Georgian, none in market; second quality, 1851, £180. Nineteen fair to middling Wallachian girls offered at £130

@ 150, but no takers; sixteen prime A1 sold in small lots to close out —terms private.

Sales of one lot Circassians, prime to good, 1852 to 1854, at £240 @ 242½, buyer 30; one forty-niner—damaged—at £23, seller ten, no deposit. Several Georgians, 1852, changed hands to fill orders. The Georgians now on hand are mostly last year's crop, which was unusually poor. The new crop is a little backward, but will be coming in shortly. As regards its quantity and quality, the accounts are most encouraging. In this connection we can safely say, also, that the new crop of Circassians is looking extremely well. His Majesty the Sultan has already sent in large orders for his new harem, which will be finished within a fortnight, and this has naturally strengthened the market and given Circassian stock a strong upward tendency. Taking advantage of the inflated market, many of our shrewdest operators are selling short.

There is nothing new in Nubians. Slow sale.

Eunuchs—None offering; however, large cargoes are expected from Egypt to-day.

I think the above would be about the style of your commercial report. Prices are pretty high now, and holders firm; but, two or three years ago, parents in a starving condition brought their young daughters down here and sold them for even twenty and thirty dollars, when they could do no better, simply to save themselves and the girls from dying of want. It is sad to think of so distressing a thing as this, and I for one am sincerely glad the prices are up again.

Commercial Morals, Especially,

Are bad. There is no getting around that. Greek, Turkish and Armenian morals consist only in attending church regularly on the appointed Sabbaths, and in breaking the ten commandments all the balance of the week. It comes natural to them to lie and cheat in the first place, and then they go on and improve on nature until they arrive at perfection. In recommending his son to a merchant as a valuable salesman, a father does not say he is a nice, moral, upright boy, and goes to Sunday School and is honest, but he says, "This boy is worth his weight in broad pieces of a hundred—for behold, he will cheat whomsoever hath dealings with him, and from the waters of Marmora to the Euxine there abideth not so gifted a liar!" How is that, for a recommendation? The Missionaries tell me that you hear encomiums like that passed upon people every day. They say of a person they admire, "Ah, he is a charming swindler and a most exquisite liar!"

Everybody lies and cheats—everybody who is in business, at any rate. Even foreigners soon have to come down to the custom of the country, and they do not buy and sell long in Constantinople till they lie and cheat like a Greek. I say like a Greek, because the Greeks are called the worst transgressors in this line. Several Americans long resident in Constantinople contend that most Turks are pretty trustworthy, but none claim that the Greeks have any virtues that a man can discover—at least without digging for them.

Amusements

I have been to one or two of the numerous beer-gardens here, but saw nothing that one might not see anywhere—a lot of people of various nationalities sitting at tables drinking beer, and half a dozen moderately pretty Bohemian girls fiddling and singing on a platform, and afterwards going around with a plate to take up a collection—and doing it, too, with that same old vain-glorious, self-important swagger that being petted and worshipped by roughs of the city and flats from the country has conferred upon the lager-beer girl in all ages of the world. When I found there was nothing national about the beer-gardens of Constantinople, I dropped them with a promptness and a moral sensitiveness which cannot be too highly commended in one so young.

Then I tried smoking the thing they call the narghili. Curse the narghili. I will meddle with it no more. It is a long-necked glass decanter, with water in it, and a pipe-bowl on top of the neck. None but Persian tobacco is ever smoked in it and nothing but charcoal will light it. One stem goes down into the other and makes a fearful blubbering when you draw and the other leads to your mouth, and is like a section of hose. You sit down flat on a carpet, tailor-fashion, with your decanter near by, and then you bend on your hose and begin. Just after you begin, you quit, and don't begin any more. You do that if you have got good sense. You see, you do not suck up the smoke with the lips, as in ordinary smoking, but by a long respiration, swelling the lungs to their utmost, just as if you heaved a powerful sigh through your mouth instead of your nose. Now, you understand that when a green-hand does that, the smoke does not discharge itself in a great volume from his nose as it ought to do, but goes in a great volume down into his lungs, his stomach, even down into his legs! And then he coughs one mighty cough, and it is as if Vesuvius had let go! For the next ten minutes he smokes at every pore, like a frame house that is on fire on the inside, and after that he lays down his hose and goes home sicker than ever he was before in all his life. These Turks can have my share. Not any more narghili for me.

I will continue the amusement business of Constantinople in some future letter.

This letter, numbered eighteen by Twain, appeared in the *Daily Alta California* of October 27, 1867. The first part of the letter was used at the beginning of Chapter VII, Volume II. "General principles" became "natural instincts"; "their points discussed" became "criticized and discussed"; "inhospitable Courts of Europe" became "courts of Europe"; "the *Alta*" became "the American metropolitan newspapers"; "getting around" became "gainsaying"; "none claim that the Greeks" became "few claim that the Greeks"; and "without digging for them" became "without a fire assay." Twain omitted the section headed "Amusements," with the exception of a few sentences about the narghile, which he worked into a passage taken from a later letter.

22. The Dogs of Constantinople

Constantinople, August, 1867.

I am half willing to believe that the celebrated dogs of Constantinople have been misrepresented—slandered. I have always been led to suppose that they were so thick in the streets that they blocked the way; that they moved about in organized companies, platoons and regiments, and took what they wanted by determined and ferocious assault; and that at night they drowned all other sounds with their terrible howlings. The dogs I see here cannot be those I have read of.

I find them everywhere, but not in strong force. The most I have found together has been about ten or twelve. And night or day a fair proportion of them were sound asleep. Those that were not asleep always looked as if they wanted to be. I never saw such utterly wretched, starving, sad-visaged, broken-hearted looking curs in all my life. It seemed a grim satire to accuse such brutes as these of taking things by force of arms. They hardly seemed to have strength enough or ambition enough to walk across the street—I do not know that I have seen one walk that far yet. They are mangy and bruised and mutilated, and often you see one with the hair singed off him in such wide and well defined tracts that he looks like a map of the new Territories. They are the sorriest beasts that breathe—the most abject—the most pitiful. In their faces is a settled expression of melancholy, an air of hopeless despondency. The patches of hair on a scalded dog are preferred by the fleas of Constantinople to a wider range on a healthier dog; and the exposed places suit the fleas exactly. I saw a dog of this kind start to nibble at a flea—a fly attracted his attention, and he started after him; the flea called for him once more, and that forever unsettled him; he looked sadly at his flea-pasture, then sadly looked at his bald spot. Then he heaved a sigh and dropped his head resignedly upon his paws. He was not equal to the situation.

The dogs sleep in the streets, all over the city. From one end of a street to the other, I suppose they will average about eight to ten to a block. Sometimes, of course, there are fifteen or twenty to a block. They do not belong to anybody, and they seem to have no close personal friendships among each other. But they district the city themselves, and the dogs of each district, whether it be half a block in extent, or ten blocks, have to remain within its bounds. Woe to him if he crosses the line! His neighbors would snatch the balance of his hair off in a second. So they say. But they don't look it.

They sleep in the streets these days. They are my compass—my guide. When I see the dogs sleep placidly on, while men, sheep, geese, and all moving things turn out and go around them, I know I am not in the great street where the hotel is, and must go further. In the Grand Rue the dogs have a sort of air of being on the lookout—an air born of being obliged to get out of the way of many carriages every day—and that expression one recognizes in a moment. It does not exist upon the face of any dog without the confines of that street. All others sleep placidly and keep no watch. They would not move, though the Sultan himself passed by.

In one narrow street (but none of them are wide) I saw three dogs lying coiled up, about a foot or two apart. A drove of a hundred sheep came along. They stepped right over the dogs, the rear crowding the front, and impatient to get on. Three dogs strung across one of these streets makes a bridge, almost. The dogs looked lazily up, flinched a little when the impatient feet of the sheep touched their raw backs—sighed, and lay peacefully down again. No talk could be plainer than that. So some of the sheep jumped over them and others scrambled between, occasionally chipping a leg with their sharp hoofs, and when the whole flock had made the trip, the dogs sneezed a little, in the cloud of dust, but never budged their bodies an inch. I thought I was lazy, but I am a steam engine compared to a Constantinople dog. But wasn't that a singular scene for a city of a million inhabitants?

Their Status

These dogs are the scavengers of the city. That is their official position, and a hard one it is. But it is their protection. But for their usefulness in partially cleansing these terrible streets, they would not be tolerated long. They eat anything and everything that comes in their way, from melon rinds and spoiled grapes up through all the grades and species of dirt and refuse to their own dead friends and relatives—and yet they are always lean, always hungry, always despondent. The people are loath to kill them—do not kill them, in fact. The Turks have an innate antipathy to taking the life of any dumb animal, it is said. But they do worse. They hang and kick and stone and scald these wretched creatures to the very verge of death, and then leave them to live and suffer.

Once a Sultan proposed to kill off all the dogs here, and did begin the work—but the populace raised such a howl of horror about it that the massacre was stayed. After a while, he proposed to remove them all to an island in the Sea of Marmora. No objection was offered, and a shipload or so was taken away. But when it came to be known that somehow or other the dogs never got to the island, but always fell overboard in the night and perished, another howl was raised and the transportation scheme was stopped.

So the dogs remain in peaceable possession of the streets. I do not say that they do not howl at night, nor that they do not attack people who have not a red fez on their heads. I only say that it would be mean for *me* to accuse them of these unseemly things who have not seen them do them with my own eyes or heard them with my own ears.

Newspaperdom in Turkey

I was a little surprised to see Turks and Greeks playing newsboy right here in the mysterious land where the giants and genii of the

Arabian Nights once dwelt—where winged horses and hydra-headed dragons guarded enchanted castles—where Princes and Princesses flew through the air on carpets that obeyed a mystic talisman—where cities whose houses were made of precious stones sprang up in a night under the hand of the magician, and where busy marts were suddenly stricken with a spell and each citizen lay or sat, or stood with weapon raised or foot advanced, just as he was, speechless and motionless, till time had told a hundred years!

It was curious to see newsboys selling papers in so dreamy a land as that. And, to say truly, it is comparatively a new thing here. The selling of newspapers had its birth in Constantinople about a year ago, and was a child of the Prussian and Austrian war.

There is one paper published here in the English language—*The Levant Herald*—and there are generally a number of Greek and a few French papers rising and falling, struggling up and falling again. You see, newspapers are not popular with the Sultan's Government. They don't understand it. The proverb says, "The unknown is always great." To the Court, the newspaper is a mysterious and rascally institution. They know what a pestilence is, because they have one occasionally that thins the people out at the rate of 2,000 a day, and they regard a newspaper as a mild form of pestilence. When it goes astray, they suppress it—pounce upon it without warning, and throttle it. When it don't go astray for a long time, they get suspicious and throttle it for luck. Imagine the Grand Vizier in solemn council with the magnates of the realm, spelling his way through the hated newspaper, and finally delivering his profound decision: "This thing means mischief—it is too darkly, too suspiciously inoffensive—suppress it! Warn the publisher that we cannot have this sort of thing; put the editor in prison!"

The newspaper business has its inconveniences in Constantinople. Two Greek papers and one French one were suppressed here within a few days of each other. No victories of the Cretans are allowed to be printed. From time to time the Grand Vizier sends a notice to the various editors that the Cretan insurrection is entirely suppressed, and although that editor knows a good deal better, he still has to print the notice. The *Levant Herald* is too fond of speaking praisefully of Americans to be popular with the Sultan, who does not relish our sympathy with the Cretans, and therefore that paper has to be particularly circumspect in order to keep out of trouble. Once the editor, forgetting the official notice in his paper that the Cretans were crushed out, printed a letter of a very different tenor, from the American Consul in Crete, and was fined $250 for it. Shortly he printed another from the same source and got imprisoned three months for his pains. I think I could get the assistant editorship of the *Levant Herald,* but I am going to try to worry along without it.

Newspapers in Naples

To suppress a paper here involves the ruin of the publisher, almost. But in Naples I think they speculate on misfortunes of that kind. Papers are suppressed there every day, and spring up the next day under a new name. During the week I staid there one paper was murdered and resurrected twice. The newsboys are smart there, just as they are elsewhere. They take advantage of popular weaknesses. When they find they are not going to sell out, they approach a citizen furtively, and say in a low voice—"Last copy, sir; double price; paper just been suppressed!" The man buys it, of course, and finds nothing in it. They do say—I do not vouch for it—but they do say that men sometimes print a vast edition of a paper, with a ferociously seditious article in it, distribute it quickly among the newsboys, and clear out till the Government's indignation cools. It pays well. Confiscation don't amount to anything. The type and presses are not worth taking care of.

There is only one English newspaper in Naples. It has seventy subscribers. The publisher is getting rich very deliberately—very deliberately indeed.

Turkish Lunch

I never want another one. The cooking apparatus was in the little lunch room, near the bazaar, and it was all open to the street. The cook was dirty, and so was the table, and it had no cloth on it. The fellow took a mass of sausage-meat and coated it round a wire and laid it on a charcoal fire to cook. When it was done, he laid it aside and a dog walked sadly in and nipped it. He smelt it first, and probably recognized the remains of a friend. The cook took it away from him and laid it before us. Brown said, "I pass"—he plays euchre sometimes—and we all passed in turn. Then the cook baked a broad, flat, wheaten cake, greased it well with the sausage, and started to bring it to us. It dropped in the dirt, and he picked it up and polished it on the seat of his breeches, and laid it before us. Brown said, "I pass." We all passed and called a new deal. He put some eggs in a frying pan, and stood pensively prying slabs of meat from between his teeth with a fork. Then he used the fork to turn the eggs with—and brought them along. Brown said, "I pass." All followed suit. We did not know what to do, and so we ordered a new ration of sausage. The cook got out his wire, apportioned a proper amount of sausage-meat, spit on his hands and fell to work. This time, with one accord, we all passed out. We paid and left. That is all I learned about Turkish lunches. A Turkish lunch is good, no doubt, but it has its weak points.

This letter, numbered nineteen by Twain, appeared in the *Daily Alta California* of October 29, 1867. It was used in Chapter VII of Volume II. "Patches of hair" became "hairless patches"; "got imprisoned" became "was imprisoned"; "during the week I staid there" became "during the ten days or a fortnight we staid there"; "are not going to sell out" became "are not likely to sell out"; "furtively" became "mysteriously"; "the cook was dirty" became "the cook was slovenly"; "Brown" became "Jack"; "started to bring it to us" became "started toward us with it"; "on the seat of his breeches" became "on his breeches"; "we all passed and called a new deal" became "we all passed"; and "its weak points" became "its little drawbacks." There were other minor revisions—both in this letter and in all the others. "When it don't go astray" and "confiscation don't" survived in the book.

23. A Genuine Turkish Bath

Constantinople, Aug. 31, 1867.

When I think how I have been swindled by books of Oriental travel, I want a tourist for breakfast. For years and years I have dreamed of the wonders of the Turkish bath; for years and years I have promised myself that I would yet enjoy one. Many and many a time, in fancy, I have lain in the marble bath, and breathed the slumbrous fragrance of eastern spices that filled the air; then passed through a weird and complicated system of pulling and hauling, and drenching and scrubbing, by a gang of naked savages who loomed vast and vaguely through the steaming mists, like demons; then rested for a while on a divan fit for a King; then passed through another complex ordeal, and one more fearful than the first; and finally, swathed in soft fabrics, was conveyed to a princely saloon and laid upon a bed of eider down, where eunuchs, gorgeous of costume, fanned me while I drowsed and dreamed, or contentedly gazed at the rich hangings of the apartment, the soft carpets, the sumptuous furniture, the pictures; and drank delicious coffee, smoked the soothing narghali [narghile], and dropped, at the last, into tranquil repose, lulled by sensuous odors from unseen censors [censers], by the gentle influence of the narghili's Persian tobacco, and by the music of fountains that counterfeited the pattering of Summer rain.

That was the picture, just as I got it from incendiary books of travel. It was a poor, miserable fraud. The reality is no more like it than the Five Points are like the Garden of Eden. They received me in a great court, paved with marble slabs; around it were broad galleries, one above another, carpeted with seedy matting, railed with unpainted balustrades, and furnished with huge, rickety chairs, cushioned with rusty old mattresses indented with impressions left by the forms of nine successive generations of men who had reposed upon them. The place was vast, naked, dreary—its court a barn, its galleries stalls for human horses. The cadaverous, half-nude varlets that served in the establishment had nothing of poetry in their appearance, nothing of romance, nothing of Oriental splendor. They shed no entrancing odors—just the contrary. Their hungry eyes and their lank forms continually suggested one glaring, unsentimental fact—they wanted a "square meal."

I went up into one of the racks and undressed. An unclean starveling wrapped a gaudy table-cloth about my loins, and hung a white rag over my shoulders. If I had had a tub then, it would have come natural to me to take in washing. I was then conducted down stairs into the wet, slippery court, and the first things that attracted my attention were my heels. My fall excited no comment. They expected it, no doubt. It belonged in the list of softening, sensuous influences peculiar to this home of eastern luxury. It was softening enough, certainly, but its application was not happy. They now gave me a pair of wooden clogs—benches in miniature, with leather straps over them to confine my feet (which they would have done, only I do not wear No. 13s). These things dangled uncomfortably by the straps when I lifted up my feet, and came down in awkward and unexpected places when I put them on the floor again, and sometimes turned sideways and wrenched my ankles out of joint. However, it was all Oriental luxury, and I did what I could to enjoy it.

They put me in another part of the barn and laid me on a stuffy sort of pallet, which was not made of cloth of gold or Persian shawls, but was merely the unpretending sort of thing I have seen in the negro quarters of Arkansas. There was nothing whatever in this dim marble prison but five more of these biers. It was a very solemn place. I expected that the spiced odors of Araby were going to steal over my senses now, but they didn't. A copper-colored skeleton, with a rag around him, brought me a glass decanter of water, with a lighted tobacco pipe in the top of it, and a pliant stem a yard long, with a brass mouth-piece to it. It was the famous "narghili" of the East—the thing the Grand Turk smokes in the pictures. This began to look like luxury. I took one blast at it, and it was sufficient. The smoke all went down my throat. It came back in convulsive snorts through my nose. It had a vile taste, and the taste of a thousand infidel tongues that remained on that brass mouth-piece was viler still. I was getting discouraged. Whenever hereafter I see the cross-legged Grand Turk smoking his narghili, in pretended bliss, on the outside of a paper of Connecticut tobacco, I shall know him for the shameless humbug he is.

This prison was filled with hot air. When I had got warmed up sufficiently to prepare me for a still warmer temperature, they took me where it was—into a marble room, wet, slippery, and steamy, and laid me out on a raised platform in the center. It was very warm. Presently my man sat me down by a tank of hot water, drenched me well, gloved his hand with a coarse mitten, and began to polish me all over with it. I began to smell disagreeably. The more he polished, the worse I smelt. It was alarming. I said to him: "I perceive that I am pretty far gone. It is plain that I ought to be buried without any unnecessary delay. Perhaps you had better go after my friends at once, because the weather is warm, and I cannot 'keep' long." He went on scrubbing, and paid no attention. I soon saw that he was reducing my size. He bore hard on his mitten, and from under it rolled little cylinders, like maccaroni. It could not be dirt, for it was too white. He pared me down in this way for a long time. Finally I said: "It is a tedious process; it will take hours to trim me to the size you want me. I will wait; go and borrow a jack-plane." He paid no attention at all.

After a while he brought a basin, some soap, and something that seemed to be the tail of a horse. He made up a prodigious quantity of soap-suds, deluged me with them from head to foot without warning me to shut my eyes, and then swabbed me viciously with the horse-tail. Then he left me there, a statue of snowy lather, and went away. When

I got tired of waiting, I went and hunted him up. He was propped against the wall, in another room, asleep. I woke him. He was not disconcerted. He took me back and flooded me with exhausting hot water, then turbaned my head, swathed me with dry table-cloths, and conducted me to a laticed chicken-coop in one of the galleries, and pointed to one of those Arkansas beds. I mounted it, and vaguely expected the odors of Araby again. They did not come. The blank, unornamented coop had nothing about it of that Oriental voluptuousness one reads of so much. It was more suggestive of the county hospital than anything else. The skinny servitor brought a narghili, and I got him to take it out again without wasting any time about it. Then he brought the world-renowned Turkish coffee that poets have sung so rapturously for many generations, and I seized upon it as the last hope that was left of my old dreams of Eastern luxury. It was another swindle. Of all the unchristian beverages that ever passed my lips, Turkish coffee is the worst. The cup is small, it is smeared with grounds; the coffee is black, thick, unsavory of smell, and execrable in taste. The bottom of the cup has a muddy sediment in it half an inch deep. This goes down your throat, and portions of it lodge by the way and produce a tickling aggravation that keeps you barking and coughing for an hour.

Here endeth my experience of the celebrated Turkish bath, and here also endeth my dream of the bliss the mortal revels in who passes through it. It is a malignant swindle. The man who enjoys it is qualified to enjoy anything that is repulsive to sight or sense, and he that can invest it with the charm of poetry is able to do the same with anything else in the world that is tedious, and wretched, and dismal, and nasty.

As for the Dancing Dervishes, they are a delusion and a folly. They are a pack of miserable lunatics in long robes, who spin round, and round, and round, with closed eyes and arms elevated and extended, and look as ridiculous as it is possible for any creature to look. They keep time to a caterwauling of barbarous instruments and more barbarous human voices, and travelers call the stupid performance and its infamous accompaniments "impressive." So would be a carnival of idiots and tom-cats.

The Dervishes are so holy that you must take your boots off when you enter their menagerie—their mosque, if you like it better. There are 300 visitors, 600 bare feet, and no two of them emit a similar fragrance. Here you have 600 different smells to start with. There are 30 Dervishes; they spin around a large, close room nine times and exhale a different odor every time, and a meaner one. So there you have 870 separate and distinct smells, and any one of them worse than a burning rag factory. Truly it is very impressive. The Dancing Dervishes are the dreariest, silliest humbugs in all the Orient. They know it as well as anybody. Yet every ass that comes here from a distant land rushes there to see them, just as I did, and then rushes to the photographer's and buys their pictures—which I did not do. I wish I were Sultan for one day. I would hang all the Dervishes for 40 minutes, and if they did not behave themselves after that I would be severe with them.

The books of travel have shamefully deceived me all these years, but they can never do it more. The narghili, the dervishes, the aromatic coffee, the Turkish bath—these are the things I have accepted and believed in, with simple, unquestioning faith, from boyhood; and, behold, they are the poorest, sickest, wretchedest humbugs the world can furnish. Wonders, forsooth! What is Turkish coffee to the coffee at home? What is a narghili to a meerschaum? What is a Turkish bath in Constantinople to a Russian one in New-York? What are the dancing dervishes to the negro minstrels?—and Heaven help us, what is Oriental splendor to the Black Crook? New-York has fifty wonders where Constantinople has one!

This letter, printed in the *New York Tribune* on October 25, 1867, was used in Volume II, Chapter VII, immediately following Letter 22. "Was conveyed" became "been conveyed," and "fraud" became "imposture." "The smoke all went down my throat. It came back in convulsive snorts through my nose" became "the smoke went in a great volume down into my stomach, my lungs, even into the uttermost parts of my frame. I exploded one mighty cough, and it was as if Vesuvius had let go. For the next five minutes I smoked at every pore, like a frame house that is on fire on the inside. Not any more Narghili for me"—which Mark Twain took, with revisions, from a rejected passage at the end of Letter 21. "Statue of snowy lather" became "snowy statue of lather," and "another swindle" became "another fraud." The account of the dancing dervishes and the remainder of the letter were omitted—Twain had already described the dancing dervishes in a passage taken from Letter 20.

24. Sebastopol

Sebastopol, August 22d.

This is probably the worst battered town in Russia or anywhere else. But we ought to be pleased with it, nevertheless, for we have been in no country yet where we have been so kindly received, or where we felt that to be Americans was a sufficient *visé* for our passports. The moment the anchor was down, the Governor of the town immediately despatched an officer on board to inquire if he could be of any assistance to us, and to invite us to make ourselves at home in Sebastopol! If you know Russia, you know that this was a wild stretch of hospitality. They are usually so suspicious of strangers that they worry them to death with the delays and aggravations incident to a complicated passport system. Had we come from any other country we could not have had permission to enter Sebastopol and leave again under three days—but we were at liberty to go and come when and where we pleased. Everybody in Constantinople warned us to be very careful about our passports, see that they were strictly *en regle*, and never to mislay them for a moment; and they told us of numerous instances of Englishmen and others who were delayed days, weeks, and even months, in Sebastopol, on account of trifling informalities in their passports, and for which they were not to blame. I had lost my passport, and was travelling under my room-mate's, who stayed behind in Constantinople to await our return. To read the description of him in that passport and then look at me, any man could see that I was no more like him than I am like Hercules. So I went into the harbor of Sebastopol with fear and trembling—full of vague, horrible apprehensions—I went sneaking about with dread in my soul and a sickly grin on my face which I was trying to pass off for gaiety—and finally my soul went down into my boots, and I made up my mind that I was going to be found out and hung. But all that time my true passport had been floating gallantly overhead—and behold it was only the Stars and Stripes. They never asked us for any other.

We have had a great many Russian and English gentlemen and ladies on board to-day, and the time has passed cheerfully away. They were all happy spirited people, and I never heard our mother tongue sound so pleasantly as it did when it fell from those English lips in this far-off land. I talked to the Russians a good deal, just to be friendly, and they talked to me from the same motive; I am sure that both enjoyed the conversation, but blast the word of it either of us understood. I did most of my talking to those English folks, though, and I am sorry we cannot carry some of them along with us.

We have gone whithersoever we chose, to-day, and have met with nothing but the kindest attentions. Nobody ever inquired whether we had any passports or not. More than that, every port charge has been remitted in favor of our ship. The authorities have declined to receive a cent.

A Distinguished Invitation

Several of the officers of the Government have insisted on our taking the ship to a little watering-place thirty miles from here, and paying the Emperor of Russia a visit. He is rusticating there. These officers said they would take it upon themselves to insure us a cordial reception. They said if we would go, they would not only telegraph the Emperor, but send a special courier overland to announce our coming. Our time is so short, though, and more especially our coal is so nearly out, that we judged it best to forego the rare pleasure of holding social intercourse with an Emperor. I am mighty sorry about this, because I never got a chance to take a drink with the King of the Sandwich Islands, and now that I have got a show at an Emperor, I don't like to lose it. It would do me proud to clink glasses with him just once, and say "Here's luck!" Why, with my experience, I could give that man some ideas about governing a kingdom that would be worth a thousand dollars to him—upon my word. However, let it pass. I am out of luck again, I suppose. If I could only get a chance at an Emperor once, he might want to adopt a likely young man, but—let it pass, let it pass.

The Battered Town

Ruined Pompeii is in good condition compared to Sebastopol. Here, you may look in whatsoever direction you please, and your eye encounters scarcely anything but ruin, ruin, ruin!—fragments of houses, crumbled walls, torn and ragged hills, devastation everywhere! It is as if a mighty earthquake had spent all its terrible forces upon this one little spot. For eighteen long months the storms of war beat upon the helpless town, and left it at last the saddest wreck that ever the sun has looked upon. Not one solitary house escaped unscathed—not one remained habitable, even. Such utter and complete ruin I could not have conceived of. The houses were all solid, dressed stone structures; most of them were ploughed through and through by cannon balls—unroofed and cut down from eaves to foundation—and now a row of them, half a mile long, looks merely like an endless procession of battered chimneys. No semblance of a house remains in such as these. Some of the larger buildings had corners knocked off; pillars cut in two; cornices smashed; holes driven straight through the walls. Many of these holes are as round and as cleanly cut as if they had been made with an auger. Others are half pierced through, and the clean impression is there in the rock, as smooth and as shapely as if it were done in putty. Here and there a ball still sticks in a wall, and from it iron stains trickle down and discolor the stone.

The Battle-Fields

They were pretty close together. The Malakoff tower is on a hill which is right in the edge of the town. The Redan was within rifle-shot of the Malakoff; Inkerman was a mile away; and Balaklava removed but an hour's ride. The French trenches, by which they approached and invested the Malakoff, were carried so close under its sloping sides that one might have stood by the Russian guns and tossed a stone into them. Repeatedly, during three terrible days, they swarmed up the little Malakoff hill, and were beaten back with terrible slaughter. Finally, they captured the place, drove the Russians out, and they tried to retreat into the town, but the English had taken the Redan, and shut them off with a wall of flame; there was nothing for them to do but go back and retake the Malakoff or die under its guns. They did go back; they took the Malakoff and retook it three times, but their desperate valor could not avail, and they had to give up at last.

These fearful fields, where such tempests of death used to rage, are peaceful enough now; no sound is heard, hardly a living thing moves about them, they are lonely and silent—their desolation is complete.

Relic Hunting

There was nothing else to do, and so everybody went to hunting relics. They have stocked the ship with them. They brought them from the Malakoff, from the Redan, Inkerman, Balaklava—everywhere. They have brought cannon balls, broken ramrods, fragments of shell—iron enough to freight a sloop. Some have even brought bones—brought them laboriously from great distances, and were grieved to hear the surgeon pronounce them only the bones of mules and oxen.

I never supposed that Brown would lose an opportunity like this. He brought a sackful on board and started after another. I stopped him. He has already turned the state-room into a museum of worthless trumpery, which he has gathered up in his travels. He is labelling his trophies, now. I picked up one a while ago, and found it marked "Fragment of a Russian General." I carried it out to get a better light upon it—it was but a couple of teeth and part of the jaw-bone of a horse! I said, with some asperity:

"Fragment of a Russian General! This is absurd. Are you never going to learn any sense?"

He only said: "Go slow—the old woman won't know any different."

This fellow gathers mementoes with a perfect recklessness, nowadays; mixes them all up together, and then serenely labels them without any regard to truth, propriety, or even plausibility. I have found him breaking a stone in two, and labelling half of it, "Piece broken from the pulpit of Demosthenes," and the other half "Darnick [Dornick] from the Tomb of Abelard and Heloise." I have known him to gather up a handful of pebbles by the roadside, and bring them on board ship and label them as coming from twenty celebrated localities five hundred miles apart. I remonstrate against these outrages upon reason and truth, of course, but it does no good. I get the same tranquil, unanswerable reply every time:

"It don't signify—the old woman won't know any different."

Ever since we three or four fortunate ones made that midnight trip to Athens, it has afforded him genuine satisfaction to give everybody in the ship a pebble from the Mars-hill where St. Paul preached. He got all those pebbles on the sea shore, abreast the ship, after he came back. However, it isn't of any use for me to expose the swindle—it affords him pleasure, and does no harm to anybody. He says he never expects to run out of mementoes of St. Paul as long as he is in reach of a sand-bank. Well, he is no worse than others. I notice that all travellers supply deficiencies in their collections in the same way. I shall never have any confidence in such things again while I live.

This letter, numbered twenty by Twain, appeared in the *Daily Alta California* of November 1, 1867. It was used as Chapter XIII in Volume II. Twain provided an introductory paragraph. "Worry them to death" became "worry them excessively." The sentence beginning "So I went into the harbor of Sebastopol" was shortened from sixty-seven words to twenty-eight. "Hung" became "hanged"; "the Stars and Stripes" became "our flag"; and "blast the word" became "never a word." The sentence beginning "More than that, every port charge" and the following sentence were omitted. "Have insisted on our taking" became "have suggested that we take." The sentence beginning "I am mighty sorry about this" and all the remainder of the paragraph were omitted. "Brown" became "Blucher." After "the old woman won't know any different," Twain added "(His aunt)." "Piece broken" became "chunk busted"; "after he came back" became "but professes to have gathered them from one of our party"; and "swindle" became "deception."

25. Arrival in Odessa

Odessa, Russia, August 22d.

We have got so far east, now—a hundred and fifty-five degrees of longitude from San Francisco—that my watch cannot keep the hang of the time any more. It has got discouraged and stopped. I think it did a wise thing. The difference in time between Sebastopol and Sacramento is enormous. When it is six o'clock in the morning here, it is week before last in California. Counting one or two detours from the straight line, this watch has travelled considerably more than ten thousand miles east from San Francisco, and as neither of us are accustomed to wandering very far from home, we are excusable for getting a little tangled as to time. I have ciphered it out far enough to know, that with a good deal over ten hours' difference between this place and the Pacific the sun is rising here when it is setting in San Francisco, or it is rising in San Francisco when it is setting here, I cannot tell which. These distractions and distresses about the time have worried me so much that I was afraid my mind was so much affected that I never would have any appreciation of time again; but when I noticed how handy I was yet about comprehending when it was dinner-time, a blessed tranquillity settled down upon me and I am tortured with doubts and fears no more.

Odessa

This is about twenty hours' run from Sebastopol and is the most northerly port in the Black Sea. We came here to get coal, principally. The city has a population of 133,000, and is growing faster than [any] other small city out of America. It is a free port, and is the great grain mart of this particular part of the world. Its roadstead is full of ships.

Engineers are at work, now, turning this open roadstead into a spacious artificial harbor. It is to be almost enclosed by massive stone piers, one of which will extend into the sea over 3,000 feet in a straight line. Sir Charles Hartley, a very distinguished English engineer, won the $8,000 prize for the best plan for the new harbor, and he was shrewd enough to leave some of the instructions as to the mode of building it obscure enough to render it best for the Government to accept his bid for its construction. It is a comfortable speculation. He is to complete it in five years, and gets $5,000,000 for it.

Suggestions of Home

I have not felt so much at home for a long time as I did when I "raised the hill" and stood in Odessa for the first time. It looked just like an American city; fine, broad streets, and straight as well; low houses (two or three stories), wide, neat, and free from any quaintness of architectural ornamentation; locust trees bordering the sidewalks (they call them acacias); a stirring, business-look about the streets and the stores; fast walkers; a familiar *new* look about the houses and everything; yea, and a driving and smothering cloud of dust that was so like a message from our own dear native land that we could not refrain from shedding a few grateful tears and swearing in the old time-honored way. Look up the street or down the street, this way or that way, we saw only America! There was not one thing to remind us that we were in Russia. We walked for some little distance, revelling in this home vision, and then we came upon a church and a hack driver, and lo! the illusion vanished! The church had a slender-spired dome that rounded inward at its base, and looked like a boy's peg-top turned upside down, and the hack-man seemed to be dressed in a long petticoat without any hoops. These things were essentially foreign, and so were the carriages—but everybody knows about these things, and there is no occasion for my describing them.

Loafing

We were only to stay here a day and a night and take in coal; we consulted the guide-books and were rejoiced to know that there were no sights in Odessa to see; and so we had one good, untrammelled holiday on our hands, with nothing to do but idle about the city and enjoy ourselves. We prowled through the markets and criticized the fearful and wonderful costumes from the back country; examined the populace as far as eyes could do it; and closed the entertainment with an ice-cream debauch. We do not get ice-cream everywhere, and if we do, we are apt to dissipate to excess.

We only found two pieces of statuary, and this was another blessing. One was a bronze image of the Duc de Richelieu, grand nephew of the splendid Cardinal. It stood in a spacious, handsome promenade, overlooking the sea, and from its base a vast flight of stone steps led down to the harbor—two hundred of them, fifty feet long, and a wide landing at the bottom of every twenty. It is a noble staircase, and from a distance the people toiling up it looked like insects. I mention this statue and this stairway because they have their story. Richelieu founded Odessa—watched over it with paternal care—labored with a fertile brain and a wise understanding for its best interests—spent his fortune freely to the same end—endowed it with a sound prosperity, and one which will yet make it one of the great cities of the Old World—built this noble stairway with money from his own private purse—and—. Well, the people for whom he had done so much, let him walk down these same steps, one day, unattended, old, poor, without a second coat to his back; and when years afterwards, he died in Sebastopol in poverty and neglect, they called a meeting, subscribed liberally, and immediately erected this tasteful monument to his memory, and named a great street after him. It reminds me of what Robert Burns' mother said when they erected a stately monument to his memory: "Ah, Robbie, ye asked them for bread and they hae gi'en ye a stone."

Cheerful Bathing

If there is one thing that is really cheerful in the world, it is cheerfulness. I have noticed it often. And I have noticed that when a man is right down cheerful, he is seldom unhappy for the time being. Such is the nature of man. Now I have often thought that our style of bathing was rather reserved than otherwise, and lacked many elements of cheerfulness. But you cannot say that of the Russian style. I watched a party of them at it this afternoon in the harbor, and it is really nice. The men and women, and boys and girls, all go in together, along about noon, and the men don't wear anything at all, the boys don't, the little girls don't, and the young women and the old women usually wear a single white thin garment with ruffles around the top of it and short sleeves, (which I have forgotten the name of it,) but this would be a very good apology for a bathing dress, if it would only stay down. But it don't do it. It will float up around their necks in the most scandalous way, and the water is clear, and yet they don't seem to know enough to kick up the mud on the bottom. I never was so outraged in my life. At least a hundred times, in the seven hours I stayed there, I would just have got up and gone away from there disgusted, if I had had any place to go to. Several times I had a mind to go anyhow. Why, those young ladies thought no more of turning somersaults, when I was not looking, than nothing in the world. Incensed as I was, I was compelled to look, most of the time, during this barbarous exhibition, because it forced them to make a show of modesty, at least. Yet it wouldn't even have accomplished that, if they hadn't been so fond of show naturally.

Well, you can't conceive of it. It was awful. But sometimes my outraged feelings were crowded down by my fears for the safety of those girls. They were so reckless. One splendid-looking young woman went in with nothing on but a shawl, and she kept it wrapped around her so that I was afraid all the time that she would tangle her feet in its long fringes and drown herself. My solicitude became so unbearable at last that I went and signified to her that if she wanted to take off her shawl I would hold it for her. But she only kicked up her heels and dived out of sight. I just took her to be one of your high-flyer, mock-modest kind, and left her to her fate. But she was the handsomest girl in the party, and it was a pity to see her endangering her life in that way.

I said to Brown: "It makes my heart bleed to look upon this unhallowed scene."

"We better go, then," he said. "If you stay here seven more hours you might bleed to death."

So we went away. But it was marvellously cheerful bathing.

The Die Is Cast

The people of Odessa have warmly recommended us to go and call on the Emperor, as did the Sebastopolians. They have telegraphed his Majesty, and he has signified his perfect willingness to grant us an audience. So we are getting up the anchors and preparing to sail to his watering-place. What a scratching around there is going to be, now! what a holding of important meetings and appointing of solemn committees!—and what a furbishing up of claw-hammer coats and white silk neck-ties! As this fearful ordeal we are about to pass through pictures itself to my fancy in all its dread sublimity, I begin to feel my fierce desire to take a drink with a genuine Emperor cooling down and passing away. What am I going to do with my hands? What am I going to do with my feet? What in the world am I going to do with myself? The Consul says we must stand in a row and be perfectly civil, and the Emperor and a long file of gorgeously caparisoned Dukes and Princes and Generals will march in stately procession before us, and bow as they go. We must bow low, and smile—smile a smile of friendly interest, of affection, of admiration—a smile which must be so comprehensive that it shall seem that through us, all America smiled! If the Emperor speaks to any he in the party, that man must talk back, but do it with a world of deference and good-breeding. All right—but if he says anything to me in Russian I shall have to pass. And the Consul says that we must invite the Emperor to come on board and take a trip; and if he accepts, we must all vacate the ship, and give her up entirely to his control as long as he wants her. His family and suite will number a hundred and fifty, and fill her full. If he chooses to invite half a dozen of us to accompany his party, we must gratefully accept—the others must stay ashore. But the Emperor must be sole lord of the vessel for the time being. Very well, I do not consider that it is taking any chances. The Emperor is one of the most responsible men in Europe.

And the Consul also says that if the Emperor takes a trip, he will doubtless invite our whole tribe to dine with him at the palace two or three days afterward. Well, we are bound for Palestine anyhow. (A pun will be observed in the last sentence.) We are all tired of ship fare. We are all mighty hungry. I foresee that the Emperor is going to bring a famine upon himself if he invites this gang to dinner, but it is his own fault. Nobody will be to blame but himself. Think of the way those varlets will waltz through the Imperial bill of fare!

This letter, numbered twenty-one by Twain, appeared in the *Daily Alta California* of November 3, 1867. It was used in Chapter IX of Volume II. Eighty-four words were deleted from the middle of the first paragraph, and the last three sentences of the second paragraph were omitted. "Could not refrain from shedding a few grateful tears and swearing in the old time-honored way" became "could hardly refrain from shedding a few grateful tears and execrations in the old time-honored American way"; "boy's peg-top" became "turnip"; and "prowled" became "sauntered." Twain omitted the section headed "Cheerful Bathing." "Perfect willingness" became "willingness"; "take a drink" became "converse"; and "What am I going to do?" became "What am I to do?" The chapter ends with "What in the world am I to do with myself?" The remainder of the letter was omitted.

26. A Visit to the Emperor of Russia

Yalta, Russia, Aug. 26, 1867.

The passengers on board the American steam yacht Quaker City have been paying a pleasant, informal visit to His Majesty, the Autocrat of all the Russias, at his Summer palace near this village. We were not smothered with attentions at Constantinople. America is in bad odor there, on account of her outspoken sympathy with the Cretans. But we found a different atmosphere in Russia. At Sebastopol we were received with great cordiality, and were not even asked to show our passports—a singular thing to occur in a Russian port. We were surprised because we had been warned that those documents would be called for and strictly scrutinized about every 40 minutes while we remained in the Czar's territories. One of the passengers began to inquire into the matter. The Russian officer he spoke to explained it in a very few words, and very gracefully. He said: "Yonder is your passport—the flag you are flying is sufficient!"

The Sebastopolitans said the Emperor of Russia was spending the Summer at the little watering-place of Yalta, 40 miles away, and warmly recommended us to take the ship there and visit him. They said they could insure us a kind reception. They insisted on telegraphing and also sending a courier overland to announce us. But we had been told that the great Viceroy of Egypt had had his visit there almost for nothing a few days before, and we were modest enough to have our doubts. So we went our way to Odessa, 200 miles distant. Again we were well received, and again they said "Go and see the Emperor." Finally the Governor-General telegraphed the court, a prompt reply was returned, and we sailed toward Yalta. A great question had to be solved: What is to be done and how are we to do it?

We had the United States Consul on board—the Odessa Consul. We assembled all hands in the cabin and commanded him to tell us what we must do to be saved, and tell us quickly. He made a speech. The first thing he said fell like a blight upon every hopeful spirit: he had never seen a court reception! (Three groans for the Consul.) But he said he had seen receptions at the Governor-General's in Odessa, and had often listened to people's experiences of receptions at the Russian and various other courts, and believed he knew pretty well what sort of ordeal we were about [to] essay. (Hope budded again.) He said we were many; the Summer palace was small—a mere mansion; doubtless we should be received in Summer fashion—in the garden: we would stand in a row, all the gentlemen in swallow-tail coats, white kids and white neck-ties, and the ladies in light-colored silks, or something of that kind; at the proper moment—12 meridian—the Emperor, attended by his suite arrayed in splendid uniforms, would appear and walk slowly along the line, bowing to some, and saying two or three words to others. At the moment His Majesty appeared, a universal, delighted, enthusiastic smile ought to break out like an epidemic among the passengers—a smile of love, of gratification, of admiration—and with one accord. The party must begin to bow—not obsequiously, but respectfully, and with dignity, at the end of 15 minutes the Emperor would go in the house, and we could shin along home again. We felt immensely relieved. It seemed, in a manner, easy. There wasn't a man in the party but believed that with a little practice he could stand in a row, especially if there were others along; there wasn't a man but believed he could bow without tripping on his coat-tail and breaking his neck; in a word, we came to believe we were equal to any item in the performance except that complicated smile. The counsel [consul] also said that we ought to draft a little address to the Emperor, and present it to one of his aides-de-camp, who would forward it to him at the proper time. Therefore, five of us were appointed to prepare the document, and the 50 others went sadly smiling about the ship. During the next twelve hours we had the general appearance, somehow, of being at a funeral where everybody was sorry the death had occurred, but glad it was over—where everybody was smiling, and yet broken-hearted. The Consul's closing statement was that it would be etiquette to invite the Emperor to visit the ship, and that he would respectfully decline, as usual.

A committee went ashore to wait on his Excellency the Governor-General, and learn our fate. At the end of three hours of boding suspense they came back and said the Emperor would receive us at noon the next day—would send carriages for us—would hear the address in person. The Grand Duke Michel [Michael] had sent to invite us to his palace also—both desired to visit the ship the following day with their families, the weather permitting. Counterfeited smiles never gave place to real ones so suddenly before! Any man could see that there was an intention here to show that Russia's friendship for America was so genuine as to render even her private citizens objects worthy of kindly attentions.

At the appointed hour we drove out three miles, and assembled in the handsome garden in front of the Emperor's palace. In five minutes the Autocrat came out, and with him the Empress, the Grand Duchess Marie (her daughter, a pretty, blue-eyed, fair-haired girl of 14), and a little Grand Duke, about 10 years old. With them came a few princes and great dignitaries in handsome, but not gaudy uniforms. We took off our hats. I smiled a reckless smile at the finest uniform, but I found it was only the Lord High Admiral, and so I had to smile it all over again. If I had had any sense I might have known that the Imperial family would be the plainest dressed personages on the spot. The Consul read the address to the Emperor and then handed it to him. He said a word or two in reply, and passed the document to a court dignitary. This is the address:

To His Imperial Majesty ALEXANDER II., *Emperor of Russia:*

We are a handfull of private citizens of America, traveling simply for recreation—and unostentatiously, as becomes our unofficial state—and, therefore, we have no excuse to tender for presenting ourselves before your Majesty, save the desire of offering our grateful acknowledgments to the lord of a realm, which through good and through evil report, has been the steadfast friend of the land we love so well.

We could not presume to take a step like this, did we not know well that the words we speak here, and the sentiments wherewith they are freighted, are but the reflex of the thoughts and the feelings of all our countrymen, from the green hills of New England to the shores of the far Pacific. We are few in number, but we utter the voice of a nation!

One of the brightest pages that has graced the world's history since written history had its birth was recorded by your Majesty's hand when it loosed the bonds of twenty millions of men; and Americans can but esteem it a privilege to do honor to a ruler who has wrought so great a deed. The lesson that was taught us then we have profited by, and are free in truth to-day, even as we were before in name. America owes much to Russia—is indebted to her in many ways, and chiefly for her unwavering friendship in seasons of our greatest need. That that friendship may still be hers in times to come we confidently pray; that she is and will be grateful to Russia and to her sovereign for it, we know full well; that she will ever forfeit it by any unpremeditated, unjust act or unfair course, it were treason to believe.

SAM L. CLEMENS, WM. GIBSON,
TIMOTHY D. CROCKER, S. A. SANFORD,
COL. P. KINNEY, U. S.A.,
Committee on behalf of the passengers of the steamer Quaker City.

The Emperor had on a white cloth cap, and white cloth coat and pantaloons, all of questionable fineness. The Empress and her daughter wore simple suits of foulard, with a little blue spot in it, blue trimmings, low-crowned straw hats trimmed with blue velvet, linen collars, clerical neck-ties of muslin, blue sashes, flesh-colored gloves, parasols—lady readers will take due notice. The exceeding simplicity of these dresses would insure them against creating a sensation in Broadway. The little Grand Duke wore a red calico blouse and a straw hat, and had his pantaloons tucked into his boots. Simplicity of costume and kingly stateliness of manner cannot go very well together, and I was curious to see how the Imperial party would act. They acted as if they had never been used to anything finer. They were as free from any semblance of pride or haughtiness as if their house had always been a village minister's house. They conversed freely and unconstrainedly with anybody and everybody that came along (they all speak English) and so did the great officers of the Empire that were with them. Our party of Americans who were so distressed the day before, as to how they were going to get through this severe trial with credit, suddenly found themselves entirely at home and comfortable.

The 15-minutes audience pleasantly augmented itself to half an hour, and then, instead of dismissing the guests, the Autocrat of all the Russias and his family transformed themselves into ushers, and led our tribe into the palace dining-room, into the library, the private chapel, the sitting-rooms, private writing-room—all over the establishment, in fact. I cannot recollect half the places. There was no hurry; there were plenty of affable Dukes and Princes, and Admirals to answer questions, and this part of the programme insensibly wore out another half hour, and something over. When there was nothing more to see, the Imperial family bade the guests good-by "till to-morrow," and we departed for the palace of the Grand Duke Michael. The young Grand Duchess, however, went to another door and bowed at the party in detail as they passed by. If you have ever called on an Emperor you will remember that little attentions not strictly in the bill were the very ones that went furthest toward making you feel comfortable. That young girl's pleasant face, its expression of friendly interest, and her timid bow, were not calculated to make any one feel like a tiresome nuisance. In my own case I know this was so. It struck me forcibly at the time that I had seldom felt so little like a nuisance before.

It is singular, but for the moment I forgot that before all this leave-taking occurred we were invited to the palace of the crown-prince of Russia (aged twenty), and shown all through it with the same absence of hurry as was the case at his father's mansion.

A drive of twenty minutes brought us to the beautiful park and gardens and the elegant palace of the Grand-Duke Michael. The first persons we saw there were the Empress and her daughter. They had come by a nearer road, I suppose. Whether justly or not, we chose to consider this as a mark that they were not altogether tired of us yet. The introduction to the Grand Duke and his Duchess was hardly over when the Emperor arrived himself. This was about as cheerful as it could be. He caught up his brother's little children and kissed them affectionately. I could not help noticing that, because it was so little like what we had reason to expect from the stern Russian Bear we read about so much.

The Grand Duchess was as simply dressed as the Empress—was as gentle and unreserved, and as ready to talk with everybody. Her husband was just like her in these respects—a splendid looking man, over six feet high, well formed, and endowed with as kingly a presence as one could wish to see. He wore a handsome Cossack uniform, and looked the military commander to a charm. He it was who crushed out, in a two-months' campaign, the Caucasian war, that had lasted 60 years, and won the coveted first-degree cross of the Order of St. George—the only man who has been so decorated in 200 years. It is a distinction that can be achieved, but the terms are not easy—dauntless courage, exalted military genius, and—success.

There was but little ceremony here. We were shown through the palace in the free-and-easy way we had already got accustomed to, and then our friends, the Princes, and Generals, and Baronesses, conducted the gang all about the lawns and groves of the park. I enjoyed it. I had reached my level at last. If there is one thing that I am naturally fitted for, it is to converse with Dukes. I got along well. They could not understand the subtleties of an American joke, it is true, and so they generally laughed in the wrong place. However, it wasn't any matter—they were inferior jokes anyhow, and some of them very old.

Some of us lingered in the grounds a good while, and when we got back we found the balance of the mob scattered about the reception-room and the verandahs, sitting at little tables, and drinking tea and wine and eating bread and cheese and cold meats with the Grand Duke, who ate at one table a while and then at another, and kept the conversation and the destruction of provisions going with a zeal which was perfectly astonishing in the brother of an Emperor. I did not suppose that the brothers of autocrats were so much like other people. Some people have curious ways about them. This sort of thing may have suited His Imperial Highness, but if I were a Grand Duke I wouldn't eat with those varlets. As the circumstances stood, however, I took a hand. They give you a lemon to squeeze into your tea there, or iced milk if you prefer it. The former is best. The Grand Duke's tea was delicious. It is brought overland from China. It injures the article to transport it by sea.

Well, to cut a long story short, it was a chatty, sociable tea-party, and free from restraint. Whoever chose got up and walked about and talked, and in all human probability would have been allowed to whistle if he had wanted to. And it was a pleasant picnic all through, from the time we left the ship till we got back again. We had spent nearly half a day with the heads of the Russian Empire, and it had seemed as if we were merely visiting a party of ordinary friends. There was not one of them but had said the kindest things about America, and said them with an earnestness that proved their sincerity—not one but had done everything he could to make us feel contented and at home. I fear for our less liberal hospitality. If they visit the ships they will find a sign up: "No smoking abaft the wheel"—but the Grand Duke passed around his box of cigars in his own reception-room. And there was another incident that shows how little he was inclined to put on airs, and how genuine the seeming cordiality of our reception was. This lordly brother of an Emperor, and himself sub-chief of half an empire, came down on his horse to Yalta, three miles, when we first came ashore, and escorted our procession all the way to the palace, keeping a sharp look-out, and dispatching his aids hither and thither to furnish assistance whenever it was needed; and, being dressed in an unpretentious uniform, nobody ever suspected who he was until we recognized him in his own palace. I doubt if he goes about escorting a rabble of plain civilians every day.

You may possibly think that our party tarried too long, or did other improper things, but such was not the case. Their going and coming, and all their movements, were quietly regulated by the imperial master of ceremonies. Mr. M. Curtin, our Secretary of Legation at St. Petersburgh, was present, and his advice was frequently asked and followed. The company felt that they were occupying an unusually responsible position—they were representing the people of America, not the Government—and therefore they were especially anxious to perform their high mission with credit.

On the other hand, the Imperial families, no doubt, considered that in entertaining us they were more especially entertaining the people of America than they could by showering attentions on a whole platoon of ministers plenipotentiary; and therefore they gave to the event its fullest significance, as an expression of good will and friendly feeling toward the entire country. We took the kindnesses we received as attentions thus directed, of course, and not to ourselves as a party. That we felt a personal pride in being received as the representatives of a great people, we do not deny; that we felt a national pride in the warm cordiality of that reception, cannot be doubted. The address and an account of the proceedings have already been forwarded to various Russian newspapers for publication, and thus our little holiday adventure is invested with a degree of political significance. It is well. We represented only the true feeling of America toward Russia when we thanked her, through her Chief, for her valuable friendship in times past and hoped that it would continue.

The sea has been very rough to-day, but still many Russian nobles, civilians, and officers of the army and navy have visited the ship. Among them were Baron Wrangel, formerly Russian Embassador at Washington, the Admiral and several Vice-Admirals of the Russian fleets, and Gen. Todtleben, the honored defender, for 18 trying months, of Sebastopol. For his distinguished services there he has been decorated with the crosses of the third and fourth degree of the Order of St.

George. By invitation we visited the Empress's yacht this morning, and afterward brought back the captains of that vessel and of one of the Emperor's yachts to breakfast with us. We have visitors on board all the time, and if we only had the boundless politeness these Russians are naturally gifted with we could entertain them well. They are able to make themselves pleasant company, whether they speak one's language or not, but our tribe can't think of anything to do or say when they get hold of a subject of the Czar who knows only his own language. However, one of our ladies, from Cleveland, Ohio, is a notable exception to this rule. She escorts Russian ladies about the ship, and talks and laughs with them, and makes them feel at home. They comprehend no word she utters, but they understand the good-will and the friendliness that are in the tones of her voice. I wish we had more like her. They all try, but none succeed so well as she.

The Emperor is very tall and slender—spare, one may say—and his bearing is full of dignity and easy self-possession. An unbending will is stamped upon his face, and yet when he smiles his blue eyes are as gentle as a woman's. His hair and whiskers are very light. He is 48 years old, but looks about 53 or 54.

The Grand Duke Michael is very tall and well shaped; has a blue eye that must beam with a wicked light when he is angry, though it is lively and pleasant enough under peaceable circumstances; his whiskers and mustache (a modification of the Dundreary pattern) are light, and he cuts his hair as close as plush, and don't curl it. He is as straight as an Indian, and if ever a man looked what they call "born to command," he does. His is the stateliest figure in Europe, I am willing to believe. His courtly grace, his fine military bearing, his varied accomplishments, and his knightly achievements make of him a Russian Sir Philip Sydney. He is greatly beloved in Russia.

The Czar and his brother would be marked in a crowd as great men and good ones. The Emperor Napoleon would be marked in a crowd as a great man and a cunning one. The Sultan of Turkey would not be marked in a crowd at all. I want to see one more assortment of Kings and average them, and then I shall be satisfied.

The day is drawing to a close, and the sea is so rough that the Emperor will certainly not visit the ship. Baron Ungern-Sternberg, the director of all the Russian railways, has come on board, and is evidently at home with the passengers. He has traveled a great deal in America. He is preparing to web the Empire with railroads. Prince

Dalgorouki and Count Festetics, members of the Emperor's Court, are also here, and we are getting ready to fire a salute for the Governor-General, who will be along directly with his family. They are laying carpets on the pier for them to walk on. They might have done that for the poet, but I suppose they didn't know he was here.

We shall have a champagne spree directly, I suppose, and then bid our guests and Russia farewell, and sail for the Sublime Porte. We have got so used to Princes now, that it is going to be hard work, during the next few days, to get down to the level of the common herd again.

Only a few paragraphs from this letter, printed in the *New York Tribune* of September 19, 1867, were used, since so much of the same information was given in the *Alta* letters. The first passage used begins with the third paragraph of the letter. "An epidemic" became "a rash." The period after "accord" was probably a printer's error; it became a comma in the book. "Shin" became "run," and "five of us" became "five gentlemen." After "smiling about the ship," Twain added "practising." The sentence beginning "The Consul's closing statement" was omitted; "both desired to visit the ship the following day with their families, the weather permitting" and the following sentence were omitted also.

Very long passages from other letters were inserted immediately after the sentence "At the appointed hour we drove out three miles, and assembled in the handsome garden in front of the Emperor's palace," and nothing more was used from this letter until we come, far down, to the paragraph beginning "You may possibly think that our party tarried too long"—and then only that paragraph and the first two-thirds of the next paragraph were used. The remainder of the letter was omitted. The sentence beginning "Their going and coming" and the following sentence were omitted. Especially anxious" became "careful to do their best."

27. More About Alexander II

Yalta, August 27th.

We anchored here day before yesterday. To me the place was a vision of California. The tall, gray mountains that back it, their sides bristling with pines—cloven with ravines—here and there a hoary rock towering into view—long, straight streaks sweeping down from the summit to the sea, marking the passage of some avalanche of former times—all these were as like what one sees in the Sierras as if the one were a portrait of the other. The little village of Yalta nestles at the foot of an amphitheatre which slopes backward and upward to the wall of hills, and looks as if it might have sunk quietly down to its present position from a higher elevation. This depression is covered with the great parks and gardens of noblemen, and through the mass of green foliage the bright colors of their palaces bud out here and there like flowers. It is a beautiful spot.

The first thing we did was to send a Committee on shore to confer with the Governor-General concerning our reception, and to present to him a brief address for the Emperor which our Consul had advised us to prepare, and which a Committee of the cheekiest of us had been ordered to draft. Why they should have made me Chairman of a Committee whose main talent was to consist of cheek, was an injustice which to me was as strange as it was painful. I accepted the office, but I did it under protest. I did it partly because I was more familiar with Emperors than the other passengers, and therefore able to write to such people with an easier grace than they, and partly because I thought that if I could spread it around that I had been corresponding with the Emperor of Russia, may be it would make my photograph sell.

Well, the Governor-General said that his Majesty would receive our whole party the next day at noon, at his summer palace—that etiquette would be waived and the address read and presented to him in person, at that time—that the Grand Duke Michael (his brother) had extended an invitation to the party to visit him at his palace on the same day, and that on the following day they and their families desired to visit the ship if the sea were smooth. He said we must disembark at half past ten or eleven and ride to the palace (three miles) in carriages which would be provided for us.

So the whole ship's company turned out at about 7 o'clock yesterday morning, and dressed from that time until 11. We got ashore, then, and drove to the Czar's mansion. It stood in the midst of a mixture of lawn, flower-garden and park, and was as snugly located as possible, almost. Its architecture is simple, but handsome and attractive, and its porches, stairways and windows are so clothed with vines and flowers, that the place looked like a cosy home, not a chilly palace.

The Reception

We formed a circle under the trees before the door, for there was no one room in the house able to accommodate our seventy-five persons comfortably, and in a few minutes the imperial family came out bowing and smiling, and stood in our midst. A number of great dignitaries of the Empire, in undress uniforms, came with them. With every bow, his Majesty said a word of welcome. I copy these speeches. There is character in them—Russian character—which is politeness itself, and the genuine article. The French are polite, but it is often mere ceremonious politeness. A Russian always imbues his polite things with a heartiness, both of phrase and expression, that compels belief in their sincerity. As I was saying, the Czar punctuated his speeches with bows: "Good morning—I am glad to see you—I am gratified—I am delighted—I am happy to receive you!" If he had said he was proud to receive that gang, I would not have believed a word of it. But he might have been happy—he looked it. All hands took off their hats, and the Consul inflicted the Address on him. He bore it with unflinching fortitude; then took the rusty looking document and handed it to some great officer or other, to be filed away among the archives of Russia—in the stove, perhaps. He thanked us for the Address, and said he was very much pleased to see us, especially as such friendly relations existed between Russia and the United States. The Empress said the Americans were favorites in Russia, and she hoped the Russians were similarly regarded in America. These were all the speeches that were made, and I recommend them to parties who present the San Francisco police with gold watches, as models of brevity and point. After this the Empress went and talked sociably (for an Empress) with various ladies around the circle, several gentlemen entered into a disjointed general conversation with the Emperor, the Dukes and Princes, Admirals and Maids of Honor dropped into free-and-easy chat with first one and then another of our party, and whoever chose stepped forward and spoke with the modest little Grand Duchess Marie, the Czar's daughter, who is fourteen years old, light-haired, blue-eyed, unassuming and pretty. Everybody talks English. Being after information more than anything else, I captured a fine old gentleman who seemed perfectly willing to be bored with questions, and bored him good. I kept it up, and bored him at many times and in many places during the afternoon. But I did not know he was the Lord High Admiral of Russia. I took him for a lieutenant in the army. But he was very affable and polite, and liked to talk. He was posted on everything, too.

If these dignitaries had come out in their trotting harness, and blazing with orders and decorations, and had assumed a courtly grandeur of bearing and speech, they would have put our light out in the twinkling of an eye—they would have extinguished us like setting a church down on a tallow candle. But they knew better. They guessed our style—they gauged us, and came at us accordingly. They dressed for the occasion. When, in the course of that half-hour's chat, the Countesses and Baronesses and Duchesses of the household got mixed up with our ladies, you could not tell them apart, except that our ladies were the finest dressed and looked the most showy. All the Admirals, and Dukes, and Princes, and Generals were Lieutenants to me; just as in Italy, I couldn't tell the policemen from the Marshals of the Kingdom. You couldn't tell which was the Empress of Russia without having her pointed out; the only way to find the Emperor was to hunt for the man that had the plainest clothes. I think any question asked with a kingly air would have stricken any of our party speechless; but the homespun simplicity of voice and manner of all the imperial party broke the ice at once and set every tongue going with a cheerful vivacity that had no suspicion of embarrassment about it. They were not five minutes in forgetting that they were in a helpless and desperate situation.

The Imperial Wardrobe

The Emperor wore a cap, frock coat and pantaloons, all of some kind of plain white drilling—cotton or linen—and sported no jewelry or any insignia whatever of rank. No costume could be less ostentatious. He is very tall and spare, and a determined looking man, though a very pleasant looking one, nevertheless. It is easy to see that he is kind and affectionate. There is something very noble in his expression when his cap is off. There is none of that cunning in his eye that all of us noticed in Louis Napoleon's.

The Empress and the little Grand Duchess wore simple suits of foulard (or foulard silk—I don't know which is proper,) with a small blue spot in it; the dresses were trimmed with blue; both ladies wore broad blue sashes about their waists; linen collars and clerical ties of muslin; low-crowned straw hats trimmed with blue velvet; parasols and flesh colored gloves. The Grand Duchess had no heels on her shoes. I do not know this of my own knowledge, but one of our ladies told me so. I was not looking at her shoes. I was only too proud to observe that she wore her own hair, plaited in thick braids against the back of her head, instead of the hated thing they call a waterfall, which is about as much like a waterfall as a canvas-covered ham is like a cataract.

Taking the kind expression that is in the Emperor's face and the gentleness that is in his young daughter's into consideration, I wondered if it would not tax the Czar's firmness to the utmost to condemn a supplicating wretch to misery in the wastes of Siberia if she pleaded for him. Every time their eyes met, I saw more and more what a tremendous power that weak, diffident school-girl could wield if she chose to do it. Many and many a time she might rule the Autocrat of Russia, whose lightest word is law to 70,000,000 of human beings! She was only a girl, and she looked like a thousand others I have seen, but never a girl provoked such a novel and peculiar interest in me before. A strange, new sensation is a rare thing in this hum-drum life, and verily I had it here. There was nothing stale or worn out about the thoughts and feelings the situation and circumstances created. It seemed strange—stranger than I can tell—to think that the central figure in the cluster of men and women, chatting here under the trees like the most ordinary people in the land, was a man who could open his lips and ships would fly through the waves, locomotives would speed over the plains, couriers would hurry from village to village, a hundred telegraphs would flash the word to the four corners of an Empire that stretches its vast proportions over a seventh part of the world, and a countless multitude of men would spring to do his bidding. I had a sort of vague desire to examine his hands and see if they were of flesh and blood, like other men's. Here was a man who could do this wonderful thing, and yet if I chose to do it I could knock him down. The case was plain, but it seemed preposterous, nevertheless—as preposterous as trying to knock down a mountain or wipe out a continent. If this man sprained his ankle, a million miles of telegraph would carry the news over mountains—valleys—uninhabited deserts—under the trackless sea—and ten thousand newspapers would prate of it; if he were grievously ill, all the nations would know it before the sun rose again; if he dropped lifeless where he stood, his fall might shake the thrones of half a world! If I could have stolen a button off his coat, I would have done it. When I meet a man like that, I want something to remember him by.

Imperial Condescension

As a general thing, we have been shown through palaces by some plush-legged filagreed flunkey or other, who charged a franc for it;

but after talking with the company half an hour, the Emperor of Russia and his family conducted us all through their elegant mansion themselves. They made no charge. They seemed to take a real pleasure in it. There was condescension for you. It even touched Brown. He said, "The idea of him trotting them beats through here himself! Some of 'em won't know any better than to offer him a *pour boire!* I wish I was Emperor about a minute—you'd see some of these roosters climb that fence!" You notice that word. It pains you. But you cannot conceive how it pains me. Yet I am obliged to hear it every day. I have talked to Brown a great deal about it, but it does no good. He forgets himself right away and uses it again. That time we saw the Pope, he touched up an English gentleman with his umbrella and said: "Which is him? The rooster with the bald head?" And when the gentleman scowled upon him, he said: "It's all right, you know—I thought may be it was that other duck that's got a red hat on." These things distress me beyond expression.

We spent half an hour idling through the palace, admiring the cosy apartments and the rich but eminently home-like appointments of the place, and then the Imperial family bade our mob good-bye, and said they would see them again on board the ship.

An invitation was extended to us to visit the palace of the eldest son, the Crown Prince of Russia, which was near at hand. The young man was absent, but the Dukes and Countesses and Princes went over the premises with us as leisurely as was the case at the Emperor's, and conversation continued as lively as ever. Brown said he knew the gang would nip something—such was his expression—but they did not. They behaved themselves in the most creditable manner.

It was a little after one o'clock, now. We drove to the Grand Duke Michael's, a mile away, in response to his invitation previously given. Of this, more anon.

The Address

As it has been sent to various Russian papers for publication—so I am told—you may as well print it yourself. Inasmuch as the Emperor approved the document, I hope you will allow me as much for it as if you had ordered me to write it yourself. The passengers approved it also—all except one. He objected to "your Majesty"—said it might be right enough, but still it looked like we were fishing for an invitation to dinner:

To His Imperial Majesty, Alexander II, Emperor of Russia:

We are a handful of private citizens of the United States, travelling simply for recreation—and unostentatiously, as becomes our unofficial state—and, therefore, we have no excuse to tender for presenting ourselves before your Majesty save the desire of offering our grateful acknowledgments to the lord of a realm which, through good and through evil report, has been the steadfast friend of the land we love so well.

We could not presume to take a step like this, did we not know well that the words we speak here, and the sentiments wherewith they are freighted, are but the reflex of the thoughts and the feelings of all our countrymen, from the green hills of New England to the shores of the far Pacific. We are few in number, but we utter the voice of a nation!

One of the brightest pages that has graced the world's history, since written history had its birth, was recorded by your Majesty's hand when it loosed the bonds of twenty millions of men; and Americans can but esteem it a privilege to do honor to a ruler who has wrought so mighty a deed. The lesson taught us then we have profitted by, and are free in truth, to-day, even as we were before in name. America owes much to Russia—is indebted to her in many ways—and chiefly for her unwavering friendship in seasons of our greatest need. That that friendship may still be hers, we confidently pray; that she is and will be grateful to Russia and to her sovereign for it, we know full well; that she will ever forfeit it by any premeditated unjust act, or unfair course, it were treason to believe.

SAM. L. CLEMENS,
WM. GIBSON,
A. N. SANFORD,
TIMOTHY D. CROCKER,
COL. P. KINNEY, U. S. A.,

Committee on behalf of the passengers
of the American steam yacht *Quaker City*.

This address will be copied into the various newspapers of Europe, and so I am perfectly satisfied, now, that my photographs will sell.

Our little unpretending visit of a few untitled American scrubs, instead of being [of] no consequence, except as a fifteen minutes' bore to the Czar, which was all we expected, begins to assume a national importance. I will observe, in this connection, that the price of photographs in Constantinople is twenty francs a dozen—say four dollars.

This letter, numbered twenty-two by Twain, appeared in the *Daily Alta California* of November 6, 1867. It was used in Chapter X of Volume II, along with parts of Letter 26. "California" became "the Sierras." The second, third, and fourth paragraphs were omitted. The sentence beginning "If he had said he was proud to receive that gang" and the following sentence were omitted. "The San Francisco police" became "policemen." The long passage beginning "Being after information more than anything else" and extending through the following paragraph was omitted. "Only too proud" became "glad," and "hated thing" became "uncomely thing." The passage beginning "There was condescension for you" and extending to the end of the paragraph was omitted. The Imperial family bade our mob good-bye, and said they would see them again on board the ship" became "the imperial family bade our party a kind good-bye, and proceeded to count the spoons." The sentence beginning "Brown said he knew the gang" and the following sentence were omitted. "Of this, more anon," the address to the Emperor, and the remainder of the letter were omitted. (The first paragraph of the address to the Emperor was quoted in the next chapter.)

28. Guests of the Grand Duke

Yalta, Russia, August 27th.

We arrived there in twenty minutes from the Emperor's. It is a lovely place. The beautiful palace nestles among the grand old groves of the park—the park sits in the lap of the picturesque crags and hills, and both look out upon the breezy ocean. In the park are rustic seats, here and there, in secluded nooks that are dark with shade; there are rivulets of crystal water; there are lakelets, with inviting, grassy banks; there are glimpses of sparkling cascades through openings in the wilderness of foliage; there are streams of clear water gushing from mimic knots on the trunks of forest trees; there are miniature marble temples perched upon gray old crags; there are airy lookouts whence one may gaze upon a broad expanse of landscape and ocean. The palace is modelled after the choicest forms of Grecian architecture, and its wide colonnades surround a central court that is banked with rare flowers that fill the place with their fragrance, and in their midst springs a fountain that cools the summer air, and may possibly breed mosquitoes, but I do not think it does.

The Grand Duke and his Duchess came out and the presentation ceremonies were as simple as they had been at the Emperor's. In a few minutes conversation was under way, as before. The Empress appeared in the verandah, and the little Grand Duchess came out into the crowd. They had beaten us there. It was pleasant to know that they were not in a hurry to get rid of us. In a few minutes the Emperor came himself on horseback. It was very jolly. You can appreciate it if you have ever visited royalty and felt occasionally that possibly you might be wearing out your welcome—though as a general thing, I believe, royalty is not scrupulous about discharging you when it is done with you.

The Grand Duke is the third brother of the Emperor, is about thirty-seven years old, perhaps, and is the princeliest figure in Russia. He is even taller than the Czar, as straight as an Indian, and bears himself like one of those gorgeous knights we read about in romances of the Crusades. He looks like a great-hearted fellow who would pitch an enemy into the river in a moment, and then jump in and risk his life fishing him out again. The stories they tell of him show him to be of a brave and generous nature. He must have been determined to prove that Americans were welcome guests in the imperial palaces of Russia, because he rode all the way to Yalta and escorted our procession to the Emperor's himself, and kept his Aids scurrying around clearing the road and offering assistance wherever it could be needed. We were rather familiar with him then, because we didn't know who he was. We recognized him now, and appreciated the friendly spirit that prompted him to do us a favor that any other Grand Duke in the world would have scorned to do. He had plenty of servitors whom he could have sent, but he chose to attend to the matter himself.

The Grand Duke was dressed in the handsome and showy uniform of a Cossack officer. The Grand Duchess had on a white alpaca robe, with the seams and gores trimmed with black barb lace, and a little gray hat with a feather of the same color. She is young, rather pretty, modest and unpretending, and full of winning politeness.

Our party marched all through the house, as usual, and then the nobility escorted them all over the grounds, and finally brought them back to the palace about half-past 2 o'clock to breakfast. They called it breakfast, but we would have called it luncheon. It consisted of two kinds of wine, tea, bread, cheese, and cold meats, and was served on the centre tables in the reception room and the verandahs—anywhere that was convenient; there was no ceremony. It was a sort of a free blow-out, like a picnic. I had heard before that we were to breakfast there, but Brown said he believed Drake's boy had suggested it to his Imperial Highness. I reckon not—though it would be like him. Drake's boy is the famine-breeder of the ship. He is always hungry. They say he goes about the staterooms when the passengers are out, and eats up all the soap. And they say he eats oakum. They say he will eat anything he can get between meals, but he prefers oakum. He don't like oakum for dinner, but he likes it for a lunch, at odd hours, or anything that way. It makes him very disagreeable, because it makes his breath smell like the sigh of a buzzard, and keeps his teeth all stuck up with tar. Drake's boy may have suggested the breakfast, but I hope he did not. It went off well, anyhow. The illustrious host moved about from place to place, and helped to destroy the provisions and keep the conversation lively, and the Grand Duchess talked with the verandah parties and such as had satisfied their appetites, and straggled out from the reception-room. When the Consul and our Secretary to the Legation at the Imperial Court said it was time to go (we kept ourselves posted all the time,) we bade the Grand Duke and the Grand Duchess good-bye, and cleared out.

We had spent the best part of half a day in the home of royalty, and had been as cheerful and comfortable all the time as we could have been in the ship. I would as soon have thought of being cheerful in Abraham's bosom as in the palace of an Emperor. I supposed that Emperors were terrible people. I thought they never did anything but wear magnificent crowns and red velvet dressing-gowns, with dabs of wool sowed [sewed] on them in spots, and sit on thrones and scowl at the flunkies and the people in the parquette, and order Dukes and Duchesses off to execution. I find, however, that when one is so fortunate as to get behind the scenes and see them at home and in the privacy of their firesides, they are strangely like common mortals. They are pleasanter to look upon then than they are in their theatrical aspect. It seems to come as natural to them to dress and act like other people as it is to put a friend's cedar pencil in your pocket when you are done using it. But don't you know, I can never have any confidence in the tinsel kings of the theatre after this? It will be a great loss. I used to take such a thrilling pleasure in them! But, hereafter, I will turn me sadly away and say: "This won't answer—this isn't the style of king that I am acquainted with!" When they prance around the stage in jewelled crowns and splendid robes I shall feel bound to observe that all the Emperors that ever *I* was personally acquainted with wore the commonest sort of clothes, and didn't prance. And when they come on the stage attended by a vast body-guard of supes in helmets and tin breastplates, it will be my duty as well as my pleasure to inform the ignorant that no crowned head of my acquaintance has a soldier anywhere about his house or his person.

"Saved as by Fire"

Under Providence we have been spared one humiliation here. Our poet has been rigidly suppressed, from the time we let go the anchor. We have only three uncouth characters on board, and the poet is one of them. He is a shameless old idiot who writes the most diabolical rhymes one can imagine, and shoves them under doors, hands them to Consuls by the ream, and waylays foreigners in out-of-the-way places when no succor is near, and inflicts his verses on them. That they do not understand English is nothing to him. He is inexorable. His only aim seems to be to save three cents when he can do it by going cold or hungry, and to flood Europe with his infernal poetry. Knowing that we watch him and try in every way to circumvent him, he has become wary of late, and employs all manner of surreptitious means to circulate his trash. When it was announced that we were going to visit the Emperor of Russia, the fountains of his great deep were broken up and he rained ineffable bosh for four and twenty hours. The anxiety as to what we were going to do with ourselves was suddenly transformed into anxiety about what we were going to do with our poet. The problem was solved at last. Two alternatives were offered him —he must either swear a dreadful oath that he would not issue a line of his vile poetry while he was in the Czar's dominions, or else remain under guard on board the ship until we were safe at Constantinople again. He fought the dilemma long, but yielded at last, with a heavy heart. It was a great deliverance. Perhaps you would like a specimen of his style:

Save us and sanctify us, and finally, then,
*See good provisions we enjoy while we journey to Jerusa*lem.
For so man proposes, which it is most true,
And time will wait for none, nor for us too.

He will grind you out that kind of rubbish by the yard, and cast it off to kings and princes, with his name signed in full at the bottom. However, we ought not to be too hard on him. For aught we know, God made him. It is even possible that He made him for some wise purpose. That the poet has failed to fill the bill is matter for regret, but not for execration. Still, while we cannot disguise the truth that he is a failure, let us at least be charitable, and hope that he is doing his level best.

Distinguished Visitors

The sea has been unusually rough all day, and no one is expecting the Emperor on board the ship. I make no doubt that the invitation he extended to himself and family to visit the vessel was only a little stretch of politeness, and that he really had very little idea of coming. Others think differently. I don't suppose any of us know enough about imperial etiquette to be able to express an opinion on the subject that would sell for much in the market.

However, we have had a lively time of it, anyhow. We have had such a run of visitors all day, so Brown says, that "if we had been a bank we would have been busted." The Governor-General came, and we received him with a salute of nine guns. He brought his family with him. I observed that carpets were spread from the pier-head to his carriage for him to walk on, though I have seen him walk there without any carpet when he wasn't on business. I thought maybe he had what the accidental insurance people might call an extra-hazardous polish ("policy"—joke, but not above mediocrity,) on his boots, and wanted to protect them, but I examined and could not see that they were blacked any better than usual. It may have been that he had forgotten his carpet, before, but he hadn't it with him, anyhow. He was an exceedingly pleasant old gentleman; we all liked him, especially Brown. When he went away, Brown invited him to come again and fetch his carpet along.

Prince Dalgorouki and a Grand Admiral or two, whom we had seen yesterday at the reception, came on board also. I was a little distant with these parties, at first, because always when I have been visiting Emperors I don't like to be too familiar with people I only know by reputation, and whose moral characters and standing in society I cannot be thoroughly acquainted with. I judged it best to be a little offish, at first. I said to myself, Princes and Counts and Grand Admirals are very well, but they are not Emperors, and one cannot be too particular about who he associates with.

Baron Wrangel came, also. He used to be Russian Ambassador at Washington. I told him I had an uncle who fell down a shaft and broke himself in two, as much as a year before that. That was a falsehood, but then I was not going to let any man get ahead of me on astonishers and surprising adventures, merely for the want of a little invention. The Baron is a fine man, and is said to stand high in the Emperor's confidence and esteem.

Baron Ungern-Sternberg, a boisterous, whole-souled, jolly old brick of a nobleman, came with the rest. He is a man of progress and enterprise—and representative man of the age—what is called a "rustler," in California. He is the Chief Director of the railway system of Russia—a sort of railroad king. In his line he is making things move right along in this country. He has travelled extensively in America. He said he tried convict labor on his railroads and with perfect success. He says they work well, and are quiet and peaceable. He observed that he employs nearly then [ten] thousand of them now. This appeared to be another call on my resources. I could not let any astonishers pass. I was equal to the emergency. I said we had eighty thousand convicts employed on the railways in California—all of them under sentence of death for murder in the first degree. That closed *him* out.

We had General Todleben, the famous defender of Sebastopol, during the siege, and many inferior army and also navy officers, and a number of unofficial Russian ladies and gentlemen. Naturally, a champagne blow-out was in order, and was accomplished without loss of life. Toasts and jokes were discharged freely, but no speeches were made save one thanking the Emperor and the Grand Dukes, through the Governor General for our hospitable reception, and one by the Governor General in reply, in which he returned the Emperor's thanks for the speech, etc., etc.

I suppose we shall sail now, right away.

This letter, numbered twenty-three by Twain, appeared in the *Daily Alta California* of November 10, 1867. It was also used in Chapter X. After "They had beaten us there," Twain inserted "It was pleasant to know that they were not in a hurry to get rid of us"—a rather similar sentence occurs in a rejected passage in Letter 26. "Jolly" became "pleasant"; "determined to prove" became "desirous of proving," and "a free blowout like a" was omitted. "Brown" became "Blucher"; "reckon" became "think"; "he don't" became "he does not"; and "makes his breath smell like the sigh of a buzzard" became "makes his breath bad." Twain omitted the sentence beginning

"When the Consul and our Secretary to the Legation" and substituted two short paragraphs, one of which was reworded slightly from a rejected passage in Letter 26. "Prance" became "swagger." Just before the passage about the poet two paragraphs from Letter 26 were inserted. In the passage about the poet only the second of the first eight sentences was retained. "Vile poetry" became "poetry." "Perhaps you would like" became "perhaps the savage reader would like"—and Twain added a few humorous sentences explaining his use of "savage." The paragraph following the "poem" was deleted. All but the first eight words of the next paragraph was deleted also. In the next paragraph Brown's statement was omitted. Toward the end of the paragraph "Brown" became "Blucher"; "Who he associates with" became "whom he associates with"; "get ahead of me on astonishers and surprising adventures" became "eclipse me on surprising adventures"; and "jolly old brick of a nobleman" became "old gentleman." "What is called a 'rustler,' in California" was deleted. "Tried" became "has tried." "I could not let any astonishers pass" was deleted. "Railways in California" became "railways in America," and "blow-out" became "luncheon." The last sentence was deleted.

29. Smyrna

Smyrna, Asia Minor, Sept. 5th, 1867.

This is a closely packed city of 130,000 inhabitants, and, like Constantinople, it has no outskirts. It is as closely packed at its outer edges as it is in the centre, and then the habitations leave suddenly off and the plain beyond seems houseless. It is just like any other Oriental city. That is to say, its moslem houses are heavy and dark, and as comfortless as so many tombs; its streets are crooked, rudely and roughly paved, and as narrow as an ordinary staircase; the streets uniformly carry a man to any other place than the one he wants to go to, and surprise him by landing him in the most unexpected localities; business is chiefly carried on in great covered bazaars, celled like a honeycomb with innumerable shops no larger than a common closet, and the whole hive cut up into [a] maze of alleys about wide enough to accommodate a laden camel, and well calculated to confuse a stranger and eventually lose him; everywhere there is dirt, everywhere there are fleas, everywhere there are lean, broken-hearted dogs; every alley is thronged with people; wherever you look, your eye rests upon a wild masquerade of extravagant costumes; the work-shops are all open to the streets, and the workmen visible; all manner of sounds assail the ear, and over them all rings out the muezzin's cry from some tall minaret, calling the faithful vagabonds to prayer; and superior to the call to prayer, the noises in the streets, the interest of the costumes

—superior to everything, and claiming the bulk of attention first, last, and all the time—is a combination of Mohammedan stinks, to which the stench of a Chinese quarter would be as pleasant as the roasting odors of the fatted calf to the nostrils of the returning Prodigal. Such is Oriental luxury—such is Oriental splendor! We read about it all our days, but we comprehend it not until we see it.

The Biblical "Crown of Life"

Smyrna is a very old city. Its name occurs several times in the Bible, one or two of the disciples of Christ visited it, and here was located one of the old original seven apocalyptic churches spoken of in Revelations. These churches were symbolized in the Scriptures as Candlesticks, and on certain conditions there was a sort of implied promise that Smyrna should be endowed with a "crown of life." She was to "be faithful unto death"—those were the terms. She has not kept up her lick right straight along, but the pilgrims that wander hither consider that she has come near enough to it to save her, and so they point to the fact that Smyrna to-day wears her crown of life, is a great city, with a great commerce and full of energy, while the cities wherein were located the other six churches and to which no crown of life was promised, have perished and have vanished from the earth. So Smyrna really still possesses her crown of life, in a business point of view. Her career, for eighteen centuries, has been a chequered one, and she has been under the rule of princes of many creeds, yet there has been no season during all that time, as far as we know, that she has been without her little community of Christians "faithful unto death." Hers was the only Church against which no threats were implied in the Revelations, and the only one which survived.

With Ephesus, forty miles from here, where was located another of the seven churches, the case was different. The "Candlestick" has been removed from Ephesus. Her light has been put out. Christian pilgrims, always too prone to find prophecies in the Bible where none exist, speak cheerfully and complacently of poor, ruined Ephesus as the victim of prophecy. And yet there is no sentence that promises, without due qualification, the destruction of the city. The words are:

"Remember, therefore, from whence thou art fallen, and repent, and do the first works; or else I will come unto thee quickly, and will remove thy candlestick out of his place, except thou repent."

That is all; the other verses are singularly complimentary to Ephesus. The threat is qualified. There is no history to show that she did not repent. But the cruelest habit the modern prophecy-fulfillers have, is that one of coolly and arbitrarily fitting a prophetic shirt on to the wrong man. They do it without regard to rhyme or reason. Both the cases I have just mentioned are instances in point. Those "prophecies" are distinctly levelled at the "*churches* of Ephesus, Smyrna," etc., and yet the pilgrims invariably make them refer to the *cities* instead. No crown of life is promised to the town of Smyrna and its commerce, but to the half-dozen of Christians who formed its "Church." If they were "faithful unto death," they have their crown now—but I don't care if they had fagged themselves out in the good work, and gone to all manner of preposterous lengths of faithfulness, they would still have found that they couldn't ring in the city for a crown of life. That would have been crowding things too much. If they could have shown that the promise included the city, too, it would have raised real estate faster than a railroad. These remarks are eminently practical, I know, but still there is reason in them. This fashion of ciphering out fulfilments of prophecy where that "prophecy" consists of mere "ifs," is absurd. Why, suppose a thousand years from now, a malarious swamp takes up a ranch in that shallow harbor of Smyrna, or something else kills the town; and suppose, also, that within that time the swamp that has filled the renowned harbor of Ephesus and rendered her ancient site deadly and uninhabitable to-day, becomes hard and healthy ground; suppose the natural consequence ensues, to wit: that Smyrna becomes a melancholy ruin, and Ephesus is rebuilt. What will the prophecy-fulfillers say? They would coolly skip over our age of the world, and say: "Smyrna was not faithful unto death, and so her crown of life was denied her; Ephesus repented, and lo! her candlestick was not removed. Behold these evidences! How wonderful is prophecy!"

Smyrna has been utterly destroyed six times. If her crown of life had been an insurance policy, she would have rushed to collect on it the first time she fell. But she holds it on sufferance and by a complimentary construction of language which does not refer to her. Six different times, however, I suppose some infatuated prophecy-sharp blundered along and said, to the infinite disgust of Smyrna and the Smyrniotes: "In sooth, here is astounding fulfilment of prophecy! Smyrna hath not been faithful unto death, and behold her crown of life is vanished from her head. Verily, these things be astonishing!"

The ship is full of books concerning the Holy Land, and holy places, and every other place on earth, and you cannot be surprised to know that I have read whole volumes of the far-fetched conclusions of these curious prophecy-fulfillers. I will not trust myself to speak of them further than to say that it is noteworthy how much extravagance of ideas, language, argument and conclusion will be cheerfully tolerated in a man when he is treating a Scriptural subject. He may rave like a very lunatic, and yet escape criticism. I expect that is as much as I had better say. I have been taught to revere the Scriptures, and that reverence is pretty firmly grounded. Perhaps it would have been well to teach me to revere their commentators. Some of them I don't. I am very sure of that.

The People

A portion of the city is pretty exclusively Turkish; the Jews have a quarter to themselves; the Franks another quarter; so, also, with the Armenians. The Armenians, of course, are Christians. Their houses are large, clean, airy, handsomely paved with tessalated marble, and in the centre of many of them is a square court, which has in it a rich flower-garden and sparkling fountain; the doors of all the rooms open on this. A very wide hall leads to the street door, and in this the women sit, the most of the day. In the cool of the evening they dress up in their trotting harness and show themselves at the door. They are all comely of countenance, every angel of them, and exceedingly neat in dress and cleanly; they look as if they were just out of a bandbox. Some of the young ladies—many of them, I may say—are even very beautiful; they average better than American girls—which treasonable words, I pray may be forgiven me. They are very sociable, and will smile back when a stranger smiles at them, will bow back when he bows and talk back if he speaks to them. No introduction is required. An hour's chat at the door with a pretty girl one never saw before, is easily obtained, and is very pleasant. I have tried it. I could not talk anything but English, and the girl knew nothing but Greek, or Armenian, or some such barbarous tongue, but we got along very well. I find that in cases like these, the fact that you cannot comprehend each other isn't much of a drawback. In that Russian town of Yalta I danced an astonishing sort of dance an hour long, and one I had never heard of before, with the most beautiful girl that ever lived, and we talked incessantly, and laughed exhaustingly, and neither one ever knew what the other was driving at. But it was splendid. There were twenty people in the set, and the dance was very lively and complicated. It was complicated enough without me—with me it was an astonisher. I just carelessly threw in a figure every now and then that made those Russians ashamed of themselves. But I have never ceased to think of that girl. I have written to her, but I cannot direct the epistle because her name is one of these nine-jointed Russian affairs, and there are not letters enough in our alphabet to hold out. I am not reckless enough to try to pronounce it when I am awake, but I make a stagger at it in my dreams, and get up with the lockjaw every morning. I am fading. I don't take my meals now, only off and on. Her dear name haunts me still in my dreams. It is awful on teeth. It never comes out of my mouth but it fetches an old snag along with it. And then the lockjaw closes down on it and nips off a couple of the last syllables—but they taste good. I am fading. Soon I shall be no more. I want to leave my property to some blind asylum. It won't make any difference to them if they can't see it.

The Camels Are Coming

Coming through the Dardanelles a few weeks ago, we saw camel trains on shore with the glasses, but we were never close to one till we got to Smyrna. I don't think much of Leander, now, who swam the Hellespont (the Dardanelles,) to see his squaw. I mean I do not think much of his feat, and Lord Byron's boasted imitation of it. It was nothing at all. I could swim that creek with all my property on my back. But I was speaking of the camels. They are very much larger than the scrawny specimens one sees in the menagerie. They are as large as those we have had in California so long. They stride along these streets, in single file, a dozen in a train, with heavy loads on their backs, and a fancy-looking negro in Turkish costume, or an Arab, preceding them on a little donkey and completely overshadowed and rendered insignificant by the huge beasts. To see a camel train laden with the spices of Arabia and the rare fabrics of Persia come marching through the narrow alleys of the bazaar, among porters with their burdens, money-changers, lamp-merchants, Alnaschars in the glassware business, portly cross-legged Turks smoking the famous narghili, and the crowds drifting to and fro in the fanciful costumes of the East, is a genuine revelation of the Orient. The picture lacks nothing. It casts you back at once into your forgotten boyhood, and again you dream over the wonders of the Arabian Nights; again your companions are princes, your lord is the Caliph Haroun Al Raschid, and your servants are terrific giants and genii that come with smoke, and lightning, and thunder, and go as a storm goes when they depart!

This letter, numbered twenty-four by Twain, appeared in the *Daily Alta California* of November 17, 1867. It was used in Chapter XI, Volume II. "Stinks" became "stenches"; "stench" became "smell"; "lick right straight" became "faith straight"; "have perished and have vanished" became "have vanished"; "where none exist" became "and often where none exist"; and "prophecy-fulfillers" became "prophecy-savants." The passage beginning "But I don't care" and ending with "still there is reason in them" was completely rewritten in almost the same number of words. "Ciphering" became "delving"; "is absurd" became "trenches upon the absurd"; "takes up a ranch" became "builds itself up"; and "prophecy-sharp" became "prophecy-enthusiast." The paragraph beginning "The ship is full of books" was deleted and another paragraph was substituted for it. "Trotting harness" became "best raiment." "Every angel of them" was deleted. "The most beautiful girl that ever lived" became "a very pretty girl"; "an astonisher" became "more so"; "made those Russians ashamed of themselves" became "surprised those Russians"; and "only off and on" became "with any sort of regularity." Twain deleted "I am fading" and the next three sentences, the sentences referring to Leander and Lord Byron, and "They are as large as those we have had in California so long."

30. Smyrna's Lions

Smyrna, Asia Minor, Sept. 6, 1867.

We inquired, and learned that the lions of Smyrna consisted of the ruins of the ancient citadel, whose broken and prodigious battlements frown upon the city from a lofty hill just in the edge of the town—the Mount Pagus of scripture, they call it; the site of that one of the Seven apocalyptic Churches of Asia which was located here in the first century of the Christian era; and the grave and the place of martyrdom of the venerable Polycarp, who suffered in Smyrna for his religion some eighteen hundred years ago.

We took little donkeys and started. Polycarp did not amount to anything save in its character as a holy place and one around which cluster the traditions and associations of a hoary antiquity. I know nothing about Polycarp, except that he served his Lord for three-score and six years and then was thrown to the wild beasts because he refused to forswear his allegiance.

The "Seven Churches"—thus they abbreviate it—were jolly enough. We rode there—about a mile and a half in the sweltering sun—and visited a little Greek church which they said was built upon the ancient site; and we paid a small fee, and the holy attendant gave each of us a little wax candle as a remembrance of the place, and I put mine in my hat and the sun melted it and the grease all ran down the back of my neck; and so now I have not got anything left but the wick, and it is a sorry and a wilted-looking wick at that.

I argued with all my might that the "church" mentioned in the Bible meant a party of Christians, and not a building; that the Bible spoke of them as being very poor—so poor, I thought, and so subject to persecution (as per Polycarp's martyrdom) that in the first place they probably could not have afforded a church edifice, and in the second couldn't have dared to build it in the open light of day if they could; and finally, that if they had had the privilege of building it, common judgment would have suggested that they build it somewhere near the town. But they ruled me down and scouted my evidences. However, retribution came to them afterward. They found that they had been led astray and had gone to the wrong place; they discovered that the accepted site is in the city.

Riding through the town, we could see marks of the six Smyrnas that have existed here and been burned up by fire or knocked down by earthquakes. The hills and the rocks are rent asunder in places, excavations expose great blocks of building-stone that have lain buried for ages, and all the mean houses and walls of modern Smyrna along the way are spotted white with broken pillars, capitals and fragments of sculptured marble that once adorned the lordly palaces that were the glory of the city in the olden time.

Mysterious Oyster Mine

The ascent of the hill of the citadel is very steep, and we proceeded rather slowly. But there were matters of interest about us. In one place, five hundred feet above the sea, the perpendicular bank on the upper side of the road was ten or fifteen feet high, and exposed three veins of oyster shells, just as you have seen quartz veins exposed in the cutting of a road in California. The veins were about eighteen inches thick and two or three feet apart, and they slanted along downward for a distance of thirty feet or more, and then disappeared where the cut joined the road. Heaven only knows how far a man might trace them by "stripping." They were clean, nice oyster-shells, large, and just like any other oyster-shells. They were thickly massed together, and none were scattered above or below the veins. Each one was a well-defined lead by itself, and without a spur. My first instinct was to set up the usual—

Notice:

We the undersigned, claim five claims of two hundred feet each, (and one for discovery,) on this ledge or lode of oyster-shells, with all its dips, spurs, angles and sinuosities, and fifty feet on each side of the same, to work it, etc., etc., according to the mining laws of Smyrna.

They were such perfectly natural-looking leads that I could hardly keep from taking them up. Among the oyster-shells were mixed many fragments of ancient, broken crockeryware. Now how did those masses of oyster-shells get there? I cannot figure it out. Broken crockery and oyster-shells are suggestive of restaurants—but then they could have had no such places away up there on that mountain side in our time, because nobody has lived up there. A restaurant would not pay in such a stony, forbidding, desolated place. And, besides, there wasn't any champagne corks among the shells. If there ever was a restaurant there, it must have been in Smyrna's palmy days, when the hills were covered with houses. I could stand one restaurant, on those terms; but then how about the three? Did they have restaurants there at three different periods of the world?—because there are two or three feet of solid earth between the oyster leads. Evidently, the restaurant solution won't answer.

The hill might have been the bottom of the sea, once, and got lifted up, with its oyster-beds, by an earthquake—but, then, how about the crockery? And, moreover, how about *three* oyster-beds, one above another, and thick strata of good, honest earth between?

That theory will not do. It is just possible that this hill is Mount Ararat, and that Noah's Ark rested here, and he ate oysters and threw the shells overboard. But that will not do, either. There are the three layers again and the solid earth between—and, besides, there were only eight in Noah's family, and they could not have eaten all these oysters in the two or three months they staid on top of that mountain.

The beasts—however, it is simply absurd to suppose he didn't know any more than to feed the beasts on oyster suppers. He couldn't afford it, anyhow. He had been out eleven months, and they must all have been on short rations for some time.

It is painful—it is even humiliating—but I am reduced at last to one slender theory: that the oysters climbed up there of their own accord. But what object could they have had in view—what did they want up there? What could any oyster want to climb a hill for? To climb a hill must necessarily be fatiguing and annoying exercise for an oyster. The most natural conclusion would be, that the oysters climbed up there to look at the scenery. Yet when you come to reflect upon the nature of an oyster, it seems plain that he does not care for scenery. An oyster has no taste for such things; he cares nothing for the beautiful. An oyster is of a retiring disposition and not boisterous—not even cheerful above the average, and never enterprising. But above all, an oyster does not take any interest in scenery—he scorns it. What have I arrived at, now? Simply at the point I started from—namely: those oyster shells are there, in regular layers, five hundred feet above the sea, and no man knows how they got there. I have hunted up the guidebooks, and the gist of what they say is this: "They are there, but how they got there is a mystery."

Millerism

Twenty-five years ago, a multitude of lunatics in America put on their ascension shirts, took a tearful leave of their friends, and got ready to fly up into heaven at the first toot of the trumpet. But the angel did not blow it. Miller's resurrection day failed to come to time. The Millerites were a disgusted community. I did not suspect that there were Millers in Asia, but a gentleman tells me that they had it all set for the world to come to an end one day about three years ago. There was much buzzing and preparation for a long time previously, and it culminated in a wild excitement at the appointed time. A vast number of the populace ascended this citadel hill early in the morning, to get out of the way of the general destruction, and many of the infatuated closed up their shops and retired from all earthly business. But the strange part of it was that about three in the afternoon, while this gentleman and his friends were at dinner in the hotel, a terrific storm of rain, accompanied by thunder and lightning, broke forth and continued with dire fury for two or three hours. It was a thing unprecedented in Smyrna at that time of year, and scared some of the most skeptical. The streets ran rivers and the hotel floor was flooded with water. The dinner had to be suspended. When the storm finished and left everybody drenched through and through, and melancholy and half-drowned, the ascensionists came down from the mountain as dry as so many charity-sermons! They had been looking down upon the fearful storm going on below, and really believed that their proposed destruction of the world was proving a grand success.

The Smyrna R. R.

A railway here in Asia—in the dreamy realm of the Orient—in the fabled land of the Arabian Nights—is a funny thing to think of. And yet they have got one already, and are building another. The present one is well built and well conducted, by an English Company, but is not doing an immense amount of business. The first year it carried a good many passengers, but its freight list only comprised 800 pounds of figs!

It runs almost to the very gates of Ephesus—a town great in all ages of the world—a city familiar to readers of the Bible, and one which was as old as the hills when the disciples of Christ preached in its streets. It dates back to the shadowy ages of tradition, and was the birth-place of gods renowned in Grecian mythology. The idea of a locomotive tearing through such a place as this, and waking the phantoms of its old days of romance out of their dreams of dead and gone centuries, is curious enough. We journey thither to-morrow to see the celebrated ruins.

This letter, numbered twenty-five by Twain, appeared in the *Daily Alta California* of November 21, 1867. It became Chapter XII, Volume II. Twain omitted all of the second paragraph except the first sentence and inserted "We saw Polycarp's tomb, and then hurried on." "Were jolly enough" became "came next on the list"; "have not got" became "have not"; "I argued with all my might" became "several of us argued as well as we could"; "they ruled me down" became "the elders of the ship's family ruled us down"; "California" became "Nevada or Montana"; "figure it out" became "determine"; "there wasn't any champagne corks" became "there were no champagne corks"; "stand one restaurant" became "believe in one restaurant"; and "got lifted up" became "been lifted up." "He couldn't afford it, anyhow" and the next sentence were deleted. "Lunatics" became "people"; "shirts" became "robes"; "toot" became "blast"; "failed to come to time" became "was a failure"; "a disgusted community" became "disgusted"; "funny" became "strange"; and "have not" became "have."

31. Bygone Magnificence

Ephesus, Asia Minor, Sept. 8th, 1867.

On a high, steep hill, toward the sea, is a gray ruin of ponderous blocks of marble, wherein, tradition says, St. Paul, was imprisoned eighteen centuries ago. From these old walls you have the finest view of the desolate scene where once stood Ephesus, the grandest city of ancient times, and whose Temple of Diana was so noble in design, and so exquisite of workmanship, that it ranked high in the list of the seven wonders of the world.

Behind you is the sea; in front is a level green valley (a marsh, in fact,) extending far away among the mountains; to the right of the front view is the old citadel of Assyalook [Ayassoluk], on a high hill; the ruined Mosque of the Sultan Selim stands near it in the plain (this is built over the grave of St. John, and was formerly a Christian Church;) further toward you is the hill of Pion [Prion], around whose front is clustered all that remains of the ruins of Ephesus that still stand; divided from it by a narrow valley is the long, rocky, rugged mountain of Coressus. The scene is a pretty one, and yet desolate—for in that wide plain no man can live, and in it is no human habitation. But for the crumbling arches and monstrous piers and broken walls that rise from the foot of the hill of Pion, one could not believe that in this place once stood a city whose renown is older than tradition itself. It is incredible to reflect that things as familiar all over the world to-day as household words, belong in the history and in the shadowy legends of this silent, mournful solitude. We speak of Apollo and of Diana—they were born here; of the metamorphosis of Syrinx into a reed—it was done here; of the great god Pan—he dwelt in the caves of this hill of Coressus; of the Amazons—this was their best prized home; of Bacchus and Hercules—both fought the warlike women here; of the Cyclops—they laid the ponderous marble blocks of some of the ruins yonder; of Homer—this was one of his many birthplaces; of Cimon of Athens; of Alcibiades, Lysander, Agesilaus—they visited here; so did Alexander the Great; so did Hannibal and Antiochus, Scipio, Lucullus and Sylla; Brutus, Cassius, Pompey, Cicero and Augustus; Antony was a judge in this place, and left his seat in the open Court, while the advocates were speaking, to run after Cleopatra, who passed the door; from this city they sailed on pleasure excursions, in galleys with silver oars and perfumed sails, and with companions [companies] of beautiful girls to serve them, and actors and musicians to amuse them; in days that seem almost modern, so remote are they from the early history of this city, Paul the Apostle preached the new religion here, and so did John, when many men still lived who had seen the Christ; here Mary Magdalen died, and here the Virgin Mary ended her days with John, albeit Rome has since judged it best to locate her grave elsewhere; six or seven hundred years ago—almost yesterday, as it were—troops of mail-clad Crusaders thronged the streets; and to come down to trifles, we speak of meandering streams, and find a new interest in a common word when we discover that the crooked river Meander, in yonder valley, gave it to our dictionary. It makes me feel as old as these dreary hills to look down upon these moss-hung ruins, this historic desolation. One may read the Scriptures and believe, but he cannot go and stand yonder in the ruined theatre and in imagination people it again with the vanished multitudes who mobbed Paul's comrades there and shouted, with one voice, "Great is Diana of the Ephesians!" The idea of a shout in such a solitude as this almost makes one shudder.

It was a wonderful city, this Ephesus. Go where you will about these broad plains, you find the most exquisitely sculptured marble fragments scattered thick among the dust and weeds, and protruding from the ground, or lying prone upon it, are beautifully fluted columns of porphyry and all precious marbles; and at every step you find elegantly carved capitals and massive bases, and polished tablets engraved with Greek inscriptions. It is a world of precious relics, a wilderness of marred and mutilated gems. And yet what are these things to the wonders that lie buried here under the ground? At Constantinople, at Pisa, in the cities of Spain, are great mosques and cathedrals, whose grandest columns came from the temples and palaces of Ephesus, but one has only to scratch the ground here to match them. We shall never know what magnificence is until this imperial city is laid bare to the sun.

The finest piece of sculpture I have ever seen, and the one that impressed me most, (for I do not know much about art and cannot get into ecstacies over it,) is one that lies in this old theatre of Ephesus which St. Paul's riot has made so celebrated. It is only the headless body of a man, clad in a coat of mail, with a Medusa head upon the breast-plate, but such dignity and majesty were never thrown into a form of stone before.

What builders they were, these men of antiquity! The massive arches of some of these ruins rest upon piers that are fifteen feet square and built entirely of solid blocks of marble, some of which are as large as a Saratoga trunk, and some the size of a boarding-house sofa. They are not shells or shafts of stone filled inside with rubbish, but the whole pier is a mass of solid masonry. Vast arches, that may have been the gates of the city, are built in the same way. They have braved the storms and sieges of three thousand years, and have been shaken by many an earthquake, but still they stand. When they dig alongside of them, they find ranges of ponderous masonry that are [as] perfect in every detail as they were the day those old Cyclopian giants finished them. An English Company is going to excavate Ephesus, and then!

The Story of the Seven Sleepers

In the Mount of Pion, yonder, is the Cave of the Seven Sleepers. Once upon a time, about fifteen hundred years ago, seven young men lived near each other in Ephesus, who belonged to the despised sect of the Christians. It came to pass that the good King Maximilianus, (I am telling this story for nice little boys and girls,) it came to pass, I say, that the good King Maximilianus got to persecuting the Christians, and as time rolled on he made it very warm for them. So the seven young men said one to the other, let us get up and dust. And they got up and dusted. They tarried not to bid their fathers and mothers good-bye, or any friend they knew. They only took certain moneys which their parents had, and garments that belonged unto their friends, whereby they might remember them when far away; and they took also the dog Ketmehr, which was the property of their neighbor Malchus, because the beast did run his head into a noose which one of the young men was carrying carelessly, and they had not time to release him; and they took also certain chickens that seemed lonely in the neighboring coops, and likewise some bottles of curious liquors that stood near the grocer's window; and then they departed from the city. By and by they came to a marvellous cave in the Hill of Pion, and entered into it and feasted, and presently they hurried on again. But they forgot the bottles of curious liquors, and left them behind. They travelled in many lands, and had many strange adventures. They were virtuous young men, and lost no opportunity that fell in their way to make their livelihood. Their motto was in these words, namely,

"Procrastination is the thief of time." And so, whenever they did come upon a man who was alone, they said, "Behold, this person hath the wherewithal—let us go through him." And they went through him. At the end of five years they had waxed tired of travel and adventure, and longed to revisit their old home again and hear the voices and see the faces that were dear unto their youth. Therefore they went through such parties as fell in their way where they sojourned at that time, and journeyed back toward Ephesus again. For the good King Maximilianus was become converted unto the new faith, and the Christians rejoiced because they were no longer persecuted. One day as the sun went down, they came to the cave in the Mount of Pion, and they said, each to his fellow, Let us sleep here, and go and feast and make merry with our friends when the morning cometh. And each of the seven lifted up his voice and said, It is a whiz. So they went in, and lo, where they had put them, there lay the bottles of strange liquors, and they judged that age had not impaired their excellence. Wherein the wanderers were right, and the heads of the same were level. So each of the young men drank six bottles, and behold they felt very tired, then, and lay down and slept soundly.

When they awoke, one of them, named Johannes Smithianus said, "We are naked." And it was so. Their raiment was all gone, and the money which they had gotten from a stranger whom they had proceeded through as they approached the city, was lying upon the ground, corroded and rusted and defaced. Likewise the dog Ketmehr was gone, and nothing save the brass that was upon his collar remained. They wondered much at these things. But they took the money, and they wrapped about their bodies some leaves, and came up to the top of the hill. Then they were perplexed. The wonderful temple of Diana was gone; many grand edifices they had never seen before stood in the city; men in strange garbs moved about the streets, and everything was changed.

Johannes said, It hardly seems like Ephesus. Yet here is the great gymnasium; here is the mighty theatre, wherein I have seen 70,000 men assembled; here is the Agora; there is the font where the sainted John the Baptist immersed the converts; yonder is the prison of the good St. Paul, where we all did use to go to touch the ancient chains that bound him and be cured of our distempers; I see the tomb of the disciple Luke, and afar off is the church wherein repose the ashes of the holy John, where the Christians of Ephesus go twice a year to gather the dust from the tomb, which is able to make bodies whole again that are corrupted by disease, and cleanse the soul from sin; but see how the wharves encroach upon the sea, and what multitudes of ships are anchored in the bay; see, also, how the city hath stretched abroad, far over the valley behind Pion, and even unto the walls of Ayassa look; and lo, all the hills are white with palaces and ribbed with colonnades of marble. How mighty is Ephesus become!

And wondering at what their eyes had seen, they went down into the city and purchased garments and clothed themselves. And when they would have passed on, the merchant bit the coins which they had given him, with his teeth, and turned them about and looked curiously upon them, and cast them upon his counter, and listened if they rang; and then he said, "These be bogus." And they said "Depart thou to Hades," and went their way. When they were come to their houses, they recognized them, albeit they seemed old and mean; and they rejoiced and were glad. They ran to the doors, and knocked, and strangers opened, and looked inquiringly upon them. And they said, with great excitement, while their hearts beat high, and the color in their faces came and went, "Where is my father? Where is my mother? Where are Dyonisius and Serapion, and Pericles, and Decius?" And the strangers that opened said, "We know not these." The seven said, "How, you know them not? How long have ye dwelt here, and whither are they gone that dwelt here before ye?" And the strangers said, "Ye play upon us with a jest, young men; we and our fathers have sojourned under these roofs these six generations; the names ye utter rot upon the tombs, and they that bore them have run their brief race, have laughed and sung, have borne the sorrows and the weariness that were allotted them, and are at rest; for nine-score years the summers have come and gone, and the autumn leaves have fallen, since the roses faded out of their cheeks and they laid them to sleep with the dead.

The seven young men wept and turned them away from their homes, and the strangers shut the doors upon them. The wanderers marvelled greatly, and looked into the faces of all they met, as hoping to find one that they knew; but all were strange, and passed them by and spake no friendly word. They were sore distressed and sad. Presently they spake unto a citizen and said, "Who is King of Ephesus?" And the citiizen answered and said, "Whence come ye that ye know not that great Laertius reigns in Ephesus?" They looked one at the other, greatly perplexed, and presently asked again, "Where, then, is the good King

Maximilianus?" The citizen moved him apart, as one who is afraid, and said, "Verily these men be mad, and dream dreams, else would they know that the King whereof they speak is dead above two hundred years agone."

Then the scales fell from the eyes of the seven, and one said, Alas, that we drank of the curious liquors. They have made us weary, and in dreamless sleep, these two long centuries have we lain. Our homes are desolate, our friends are dead. Behold, the jig is up—let us ante up and pass the buck. And that same day they went and laid them down and died.

Such is the story of the Seven Sleepers, (with slight variations,) and I know it is true, because I have seen the cave myself.

So firm a faith had the ancients in this legend, that as late as eight or nine hundred years ago, learned travellers held it in superstitious fear. Two of them record that they ventured into it, but ran quickly out again, not daring to tarry lest they should fall asleep and outlive their great grand children a century or so. Even at this day the ignorant denizens of the neighboring country prefer not to sleep in it.

This letter, numbered twenty-six by Twain, appeared in the *Daily Alta California* of November 24, 1867. It was used in Chapter XIII, Volume II. "Grandest city" became "proudest city." After "so did John," Twain inserted a passage, including a Scriptural quotation. "Got to persecuting" became "fell to persecuting"; "dust" became "travel"; and "ante up and pass the buck" became "die." After "laid them down and died," Twain inserted a passage of about eighty words.

32. Camping Out

In Camp, Mountains of Lebanon,
Syria, September 11th, 1867.

For the last two months we have been in a worry about one portion of this Holy Land pilgrimage. I refer to transportation service. We knew very well that Palestine was a country which did not do a large passenger business, and every man we came across who knew anything about it gave us to understand that not half of our party would be able to get dragomen and animals. As far as I was individually concerned, I did not bother much about the matter, but Brown, who had somehow imbibed a vague notion that a dragoman was some kind of a rare and mysterious beast like a rhinosceros or a mastodon, was greatly distressed. At Constantinople everybody fell to telegraphing the American Consuls at Alexandria and Beirout to give notice that we wanted dragomen and transportation. We were desperate—would take horses, jackasses, cameleopards [camelopards], kangaroos—anything. At Smyrna, more telegraphing was done, to the same end. Also, fearing for the worst, we telegraphed for a large number of seats in the diligence for Damascus, and horses for the ruins of Baalbec.

As might have been expected, a notion got abroad in Syria and Egypt that the whole population of the Province of America (the Turks consider us a trifling little province in some unvisited corner of the world,) were coming to the Holy Land—and so, when we got to Beirout yesterday, we found the place full of dragomen and their outfits. We had all intended to go by diligence to Damascus, and switch off to Baalbec as we went along—because we expected to rejoin the ship at Mount Carmel, and take to the woods from there. However, when our own private party of eight found that we could just as well make the through trip from Beirout, we adopted that programme. We have never been much trouble to a Consul before, but we have been a fearful bother to our Consul at Beirout. I mention this because I cannot help admiring his patience, his industry, and his accommodating spirit. I mention it also, because I think some of our gang did not give him as full credit for his excellent services as he deserved.

Well, out of our eight, three were selected to attend to all business connected with the expedition. The rest of us had nothing to do but look at the beautiful city of Beirout, with its bright, new houses nestled among a wilderness of green shrubbery spread abroad over an upland that sloped gently down to the sea; and also at the mountains of Lebanon that environ it; and likewise to bathe in the transparent blue water that rolled its billows about the ship (we did not know there were sharks there). We had also to range up and down through the town and look at the costumes; these are picturesque and fanciful, but not so varied as at Constantinople and Smyrna; the women here add an agony—in the two former cities the sex wear a thin veil which one can see through and often expose their ancles [ankles], but at Beirout they cover their entire faces with dark-colored or black veils, so that they look like mummies, and then expose their breasts to the public. A young gentleman (I believe he was a Greek,) volunteered to show us around the city, and said it would afford him great pleasure, because he was studying English and wanted practice in that language. When we had finished the rounds, however, he called for remuneration—said he hoped the gentlemen would give him a trifle in the way of a few piastres (equivalent to a few five cent pieces). We did so. The Consul was surprised when he heard it, and said he knew the young fellow's family very well, and that they were an old and highly respectable family and worth a hundred and fifty thousand dollars! Some people, so situated, would have been ashamed of the berth he had with us and his manner of sneaking into it.

At the appointed time our business committee reported, and said all things were in readiness—that we were to start to-day, with horses, pack animals and tents, and go to Baalbec, Damascus, the Sea of Tiberias thence southward by the way of the scene of Jacob's Dream and other notable Bible localities to Jerusalem—from thence probably to the Dead Sea, but possibly not—and then strike for the ocean and rejoin the ship three or four weeks hence at Joppa; terms, five dollars a day a piece, in gold, and everything to be furnished by the dragoman. They said we would live as well as at a hotel. I had read something like that before, and didn't shame my judgment by believing a word of it. I said nothing, however, but just packed up a blanket and a shawl to sleep in, pipes and tobacco, two or three woollen shirts, a portfolio, a guide-book (the same being a Bible), a deck of cards and a tooth-brush. I also took along a towel and a cake of soap, to inspire respect in the Arabs, who would take me for a king in disguise.

We were to select our horses at 3 P. M. At that hour Abraham, the dragoman, marshalled them before us. With all solemnity I set it down here, that those horses were the hardest lot I ever did come across, and their accoutrements were in exquisite keeping with their style. One brute had an eye out; another had his tail sawed off close, like a jack-ass rabbit, and was proud of it; another had a bony ridge running from his neck to his tail, like one of those ruined aqueducts one sees about Rome, and then had a neck on him like a bowsprit; they all limped, and had sore backs, and likewise raw places and old scales scattered about their persons like brass nails in an old hair trunk; their gaits were marvellous to contemplate, and replete with variety—under way the procession looked like a fleet in a storm. It was fearful. Brown shook his head and said:

"That dragon's going to get himself into trouble fetching these old crates out of the hospital the way they are, unless he's got a permit."

I said nothing. The display was exactly according to the guide-book, and were we not travelling by the guide-book? I selected a certain horse because I thought I saw him shy, and I thought that a horse that had spirit enough to shy was not to be despised. However, and I have found out since, that it must have been a mistake. He never shied—he only staggered.

Pilgrim Style

At 6 o'clock P. M. we came to a halt here on the breezy summit of a beautiful mountain overlooking the sea and the beautiful valley where dwelt some of those enterprising Phenicians of ancient times we read so much about; all around us are what were once the dominions of Hiram, King of Tyre, who furnished timber from the cedars of these Lebanon hills to build portions of King Solomon's Temple with.

Shortly after six, our pack train arrived. I had not seen it before, and a good right I had to be astonished. We had nineteen serving men and twenty-six pack mules! It was a perfect caravan. It looked like one, too, as it wound among the rocks. I wondered what in the very mischief we wanted with such a vast turn-out as that, for eight men. I wondered awhile, but soon I began to hanker for a tin plate, and some bacon and beans. You know, I had camped out many and many a time before, and knew just what was coming. I went off, without waiting for serving men, and unsaddled my horse, and washed such portions of his ribs and his spine as projected through his hide, and when I came back, behold five stately circus tents were up—tents that were brilliant within, with blue, and gold, and crimson, and all manner of splendid adornment! I was speechless. Then they brought eight little iron bedsteads, and set them up in the tents; they put a soft mattress and pillows and good blankets and two snow-white sheets on each bed. Next, they rigged a table about the centrepole, and on it placed pewter pitchers, basins, soap and the whitest of towels—one set for each man; they pointed to pockets in the tent, and said we could put our small traps in them for convenience, and if we needed pins or such things, they were sticking everywhere. Then came the finishing touch—they spread nice carpets on the floor! I simply said, "If you call this camping out, all right—but it isn't the style I am used to; my little baggage that I brought along is at a discount."

It grew dark, and they put candles on the tables—candles set in bright, new, brazen candlesticks. And soon the bell—a genuine, simon-pure bell—rung, and we were invited to "the saloon." I had thought before that we had a tent or so too many, and now here was one, at least, provided for; it was to be used for nothing but an eating-saloon. Like the others, it was high enough for a family of giraffes to live in, and was very handsome and clean and bright-colored within. It was a gem of a place. A table for eight, and eight canvas chairs; a table-cloth and napkins whose whiteness and whose fineness laughed to scorn the things we were used to in the great excursion steamer; soup-plates, dinner-plates—everything, you understand, in the handsomest kind of style. It was wonderful! And they call *this* camping out! Those stately fellows in baggy trowsers and turbaned fezzes brought in a dinner which consisted of roast mutton, roast chicken, roast goose, potatoes, bread, tea, pudding, apples and delicious grapes; the viands were better cooked than any we had eaten for weeks and the table made a finer appearance, with its large silver candlesticks and other finery, than any table we had sat down to for a good while, and yet that eternally polite dragoman, Abraham, came bowing in and apologizing for the whole affair, on account of the unavoidable confusion of getting under way for a very long trip, and promising to do a great deal better in future! We took up a club and drove him out.

It is midnight, now, and we break camp at six in the morning. Of course I must turn in at once.

They call this camping out. At this rate it is a glorious privilege to be a pilgrim to the Holy Land.

This letter, numbered twenty-seven by Twain, appeared in the *Daily Alta California* of December 1, 1867. It was used in Chapter XIV, Volume II, beginning with the fourth paragraph of the chapter and filling the remainder of it. The sentence beginning "As far as I was individually concerned" was deleted. "Rejoin the ship at Mount Carmel" became "rejoin the ship, go to Mount Carmel"; "we could just as well make the through trip from Beirout" became "it was possible, and proper enough, to make the 'long trip' "; "bother" became "nuisance"; "gang" became "ship's company"; "sneaking" became "crawling"; and "a guide-book (the same being a Bible)" became "a guide-book, and a Bible." "A deck of cards and a tooth-brush" was deleted. "Jackass rabbit" became "rabbit," and "Brown" became "Blucher." The sentence beginning "However, and I have found out since" and the following sentence were deleted. "Beautiful mountain" became "shapely mountain"; "beautiful valley" became "handsome valley"; "hanker for" became "long for"; "traps" became "trifles"; "silver" became "German-silver"; and "eternally polite" became "polite." "We took up a club and drove him out" and "Of course I must turn in at once" were deleted.

33. All About Joshua

In Camp near Temnin el Foka,
Valley of Lebanon, Sept. 12th.

The night shall be filled with music,
And the cares that infest the day
Shall fold their tents like the Arabs,
And as silently steal away.

I slept very soundly last night, yet when the dragoman's bell rang at half-past five this morning and the cry went abroad of "Ten minutes to dress for breakfast!" I heard both. It surprised me, because I have not heard the breakfast gong in the ship for a month, and whenever we have had occasion to fire a salute at daylight I have only found it out in the course of conversation afterward. However, camping out, even though it be in a gorgeous tent, makes one fresh and lively in the morning—especially if the air you are breathing is the cool, fresh air of the mountains.

I was dressed within the ten minutes, and came out. The saloon tent had been stripped of its sides, and had nothing left but its roof; so when we sat down to table we could look over a noble panorama of mountain, sea and hazy valley. And sitting thus, the sun rose slowly up and suffused the picture with a world of rich coloring. Hot mutton chops, fried chicken, omelettes, fried potatoes and coffee—all excellent. This was the bill of fare. It was sauced with a savage appetite purchased by hard riding the day before, and refreshing sleep in a pure atmosphere. As I called for my second cup of coffee, I glanced over my shoulder, and behold our white village was gone—the splendid tents had vanished like magic! It was wonderful how quickly those Arabs had "folded their tents"; and it was wonderful, alas, how quickly they got the thousand odds and ends of the camp together and disappeared with them.

By half-past six we were under way, and all the Syrian world seemed to be under way also. The road was filled with mule trains and long processions of camels. This reminds me that I have been trying for some time to think what a camel looks like, and now I have made it out. When he is down on all his knees, flat on his breast to receive his load, he looks like a goose swimming; and when he is upright he looks like a bob-tailed ostrich with fore-legs to it. Camels are not beautiful, and their long under lip gives them an exceedingly "gallus" expression. They have immense, flat, forked cushions of feet, that make a track in the dust like a pie with a slice cut out of it. They are not particular about their diet. They would eat a tomb-stone if they could bite it. A thistle grows about here which has needles on it that would pierce through leather, I think; if one touches you, you can find relief in nothing but profanity. The camels eat these. They show by their actions that they enjoy them. I expect it would be a real treat to a camel to have a keg of nails for supper.

"*Jerico*"

While I am speaking of animals, I will mention that I have got a horse by the name of "Jerico." He is a mare. I have seen remarkable horses before, but none so remarkable as this. I wanted a horse that could shy, and this one fills the bill. I had an idea that shying indicated spirit. If I was correct, I have got the most spirited horse on earth. He shies at everything he comes across, with the utmost impartiality. He appears to have a mortal dread of telegraph poles, especially; and it is fortunate that these are on both sides of the road, because as it is now, I never fall off twice on the same side. If I fell on the same side always, it would get to be monotonous after a while. This creature has got scared at everything he has seen to-day, except a hay wagon. He walked up to that with an intrepidity and recklessness that were astonishing. And it would fill any one with admiration to see how he preserves his self-possession in the presence of a barley sack. This daredevil bravery will be the death of this horse some day.

He is not particularly fast, but I think he will get me through the Holy Land. He has only one fault. His tail has been chopped off or driven up, and he has to fight the flies with his heels. This is all very well, but when he tries to kick a fly off the top of his head with his hind foot, it is too much variety. He is going to get himself into trouble that way, some day. He reaches around and bites my legs, too. I don't care particularly about that, only I don't like to see a horse too sociable.

I think the owner of this prize had a wrong opinion about him. He had an idea that he was one of those fiery, untamed steeds, but he is not of that character. I know the Arab had this idea, because when he brought the horse to me for inspection in Beirout, he kept jerking at the bridle and shouting in Arabic, "Ho! will you? Do you want to run away, you ferocious beast, and break your neck?" when all the time the horse was not doing anything in the world, and only looked like he wanted to lean up against something and think. Whenever he is not shying at things, or reaching after a fly, he wants to do that yet. How it would surprise his owner to know this.

Bible Land

We have been in a historical section of country all day. At noon we camped three hours and took luncheon at Mekseh, near the junction of the Lebanon Mountains and the Jebel el Kuneiyiseh, and looked down into the immense, level, garden-like Valley of Lebanon. To-night we are camping near the same valley, and have a very long sweep of it in view. We can see the long, whale-backed ridge of Mount Hermon projecting above the eastern hills. The "dews of Hermon" are falling upon us now, and the tents are almost soaked with them.

Over the way from us, and higher up the valley, we can discern, through the glasses, the faint outlines of the wonderful ruins of the Baalbec, the Baal-Gad of Scripture. Joshua, and another gentleman, whose name has escaped me, were the two spies who were sent into this land of Caanan from Egypt to report upon its character—I mean they were the spies who reported favorably—which report was received, and the committee discharged. They took back with them some specimens of the grapes of this country, and in the children's picture-books they are always represented as bearing one monstrous bunch swung to a pole between them, a respectable load for a pack-train. The Sunday school books stretched it a little. The grapes are most excellent to this day, but the bunches are not as large as those in the pictures. I was surprised and hurt when I saw them, because those colossal bunches of grapes was one of my most cherished juvenile traditions.

Well, Joshua reported favorably, and the children of Israel started out, with Moses at the head of the general government, and Joshua in command of the army, of 600,000 fighting men. Of women and children and civilians there was a countless swarm. Of all that mighty host none but Joshua ever lived to set his foot in the Promised Land. They wandered forty years in the desert, and then old Moses, the gifted warrior, poet, statesman and philosopher, went up into Pisgah and met his mysterious fate. Where he was buried no man knows:

... no man dug that sepulchre,
And no man saw it e'er—
For the Sons of God upturned the sod
And laid the dead man there!

Then Joshua started on his terrible raid, and from Jericho clear to this Baal-Gad, over here, he swept the land like the Genius of Destruction. He slaughtered the people, laid waste their soil, and razed their cities to the ground. He wasted thirty-one Kings, also. One may call it that, though really it can hardly be called wasting them, because there were always plenty of Kings in those days, and to spare. At any rate, he closed out thirty-one Kings, and divided up their realms among his Israelites. He divided up this valley stretched out here before us, and so it was once Jewish territory. They have long since disappeared from it, however.

Down yonder, an hour's journey from here, we passed through an Arab village of stone dry-goods boxes (they look like that,) where old father Noah's tomb lies under lock and key. (Noah was the party who built the ark.) Over these old hills and valleys the ark that contained all that was left of a vanished world once floated.

Noah's tomb is built of stone, and is covered with a long stone building. Bucksheesh let us in. The building had to be long, because the grave of the honored old navigator is two hundred and ten feet long itself! It is only about four feet high, though. The proof that this is the genuine spot where Noah was buried can only be doubted by uncommonly incredulous people. The evidence is pretty straight. Shem, the son of Noah, was present at the burial, and showed the place to his descendants, who transmitted the knowledge to his [their] descendants, and the lineal descendants of these introduced themselves to us to-day. It was pleasant to make the acquaintance of members of so respectable a family. It was a thing to be proud of. It was the next thing to being acquainted with Noah himself.

Noah's memorable voyage will always possess a living interest for me, henceforward.

An Unfortunate People

If ever an oppressed race existed, it is this one we see fettered around us under the inhuman tyranny of the Ottoman Empire. I wish Europe would let Russia tone Turkey down a little. The Syrians are very poor, and yet they are ground down by a system of taxation that would drive any other nation frantic. Last year their taxes were heavy enough, in all conscience—but this year they have been increased by the addition of taxes that were forgiven them in times of famine in former years. On top of this the Government has levied a tax of *one-tenth* of the whole proceeds of the land. This is only half the story. The Pacha of a Pachalia does not bother himself with appointing Tax Collectors. He figures up what all these taxes ought to amount to in a certain district. Then he farms the collection out. He calls the rich men together, the highest bidder gets the speculation, pays the Pacha on the spot, and then sells out to smaller fry, who sell in turn to a piratical horde of still smaller fry. These latter compel the peasant to bring his little trifle of grain to the village, at his own cost. It must be weighed, the various taxes set apart and the remainder returned to the producer. But the Collector delays this duty day after day, while the producer's family are perishing for bread; at last the poor wretch, who cannot but understand the game, says take a quarter—take half—take two-thirds, if you will, and let me go! It must be the most outrageous state of things in all the world.

These people are naturally good-hearted and intelligent, and with education and liberty, would be a happy and contented race. They often appeal to the stranger to know if the great world will not some day come to their relief and save them. The Sultan has been lavishing money like water in England and Paris, but his subjects are sweating for it now.

More Splendor

This style of camping out bewilders me. We have got boot-jacks and a bath-tub, now, and yet all the mysteries the pack-mules carry are not revealed. Brown has come to believe, at last, that the dragoman has got Aladdin's lamp hidden about his person, and has ceased to be surprised at anything. He has gone out now to inquire if the dragoman has brought a piano along.

This letter, numbered twenty-eight by Twain, appeared in the *Daily Alta California* of December 4, 1867. It became Chapter XV in Volume II. Twain provided three introductory sentences, giving to Temnin-el-Foka the name of Jacksonville. "Got . . . together" became "gathered . . . together," and "a bob-tailed ostrich with fore-legs to it" became "an ostrich with an extra set of legs." To "gallus," Twain attached this footnote: "Excuse the slang—no other word will describe it." "I expect" became "I suppose"; "have got a horse" became "have a horse"; "has got scared at everything" became "has scared at everything"; "or driven up" became "or else he has sat down on it too hard, some time or other"; "Joshua, and another gentleman, whose name has escaped me" became "Joshua and another person"; and "from Egypt" became "by the children of Israel."

"Which report was received, and the committee discharged" was deleted. "Stretched" became "exaggerated"; "bunches of grapes was" became "bunches of grapes were"; "started out" became "journeyed on"; "none but Joshua ever lived to set his foot" became "none but the two faithful spies ever lived to set their feet"; "started on his terrible raid" became "began his terrible raid"; "closed out thirty-one Kings" became "destroyed thirty-one kings"; "They have long since disappeared" became "The Jews have long since disappeared"; and "Noah was the party who built the ark" became "Noah built the ark." After "all that was left of a vanished world once floated," Twain added two sentences. After the statements about the size of Noah's tomb, Twain inserted "He must have cast a shadow like a lightning-rod." "Tone Turkey down a little" became "annihilate Turkey a little—not much, but enough to make it difficult to find the place again without a divining-rod or a diving-bell"; "Pacha of a Pachalia" became "Pasha of a Pashalic"; "It must be the most outrageous state of things in all the world" became "It is a most outrageous state of things"; "sweating for it" became "suffering for it"; and "we have got" became "we have." After "are not revealed," Twain added "What next?" and deleted the last two sentences of the letter.

34. Portrait of a Syrian Village

In Camp, Eight Hours Beyond Damascus, September 17th

That is the cheapest way to put it, perhaps. There is a Syrian village of the usual style near here, and I think they spell it Kaf'r Houer, but I do not know. It don't matter, though. Most people don't care anything about names, and cannot recollect them after they hear them. When I say that that village is of the usual style, I mean to insinuate that all Syrian villages within fifty miles of Damascus are alike—so much alike that it would require more than human intelligence to tell wherein one differed from another. A Syrian village is a hive of huts one story high (six feet,) and as square as a dry goods box; it is mudplaster all over, flat roof and all, and generally white-washed after a fashion. The same roof often extends over half the town, covering many of the streets, which are generally about a yard wide. When you ride through one of these villages at noonday, you first meet a melancholy dog, that looks up at you and silently begs that you won't run over him, but he does not offer to get out of the way; next you meet a young boy without any clothes on, and he holds out his hand and says "Bucksheesh!"—he don't really expect a cent, but then he learned to say that before he learned to say mother, and now he cannot break himself of it; next you meet a woman with a black veil drawn closely over her face, and her bust exposed; finally, you come to several sore-eyed children and children in all stages of mutilation and decay; and sitting humbly in the dust, and all fringed with filthy rags, is a poor devil whose arms and legs are gnarled and twisted like grapevines. These are all the people you are likely to see. The balance of the population are asleep within doors, or abroad tending goats in the plains and on the hill sides. The village is built on some poor little water-course (water is a scarce article in this country), and about it is a little fresh-looking vegetation. Beyond this charmed circle, for miles on every side, stretches a weary desert of sand and gravel, which produces a gray bunchy shrub like sage-brush. A Syrian village is the sorriest sight in the world, and its surroundings are eminently in keeping with it.

Nimrod, the Mighty Hunter

I would not have gone into this dissertation upon Syrian villages but for the fact that Nimrod, the Mighty Hunter of Scriptural notoriety, is buried in this one close to which our tents are pitched, and I wanted you to know about how he is located. Like Homer, he is said to be buried in many other places, but this is the only true and genuine place where he is planted.

Nimrod was a brick. When the original tribes were dispersed, more than four thousand years ago, Nimrod and a large party travelled three or four hundred miles, and preëmpted a claim where the great city of Babylon afterwards stood. Nimrod built that city. He also began to build the famous Tower of Babel, but circumstances over which he had no control put it out of his power to finish it. He ran it up eight stories high, however, and two of them still stand, at this day—a huge mountain of brickwork, rent down the centre by earthquakes, and seared and vitrified by the lightnings of an angry God. But the vast ruin will still stand for ages, to shame the puny labors of these modern generations of men. Its huge compartments are tenanted by owls and lions, and old Nimrod lies neglected in this wretched village, far from the scene of his grand enterprise. He did the best he could with his little tower, but they rung in too many languages on him. When things got so mixed that when a mason sung out for bricks and they brought him mortar, Nimrod saw that the game was up with him, and so he settled with the hands and left destroying Time a job of fifty centuries to worry over.

Baalbec

But I am getting along too fast. When I wrote last we were approaching Baalbec, a noble ruin whose history is a sealed book. It has stood there for thousands of years, the wonder and admiration of travellers—but who built it, or when it was built, are questions that may never be answered. One thing is very sure, though. Such grandeur of design, and such matchless grace of execution, as one sees in the temples of Baalbec, have not been equalled or even approached in any work of men's hands that has been built within twenty centuries past.

The great Temple of the Sun, the Temple of Jupiter, and several smaller temples, are clustered together in the midst of one of these miserable Syrian villages, and look strangely enough in such plebian company. These great temples are built upon massive substructions that might support a world, almost; the materials used are blocks of stone as large as an omnibus—very few, if any of them, are smaller than a carpenter's tool chest—and these substructions are traversed by tunnels through which a train of cars could pass. With such foundations as these, it is little wonder that Baalbec has lasted so long. The Temple of the Sun is nearly three hundred feet long and one hundred and sixty wide. It had fifty-four columns around it, but only six are standing now—the others lie broken at its base, a confused and picturesque heap. The six columns are perfect, as also are their bases—Corinthian capitals and entablature—and six more shapely columns do not exist. The columns and the entablature together are ninety feet high—a prodigious altitude for shafts of stone to reach, truly—and yet one only thinks of their beauty and symmetry when looking at them; the pillars look slender and delicate, the entablature, with its elaborate sculpture, looks like rich stucco work. But when you have gazed aloft till your eyes are weary, you glance at the great fragments of pillars among which you are standing, and find that they are eight feet through; and with them lie beautiful capitals apparently as large as a small cottage; and also single slabs of stone, superbly sculptured, that are four or five feet thick and would completely cover the floor of any ordinary parlor. You wonder where these monstrous things came from, and it takes you some little time to satisfy yourself that the airy and graceful fabric that towers above your head is made up of their mates. It seems too preposterous.

The Temple of Jupiter is a smaller ruin than the one I have been speaking of, and yet is immense. It is in a tolerable state of preservation. One row of nine columns stands almost uninjured. They are sixty-five feet high and support a sort of porch or roof, which connects them with the roof of the building. This porch-roof is composed of tremendous slabs of stone which are so superbly sculptured on the under side that the work looks like a finely finished fresco from below. One or two of these slabs had fallen, and again I wondered if the gigantic masses of carved stone that lay about me were no larger than those above my head. Within the temple, the ornamentation was magnificent and colossal. What a wonder of architectural beauty and grandeur this edifice must have been when it was new! And what a noble picture it and its statelier companion, with the chaos of mighty fragments scattered about them, makes in the moonlight!

I cannot conceive how those immense blocks of stone were ever hauled from the quarries, or how they were ever raised to the dizzy heights they occupy in the temples. And yet these sculptured blocks are trifles in size compared with the rough-hewn blocks that form the wide verandah or platform which surrounds the Great Temple. One stretch of that platform, 200 feet long, is composed of blocks of stone as large, and some of them larger, than a street car. They surmount a wall about ten or twelve feet high. I thought those were large rocks, but they sank into insignificance compared with those which formed another section of the platform. These were three in number, and I thought that each of them was about as large as four street cars. In combined length these three stones stretch nearly 200 feet; they are 13 feet square; two of them are 64 feet long each, and the third is 69. They are built into the massive wall some 20 feet above the ground. They are there, but how they got there is the question. I have seen the hull of a steamboat that was smaller than one of those stones. All these great walls are as exact and shapely as the flimsy things we build of bricks in these degenerate days. A race of gods or of giants must have inhabited Baalbec many a century ago. Men like the men of our day could hardly rear such temples as these.

I went to the quarry from whence the stones of Baalbec were taken. It was about a quarter of a mile off, and down hill. In a great pit lay the mate of the largest stone in the ruins. It lay there just as the giants of that old forgotten age had left it when they were called hence—just as they had left it to remain for thousands of years, an eloquent rebuke unto such as are prone to think slightingly of the men who lived before them. This enormous block lies there, neatly squared and ready for the builders' hands—a solid mass fourteen feet by seventeen, and seventy feet long! Two buggies could be driven abreast of each other, from one end of it to the other, and have room enough for a man or two to walk on either side. Three such stones laid side by side in Platt's Hall would leave small room for an audience. One might step upon them from the galleries, I think.

You might swear that all the John Smiths and George Wilkinsons, and all the other pitiful nobodies between Kingdom Come and Baalbec would inscribe their poor little names upon the walls of Baalbec's magnificent ruins, and would add the town, the county, and the State they came from—and swearing thus, you would be correct. It is a pity some great ruin does not fall in and flatten out some of these cattle and scare their tribe out of ever giving their names to fame upon any walls again, save those of the water-closets where they were wont to inscribe them before they wandered from their native land.

Trouble Brewing

I was going to write about the ancient city of Damascus, but this last new horse I have got is trying to break his neck over the tent-ropes, and I shall have to go out and anchor him. Jericho and I have parted company. The new horse is not much to boast of, I think. One of his hind legs bends the wrong way, and the other one is a straight and stiff as a tent pole. Most of his teeth are gone, and he is as blind as a bat. His nose has been broken at some time or other, and is arched like a culvert now. His under lip hangs down like a camel's, and his ears are chopped off close to his head. I had some trouble at first to find a name for him, but I finally concluded to call him Baalbec, because he is such a magnificent ruin. I cannot keep from talking about my horses, because I have a very long and tedious journey before me, and they naturally occupy my thoughts about as much as matters of apparently much greater importance. And while I am writing about him, Baalbec has tripped again and caved in one side of the tent, and I am just as good as out of doors. I shall have to go out and see about this.

This letter, numbered twenty-nine by Twain, appeared in the *Daily Alta California* of December 8, 1867. The first two parts of the letter, the portrait of the Syrian village and the story of Nimrod, were used in Chapter XVIII, Volume II, beginning in the seventh paragraph. The first four sentences were omitted. "Poor little water-course" became "consumptive little water-course"—and the following words in parenthesis were omitted. "This one close to which our tents are pitched, and I wanted you to know" became "Jonesborough, and I wished the public to know"; and "where he is planted" became "his ashes inhabit." "Nimrod was a brick" was deleted. "Preëmpted a claim" became "settled," and "a huge mountain" became "a colossal mass." The last two sentences about Nimrod were deleted.

The section on Baalbec was used in Chapter XVI, Volume II, beginning with the fourth paragraph of the chapter. "Matchless grace" became "grace"; "superbly sculptured" became "finely sculptured"; "finely finished fresco" became "fresco"; "magnificent" became "elaborate"; and "it and its statelier companion . . . makes" became "it and its statelier companion . . . make." Between the sentence ending "as four street cars" and that beginning "In combined length" Twain inserted thirty-six words elaborating on the comparison. "These degenerate days" became "these days" and "neatly squared" became "squared." The sentence beginning "Three such stones laid side by side" and the following sentence were deleted. "Cattle" became "reptiles," and "upon any walls again, save those of the water-closets where they were wont to inscribe them before they wandered from their native land" became "upon any walls or monuments again, forever." The last paragraph (about the new horse, Baalbec) was used near the end of Chapter XVIII, Volume II, although the last two sentences were omitted.

35. Damascus the Eternal

Banias, September, 1867.

Though old as history itself, thou art fresh as the breath of spring, blooming as thine own rosebud, and fragrant as thine own orange-flower, O Damascus, pearl of the East!

Damascus dates back anterior to the days of Abraham, and is the oldest city in the world. It was founded by Uz, the grandson of Noah. "The early history of Damascus is shrouded in the mists of a hoary antiquity." Leave the matters written of in the first eleven chapters of the Old Testament out, and no recorded event has occurred in the world but Damascus was in existence to receive the news of it. Go back as far as you will into the vague Past, there was always a Damascus. In the writings of every century for more than four thousand years, its name has been mentioned and its praises sung. To Damascus, years are only moments, decades are only flitting trifles of time. She measures time, not by days and months and years, but by the empires she has seen rise, and prosper and crumble to ruin. She is a type of immortality. She saw the foundations of Baalbec, and Thebes and Ephesus laid; she saw them grow into mighty cities, and amaze the world with their grandeur—and she has lived to see them desolate, deserted, and given over to the owls and the bats. She saw the Israelitish Empire exalted, and she saw it annihilated. She saw Greece rise and flourish two thousand years, and die. In her old age she saw Rome built; she saw it overshadow the world with its power; she saw it perish. The few hundreds of years of Genoese and Venitian might and splendor were, to grave old Damascus, only a trifling scintillation hardly worth remembering. Damascus has seen all that has ever occurred on earth, and still she lives. She has looked upon the dry bones of a thousand Empires, and will see the tombs of a thousand more before she dies. Though another claims the name, old Damascus is by right the Eternal City.

Mahomet's Paradise, and the Bible's

We arrived, after a long day's ride in a scorching sun, upon a high mountain overlooking the city, and as the glare of day mellowed into twilight, we looked down upon a picture which is celebrated all over the world. I think I have read about four hundred times that when Mahomet was a simple camel driver he reached this point and looked down upon Damascus for the first time, and then called at the office and got his money. He said man could enter only one paradise; he preferred to go to the old regular one above. So he sat down there and feasted his eyes upon the earthly paradise of Damascus, and then went away without entering its gates. They have erected a tower on the hill to mark the spot where he stood.

Damascus *is* beautiful from the mountain. It is beautiful even to foreigners accustomed to luxuriant vegetation, and I can easily understand how unspeakably beautiful it must be to eyes that are only used to the God-forsaken barrenness and desolation of Syria. I should think a Syrian would go wild with ecstacy when such a picture bursts upon him for the first time.

In a vast level plain Damascus sits, a great snow-white city nestling in the heart of a sea of brilliant green shrubbery that stretches for fifteen miles up and down the plain and is five or six miles wide. Outside of that billowy expanse of shining foliage is the desert—pure, unadulterated, yellow sand, apparently, and smooth as velvet, and threaded far away with fine lines that stand for roads, and dotted with creeping mites that we know are camel-trains and journeying men—and fencing in the desert are bald, bare mountains that have no green thing about them to soften their forbidding aspect. From Mahomet's stand-point you have the wall of dreary mountains, the wide, yellow desert, the dense mass of rich green foliage and the great white city with its hundred domes and its forest of minarets, gleaming out of the midst of it. You have these for a picture—and when you think of the leagues of blighted, blasted, sandy, rocky, sun-burnt, ugly, dreary, infamous country you have ridden over to get here, you think it is the most beautiful, beautiful picture that ever human eyes rested upon in all the world! If I were to go to Damascus again, I would camp on Mahomet's hill about a week, and then go away. There is no need to go inside the walls. The Prophet was wise without knowing it when he decided not to go down into the Paradise of Damascus.

There is an honored old tradition that the immense garden which Damascus stands in was the Garden of Eden, and modern writers have gathered up many chapters of evidence tending to show that it really was the Garden of Eden, and that the Rivers Pharpar and Abana are the "two rivers" that watered Adam's Paradise. It may be so, but it is not Paradise now, and one would be as happy outside of it as he would be likely to be within. It is so crooked and cramped and dirty that one cannot realize that he is in the splendid city he saw from the hill top. The gardens are hidden by high mud walls, and the Paradise is become a very sink of polution and uncomeliness. Damascus has plenty of clear, pure water in it, though, and this is enough, of itself, to make an Arab think it beautiful and blessed. Water is scarce in blistered Syria. We run railways by our large cities in America; in Syria they curve the roads so as to make them run by the meagre little puddles they call "fountains," and which are not found oftener on a journey than every four hours. But the "rivers" of Pharpar and Abana of Scripture (they do not amount to quite as much as the Carson and the Humboldt) run through Damascus, and so every house and every garden have their sparkling fountains and rivulets of water. With her forest of foliage and her abundance of water, Damascus must be a wonder of wonders to the Bedouin from the deserts. Damascus is simply an oasis—that is what it is. For four thousand years its waters have not gone dry or its fertility failed. Now you understand why the city has existed so long. It could not die. So long as its waters remain to it away out there in the midst of that howling desert, so long will Damascus live to bless the sight of the tired and thirsty wayfarer.

In Damascus they just think there are no such rivers in all the world as their little Abana and Pharpar. The Damascenes have always thought that way. In II Kings, chapter 5, Naaman brags most ridiculously about them. That was three thousand years ago. He says: "Are not Abana and Pharpar Rivers of Damascus better than all the waters of Israel? May I not wash in them and be clean?" But perhaps you never heard the story. I will give it you.

The Story of Naaman

Major General Naaman was the Commander-in-Chief of the Syrian armies and wore the brass collar. He was the pet of the King, and had much shekels, and lived in a two-story house and put on more style than any man in Damascus. "He was a mighty man in valor, but he was a leper." (Strangely enough, the house they point out to you now as his, has been turned into a leper hospital, and the inmates expose their horrid deformities and hold up their ghastly hands and beg for "bucksheesh" when you enter.) A little captive Israelitish maid servant of Naaman's wife remarked one day that if the Prophet Elisha, who was living down in Samaria somewhere, would only take hold of Naaman's case, he could cure him. This came to the ears of Naaman's friend, the King, and he at once (on such slim evidence), sent his sick Major General off to Elisha with bucksheesh enough to pay ten thousand doctor's bills, viz: "ten talents of silver, and six thousand pieces of gold and ten changes of raiment." This would naturally look like a pretty good thing for Elisha, who was the successor of a prophet who had been fed by the ravens, and who was in indifferent circumstances himself. But it never started the enthusiasm in Elisha once. Naaman thought the prophet would rush down and invite him in and make a great fuss over him, and all that sort of thing, but he never did anything of the kind. He just said, in his careless way, that about the best thing the old party could do would be to go and wash himself—wash himself in the Jordan—and with a happy facetiousness, he suggested that he had better wash *seven* times—for Elisha had been to Damascus, and knew it was not a clean place by any means. But, to wash in the

Jordan! That was what stuck in Naaman's craw. It was then that he said: "Are not Abana and Pharpar, rivers of Damascus, better than all the waters of Israel? may I not wash in them and be clean?" And he told his eunuch to drive on. He was very wroth.

However, his servants got around him and persuaded him, and he did finally travel a good deal out of his way and dip seven times in the Jordan. He was surprised to find himself entirely cured. He was a just man and a gentleman, and he drove back at once to acknowledge the service that had been done him, and to atone for his former ungracious conduct as well as he could. But a greater surprise was in store for him: he offered the prophet bucksheesh, and it was refused. (It hardly seems possible that this could have occurred in Syria. Why, in Syria, if a person even looks at you he expects a piastre or two for bucksheesh, and if he smiles, he charges double.) Naaman offered his bucksheesh again, and again it was refused. Naaman was astonished. It came near giving him a relapse. Then he said he knew that Elisha's God must be the true God. After this he went his way.

But Gehazi, the prophet's servant (prophets paid not high wages in those days), said, "Behold, my master hath spared Naaman, this Syrian, in not receiving at his hands that which he brought; but as the Lord liveth I will run after him and take somewhat of him."

He would take "somewhat" of him. He was outraged at the prophet's loose way of doing business. So he ran after Naaman, and put up an absurd story about two young men of the sons of the prophets having just arrived on a bit of a tear from Mount Ephraim, and said, "Give them, I pray thee, a talent of silver and two changes of linen." Naaman gave him double as much as he asked, and Gehazi returned back home, following the two servants of Naaman that carried the silver—for there were two men's loads of it. And when he came to the tower, he bestowed the treasure within and discharged the men. Then he chuckled to himself as one that had done a good thing and knoweth to go slow and keep shady about it; and he went and stood before Elisha his master, and said in his singular way of speaking, that he hadn't been "any whither." But Elisha capped that. He knew better. He knew everything. So, he pronounced a curse upon him which was as terrible as it was well deserved:

"The leprosy therefore of Naaman shall cleave unto thee and unto thy seed forever. And he went out from his presence a leper as white as snow!"

One cannot appreciate the horror of that curse until he looks upon leprosy in all its ghastliness, in Naaman's ancient dwelling there in Damascus. Bones all twisted out of shape, great knots protruding from face and body, joints decaying and dropping away—I pass.

This letter, numbered thirty by Twain, appeared in the *Daily Alta California* of December 15, 1867. It was used in Chapter XVII, Volume II. The quotation at the beginning and the next paragraph were moved down to a position below the four following paragraphs, and immediately following them (in their new position) Twain inserted Letter 36. The remainder of this letter (in drastically reduced form) then completed the chapter.

"Mahomet" became "Mohammed"; called at the office and got his money" became "made a certain renowned remark"; and "old regular one above" became "one above." The paragraph beginning "In a vast, level plain Damascus sits" was completely rewritten, although much of the phraseology was retained. "They do not amount to quite as much as the Carson and Humboldt" became "mere creeks"; "But perhaps you never heard the story. I will give it you" became "But some of my readers have forgotten who Naaman was, long ago"; "Major General Naaman was the Commander-in-Chief of the Syrian armies and wore the brass collar" became "Naaman was the commander of the Syrian armies"; "pet" became "favorite"; and "had much shekels, and lived in a two-story house and put on more style than any man in Damascus" became "lived in great state." The long passage beginning "A little captive Israelitish maid servant of Naaman's wife" and extending to the last short paragraph was deleted. At the end of the letter "I pass" became "horrible."

36. More of Damascus

Banias, September, 1867.

We reached the city gates that night we arrived, just at sundown—just in time to get in before the gates were closed for the night. They do say that you can get into any walled city of Syria, after night, for bucksheesh, except Damascus. But Damascus, with its four thousand years of respectability in the world, has many old fogy notions. There are no street lamps there, and the law compels all who go abroad at night to carry lanterns, just as was the case in old days, when heroes and heroines of the Arabian Nights walked the streets of Damascus, or flew away toward Bagdad on enchanted carpets.

It was fairly dark a few minutes after we got within the wall, and we went long distances through wonderfully crooked streets, eight to ten feet wide, and shut in on either side by the high mud walls of the gardens. At last we got to where lanterns could be seen flitting about here and there, and knew we were in the midst of the curious old city. In a little narrow street, crowded with our pack-mules and with a swarm of uncouth Arabs, we alighted, and through a kind of a hole in the wall entered the hotel. We stood in a great flagged court, with flowers and citron trees about us, and a huge tank in the centre that was receiving the waters of many pipes. We crossed the court and entered the rooms prepared to receive four of us. In a large marble-paved recess between the two rooms was a tank of clear, cool water, which was kept running over all the time by the streams that were pouring into it from half a dozen pipes. Nothing, in this scorching, desolate land could look so refreshing as this pure water flashing in the lamp-light; nothing could look so beautiful, nothing could sound so delicious as this mimic rain to ears long unaccustomed to sounds of such a nature. Our rooms were large, comfortably furnished, and even had their floors clothed with soft, cheerful-tinted carpets. It was a jolly thing to see a carpet again, for if there is anything drearier than the tomb-like, stone-paved parlors and bedrooms of Europe, I do not know what it is. They make one think of the grave all the time. A very broad, hard cushioned, gaily comparisoned [caparisoned] divan some twelve or fourteen feet long, extended across one side of each room, and opposite were single beds with spring mattrasses. There were great looking-glasses and marble-top tables. All this luxury was as grateful to systems and senses worn out with an exhausting day's travel, as it was unexpected—for one cannot tell what to expect in a Turkish city of even a quarter of a million inhabitants.

I do not know, but I think they used that tank between the rooms to draw drinking water from; that did not occur to me, however, until I had dipped my baking head far down into its cool depths. I thought of it then, and superb as the bath was, I was sorry I had taken it, and was about to go and explain to the landlord. A finely curled and scented poodle-dog frisked up and wiped [nipped] the calf of my leg just then, and before I had time to think, I had soused him to the bottom of the tank, and when I saw a servant coming with a pitcher I went off and left the pup trying to dig out and not succeeding very well. Satisfied revenge was all I needed to make me perfectly happy, and when I walked in to supper that first night in Damascus I was blissful. We lay on those broad divans a long time, after supper, smoking narghilies [narghilis] and long-stemmed chibouks, and talking about the infernal ride of the day, and I knew then what I had sometimes known before—

that it is worth while to get tired out, because one so enjoys resting afterward.

Damascus Street Car

In the morning we sent for donkeys. It is worthy of note that we had to *send* for these things. I said Damascus was an old fogy, and she is. Anywhere else we would have been assailed by a clamorous army of donkey-drivers, guides, peddlars and beggars—but in Damascus they so hate the very sight of a foreign Christian that they want no intercourse whatever with him; only a year or two ago, his person was not always safe in Damascus streets. It is the most fanatical Mahometan hole out of perdition. Where you see one green turban of a Hadji elsewhere, (the honored sign that my lord has made the pilgrimage to Mecca,) I think you will see a dozen in Damascus. The Damascenes are the ugliest, wickedest looking villains I have seen. All the veiled women we had seen yet, nearly, left their eyes exposed, but numbers of these in Damascus completely hid the face, and under a close-drawn black veil that made the woman look like a mummy. If ever we caught an eye exposed it was quickly hidden from our contaminating Christian vision; the beggars actually passed us by without demanding bucksheesh; the merchants in the bazaars did not hold up their goods and cry out eagerly, "Hey, John!" or "Look this, Howajii!" On the contrary, they only scowled at us and said never a word.

The narrow streets swarmed like a hive with men and women in strange Oriental costumes, and our small donkeys knocked them right and left as we ploughed through them, urged on by the merciless donkey-boys. These persecutors ran after the animals shouting and goading them for hours together; they keep the donkey in a gallop always, yet never get tired themselves or fall behind. The donkeys fell down and spilt us over their heads occasionally, but there was nothing for it but to mount and hurry on again. We got banged against sharp corners, loaded porters, camels, and citizens generally; and we were so taken up with looking out for collisions and casualties that we had no chance to look about us at all. We rode half through the city and through the famous "street which is called Straight" without seeing anything, hardly. Our bones were nearly knocked out of joint, we were wild with excitement, and our sides ached with the jolting we had got. I do not like riding in the Damascus street cars.

The Story of Paul

We were on our way to the reputed houses of Judas and Ananias. About eighteen or nineteen hundred years ago, one Saul, a native of Tarsus, was particularly bitter against the new sect called Christians, and he took out letters of marque at Jerusalem and started across the country on a furious privateering crusade against them. He went forth "breathing threatenings and slaughter against the disciples of the Lord."

"And as he journeyed, he came near Damascus, and suddenly there shined round about him a light from heaven:

"And he fell to the earth and heard a voice saying unto him, 'Saul, Saul, why persecutest thou me?' "

And when he knew that it was Jesus that spoke to him he trembled, and was astonished, and said "Lord, what wilt thou have me to do?"

He was told to arise and go into the ancient city and one would tell him what to do. In the meantime his soldiers stood speechless and awe-stricken, for they heard the mysterious voice but saw no man. Saul rose up and found that that fierce supernatural light had destroyed his sight, and he was blind, so "they led him by the hand and brought him to Damascus." He was converted. Alas! there are others that will never be convinced by any milder argument than to be struck by lightning.

Paul [Saul] lay three days, blind, in the house of Judas, and during that time he neither ate nor drank.

There came a voice to a citizen of Damascus, named Ananias (not the justly celebrated liar,) saying, "Arise, and go into the street which is called Straight, and inquire at the house of Judas for one called Saul, of Tarsus; for behold, he prayeth."

Ananias did not want to go at first, for he had heard of the enterprising Saul before, and he had his doubts about that style of a "chosen vessel" to preach the gospel of peace. However, in obedience to orders, he went into the "street called Straight" (how he ever found his way into it, and after he did, how he ever found his way out of it again, are mysteries only to be accounted for by the fact that he was acting under Divine inspiration). He found Paul and restored him, and ordained him a preacher; and from this old house that we had hunted up in the street which is miscalled Straight, he had started out on that bold missionary career which he prosecuted till his death. It was not the house of the shaky disciple who sold the Master for thirty pieces of silver. I make this explanation in justice to the gentleman, who was a far different style of man from the party just referred to. A very different style of man, and lived in a very good house. It is a pity we do not know more about him.

The Straight Street

The street called Straight is straighter than a corkscrew, but not as straight as a rainbow. St. Luke is careful not to commit himself; he does not say it is the street which is straight, but "the street which is *called* Straight." It is a fine piece of irony; it is the only facetious remark in the Bible, I believe. St. Luke probably considered it the best thing he ever said. We traversed the street called Straight a good way, and then turned off and called on Ananias; he was out; he has been out about eighteen centuries. But there is no question that a part of his house is there still; it is an old room 12 or 15 feet under ground, and its masonry is evidently ancient. If Ananias did not live there in St. Paul's time, somebody else did, which is just as well. I took a drink out of Ananias' old well, and singularly enough, the water was just as fresh as if the well had been dug yesterday. I was deeply moved. I mentioned it to the old Doctor, who is the religious enthusiast of our party, and he lifted up his eyes and his hands and said: "Oh, how wonderful is prophecy!" There isn't any prophecy about that rusty old well, but that is just his gait; when he don't know anything else to say, he always comes out with that: "Oh, how wonderful is prophecy!" I start a bogus astonisher for him every now and then, just to hear him yelp.

The Rest of the Sights

We went out toward the north end of the city to see the place where the Disciples let Paul down over the Damascus wall at the dead of night—for he got to preaching Christ so fearlessly in Damascus that the people sought to kill him, just as they would to-day for the same offence, and he had to escape and flee to Jerusalem.

Then we called at the tombs of Mahomet's children and at a tomb which purported to be that of St. George who killed the dragon, and so on out to the hollow place under a rock where Paul hid during his flight till his pursuers gave him up; and to the mausoleum of the five thousand Christians who were massacred in Damascus in 1861 by the Turks. They say those narrow streets ran blood for several days, and men, women and children were butchered indiscriminately and left to rot by hundreds all through the Christian quarter; the stench was dreadful. All the Christians who could get away fled from the city, and the Mahometans would not defile their hands by burying the "infidel dogs." The thirst for blood extended to the high lands of Hermon and Anti-Lebanon, and in a short time 25,000 more Christians were massacred and their possessions laid waste. How they hate a Christian in Damascus!—and pretty much all over Turkeydom as well! And how they will sweat for it when Russia gets after them again!

It is so[o]thing to the human heart to curse England and France for interposing to save the Ottoman Empire from the destruction it has so richly deserved for a thousand years. I want to live to see the Sultan dethroned, and his subjects scattered to the four winds of heaven. It makes me savage to see these vermin-persecuted pagans refuse to eat of food that has been cooked for us; or to eat from a dish that we have eaten from; or to drink from a goatskin which we have polluted with our Christian lips, except by filtering the water through a rag which they put over the mouth of it or through a sponge! I never hated a Chinaman as I hate these degraded Turks and Arabs, and when Russia gets ready to exterminate them a little I hope England and France will not find it good breeding or good judgment to interfere in the business.

This letter, numbered thirty-one by Twain, appeared in the *Daily Alta California* of December 22, 1867. As stated above, the letter was used in Chapter XVII, between two parts of Letter 35. "We went" became "we rode"; "Europe" became "Europe and Asia"; "dig out" became "climb out"; "blissful" became "in that condition"; "infernal ride became "dreadful ride"; "old fogy" became "old fossil"; "Mahometan hole out of perdition" became "Mohammedan purgatory out of Arabia"; "we had got" became "we had suffered"; "took out letters of marque at" became "left"; and "privateering crusade" became "crusade."

The sentence beginning "Alas! there are others" was deleted. "Ananias (not the justly celebrated liar)" became "Ananias"; "enterprising Saul" became "Saul"; "shaky disciple" became "disciple"; and "the gentleman, who was a far different style of man from the party" became "Judas, who was a far different sort of man from the person." After "it is a pity we do not know more about him," Twain inserted a paragraph of forty-seven words. "St. Luke probably considered it the best thing he ever said" was deleted.

"Called on Ananias; he was out; he has been out about eighteen centuries. But there is no question" became "called at the reputed house of Ananias. There is small question." The passage beginning "I was deeply moved" and extending to the end of the paragraph was deleted. "Got to preaching" became "preached"; "sweat for it when Russia gets after them again" became "pay for it when Russia turns her guns upon them again"; and "curse" became "abuse." The sentence beginning "I want to live to see the Sultan" was deleted. "It makes me savage to see these vermin-persecuted pagans" became "It hurts my vanity to see these pagans"; "I never hated a Chinaman as I hate" became "I never disliked a Chinaman as I do"; and "gets ready to exterminate them a little" became "is ready to war with them again." "In the business" was deleted.

37. South to Banias

Banias, September, 1867.

The last twenty-four hours we staid in Damascus I lay prostrate with a violent attack of cholera, or cholera morbus, and therefore I had a good chance and a good excuse to lay there on that wide divan and take an honest rest. I had nothing to do but listen to the pattering of the fountains and take medicine and throw it up again. It was dangerous recreation, but it was pleasanter than traveling in Syria. I had plenty of snow from Mount Hermon, and as it would not stay on my stomach, there was nothing to interfere with my eating it—there was always room for more. I enjoyed myself very well. Syrian travel has its interesting features, like travel in any other part of the world, and yet to break your leg or have the cholera adds a welcome variety to it.

We left Damascus at noon and rode across the Plain a couple of hours and then stopped a while in the shade of some fig trees to give me a chance to rest. It was the hottest day we had seen yet—the sun flowed down like the shafts of fire that stream out before a blow-pipe; the rays seemed to fall in a steady deluge on the head and pass downward like rain from a roof. I imagined I could distinguish between the floods of rays—I thought I could tell when each lot struck my head, when it reached my shoulders, and when the next lot came. It was terrible. All the desert glared so fiercely that my eyes were swimming in tears all the time. All the boys had white umbrellas heavily lined with dark green. They were a priceless blessing. I thanked God that I had one, too, notwithstanding it was packed up with the baggage and was ten miles ahead. It is madless [madness] to travel in Syria without an umbrella. They told me in Beirout (these people who always fill you up to the chin with advice) that it was madness to travel in Syria without an umbrella. It was on this account that I got one.

They told me to take the best care of it, so as to make it last the journey through. They said this was very important. Therefore the idea of losing the umbrella became such a bugbear to me, and distressed me so much that I thought it best to take it to the head mulateer and get him to send it ahead with the baggage. He did so, and I have been happy ever since. Every night, the first thing after the tents are pitched, he brings that precious umbrella for me to inspect, and then takes it back, greatly satisfied with himself when nothing is found wrong with it.

But, honestly, I think an umbrella is a nuisance anywhere when its business is to keep the sun off. No Arab wears a brim to his fez, or uses an umbrella, or anything to shade his eyes or his face, and he always looks comfortable and proper in the sun. But of all the ridiculous sights I ever have seen, our party of eight is the most so—they cut the most outlandish figure you can imagine. They travel single file; they all wear the endless white rag of Constantinople wrapped round and round their hats and dangling down their backs; they all wear thick green spectacles, with side-glasses to them; they all hold white umbrellas, lined with green, over their heads; without exception their stirrups are too short—they are the very worst gang of horsemen on earth; their animals to a horse trot fearfully hard—and lo! when these pilgrims get strung out one after the other; glaring straight ahead and breathless; bouncing high and out of turn, all along the line, and coming down one after the other like the stamps of a quartz mill; knees well up and stiff, elbows flapping like a rooster's that is going to crow, and the long file of umbrellas popping convulsively up and down—when one sees this outrageous picture exposed to the light of day, he is astounded that the gods don't get out their thunderbolts and just haze these pilgrims from Julesburg to Jericho! I do—I wonder at it. I wouldn't let any such caravan go through a country of mine.

And when the sun drops below the horizon and the boys close their umbrellas and put them under their arms, it is only a variation of the picture, not a modification of its absurdity.

But may be you can't see the wild extravagance of my panorama. You could if you were here. Here, you feel all the time just as if you were living about the year 1200 before Christ—or back to the patriarchs—or forward to the New Era. The scenery of the Bible is about you—the customs of the patriarchs are around you—the same people, in the same flowing robes, and in sandals, cross your path—the same long trains of stately camels go and come—the same old religious solemnity and silence are upon the desert and the mountains that were upon them in the old days of antiquity, and behold, intruding upon a scene like this, comes this fantastic gang of green-spectacled Yanks, with their flapping elbows and bobbing umbrellas! It is just Daniel in the lion's den with a green cotton umbrella under his arm, all over again. I wish I had a magazine under these fellows, with four or five hundred thousand barrels of powder in it.

I see that I have been digressing somewhat. However, I have had my say, and that is something, anyhow. My umbrella is with the baggage, and so are my green spectacles. They have always been there, and there they shall stay. I will not use them. I will show some respect for the eternal fitness of things. It will be rough enough to get sunstruck, without looking ridiculous into the bargain. If I fall, let me fall bearing about me the semblance of a Christian, at least.

The Old Castle

Three or four hours out from Damascus we passed the spot where they say Saul was so abruptly converted, and from this place we looked back over the scorching desert, and had our last glimpse of beautiful Damascus, decked in its robes of imperial green. After nightfall we reached our tents, just outside of the nasty Arab village of Jonesborough. Of course the real name of the place is El something or other, but I can't spell these infamous Arabic names, or pronounce them either—and so I shall just have to substitute decent Christian names for them, and I hope a charitable people will sympathize with my sorrows and pardon my conduct in this matter.

We left Jonesborough very early in the morning, and rode forever and forever and forever, it seemed to me, over parched deserts and rocky hills, hungry and with no water to drink. We had drained the goatskins dry in a little while. At noon we halted before the wretched Arab town of El Yuba Dam, perched on the side of a mountain, but the dragoman said if we applied there for water we would be attacked by the whole tribe, for they did not love Christians. We had to journey on. Two hours later we reached the foot of a tall isolated mountain, which is crowned by the crumbling castle of Banias, the stateliest ruin of that kind on earth, no doubt. It is a thousand feet long and two hundred wide, all of the most symmetrical, and at the same time the most ponderous masonry. The massive towers and bastions are more than thirty feet high, and have been sixty. From the mountain's peak its broken turrets rise above the groves of ancient oaks and olives, and look wonderfully picturesque. It is of such high antiquity that no man knows who built it or when it was built. It is utterly inaccessible, except in one place, where a bridle-path winds upward among the solid rocks to the old portcullis. The horses' hoofs have bored holes in these rocks to the depth of six inches during the hundreds and hundreds of years that the castle was garrisoned. We wandered for three hours among the chambers and crypts and dungeons of the fortress, and trod where the mailed heels of many a knightly Crusader had rang, and where Phœnician heroes had walked ages before them.

I wondered how such a solid mass of masonry could be affected even by an earthquake, and could not understand what agency had made Banias a ruin; but I found the destroyer, after a while, and then my wonder was increased ten fold. Seeds had fallen in crevices in the vast walls; the seeds had sprouted; the tender, insignificant sprouts had hardened; they grew larger and larger, and by a steady, imperceptible pressure forced the great stones apart, and now are bringing sure destruction upon a giant work that even has mocked the earthquakes to scorn! Gnarled and twisted trees spring from the old walls everywhere, and beautify and overshadow the gray battlements with a wild luxuriance of greenest foliage.

From these old towers we looked down upon a broad, level, far-reaching green valley (pleasant to look upon after the deserts,) glittering with the pools and rivulets which are the sources of the sacred river Jordan.

And as the evening drew near we clambered down the mountain, through groves of the Biblical oaks of Bashan, (for we were just stepping over the border and entering the long-sought Holy Land,) and at its extreme foot, toward the wide valley, we entered this little execrable village of Banias and camped in a great grove of olive trees near a torrent of sparkling water whose banks are splendidly arrayed in fig trees, pomegranates and oleanders in full leaf. Barring the proximity of the village, it is a sort of paradise.

The very first thing one feels like doing when he gets into camp, all burning up and dusty, is to scare up a bath. We followed the stream up to where it gushes out of the mountain side, 300 yards from the tents, and took a bath that was so icy that if I did not know this was a main source of the sacred river, I would expect harm to come of it. It was bathing at noonday in the chilly source of the Abana, "River of Damascus," that gave me the cholera, so Dr. Birch said. However, it generally does give me the cholera to take a bath.

The village of Banias stands among the ruins of the Biblical city of Cesarea Phillippi, and—

I cannot write any more. The boys have come in with a lot of specimens broken from the ruins. I wish I could stop this Vandalism. They broke off chunks from Noah's tomb; from the exquisite sculptures of the temples of Baalbec; from the houses of Judas and Ananias, in Damascus; from the tomb of Nimrod the Mighty Sport, in Jonesborough; from the worn Greek and Roman inscriptions set in the hoary walls of the Castle of Banias; and now they have been hacking and chipping these old arches here that Jesus looked upon in the flesh. God protect the Holy Sepulchre when this tribe invades Jerusalem!

This letter, numbered thirty-two by Twain, appeared in the *Daily Alta California* of December 29, 1867. The letter was used in two parts in Chapter XVIII. The chapter begins with the first part of the letter. "To lay" became "to lie"; "sun flowed" became "sun-flames shot"; "each lot" became "each flood"; and "fill you up to the chin" became "gorge you." The passage beginning "They told me to take the best care of it" and extending to the end of the paragraph was deleted. "Cut the most outlandish figure you can imagine" became "do cut such an outlandish figure." "And coming down one after the other like the stamps of a quartz mill" was deleted. "Astounded" became "amazed"; "just haze these pilgrims from Julesburg to Jericho" became "destroy them off the face of the earth"; "are upon the desert" became "rest upon the desert"; "old days of antiquity" became "remote ages of antiquity"; and "gang" became "mob."

The thirty-nine words beginning "I wish I had a magazine under these fellows" and ending "that is something, anyhow" were deleted. "They have always been there" was also deleted. "Rough enough" became "bad enough"; "the spot where they say Saul was so abruptly converted" became "the spot where Saul was so abruptly converted"; and "imperial green" became "shining green." The passage beginning "I can't spell these infamous Arabic names" and extending to the end of the paragraph became "the boys still refuse to recognize the Arab names or try to pronounce them."

At this point Twain inserted the description of the typical Syrian village and the story of Nimrod from Letter 34. He then continued with this letter ("We left Jonesborough," etc.). "Even has mocked" became "has even mocked"; "greenest foliage" became "foliage"; and "green valley" became "green plain." He rewrote the phrase "pleasant to look upon after the deserts" as a sentence: "It was a grateful vision, after so much desert." "Splendidly arrayed" became "arrayed"; "scare up a bath" became "hunt up a bath"; and "Dr. Birch" became "Dr. B——." "The village of Banias stands among the ruins" and the next thirteen words were deleted. "The boys" became "the incorrigible pilgrims"; "a lot of" became "their pockets full of"; "I wish I could stop this Vandalism" became "I wish this vandalism could be stopped"; "chunks" became "fragments"; "Mighty Sport" became "Mighty Hunter"; and "God protect the Holy Sepulchre" became "heaven protect the Sepulcher."

38. First Day in Palestine

Baldwinsville, Galilee, September, 1867.

THE REAL NAME of this place is Cesarea Phillippi, but I call it Baldwinsville because it sounds better and I can recollect it easier. One of the great drawbacks to this country is its distressing names that nobody can get the hang of. You may travel here a month, and when you get through you cannot tell where you have been, to save your life, unless you are a living, breathing geography. You may make a stagger of pronouncing these names, but they will bring any Christian to grief that tries to spell them. I have an idea that if I can only simplify the nomenclature of this country, it will be of the greatest service to Americans who may travel here in the future. Galilee is well enough, I don't propose to change that, but I can't accept of Cesarea Phillippi—it uses up too much alphabet, and there is very little music in it any how. Baldwinsville is much better.

The ruins here are not very interesting. There are the massive walls of a great square building that was once the citadel; there are many ponderous old arches that are so smothered with debris that they barely project above the ground; there are heavy-walled sewers through which the beautiful brook of which Jordan is born still runs; in the hill-side are the substructions of a costly marble temple that Herod the Great built here—patches of its handsome mosaic floors still remain; there is a quaint old stone bridge that was here before Herod's time, may be; scattered everywhere, in the paths and in the woods, are Corinthian capitals, broken porphyry pillars, and little fragments of sculpture; and up yonder in the precipice where the fountain gushes out, are well-worn Greek inscriptions over niches in the rock where in ancient times the Greeks, and after them the Romans, worshiped the Sylvan God Pan. But trees and bushes grow above many of these ruins now; the miserable huts of a little gang of filthy Arabs are perched upon the broken masonry of antiquity, the whole place has a sleepy, stupid, rural look about it, and one can hardly bring himself to believe that a busy, substantially-built city once existed here, even two thousand years ago. The place was nevertheless the scene of an event whose effects have added page after page and volume after volume to the world's history. For in this place Christ stood when he said to Peter:

Thou art Peter; and upon this rock will I build my church, and the gates of hell shall not prevail against it. And I will give unto thee the keys of the Kingdom of Heaven; and whatsoever thou shalt bind on earth shall be bound in heaven, and whatsoever thou shalt loose on earth shall be loosed in heaven.

On those little sentences have been built up the mighty edifice of the Church of Rome; in them lie the authority for the imperial power of the Popes over temporal affairs, and their god-like power to curse a soul or wash it white from sin. To sustain the position of "the only true church," which Rome claims was thus conferred upon her, she has fought and labored and struggled for many a century, and will continue to keep herself busy in the same line to the end of time. The memorable words I have quoted give to this ruined city about all the interest it possesses to people of the present day.

It seems curious enough to us to be standing on ground that was once actually pressed by the feet of the Savior. The situation is suggestive of a reality and a tangibility that seem at variance with the vagueness, and mystery, and ghostliness that one naturally attaches to the character of a God. I cannot comprehend yet that I am sitting where a God has stood, and looking upon the brook and the mountains that that God looked upon, and am surrounded by dusky men and women whose ancestors saw him, and even talked with him, face to face, and carelessly just as they would have done with any other stranger. I cannot comprehend this; the gods of my understanding have been always hidden in clouds and very far away.

The People the Disciples Knew

This morning, during breakfast, the usual assemblage of squalid humanity sat patiently without the charmed circle of the camp and waited for such crumbs as pity might bestow upon their misery. There were old and young, brown-skinned and yellow. Some of the men were tall and stalwart (for one sees nowhere such splendid looking men as here in the East) but all the women and children looked worn and sad, and distressed with hunger. They reminded me much of Indians, did these people. They had but little clothing, but such as they had was fanciful in character and fantastic in its arrangement. Any little absurd gewgaw or jimcrack [gimcrack] they had they disposed in such a way as to make it attract attention most readily. They sat in silence, and with tireless patience watched our every motion with that vile, uncomplaining impoliteness which is so truly Indian, and which makes a white man so nervous, and uncomfortable and savage that he wants to exterminate the whole tribe.

These people about us had other peculiarities, which I have noticed in the noble red man, too; they carried passengers in their hair, they were infested with fleas, and the dirt had caked on them till it amounted to bark.

The little children were in a pitiable condition—they all had sore eyes, and were otherwise afflicted in various ways. They say that hardly a native child in all the East is free from sore eyes, and that thousands of them go blind of one eye or both every year. I think this must be so, for I see plenty of blind people every day, and I don't remember seeing any children that hadn't sore eyes. And, would you suppose that an American mother could sit for an hour, with her child in her arms, and let a thousand flies roost upon its eyes all that time undisturbed? I see that every day. It makes my flesh creep. Yesterday we met a woman riding on a little jackass, and she had a child in her arms; honestly, I thought the child had goggles on as we approached, and I wondered how its mother could afford so much style. But when we drew near, we saw that the goggles were nothing but a camp-meeting of flies assembled around each of the child's eyes, and at the same time there was a detachment prospecting its nose. The flies were happy, the child was contented, and so the mother did not interfere.

As soon as the tribe found out that we had a doctor in our crowd, they began to flock in from all quarters. Dr. B., in the charity of his nature, had taken a child from a woman that sat near by, and put some sort of a wash upon its diseased eyes. That woman went off and started the whole nation, and you ought to have seen them swarm! The lame, the halt, the blind, the leprous—all the distempers that are bred of dirt and iniquity, were represented in the Congress in ten minutes, and still they came! Every woman that had a sick baby brought it along, and every woman that hadn't, borrowed one. What reverent and what worshiping looks they bent upon that dread, mysterious Power, the Doctor! They watched him take his phials out; they watched him measure the particles of white powder; they watched him add drops of one precious liquid, and drops of another; they lost not the slightest movement; their eyes were riveted upon him with a fascination that nothing could distract. I believe they thought he was gifted like a god. When each individual got his portion of medicine, his eyes were radiant with joy—not withstanding by nature they are a thankless and impassive race—and upon his face was written the unquestioning faith that nothing on earth could prevent the patient from getting well now.

Christ knew how to preach to these simple, childish, ignorant, superstitious, disease-tortured vagabonds: *he healed the sick.* They flocked to our poor human doctor this morning when the fame of what he had done to the sick child went abroad in the land, and they worshiped him with their eyes while they did not know as yet whether there was virtue in his simples or not. The ancestors of these—people precisely like them in color, dress, manners, customs, ignorance, simplicity—flocked in vast multitudes after Christ, and when they saw him make the afflicted whole with a word, it is no wonder they worshiped him. No wonder his deeds were the talk of the nation; no wonder the multitudes that followed Him were so great that at one time—30 miles from here—they had to let a sick man down through the roof because no approach could be made to the door; no wonder His audiences were so great at Galilee that He had to preach from a ship removed a little distance from the shore; no wonder that even in the desert places about Bethsaida 5,000 invaded His solitude and He had to feed them by a miracle or else see them suffer for their confiding faith and devotion; no wonder when there was a great commotion in a city in those days, one neighbor explained it to another in words to this effect: "They say that Jesus of Nazareth is come!"

He healed the sick. If a man would have crowds to attend him all the day long, let him come to Palestine and do likewise.

Well, as I was saying, the doctor distributed medicine as long as he had any to distribute, and his reputation is mighty in Galilee this day. Among his patients was the child of the Shiek's daughter—for even this poor, ragged handful of sores and sin has its royal Shiek—a poor old devil that looked as if he would be more at home in a poor-house than in the Chief Magistracy of this tribe of hopeless, shirtless savages. The princess—I mean the Shiek's daughter—was only 13 or 14 years old, and had a very sweet face and a pretty one. She was the only Syrian female we have seen yet who was not so sinfully ugly that she couldn't smile after 10 o'clock Saturday night without breaking the Sabbath. Her child was a hard lot, though—there wasn't enough of it to make a pie, and the poor little thing looked so pleadingly up at all who came near it (as if it had an idea that now was its chance or never), that we were filled with compassion which was genuine and not put on.

This letter, which appeared in the *New York Tribune* of November 9, 1867, was used in Chapter XVIII, Volume II, immediately following the last part of Letter 37. The first paragraph was deleted. "Beautiful brook" became "crystal brook"; "gang of filthy Arabs" became "crew of filthy Arabs"; "in the same line" became "in the same work"; "that that" became "which that"; "one sees nowhere" became "one hardly sees anywhere"; "they carried passengers in their hair, they were infested with fleas" became "they were infested with vermin"; "thousand flies" became "hundred flies"; "our crowd" became "our party"; "you ought to have seen" became "it was a sight to see"; "bred of dirt and iniquity" became "bred of indolence, dirt, and iniquity"; and "simple, childish, ignorant, superstitious, disease-tortured vagabonds" became "simple, superstitious, disease-tortured creatures." Twain deleted "He healed the sick. If a man would have crowds to attend him all the day long, let him come to Palestine and do likewise." "Devil" became "mummy," and "hard lot" became "hard specimen."

39. Ancient History of Dutch Flat

Williamsburgh, Canaan,
(Ain-Mellahah,) September, 1867.

About an hour's ride over a rough, rocky road, half flooded with water (which is a singular thing in the arid land of Syria,) and through a forest of oaks of Bashan (this little district was once the kingdom famous in Scripture for its oaks and its bulls,) brought us to Dutch Flat. Dutch Flat is more popularly known as Dan, and the expression "from Dan to Beersheba" makes it familiar to all peoples under the sun. To my mind, "from Dutch Flat to Beersheba" sounds infinitely better. Dan was the northern and Beersheba the southern limit of Palestine—hence the expression.

From a little mound here in the plain issues a broad stream of limpid water and forms a large shallow pool, and then rushes furiously away toward Lake Huleh and the Sea of Galilee. This fountain (every puddle in Syria is a "fountain") is an important source of the Jordan. The banks of the pond and the brook are respectably adorned with blooming oleanders, but the unutterable beauty of the spot will not throw a well-balanced man into convulsions, as the customary style of Syriac books of travel would lead one to suppose.

The small mound I have mentioned was once occupied by the Phœnician city of Laish. A party of filibusters from Zorah and Eshtool [Eshcol] captured the place, and lived there in a free and easy way, worshipping gods of their own manufacture and stealing idols from their neighbors whenever they wore their own out. Jeraboam [Jeroboam] set up a golden calf here to fascinate his people and keep them from making dangerous trips to Jerusalem to worship, which might result in a return to their rightful allegiance. With all respect for those ancient Israelites, I cannot overlook the fact that they were seldom virtuous enough to withstand the seductions of a golden calf. However, perhaps it was pleasantly suggestive of free lunch.

Some forty centuries ago the city of Sodom was pillaged by the Arab princes of Mesopotamia, and among other plunder they seized upon the patriarch Lot and brought him here on their way to their own possessions. You will remember Lot as the party whose wife was turned into a pillar of salt and left standing in this condition in the most public place in Palestine. We sympathize with the woman, because she could not but look unpleasantly conspicuous; and we feel deeply for Lot, because the circumstance could not be otherwise than irritating to him. It would irritate anybody.

The Arab Princes brought Lot to this spot which the Bible calls Dan, and father Abraham, who was pursuing them, crept softly in at dead of night, among the whispering oleanders and under the shadows of the stately oaks, and fell upon the slumbering victors and startled them from their dreams with the clash of steel. He recaptured Lot and all the other plunder.

Character of the Ranch

We moved on. We were now in a green valley, five or six miles wide and fifteen long. The streams which are called the sources of the Jordan flow through it from Lake Huleh, at its southern end, (called the "Waters of Merom" in the Old Testament,) a sheet of water about three or four miles in diameter. The Lake is surrounded by a broad marsh, grown with reeds. Between the marsh and the mountains that wall the Valley is a respectable strip of fertile land; at the end of the Valley, toward Dan, as much as half the land is solid and fertile, and watered by Jordan's sources. There is actually enough of it to make a farm. It almost warrants the unbiblical enthusiasm of the spies of that rabble of filibusters who captured Dan. They said: "We have seen the land, and behold it is very good. . . . A place where there is no want of anything that is in the earth."

Well, I suppose they were pardonable. They hadn't seen any country but Palestine, and surely this was very good for Palestine. They thought that little patch was plenty for their six hundred men and their families. They do say that in the good old Bible times Palestine had a population of six million souls—Palestine, the promised land, a small strip of rocks and deserts and mountains, not equal in [area] to the State of Massachusetts, (which one cannot always see on the map of the United States without shutting one eye, Mrs. A. J. M.)—Palestine, where every hundred acres of arable land is protected by three mountains on each side and a desert at each end to keep it from bolting for want of company. I suppose Dutch Flat struck the filibustering spies as something extraordinary in the way of wide-extended fertility. At the same time, though, they drew it just a little strong when they said it was "a place where there is no want of anything that is in the earth." That was a *little* strong. A good deal of the north end of the farm had the boulders of original creation bedded in the soil as thick as nail-heads in a hair trunk, and they are there yet. Other portions of the farm lacked many things that are in the earth, and likewise lacked the capacity to produce those things. Still, it was a good piece of country for Palestine.

Signs That Fail Not in Dry Times

When we got fairly down on the level part of the Danite farm, we came to places where we could actually run our horses. It was a notable circumstance. Wherever imperial Rome carried her banners, she left the sign and symbol of her greatness and her intelligence in roads and bridges that endure to this day. In Italy, in England, in France, in Spain, in Africa—everywhere that one wanders, he finds these footprints of the fallen Colossus. Roads are the highways of the arts, and sciences, and commerce. One can tell what a nation is if he can only see its roads. Glance at the thing for a moment. France has such magnificent roads!—miserable Spain has none; England has roads—Portugal has not; the Northern States of America are webbed with roads—the South is not. The Caesars were great. They built roads. Napoleon the First was great. He inaugurated the road system of France, and men point to some of his roads to-day as wonderful works. Napoleon the Third is great. He is opening up France from centre to circumference with countless leagues of macadamized roads that are as smooth and hard and clean as the floor of a drawing-room. Alexander II is the most genuinely great man that has ever occupied the throne of Russia. He has inaugurated a system that will completely thread his vast empire with iron rails in a very few years. But if ever the nations of Palestine were great, the proof must be sought elsewhere than in the roads they have left behind them. They never even made a trail. Their goats made paths, and they followed them. The goats made the paths four thousand years ago; and to this day the caravans follow those same old trails. Israel was not great in architecture, either. She has left no monument of that kind. She was great in sanguinary warfare—in the extermination of tribes, even to the destroying of every woman and every child. She was also great in her worship of the true God so long as He showered blessings upon her and held her to her allegiance with a rigid hand; but when He left her to herself a moment, she was great in her propensity to fly back to her golden calves.

We had been painfully clambering over interminable rocks for days together, and when we suddenly came upon this astonishing piece of rockless, level ground, every man drove the spurs into his horse and sped away with a velocity that he could surely enjoy to the utmost, but could never hope to comprehend in Palestine.

Glimpses of the Hoary Past

Here were evidences of cultivation—a rare sight in this country—an acre or two of rich soil studded with last season's dead corn-stalks of the thickness of your thumb and very wide apart. But in such a land as this it was a thrilling spectacle. Close to it was a stream, and on its banks a great herd of curious looking Syrian goats and sheep were gratefully eating gravel. I do not state this as a petrified fact—I only *suppose* they were eating gravel, because there did not appear to be anything else for them to eat. The shepherds that tended them were the very pictures of Joseph and his brethren I have no doubt in the world. They were tall, muscular, and very dark-skinned Bedouins, with inky black beards. They had firm lips, unquailing eyes, and a kingly stateliness of bearing. They wore the parti-colored half-bonnet, half hood, with fringed ends falling upon their shoulders, and the full, flowing robe barred with broad black stripes—the dress one sees in all pictures of the swarthy sons of the desert. They say these people are not the descendants of Israel, but I guess they are. These chaps would sell their younger brothers if they had a chance, I think. They have the manners, the customs, the dress, the occupation and the loose principles of the ancient stock. (They attacked our camp last night, and I bear them no good-will.) They had with them the pigmy jackasses one sees all over Syria and remembers in all pictures of the "Flight into Egypt," where Mary and the Young Child are riding and Joseph is walking alongside, towering high above the little donkey's shoulders. (That picture is marked by a gross blunder: Joseph ought to be riding and carrying the Child, and Mary ought to be walking. Whoever heard of a Syrian walking while his wife or his mother or his sister rode?—and behold, these people are exceedingly like the people who have always lived here since Abraham's days. The blunder in the picture is entirely pardonable, but it is a blunder, nevertheless.) When I see these hooded, full-robed, bearded, swarthy Arabs riding on a mighty-eared jackass the size of a young calf, and swinging their prodigious feet contentedly to and fro within four inches of the ground, and pouring forth that maddening caterwauling which they call music, my heart goes back to the old days of the patriarchs and I behold the pride of Canaan and the hope of the world—Israel the blest!

We could not stop to rest two or three hours out from our camp, of course, albeit the brook was beside us. So we went on an hour longer. We saw water, then, but nowhere in all the waste around was there a foot of shade, and we were scorching to death. "Like unto the shadow of a great rock in a weary land." Nothing in the Bible is more beautiful than that, and surely there is no place we have wandered to that is able to give it such touching expression as this blistering, naked, treeless land.

Here you don't stop just when you please, but when you can. We found water, but no shade. We travelled on and found a tree at last, but no water. We rested and lunched, and came on to this place, Ain Mellahah (Williamsburgh.) It was a very short day's run, but the dragoman don't want to go further, and has gotten up a plausible lie about the country beyond this being infested by ferocious Arabs, who would make sleeping in their midst a dangerous pastime. Well, they ought to be dangerous. They carry a rusty old weather-beaten flintlock gun, with a barrel that is longer than themselves; it has no sights on it; it will not carry farther than a brick-bat, and is not half so certain. And the great sash they wear in many a fold around their waists has two or three absurd old horse-pistols in it that are rusty from eternal disuse—weapons that would hang fire just about long enough for you to walk out of range, and then burst and blow the Arab's head off. Exceedingly dangerous these sons of the Desert are.

And yet, how they do remind one of the former glory of Israel! They live in tents of the rudest possible pattern, made of matting in localities where the materials are plenty, and of coarse black cloth elsewhere. They are so like the cheerful children of Benjamin, and Judah, and Exodus, and all those old parties of the elder days. These latter borrowed all the jewelry their loving and trusting bosom friends had, the night before they *vamosed* the Egyptian ranch, and it is not stated that they ever sent any of it back again—forgot it, likely—and these sweet-scented sons of the desert around us would waltz through this camp, if we kept no watch, and leave us neither food or raiment or horses, or a sign of the wherewithal to purchase more and save our bodies from perishing. How pleasant it is to read the stirring narratives of the old Scriptures, and revel in these scenes of the ancient patriarchal times!

This letter, numbered thirty-three by Twain, appeared in the *Daily Alta California* of January 5, 1868. It was used at the beginning of Chapter XIX. Twain deleted "which is a singular thing in the arid land of Syria"; "this little district was once the kingdom famous in Scripture for its oaks and its bulls"; and the last three sentences of the first paragraph. "Dutch Flat" became "Dan."

"Away toward Lake Huleh and the Sea of Galilee" became "onward, augmented in volume"; "this fountain (every puddle in Syria is a 'fountain')" became "this puddle"; "the banks of the pond and the brook" became "its banks, and those of the brook"; and "customary style of Syriac" became "Syrian." After "books of travel would lead one to suppose," Twain inserted a paragraph. The new paragraph contains statements about Lake Huleh and the Sea of Galilee and the phraseology "was once the kingdom so famous in Scripture for its bulls and its oaks" and "Dan was the northern and Beersheba the southern limit of Palestine—hence the expression 'from Dan to Beersheba' "—all of which had been deleted from the first two paragraphs of the letter.

"Seldom" became "not always." "However, perhaps it was pleasantly suggestive of free lunch" was deleted and "Human nature has not changed much since then" was substituted for it. "Plunder" became "prisoners." The passage beginning "you will remember Lot" and extending to the end of the paragraph was deleted. "The Arab Princes brought Lot to this spot which the Bible calls Dan" became "They brought him to Dan." "From Lake Huleh, at its southern end, (called the 'Waters of Merom' in the Old Testament,) a sheet of water about three or four miles in diameter" became "to Lake Huleh, a shallow pond three miles in diameter, and from the southern extremity of the lake the concentrated Jordan flows out." ("Lake Huleh is the Biblical 'Waters of Merom'" appears in the paragraph which Twain inserted.) "Actually enough" became "enough." "Unbiblical" was deleted. "Filibusters" became "adventurers."

"Well, I suppose they were pardonable. They hadn't seen any country but Palestine, and surely this was very good for Palestine. They thought that little patch was plenty for their six hundred men and their families" became "Their enthusiasm was at least warranted by the fact that they had never seen a country as good as this. There was enough of it for the ample support of their six hundred men and their families, too."

The passage beginning "They do say that in the good old Bible times" and extending to the end of the paragraph (over two hundred words) and the passage beginning "Wherever imperial Rome" and extending to the end of the paragraph (about three hundred and fifty words) were deleted. "Rockless, level ground" became "rockless plain"; "Palestine" became "Syria"; and "such a land as this" became "such a land." "They say these people are not the descendants of Israel, but I guess they are" was deleted. The passage of a hundred and forty-two words beginning "That picture is marked by a gross blunder" and extending to the end of the paragraph was rewritten in a paragraph of sixty-eight words. "Williamsburgh" became "the boys call it Baldwinsville"; "dragoman don't" became "dragoman does not"; and "gotten up" became "invented." The last paragraph of the letter was deleted.

40. The Fall and Rise of Joseph

Williamsburgh, Palestine,
(Ain Mellahah,) September, 1867.

All this valley of the Waters of Merom is historical. The localities about it are familiar to readers of the Old Testament and the New. A Minie rifle-shot from our camp is the lake that is called the Waters of Merom. Above its north end is Dan; from its south end flows the Jordan, some fifteen or eighteen miles, and empties into the sea of Galilee. The borders of that little sea were the home of Christ for three years; there he performed most of his miracles, and not a rod of ground exists about it but was pressed by his feet.

About fifteen hundred years before Christ, this camp ground of ours by the Waters of Merom was the scene of one of Joshua's exterminating battles. Jabin, King of Hazor (up yonder above Dan), called all the shieks about him together, with their hosts, to make ready for Israel's terrible General who was approaching.

"And when all these Kings were met together, they came and pitched together by the Waters of Merom, to fight against Israel.

"And they went out, they and all their hosts with them, much people, even as the sand that is upon the sea shore for multitude," etc. (There were probably about ten thousand—there is hardly country enough in all the land around here to support more, with their families, but still "much people" is a good figure.)

But Joshua fell upon them and utterly destroyed them, root and branch. That was his usual policy in war. He never left any chance for newspaper controversies about who won the battle. He made this valley, so quiet now, a reeking slaughter-pen.

Somewhere in this part of the country—I do not know exactly where —Israel fought another bloody battle a hundred years later. Deborah, the prophetess, told General Barak to take ten thousand men and sally forth against another King Jabin who had been doing something, I suppose. Barak came down from Mount Tabor, twenty or twenty-five miles from here, and gave battle to Jabin's forces, who were in command of one Sisera, who could not have been more than a Brigadier General—I never heard of him before. Barak won the fight, and while he was making the victory complete by the usual method of exterminating the remnant of the defeated host, Sisera fled away on foot, and when he was nearly exhausted by fatigue and thirst, one Jael, a woman he seems to have been acquainted with, invited him to come into her tent and rest himself. The weary soldier acceded readily enough, and Jael put him to bed. He said he was very thirsty, and asked his generous preserver to get him a cup of water. So she went out. Presently when he was asleep she came softly in with a hammer and drove a hideous tent-pin down through his brain. It was very funny. The gentle children of Israel, the race beloved, were full of amusing eccentricities.

Stirring scenes like these occur in this valley no more. There is not a solitary village throughout its whole extent—not for thirty miles in either direction. There are two or three small clusters of Bedouin tents, but not a single permanent habitation. One may ride ten miles, hereabouts, and not see ten human beings.

To this region one of the prophecies is applied: "I will bring the land into desolation; and your enemies which dwell therein shall be astonished at it. And I will scatter you among the heathen, and I will draw out a sword after you; and your land shall be desolate and your cities waste." No man can stand here in deserted Williamsburgh and say the prophecy has not been fulfilled.

The Story of Joseph

Without changing my date, I will observe that we have traversed some miles of desolate country, whose soil is rich enough, but is given over wholly to weeds—a silent, mournful expanse, wherein we saw only three persons—Arabs with nothing on but a course shirt. Shepherds, they were, and they charmed their flocks with the traditional shepherd's pipe—a reed instrument that made music as exquisitely infernal as these same Arabs create when they sing. I wonder if it was to this kind of scallawags the angels brought tidings that a Saviour was born? It rather staggers me to believe it. We have traversed this solitude, and are resting now at Joseph's Pit. This is a ruined Khan of the Middle Ages, in one of whose side courts is a great walled and arched pit with water in it, and this pit, one tradition says, is the one Joseph's brethren cast him into. A more authentic tradition, aided by the geography of the country, places the pit in Dothan, some two days journey from here. However, since there are many who believe in this present pit as the true one, it has its interest. I suppose your readers are very rusty about the history of Joseph. It is my duty to recount it:

Joseph had eleven brethren and a father, making twelve in all. He is dead now. Joseph was the youngest but one, and the best beloved. So well beloved was he that his father gave him a coat of many colors. They went a good deal on coats of many colors in those days. Joseph was only a thoughtless lad of seventeen, and that coat corralled his sympathies. He used to swell around and put on many frills among his brethren; insomuch that they reasoned among themselves, and said: As Jacob, our father, liveth, there is too much style about this upstart. For, behold, even before these days were they down upon him.

Not satisfied with having a coat of many colors, Joseph proceeded to further atrocities and began to dream dreams. And he had a fashion of interpreting them in a way that was very comforting to himself—in a way that seemed to foreshadow that he would one day be exalted high above his father Jacob and his other brethren. These things made the wrath of the eleven to increase by many fold, and in a greater degree than ever were they down upon him.

In the fullness of time Jacob sent his sons away up in the north country to pasture their flocks, and by and by the mails got irregular and he wondered if anything was the matter, because of his not hearing from them. So he sent Joseph to look into the matter, and, just like a boy, he started off through that vilest, rockiest, dustiest country in Asia, tricked out in his trotting harness—gotten up regardless of expense—arrayed in the pride of his heart, his beautiful claw-hammer coat of many colors.

When the other boys saw him coming they said: "Lo, here is the dreamer—let us kill him." But Reuben pleaded with tender eloquence for his innocent brother, and said: "O, pity him!" Wherefore they pitted him. And the self-same pit that they pitted him in is here in this place, even to this day. And here it will remain until the next detachment of image-breakers and tomb-desecraters arrives from the *Quaker City* excursion, and they will infallibly dig it up and carry it away with them. For behold in them is no reverence for the solemn monuments of the past, and whithersoever they go they destroy and spare not. Then the brethren sold Joseph to some Ishmaelites, at the ruling rates, ten per cent off for cash, and dabbled his coat in the blood of a kid and sent it to their father, who rent his garments and believed that his boy, the jewel of his heart and the joy of his old age, was gone from him to return no more forever.

The Ishmaelites took Joseph into Egypt, and sold him to Potiphar, an officer of the King's household, and lost money on him, which served them right. Joseph became foreman of Potiphar's affairs and prospered greatly. He had the run of the whole establishment, and was trusted to the utmost. He got into trouble with Potiphar's wife at last, and both gave in their versions of the affair, but the lady's was plausible and Joseph's was most outrageously shaky. So they threw him into prison and he staid there two years. He got to eating too much again, and consequently he got to dreaming. The same was the case with the other prisoners. They all wanted their dreams interpreted. This was Joseph's strong suit. The interpretations proved correct. This came to Pharaoh's ears, after a while, and, most luckily, just at the time when he had had a couple of curious dreams himself and had run so short of dreaming material that he dreamt them over again, which astonished him. Joseph enlightened him. He said, "Sire, your dreams signify that there are going to be seven years of extraordinary plenty in Egypt, and they will be followed by a howling famine that will distress the whole world for full seven years." Then he closed one eye and looked exceedingly shrewd out of the other, after the manner of a man who knoweth that which he is about, and said, "Behold, thou and thy servant can gather together divers and sundry shekels out of this thing—let us bear the market and buy against the season of famine." And Pharaoh said, "I perceive that thou are not of them that know not to come in when it doth rain; behold, it shall be even as thou sayest."

Wherefore he made Joseph ruler over all the land of Egypt, and gave unto him chariots and horses, and servants to wait upon him; and clothed him in sumptuous garments whereunto the coat of many colors was not so much as a circumstance. Then did Joseph show what manner of man he was. He beared the market and bought all the corn that was to be raised in Egypt for seven years to come, and stored it away. And when the first year of the famine was approaching he bought again at six months, buyer's option, and surprised the boys very greatly, for when he called his stocks they could not deliver. In that day many a man sold short and Joseph had them on the hip, and their names were posted and they forfeited their seats in the Board. And during all those years of famine, ships came from far countries that were in distress, and lo, the corn that Joseph bought at forty cents he sold it unto them at seven dollars and a half. Before a time and a half or two times had passed over their heads, Joseph and Pharaoh owned about two-thirds of Egypt; and it is estimated that if Pharaoh could have dreamed one more dream and got Joseph to interpret it, they would have shortly owned the balance of it.

By and by Jacob sent ten of his sons down to Egypt to buy corn. Joseph knew them, but never let on. He called them spies, and blackguarded them until he thought he had about got even with them for selling him out, and then he sold them corn, hid their money in their sacks, and sent them home. But he held on to Simeon, and bound him. He appeared to have a special grudge against Simeon. He said he would hold on to Simeon and crowd him all he could, until they brought down Benjamin, the one they had left home. So he made it lively for Simeon.

Jacob was sore distressed when he heard the news, but as the boys had only brought one sack of corn apiece after travelling all the way to Egypt, they necessarily ran out shortly and were morally obliged to go again. Jacob nerved his heart and parted with his young boy.

The brethren saw Joseph again, and again he knew them, but said no word. They got their corn and went away, but once more they got into trouble. Young Benjamin, with the artless simplicity of youth, nipped a silver cup, and the servant of Joseph found it in his sack. Then there was weeping and wailing and gnashing of teeth. They had to go back, though, to the palace, and then came the climax of Joseph's stirring drama! While the sorrowing strangers stood with bowed heads before the mighty lord of Egypt, he fell upon Benjamin's neck and cried: "Ha! the strawberry upon your left arm!—it is! it is my long-lost brother!" (Slow music.)

Forgiven, and the past forgotten, the brethren of Joseph rejoiced with a joy they had never known before. A feast was spread, and, surrounded by the grandeur of princely Egypt, they partook of the squarest meal that had passed their lips since the day that the famine came upon the land. Let us draw the curtain over this sacred family blow-out. It was splendid, and cordial, and never cost the brethren a cent.

One day old Jacob lifted up his eyes and saw a caravan winding its long line over the hills—a caravan like unto the caravans that bear princes and their goods. And when it was come nigh, behold his sons were with it, and they said, "These are for thee; for lo, Joseph thy son liveth, and is lord over all the land of Egypt!" The joy of Jacob, and the words that he spake, are they not written in the chronicles of the book that is called Genesis? So Jacob went down into the land of Egypt, and tripped and fell upon Joseph's neck; but Joseph caught him all right, and said, "Go slow, Governor:" and from that hour the happiness of Jacob was complete. Through Joseph, he and his sons were honored in the land all their days; and they prospered mightily, and never knew sorrow any more.

So ends the story of Joseph—the most touching and beautiful, and also the most dramatic, in the Old Testament. Of all the patriarchs, Joseph was the noblest. In his perfect character one can find no flaw. From his boyhood onward to the day of his death, he was both great and good. At one time or another of their lives, the other patriarchs did things that were not entirely creditable, but Joseph's record was clear from the beginning even unto the end.

I will go down into this gloomy pit his brethren cast him into thirty-five hundreds years ago, and drink to his honored memory a cup of its waters mingled with certain drops of the curious cordial I have brought hither from the strange lands that are beyond the sea.

This letter, numbered thirty-four by Twain, appeared in the *Daily Alta California* of January 12, 1868. It was used in Chapters XIX and XX. The first paragraph was deleted. The first part of the letter follows Letter 39, with a paragraph intervening. The passage in parentheses was deleted. "Who could not have been more than a Brigadier General" and the rest of the sentence was deleted. A sentence of twenty-seven words was substituted for "So she went out." "It was very funny" and the next sentence were deleted, and a longer passage, including Scriptural quotation, was inserted. "Williamsburgh" became "Ain Mellahah."

After the paragraph ending "and say the prophecy has not been fulfilled," Twain inserted two paragraphs to conclude Chapter XIX and then began the next chapter with the remainder of this letter. After "shirt" Twain inserted a comparison between the shirt and "the only summer garment of little negro boys on Southern plantations." The sentence beginning "I wonder if it was to this kind of scallawags" and the following sentence were rewritten. At this point Twain inserted several pages and then continued with this letter. After the sentence "However, since there are many who believe in this present pit as the true one, it has its interest" there follows—both in the letter and in the book—the story of Joseph, but Twain rewrote, condensed, and greatly improved the version in the letter. Before the story he inserted high praise of the writers of the Bible for "their simplicity of language, their felicity of expression, their pathos, and, above all, their faculty of sinking themselves entirely out of sight of the reader and making the narrative stand out alone and seem to tell itself. The censure of the *Quaker City* excursionists for their vandalism was retained, in the same language. In the book Twain also told the story of Esau and "his still sublimer generosity to the brother who had wronged him." The last paragraph of the letter was deleted.

41. Famous Holy Places

Capernaum, September, 1867.

The celebrated Sea of Galilee is not so large a sea as Lake Tahoe by a good deal—it is just about two-thirds as large. And when you speak of beauty, this sea is no more to be compared to Tahoe than a meridian of longitude is to a rainbow. The dim waters of this puddle cannot suggest the limpid brilliancy of Tahoe; those low, shaven, yellow hillocks of rocks and sand, so devoid of perspective, cannot suggest the grand peaks that compass Tahoe like a wall, and whose ribbed and chasmed fronts are clad with stately pines that seem to grow small and smaller as they climb, till one might fancy them reduced to weeds and shrubs far upward, where they join the everlasting snows. Silence and soliture brood over Tahoe; and silence and solitude brood also over this lake of Genessaret [Gennesaret]. But the solitude of the one is as cheerful and fascinating as the solitude of the other is dismal and repulsive.

In the early morning one watches the silent battle of dawn and darkness upon the waters of Tahoe with a placid interest; but when the shadows sulk away and one by one the hidden beauties of the shore unfold themselves, in the full splendor of noon, when the still surface is belted like a rainbow with broad bars of blue and green and white, half the distance from the circumference to centre; when, in lazy summer afternoons, one lies in a boat, far out to where the dead blue of the deep water begins, and smokes the pipe of peace and idly winks at the distant peaks and patches of snow from under his cap brim; when the boat drifts shoreward to the white water, and one lolls over the gunwale and gazes by the hour down through the crystal depths and notes the colors of the pebbles and averages the spots upon the school of trout a hundred feet below; when at night he sees moon and stars, mountain ridges feathered with pines, jutting white capes, bald [bold] promontories, grand sweeps of rugged scenery topped with bald, glimmering peaks, all magnificently pictured in the polished mirror of the lake, in richest, softest detail, the tranquil interest that was born with the morning deepens and deepens, by sure degrees, till it culminates at last in resistless fascination.

It is solitude, for birds and squirrels on the shore and fishes in the water are all the creatures that are near to make it otherwise, but it is not the sort of solitude to make one dreary. Come to Galilee for that. If these unpeopled deserts, these rusty mounds of barrenness, that never, never, never do shake the glare from their harsh outlines, and fade and faint into vague perspective; this melancholy ruin of Capernaum; that stupid village of Tiberias, slumbering under its three or four funeral plumes of palm trees; yonder desolate declivity where the swine of the miracle ran down into the sea, and doubtless thought it was better to swallow a devil or two and get drowned into the bargain than to have to live longer in such a place; this cloudless, blistering sky; this solemn, sailless, tintless lake, reposing within its rim of yellow hills and low, steep banks, and looking just as expressionless and unpoetical (when you leave its sublime history out of the question,) as any bath-tub on earth—if these things are not food for rock me to sleep mother, none exist, I think; if they do not make an exquisitely dismal solitude, I am not able to conceive what it is that is lacking.

They say this land is accursed; I don't think there can be any shadow of a doubt about that. And it was about as responsible a piece of cursing as ever was done, too, I take it. I am strong, very strong, in the doctrine that it was cursed. And also inclined a little to the suspicion that the curse dates from the morning of creation. It looks most uncommonly like it. I do not see any more reason to think there was ever any soil on these hills and in these deserts than I do that there was ever soil in the deserts and on the hills of Washoe. In the short valley we have left behind us, and on the table lands above and just beyond Tiberias, and here in the little plain of Genessaret, there are very respectable expanses of land that would be called rich anywhere—but the deserts sadly oversize the arable sections. This country reminds me of Washoe all the time. Take Washoe Valley, and you have this Valley of the Sources of the Jordan; take Washoe Lake and you have the Waters of Merom exactly; take the swamps that border it and you have the dwelling-place of the Bedouin goat herdsmen; take the forbidding mountains that surround the picture, and strip them of every tree, every shrub, and batter from their outlines every semblance of grace and beauty, and you have the mountains that border Merom—in a word, you have the country to perfection that comes down from Cesarea Phillippi to the Sea of Galilee. They say it is a most favorable specimen of Palestine. If it is a favorable specimen of Palestine, surely Palestine is Washoe's born mate. I have thought over such information as I could get, and ciphered it down, and as nearly as I can come at it, there is really as much good farming land in Washoe as there is in Palestine. It astounds me, but I am sure the figures are correct. It begins to make me a little shaky about Silverland. I don't know but part of the curse fell upon Washoe. What put this figuring into my head was the apparent unfertility of Syria. The idea suggested was, that if Palestine was a similar country, how did it support six millions of people in ancient times? How could Washoe do it? As nearly as one can come at it, Washoe is six times as large as Palestine, and California is twelve times as large. Now I have got it reduced to the plainest proposition in the world, viz., if Washoe, with her agricultural facilities, could support 36,000,000 persons, the present population of the United States, then I know that, industriously cultivated, Palestine could really support the 6,000,000 attributed to her in old times. And if California, (supposing she were as barren and rocky and sandy as Palestine,) could support 72,000,000 of people, the same being the population of the vast Russian Empire, which covers a seventh part of the habitable globe, then there would be no question in my mind that little Palestine *did* support a swarm of 6,000,000 human beings in the olden time. Just at present, though, it don't look promising to me. The land must have been blessed much harder then than ever it was cursed afterwards.

One of the most astonishing things that have yet fallen under my observation is the exceedingly small portion of the earth from which sprang the now flourishing plant of Christianity. The longest journey our Saviour ever performed was from here to Jerusalem—say 150 miles—about as far as from Sacramento to Carson City, I should judge.

The next longest was from here to Sidon—say about forty miles. Instead of being wide apart—as American appreciation of distances would naturally suggest—the places made so celebrated by the presence of Christ are nearly all right here in full view, and within cannon-shot of the spot where we are camped. Leaving out two or three short journeys of the Saviour, he spent his life, preached his gospel and performed his miracles within a compass no larger than an ordinary county in the United States. It is as much as I can do to get this stupefying fact through my head. Now you can imagine how it wears a man out to have to read up a hundred pages of history every two or three miles—for verily the celebrated localities of Palestine occur that close together. You cannot imagine how wearily, how bewilderingly they swarm about your path.

Historical

Something more than eighteen hundred years ago, the Saviour was born in Bethlehem of Judea, and his parents came and dwelt in the insignificant village of Nazareth, fifteen or twenty miles from here.

In this town of Capernaum, where we are, he began to tell the people of the new religion that he had brought unto the world, and also to heal the sick. There was a man here by the name of Jairus, whose daughter lay dead in his house. The Saviour entered and spoke to her and she rose up alive. Peter's wife's mother lay sick of a fever and he cured her with a touch. He also cured the servant of the centurion without even going near him. If they brought a blind man to him, he merely spoke and the man opened his eyes and saw. Many and many and many a cripple hobbled hither from the country round about here, and when he looked upon them they got upon their feet and walked whithersoever they would. He performed all measures of miracles, and his fame spread abroad in the land.

He gathered together some disciples, from this place and from one or two of the towns a rifle-shot from here, and bade them leave off fishing and go about the land and preach. Once when himself and some of these disciples were out on the lake here in a boat, a heavy storm arose and the disciples were frightened and took in their sails and woke him trembling. But he spoke to the winds and the waves and they went peacefully to rest.

But the most notable event happened yonder close to Bethsaida.

There were fed the five thousand with five loaves and two little fishes. Only five and two for five thousand.

MARK TWAIN

(Note by the Editors.—We have received a private letter from our correspondent, in which we expected some explanation of his strange conduct in presenting the above information to the public with such a confident air of furnishing news, but he offers none. He does not refer to the subject of the letter at all, except in the postscript, and then only to mention casually that he has inserted nothing in it but what can be substantiated.)

This letter, numbered thirty-five by Twain, appeared in the *Daily Alta California* of January 19, 1868. The opening passage of the letter, comparing Lake Tahoe and the Sea of Galilee, and extending through the words "if these things are not food for rock me to sleep mother, none exist, I think," was used in Chapter XXI, beginning with the eighth paragraph of the chapter. Twain supplied a footnote explaining why he measured all lakes by Tahoe. "This puddle" became "this pool"; "repulsive" became "repellent"; "averages the spots upon the school of trout" became "reveiws the finny armies gliding in procession"; "three or four funeral plumes" became "six funeral plumes"; and "as any bath-tub on earth" became "as any metropolitan reservoir in Christendom." The paragraph beginning "One of the most astonishing things that have yet fallen under my observation is the exceedingly small portion of the earth" was followed—almost verbatim at times but with revisions—at the end of Chapter XX. In the two chapters Twain made use of some of the other material in the letter, but in different language, such as the curse upon Palestine, the desolation of the region, and the comments on Capernaum and Christ's activities there and in its environs. On the whole, however, Twain made less use of this letter than most of the other letters.

42. Pious Enthusiasm of the Pilgrims

Tiberias, September, 1867.

At noon we took a swim in the Sea of Galilee—a blessed privilege in this roasting climate—and then lunched under a neglected old fig tree at the fountain they call Ain-et-Tin. As I have remarked before, every trifling rivulet that gurgles out of the rocks and sands of Palestine is dignified with the title of "fountain," and lunatics familiar with the Hudson, the great lakes and the Mississippi fall into transports of admiration over them, and exhaust their powers of composition in writing their praises. If all the poetry and nonsense that have been discharged upon the fountains and the bland scenery of Palestine were collected in a book it would make a most valuable volume to burn.

During luncheon, the pilgrim enthusiasts of our party, who had been so wild with religious ecstasy ever since they touched holy ground that they did nothing but mutter incoherent rhapsodies about how wonderful is prophecy, and that sort of thing, could scarcely eat, so anxious were they to "take shipping" and sail in very person upon the waters that had borne the vessels of the Apostles and upheld the sacred feet of the Saviour. I thought they cherished a sort of vague notion that a fervor such as theirs might peradventure earn for them a little private miracle of some kind or other to talk about when they got home. Their anxiety grew and their excitement augmented with every fleeting moment, until my fears were aroused and I began to have misgivings that in their present condition they might break recklessly loose from all considerations of prudence and buy a whole fleet of ships to sail in instead of hiring a single one for an hour, as quiet folk are wont to do. I trembled to think of the ruined purses this day's performances might result in. Never before had I known them to lose their self-possession when a question of expenses was before the tribe, and now I could not help reflecting bodingly upon the intemperate zeal with which middle-aged men are apt to surfeit themselves upon a seductive folly which they have tasted for the first time. And, yet, I did not feel that I had a right to be surprised at the state of things which was giving me so much concern. These men had been taught from infancy to revere, almost to worship, the holy places whereon their happy eyes were resting now. For many and many a year this very picture had visited their thoughts by day and floated through their dreams by night. To stand before it in the flesh—to see it as they saw it now—to sail upon the hallowed sea, and kiss the holy soil that compassed it about; these were aspirations they had cherished while a generation dragged its lagging seasons by and left its furrows in their faces and its frosts upon their hair. To look upon this picture, and sail upon this sea, they had forsaken home and its idols and journeyed thousands and thousands of miles, in weariness and tribulation. What wonder that the sordid lights of work-day prudence should pale before the glory of a hope like theirs in the full splendor of its fruition? Let them squander millions! I said—who speaks of money at a time like this?

Ah, Me!

In this frame of mind I followed, as fast as I could, the eager footsteps of the pilgrims, and stood upon the shore of the lake, and swelled, with hat and voice, the frantic hail they sent after the "ship" that was speeding by. It was a success. The toilers of the sea ran in and beached their barque. Joy sat upon every countenance.

"How much?—ask him how much, Abraham!—how much to take us all—eight of us, and you—to Bethsaida, yonder, and to the mouth of Jordan, and to the place where the swine ran down into the sea—quick!—and we want to coast around everywhere—everywhere!—all day long!—*I* could sail a year in these blessed waters!—and tell him we'll stop at Magdala and finish at Tiberias!—ask him how much?—anything—anything whatever!—tell him we don't care what the expense is!" (I said to myself, I knew how it would be.)

ABRAHAM—(interpreting) "He says two Napoleons—eight dollars."

One or two countenances fell—no matter whose. Then a pause.

"Too much!—we'll give him one!"

I never shall know how it was—I shudder yet when I think how the place is given to miracles—but in a single instant of time, as it seemed to me, that ship was twenty paces from the shore, and speeding away like a frightened thing! Eight crest-fallen creatures stood upon the shore, and this—this—after all that frenzied zeal, that o'er-mastering ecstasy! Oh, shameful, shameful ending, after such unseemly boasting! It was too much like "Ho! let me at him!" followed by a prudent "Two of you hold him—one can hold me!"

Instantly there was wailing and gnashing of teeth in the camp. The two Napoleons were offered—more if necessary—and pilgrims and dragoman shouted themselves hoarse with pleadings to the retreating boatmen to come back. But they sailed serenely away and paid no farther heed to pilgrims who had dreamed all their lives of some day skimming over the sacred waters of Galilee and listening to its hallowed story in the whisperings of its waves, and had journeyed countless leagues to do it, and—and then concluded they had better not, because it would cost a dollar apiece! Impertinent Mahommedan Arabs, to think such things of gentlemen of another faith!

Well, there was nothing to do but just submit and forego the privilege of voyaging on Genessaret [Gennesaret], after coming half around the globe to taste that pleasure. There was a time, when the Saviour taught here, that boats were plenty among the fishermen of the coasts—but boats and fishermen both are gone, now; and old Josephus had a fleet of men-of-war in these waters eighteen centuries ago—a hundred and thirty bold canoes—but they, also, have passed away and left no sign. They battle here no more by sea, and the commercial marine of Galilee numbers only two small ships, just of a pattern with the little skiffs the disciples knew. One was lost to us for good—the other was miles away and far out of hail. So we mounted the horses and rode grimly on toward Magdala, cantering along in the edge of the water for want of the means of passing over it.

How the pilgrims abused each other! Each said it was the other's fault, and each in turn denied it. No word was spoken by the sinners—even the mildest sarcasm might have been dangerous at such a time. Sinners that have been kept down and had examples held up to them, and suffered frequent lectures, and been so put upon in a moral way and in the matter of going slow and being serious and bottling up slang, and so crowded in regard to the matter of being proper and always and forever behaving, that their lives have become a burden to them, would not lag behind pilgrims at such a time as this, and wink furtively, and be joyful, and commit other such crimes, because it wouldn't occur to them to do it. Otherwise they would.

So we all rode down to Magdala, while the gnashing of teeth waxed and waned by turns, and harsh words troubled the holy calm of Galilee.

Curious Specimens of Art and Architecture

Magdala is not a beautiful place. It is thoroughly Syrian, and that is to say that it is thoroughly ugly, and cramped, squalid, uncomfortable and filthy—just the style of cities that have adorned Palestine since Jacob's time, as all writers have labored hard to prove, and have succeeded. The streets of Magdala are anywhere from three to six feet wide, and reeking with uncleanliness. The houses are from five to seven feet high, and all built upon one arbitrary plan—the ungraceful form of a dry-goods box. The sides are daubed with a smooth white plaster, and tastefully frescoed aloft and alow with disks of camel-dung placed there to dry. This gives the edifice the romantic appearance of having been riddled with cannon-balls, and imparts to it a very pleasing effect. When the artist has arranged his materials with an eye to just proportion—the small and the large flakes in alternate rows, and separated by carefully-considered intervals—I know of nothing more cheerful to look upon than a spirited Syrian fresco. Nothing in this world has such a charm for me as to stand and gaze for hours and hours upon the inspired works of these old masters. I have seen the *chef d'œuvres* of Vernet, Tintoretto, Titian and a host of others whose fame is known in every land, but few of them ever affected me like the battle-pieces of these nameless sons of Art. Yet who speaks of them? No one. Book-makers swarm through the galleries of Europe, and lavish praises with untiring lips; they invade the Holy Land and prate of temples that are gone and statues that never had a being; they seek for beauty far and wide, and when they find it glorify it—but never a page have they given to Syrian fresco. Like the lost art of painting on glass, it will pass from the knowledge of men, and then, too late, the world will mourn.

But I digress. The flat, plastered roof of the Syrian dwelling is garnished by picturesque stacks of fresco materials, which, having become thoroughly dried and cured, are placed there where it will be convenient. It is used for fuel. There is no timber of any consequence in Palestine—none at all to waste upon fires—and neither are there any mines of coal. If my description has been intelligible, you will perceive, now, that a square, flat-roofed hovel, neatly frescoed, with its wall-tops gallantly bastioned and turreted with dried camel refuse, gives to a landscape a feature that is exceedingly festive and picturesque, especially if one is careful to remember to stick in a cat wherever, about the premises, there is room for a cat to sit. There are no windows to a Syrian hut, and no chimneys. When I used to read that they let a bed-ridden man down through the roof of a house to get him into the presence of the Saviour, I generally had a three-story brick in my mind, and marvelled that they did not break his neck with the strange experiment. I perceive now, however, that they might have taken him by the heels and thrown him clear over the house without discommoding him very much. Palestine is not changed any since those days, in manners, customs, architecture or people.

Public Reception of the Pilgrims

As we rode into Magdala not a soul was visible. But the ring of the horses' hoofs roused the stupid population, and they all came trooping out—old men and old women, boys and girls, the blind, the crazy and the crippled, all in ragged, soiled and scanty raiment, and all abject beggars by nature, instinct and education. How the vermin-tortured vagabonds did swarm! How they showed their scars and sores, and piteously pointed to their maimed and crooked limbs, and begged with their pleading eyes for charity! We had invoked a spirit we could not lay. They hung to the horses' tails, clung to their manes and the stirrups, closed in on every side in scorn of dangerous hoofs—and out of their infidel throats with one accord, burst an agonizing and most infernal chorus: "Howajji, bucksheesh! howajji, bucksheesh! howajji, bucksheesh! bucksheesh! bucksheesh!" I never was in a storm like that before.

Mary Magdalene's House

As we paid the bucksheesh out to sore-eyed children and brown, buxom girls with repulsively tattooed lips and chins, we filed through the town and by many an exquisite fresco by some unsung Syrian Vernet, till we came to a bramble-infested inclosure and a Roman-looking ruin which was the veritable dwelling of St. Mary Magdalene, the friend and follower of Jesus. The guide believed it, and so did I. I could not well do otherwise, with the house right there before my eyes as plain as day. The pilgrims took down portions of the front wall for specimens, as is their honored custom, and then we departed. There was nothing else in Magdala to see—nothing else save treasures of art. We had no catalogue. We journeyed on.

We are camped in this place, now, just within the city walls of Tiberias. We went into the town before nightfall and looked at its people—we cared nothing about its houses. Its people are best examined at a distance. They are greasy Jews, Arabs and negroes. Squalor and poverty are the pride of Tiberias. The young women wear their dower strung upon a strong wire that curves downward from the top of the head to the jaw—Turkish silver coins that they have raked together or inherited. Most of these maidens were not wealthy, but some few had been very kindly dealt with by fortune. I saw heiresses there worth, in their own right—worth, well, I suppose I might venture to say, as much as nine dollars and a half. But such cases are rare. When you come across one of these, she naturally puts on airs. She won't ask for bucksheesh. She won't even permit of undue familiarity. She throws herself on her dignity and goes on serenely prospecting with her fine-tooth comb and quoting poetry just the same as if you were not present at all. Some people can't stand prosperity.

They say that the long-nosed, lanky, dyspeptic-looking bodysnatchers, with the indescribable hats on, and a long curl dangling down in front of each ear, are the old, regular, self-righteous Pharisees we read of in the Scriptures. Verily, they look it. Judging merely by their general gait, and without other evidence, one might easily suspect that self-righteousness was their strong suit.

From various authorities I have culled information concerning Tiberias. It was built by Herod Antipes [Antipas], the murderer of John the Baptist, and named after the Emperor Tiberias. It is believed that it stands upon the site of what must have been, ages ago, a city of considerable architectural pretensions, judging by the fine porphyry pillars that are scattered through Tiberias and down the lake shore southward. These were fluted, once, and yet, although the stone is about as hard as iron, the flutings are almost worn away. This modern town—Tiberias—is only mentioned in the New Testament; never in the Old.

The Sanhedrim met here last, and for three hundred years it was the metropolis of the Jews in Palestine. It is one of the four holy cities of the Israelites, and is to them what Mecca is to the Mohammedan and Jerusalem to the Christian. It has been the abiding place of many learned and famous Jewish rabbins. They lie buried here, and near them lie also 25,000 of their faith who travelled far to be near them while they lived and lie with them when they died. The great Rabbi Ben Israel spent three years here in the early part of the third century. He is dead, now.

The metaphors of the Bible have to me an aptness and a significance now that they never possessed before. I never knew but one poem by heart in my life—it was impressed upon my mind at school by the usual process, a trifle emphasized. I even discovered a new excellence in that poem now as I look out upon the still sea of Galilee and mark how these multitudes of strangely lustrous stars fling their counterfeits upon it and gem the whole broad surface with their glittering splendor:

And the sheen of his spear was like
Stars on the sea,
When the blue wave rolls
Nightly on deep Galilee.

I see the long files of burnished spear-heads stretching, rank upon rank, far away till they are lost in the mists that brood over the further shore.

The pilgrims are gone to rest, but they did not sail on Galilee. Let us not exult, but let us rather endeavor to be blandly sorrowful.

This letter, numbered thirty-six by Twain, appeared in the *Daily Alta California* of January 26, 1868. The first part was used in Chapter XX, beginning near the middle of the chapter. After "Ain-et-Tin" Twain added "a hundred yards from ruined Capernaum." "Trifling rivulet" became "rivulet"; "of Palestine is dignified with" became "of this part of the world is dubbed with"; "lunatics" became "people"; "Palestine" became "this region"; "wild with religious ecstasy" became "light-hearted and happy"; and "did nothing but" became "did little but." "About how wonderful is prophecy, and that sort of thing" was deleted. After "vessels of the Apostles" Twain deleted forty-four words, and after "might result in" he deleted twenty-one words. "Abraham" became "Ferguson," and "blessed waters" became "waters." After "countenances fell," Twain deleted "no matter whose." "That frenzied zeal" was deleted. "They had better not, because it would cost a dollar apiece" became "that the fare was too high." After "Otherwise they would," Twain inserted two sentences totaling forty-nine words. "And harsh words troubled the holy calm of Galilee" concludes that part of the letter used in Chapter XX.

The remainder of the letter was used at the beginning of Chapter XXI. "Palestine since Jacob's time" became "the country since Adam's time," and "pleasing effect" became "warlike aspect." After "spirited Syrian fresco," Twain deleted the next 155 words—down through "But I digress." "By some unsung Syrian Vernet" was deleted. "Was the veritable dwelling" became "had been the veritable dwelling." The sentence beginning "There was nothing else in Magdala to see" and the two following sentences were deleted. "Greasy Jews, Arabs and negroes" became "particularly uncomely Jews, Arabs, and negroes"; "throws herself on her dignity and goes on serenely prospecting" became "assumes a crushing dignity and goes on serenely practicing"; "regular" became "familiar"; "gait" became "style"; and "strong suit" became "specialty." After "the flutings are almost worn away," Twain inserted a sentence of seventeen words. The paragraph ending with the reference to Rabbi Ben Israel is followed by the Lake Tahoe passage from Letter 41 and the remainder of Letter 42 was omitted.

43. The Apparition

Nazareth, September, 1867.

We took another swim in the sea of Galilee last night, and another at sunrise this morning. We have not sailed, but three swims are equal to a sail, are they not? There were plenty of fish visible in the water, but we have no outside aids in this pilgrimage but "Tent Life in the Holy Land," "The Land and the Book," and other literature of like description—no fishing tackle. There were no fish to be had in the village of Tiberias. True, we saw two or three rusty vagabonds mending their nets, but never trying to catch anything with them. If you will take the trouble to glance through a few books of Palestine travel, you will notice that the authors impartially and invariably dwell with moving pathos upon this matter of seeing the fishermen mending their nets. And they always seem astonished at it. Taking the cue from the books, our pilgrims, and all other pilgrims, make it a point to be much affected when they behold this net-mending process. They all speak of it with exultant delight, and apparently with a dim notion that some how or other it is a sort of fulfilment of prophecy, or that it is a clincher or something, or is in some inscrutable way a Bulwark of Christianity. To be on Galilee and not see the fishermen mending their nets, could not be regarded in any other light than that of a calamity. Very well, we have seen it, and are happy. I suppose it is only a natural effect of all this, that a notion I was hardly conscious of myself has crept into my head that the fishermen have never done anything with their nets but mend them, from time immemorial; and now it is likely that if any of us were to see them actually engaged in fishing with them, it would strike us irresistibly as a curious and interesting phenomenon.

The Baths

We did not go to the ancient warm baths two miles below Tiberias. I had no desire in the world to go there. This seemed a little strange, and prompted me to try to discover what the cause of this unreasonable indifference was. It turned out to be simply because Pliny mentions them. I have conceived a sort of unwarrantable antipathy to Pliny and St. Paul, because it seems as if I can never ferret out a place that I can have to myself. It always and eternally transpires that St. Paul has been to that place, and Pliny has "mentioned" it. Did Pliny, with the head he had, find nothing to do but poke around mentioning things? And that inveterate St. Paul, wouldn't it have been just as convenient to him to locate somewhere? Was it necessary for them to use up everything, and never give anybody else a chance? I want to hurry through this pilgrimage and get to Egypt. It is my only hope. If St. Paul has gone and landed there, and Pliny has been depraved enough to mention that also, in his absurd way, I am a blighted community.

Ye Apparition

In the early morning we mounted and started. And then a wierd apparition marched forth at the head of the procession—a pirate, I thought, if ever a pirate dwelt upon land. It was a tall Arab, as swarthy as an Indian—young—say thirty years of age. On his head he had closely bound a gorgeous yellow and red striped silk scarf, whose ends, lavishly fringed with tassels, hung down between his shoulders and dallied with the wind. From his neck to his knees, in ample folds, a robe swept down that was a very star-spangled banner of curved and sinuous bars of black and white. Out of his back, somewhere, apparently, the long stem of a chibouk projected, and reached far above his right shoulder. Athwart his back, diagonally, and extending high above his left shoulder, was an Arab gun of Saladin's time, that was splendid with silver plating from stock clear up to the end of its measureless stretch of barrel. About his waist was bound many and many a yard of elaborately figured but sadly tarnished stuff that came from sumptuous Persia, and among the baggy folds in front the sunbeams glinted from a formidable battery of old brass-mounted horse-pistols and the gilded hilts of blood-thirsty knives. There were holsters for more pistols appended to the wonderful stack of long-haired goat-skins and Persian carpets, which the man had been taught to regard in the light of a saddle; and down among the pendulous rank of vast tassels that swung royally from that saddle, and clanging against the iron shovel of a stirrup that propped the warrior's knees up toward his chin, was a crooked, silver-clad scimetar of such awful dimensions and such implacable expression that no man might hope to look upon it and yet not shudder. The fringed and bedizened prince whose privilege it is to ride the pony and lead the elephant into a country village is poor and naked compared to this chaos of paraphernalia, and the happy vanity of the one is the very poverty of satisfaction compared to the majestic serenity, the overwhelming complacency of the other.

"*Who* is this! *What* is this?" That was the trembling inquiry all down the line.

"Our guard! From Galilee to the birth place of the Saviour, the country is infested with fierce Bedouins, whose sole happiness it is, in this life, to cut and stab, and mangle and murder unoffending Christians. Allah be with us!"

"Then hire a regiment! Would you send us out among these desperate hordes, with no salvation in our utmost need but this old turret?"

The dragoman laughed—not at the facetiousness of the similie [simile], for verily, that guide, or that courier, or that dragoman never yet lived upon earth who had in him the faintest appreciation of a joke, even though that joke were so broad and so ponderous that if it fell on him it would flatten him out like a postage stamp —the dragoman laughed, and then, emboldened by some thought that was in his brain, no doubt, proceeded to extremities and winked.

In straits like these, when a man laughs, it is encouraging; when he winks, it is positively reassuring. He finally intimated that one guard would be sufficient to protect us, but that one was an absolute necessity. It was because of the moral weight his awful panoply would have with the Bedouins. Then I said we didn't want any guard at all. If one fantastic vagabond could protect eight armed Christians and a pack of Arab servants from all harm, surely that detachment could protect themselves. He shook his head doubtfully. Then I said, just think of how it looks—think of how it would read, to self-reliant Californians, that we went sneaking through this deserted wilderness under the protection of this masquerading Arab, that would break his neck getting out of the country if a man that *was* a man ever started after him. It was a mean, low, degrading position. What were we ever told to bring navy revolvers with us for, if we had to be protected at last by this infamous star-spangled scum of the desert? These appeals were vain—the dragoman only smiled and shook his head.

I rode to the front and struck up an acquaintance with King Solomon, in all his glory, and got him to show me his lingering eternity of a gun. It had a rusty flint lock; it was ringed, and barred and plated with silver from end to end, but it was as desperately out of the perpendicular as are the billiard cues of '49 that one finds yet in service of the ancient mining camps of Calaveras and Tuolumne. The muzzle was eaten by the rust of centuries into a ragged filagree-work, like the end of a burnt-out stove pipe. I shut one eye and peered within—it was flaked with iron rust like an old steamboat boiler. I borrowed the ponderous pistols and snapped them. They were rusty inside, too— had not been loaded for a generation. I went back, full of encouragement, and reported to the guide, and asked him to discharge this dismantled fortress. It came out, then. This fellow was a retainer of the Sheik of Tiberias. He was a source of Government revenue. He was to the Empire of Tiberias what the customs are to America. The Sheik imposed guards upon travellers and charged them for it. It is a lucrative source of emolument, and sometimes brings into the National treasury as much as thirty-five or forty dollars a year.

I knew the warrior's secret now; I knew the hollow vanity of his rusty trumpery, and despised his asinine complacency. I told on him, and with reckless daring the cavalcade rode straight ahead into the perilous solitudes of the desert, and scorned his frantic warnings of the mutilation and death that hovered about them on every side.

A Distinguished Panorama

Arrived at an elevation of twelve hundred feet above the lake (I ought to mention that the lake lies six hundred feet below the level of the Mediterranean—no traveller ever neglects to flourish that fragment of news in his letters,) as bald and unthrilling a panorama as even Palestine can afford, perhaps, was spread out before us. Yet it was so crowded with historical interest, that if all the pages that have been written about it were spread upon its surface, they would flag it from horizon to horizon like a pavement. Among the localities comprised in this view, were Mount Hermon; the hills that border Cesarea Phillippi [Cæsarea Philippi], Dan, the Sources of the Jordan and the Waters of Merom; Tiberias; the Sea of Galilee; Joseph's Pit; Capernaum; Bethsaida; the supposed scenes of the Sermon on the Mount, the feeding of the multitudes and the miraculous draught of fishes; the declivity down which the swine ran to the sea; the entrance and the exit of the Jordan; Safed, "the city set upon a hill," one of the four holy cities of the Jews, and the place where they believe the real Messiah will appear when he comes to redeem the world; part of the battle-field of Hattin, where the knightly Crusaders fought their last fight, and in a blaze of glory passed from the stage and ended their splendid career forever; Mount Tabor, the traditional scene of the Lord's Transfiguration, around whose confines cluster Nazareth, Cana of Galilee, Nain, Endor, Esdraelon the storied battle-field of Palestine, Gilboa, where Saul and Jonathan fell; the Fountain of Jezreel. And down toward the southeast lay a landscape that suggested to my mind a quotation (imperfectly remembered, no doubt,) that is familiar to certain myriads of men of all nationalities, all climes and all languages this day:

"The Ephraimites, not being called upon to share in the rich spoils of the Ammonitish war, assembled a mighty host to fight against Jeptha, Judge of Israel; who, being apprised of their approach, gathered together the men of Israel and gave them battle and put them to flight. To make his victory the more secure, he stationed guards at the different fords and passages of the Jordan, with instructions to let none pass who could not say Shibboleth. The Ephraimites, being of a different tribe, could not frame to pronounce the word aright, but called it Sibboleth, which proved them enemies and cost them their lives; wherefore, forty and two thousand fell at the different fords and passages of the Jordan that day."

Hattin

We jogged along peacefully over the great caravan route from Damascus to Jerusalem and Egypt, past Lubia and other Syrian hamlets, perched, in the unvarying style, upon the summit of steep mounds and hills, and fenced round about with giant cactuses, (the sign of worthless land,) with prickly pears upon them like hams, and came at last to the battle-field of Hattin.

It is a grand, irregular plateau, and looks like it might have been created for a battle-field. Here the peerless Saladin met the Christian host some seven hundred years ago, and broke their power in Palestine for all time to come. There had long been a truce between the opposing forces, but according to the Guide-Book, Raynauld of Chattilon [Châtillon], Lord of Kerak, broke it by plundering a Damascus caravan, and refusing to give up either the merchants or their goods when Saladin demanded them. This conduct of an insolent petty chieftain stung the proud Sultan to the quick, and he swore that he would slaughter Raynauld with his own hand, no matter how, or when, or where he found him. Both armies prepared for war. Under the weak King of Jerusalem was the very flower of the Christian chivalry. He foolishly compelled them to undergo a long, exhausting march, in the scorching sun, and then, without water or other refreshment, ordered them to camp in this open plain. The splendidly mounted masses of Moslem soldiers swept round the north end of Genessaret [Gennesaret], burning and destroying as they came, and pitched their camp in front of the opposing lines. At dawn the terrific fight began. Surrounded on all sides by the Sultan's swarming battalions, the Christian Knights fought on without a hope for their lives. They fought with desperate valor, but to no purpose, the odds of heat and numbers, and consuming thirst, were too great against them. Towards the middle of the day the bravest of their band cut their way through the Moslem ranks and gained the summit of a little hill, and there, hour after hour, they closed around the banner of the Cross, and beat back the charging squadrons of the enemy.

But the doom of the Christian power was sealed. Sunset found Saladin Lord of Palestine, the Christian chivalry strewn in heaps upon the field, and the King of Jerusalem, the Grand Master of the Templars and Raynauld of Chatillon captives in the Sultan's tent. Saladin treated two of the prisoners with princely courtesy, and ordered refreshments to be set before them. When the King handed an iced Sherbet to Chatillon, the Sultan said, "It is thou that givest it to him, not I." He remembered his oath, and slaughtered the hapless Knight of Chatillon with his own hand.

It was hard to realize that this silent plain had once resounded with martial music and trembled with the tramp of armed men. It was hard to people this solitude with charging masses of cavalry, and stir its torpid pulses with the shouts of victors, the shrieks of the wounded, and the flash of banner and steel above the surging billows of battle. A desolation is here that not even imagination can grace with the pomp of life and action.

Yonder, where the glory of the setting sun kindles the western hills —supper is ready. Time and hash wait for no man.

This letter, numbered thirty-seven by Twain, appeared in the *Daily Alta California* of February 2, 1868. It was used at the beginning of Chapter XXII. "Rusty vagabonds" became "vagabonds." The sentence beginning "If you will take the trouble" and all the remainder of the paragraph were deleted. "Antipathy to" became "unfriendliness toward." The sentence beginning "Did Pliny, with the head he had" and all the remainder of the paragraph were deleted. "Californians" became "Americans"; "what . . . for" became "why"; "Calaveras and Tuolumne" became "California"; and "even Palestine" became "any land." Twain deleted the remainder of the sentence after "Lord's Transfiguration." After "imperfectly remembered, no doubt," Twain deleted the next eighteen words. "Like it might have been" became "as if it might have been," and "charging masses" became "rushing columns." The last two sentences of the letter were deleted.

44. Mount Tabor and the Prodigal Son

Nazareth, September, 1867.

We got to Tabor safely, and considerably in advance of that old iron-clad swindle of a guard. We never saw a human being on the whole route, much less lawless hordes of Bedouins. Tabor stands solitary and alone, a giant sentinel above the Plain of Esdraelon. It rises some 1400 feet above the surrounding level, a green, wooded cone, symmetrical and full of grace—a prominent landmark, and one that is exceedingly pleasant to eyes weary of the repulsive monotony of desert Syria. We climbed the steep path to its summit, through breezy glades of thorn and oak. The view presented from its highest peak was almost beautiful. Below, was the broad, level plain of Esdraelon, checkered with fields like a chess-board, and full as smooth and level, seemingly; dotted about its borders with white, compact villages, and faintly pencilled, far and near, with the curving lines of roads and trails. When it is robed in the fresh verdure of spring, it must form a charming picture, even by itself. Skirting its southern border rises "Little Hermon," over whose summit a glimpse of Gilboa is caught. Nain, famous for the raising of the widow's son, and Endor, as famous for the performances of her witch, are in view. To the eastward lies the Valley of the Jordan and beyond it the mountains of Gilead. Westward is Mount Carmel. Snow-touched Hermon in the north—the table-lands of Bashan—Safed, the holy city, gleaming white upon a tall spur of the mountains of Lebanon—a steel-blue corner of the Sea of Galilee—saddle-peaked Hattin, the traditional "Mount of Beatitudes" and the mute witness of the last brave fight of the Crusading host for Holy Cross—these fill up the picture.

To glance at the salient features of this landscape through the picturesque framework of a ragged and ruined stone window-arch of the time of Christ, thus hiding from sight all that is unattractive, is to secure to yourself a pleasure worth climbing the mountain to enjoy. One must stand on his head to get the best effect in a fine sunset, and set a landscape in a bold, strong framework that is very close at hand, to bring out all its beauty. One learns this latter truth never more to forget it, in that mimic land of enchantment, the wonderful garden of my lord the Count Pallavicini, near Genoa. You go wandering for hours among hills and wooded glens, artfully contrived to leave the impression that Nature shaped them and not man; following winding paths and coming suddenly upon leaping cascades and rustic bridges; finding sylvan lakes where you expected them not; loitering through battered mediæval castles in miniature that seem hoary with age and yet were built a dozen years ago; meditating over ancient crumbling tombs, whose marble columns were marred and broken by the modern artist that made them; stumbling unawares upon toy palaces, wrought of rare and costly materials, and again upon a peasant's hut, whose dilapidated furniture can never suggest that it was made so to order; sweeping round and round in the midst of a forest on an enchanted wooden horse that is moved by some invisible agency; traversing Roman roads and passing under majestic triumphal arches; resting in quaint bowers where unseen spirits squirt jets of water on you from every possible direction, and where even the flowers you touch assail you with a shower; boating on a subterranean lake among caverns and arches royally draped with clustering stalactites, and passing out into open day upon another lake that is bordered with sloping banks of grass, and gay with royal barges that swim at anchor in the shadow of a miniature marble temple that rises out of the clear water and glasses its white statues, its rich capitals and fluted columns in the tranquil depths. So, from marvel to marvel you have drifted on, thinking all the time that the one last seen must be the chiefest. And, verily, the chiefest wonder *is* reserved until the last, but you do not see it until you step ashore, and passing through a wilderness of rare flowers, collected from every corner of the earth, you stand at the door of one more mimic temple. Right in this place the artist taxed his genius to the utmost, and fairly opened the gates of fairy land. You look through an unpretending pane of glass, stained yellow; the first thing you see is a mass of quivering foliage, ten short steps before you, in the midst of which is a ragged opening like a gateway—a thing that is common enough in nature, and not apt to excite suspicions of a deep human design—and above the bottom of the gateway project, in the most careless way, a few broad tropic leaves and brilliant flowers. All of a sudden, through this bright, bold gateway, you catch a glimpse of the faintest, softest, richest picture that ever graced the dream of a dying Saint, since John saw the New Jerusalem glimmering among the clouds of Heaven. A broad sweep of sea, flecked with careening sails; a sharp, jutting cape, and a lofty light house on it; a sloping lawn behind it; beyond, a portion of the old "city of palaces," with its parks and hills and stately mansions; beyond these, a prodigious mountain, with its strong outlines sharply cut against ocean and sky; and over all, vagrant shreds and flakes of cloud, floating in a sea of gold. The ocean is gold, the city is gold, the meadow, the mountain, the sky—everything is golden—rich, and mellow, and dreamy as a vision of Paradise. No artist could put upon canvas its entrancing beauty, and yet, without the yellow glass, and the carefully contrived accident of a framework that cast it into enchanted distance and shut out from it all unattractive features, it was not a picture to fall into ecstasies over. Such is life, and the trail of the serpent is over us all.

There is nothing for it now but to come back to old Tabor, though the subject is tiresome enough, and I cannot stick to it for wandering off to scenes that are pleasanter to remember. I think I will skip, anyhow. There is nothing about Tabor (except you concede that it was the scene of the Transfiguration,) but some rusty old ruins, stacked up there in all ages of the world from the days of General Gideon and parties that flourished thirty centuries ago to the fresh yesterday of Crusading times. It has its Greek Convent, and the coffee there is good, but never a splinter of the true cross or shin of a hallowed saint to arrest the idle thoughts of worldlings and turn them into graver channels. A church is nothing to me that has got no relics.

The plain of Esdraelon—"the battle-field of the nations"—only sets one to dreaming of Joshua, and Benhadad, and Saul, and Gideon; Tamerlane, Tancred, Cœur de Lion and Saladin; the warrior Kings of Persia, Egypt's heroes, and Napoleon. If the magic of the moonlight could summon from the graves of forgotten centuries and many lands the countless myriads that have battled on this wide, far-reaching floor, and array them in the thousand strange costumes of their hundred nationalities, and send the vast host sweeping down the plain, splendid with plumes and banners and glittering lances, I could stay here an age to see the phantom pageant. But the magic of the moonlight is a vanity and a swindle; and whoso putteth his trust in it shall fare no better than he that betteth his substance upon "deuces *and*" when the thing the worldling calleth a flush is out against him.

The Home of the Prodigal Son

Down at the foot of Tabor, and just at the edge of the storied Plain of Esdraelon, is the wretched little insignificant village of Deburich [Deburieh], where Deborah, prophetess of Israel, lived. It is as much like Magdala as one Chinaman is like another, and therefore has its mud-hovels reeking with filth, populous with cats and fleas, and seven kinds of lice, and hath also its strangely frescoed walls, and on its roofs the everlasting towers and turrets of ornamental ordure of beasts. As Deburich is now, so has it always been. Its men are lazy, its women are slovenly, its children have sore eyes. As in the days of old, the pensive youth, in curtailed shirt and naked shins, still breathes soft nothings in the ear of his adored, while she gathers her daily camel-dung and sorts it with a critical eye. I know, because I have seen the parties at it. Every day you see the young ladies of Palestine revelling in masses of the refuse of animals with their gentle hands and putting the treasure in baskets to be dried and used for fuel. I am susceptible, but even up to this very moment I have never taken what you might seriously regard as a shine to one of these young women. They are not fastidious enough for me. I may be too particular, but such is my bias, anyway.

However, I keep wandering from my subject, to-day, somehow. This Deburich is not handsome, but it is full of interest because of the fact that the Prodigal Son was born and raised here. His history is touching and suggestive. Few of your readers have ever heard of it, I suppose.

The Prodigal Son dwelt in the village of Deburich, ages and ages ago. His parents were very wealthy. They had three hundred goats, twelve camels, some donkeys and some horned cattle. Their mansion was like the mansion of a prince; and from its roof the fuel towered high aloft and filled the soul of every man with envy—yet, with admiration, likewise, and even hate, withal. In the mansion was there nothing lacking; there was a bowl and a spoon, and also a calabash. Yet were not these people proud. In that great mansion was room for the asses, and room for the men and room for the women-kind. All these things were before the Prodigal every day. From the days of his infancy naught knew he but luxury. He had two shirts that were his own—shirts that hung far down about his calves, and caused him to be admired by maidens, and even by the aged and the prophets. Elsewhere, in all the coasts of Galilee, was not another swell like unto him. When he passed by, all men bowed low, and said, Behold it is the rich man's son. He wrought not with his hands, yet every seventh day he ate of the broth of goat's meat and the luscious milk of asses. He lacked not anything that human heart could wish. But yet in elegant leisure and high living there is a bane that destroyeth happiness and maketh the cheerful spirit to droop. Wherefore, in the fulness of time, the Prodigal took to himself his share of his father's goods, and went away like many other foolish pilgrims, to travel and see strange lands that they know naught about, and are too stupid to learn.

So he journeyed to a far country and squandered his substance in riotous living. Strong drink betrayed his judgment, and in the end fell he a prey to the ravening tiger.

Then went he to the Publican that erst had welcomed him with joy and gladness, and said, Behold, thy servant is naked and hungry, and penniless, and like to die with thirst; open thy gates, I pray thee. But the Publican laughed him to scorn, and said, Get thee to honest labor —put shekels in thy purse.

So he wrought in the field for a hard master, and fain would have eaten the husks wherewith he fed the swine. At last he said, I have seen the great world, and it is deceitful and frought with sorrow. I will arise and go to my father. And when his father saw him afar off he ran and fell upon his neck and kissed him, and said, Bring forth the fatted calf and kill it, for my son that was lost is found. And he put a garment about his nakedness, and shoes upon his feet, and a ring upon his hand, and said, Let us feast and be merry. And when the Prodigal's brother heard these things, he said, I have labored for you faithfully, yet have you never given me a kid to make merry with my friends. And he liked it not.

I have said before, that a few days' sojourn in Syria and Palestine has given to Bible language a newer and fuller significance for me than it had before. I understand the Prodigal, now. They killed *the* fatted calf for him on this most momentous occasion that had ever happened in his father's family—showing that to have a fatted calf served up, was in all respects as grand a thing as a Shampagne blow-out is with us to-day. These present citizens of Palestine would so regard it at the present time. It is precious few of them that have got a fatted calf among their riches, and precious few that ever taste so great a luxury. I never could comprehend before why the old party, the Prodigal's father, laid so much stress on the fatted calf. The subject hardly seemed to me to warrant such a flourish as he gave to it. It sounded too much like Who cares for expenses? and then squandering forty cents. But truly I perceive now that the old man came down, to the most gorgeous tune that was possible to his gamut.

And the brother complained that he had never been given a kid, so that he could have a princely revel with his friends. The young Palestine gentleman of to-day fares no better. To give one of them a kid banquet would be to make him so airy and stuck up that there would be no such thing as living with him.

They gave the Prodigal "shoes"—worth a dollar and a half a

thousand, and yet more indulged in by villagers who are inclined to put on a good deal of style than any other. And they clothed the Prodigal. Yet if they gave him more than one suit it was an event worth recording particularly. The beaux of Palestine can seldom afford much fine raiment. Shirts are a trifle scarce.

When I was in Sunday School I always regarded that Prodigal Son as the stupidest youth that ever lived, to go away from his father's palace where he had a dozen courses for dinner, and wore handsome clothes, and had fast horses, and dogs, and plenty of money to spend, and could go to the circus whenever he wanted to (I had an idea that this was a peculiar privilege of rich men's sons all the world over), and travel off to some strange land and get swamped and have to feed hogs for a living. But I always rejoiced to think he went back home again, and I took pleasure in thinking he must have appreciated its riches and its luxury so unspeakably then. I could not understand the fatted calf, but I never allowed him to interfere materially with the unities of my romance. But my dream is over, now. It was just about an even matter between the Prodigal's two homes. If he had had a shirt and something to eat when he was feeding swine, the difference between that place and his old home would not have paid for the trouble of the journey back again—save that one was *home* and the other was not.

This letter, numbered thirty-eight by Twain, appeared in the *Daily Alta California* of February 9, 1868. It was used in Chapter XXII, immediately following Letter 43. "Got to" became "reached"; "weary of" became "surfeited with"; "broken by the modern artist" became "broken purposely by the modern artist"; "can never suggest" became "would never suggest"; "squirt" became "discharge"; "royal barges" became "patrician barges"; "among the clouds" became "above the clouds"; "rusty old ruins" became "gray old ruins"; "shin" became "bone"; and "has got" became "has." After "Napoleon," Twain added "for they all fought here." "Swindle" became "fraud." After "whoso putteth his trust in it shall," Twain deleted the remainder of the sentence and substituted for it "suffer sorrow and disappointment." "Wretched little insignificant" became "insignificant." For the sentence beginning "It is as much like Magdala as one Chinaman is like another," Twain substituted "It is just like Magdala," and he omitted the remainder of the letter (the story of the Prodigal Son).

45. Nazareth

Nazareth, September, 1867.

We descended from Mount Tabor, crossed a deep ravine, and followed a hilly, rocky, villainous road to Nazareth—distant two hours.

All distances in the east are measured by hours, not miles. A good horse will walk three miles an hour over nearly any kind of a road; therefore, an hour, here, always stands for three miles. This method of computation is bothersome and annoying; and until one gets thoroughly accustomed to it it seems to carry no intelligence to his mind until he has stopped and translated the pagan hours into Christian miles, just as people do with the spoken words of a foreign language they are acquainted with but not familiarly enough to catch the meaning in a moment. Distances travelled by human feet are also estimated by hours and minutes, though I do not know what the base of the calculation is. In Constantinople you ask "How far is it to the Consulate?" and they answer, "About ten minutes." "How far is it to the Lloyd's Agency?" "Quarter of an hour?" [*sic*] "How far is it to the lower bridge?" "Four minutes." I cannot be positive about it, but I think that there, when a man orders a pair of pantaloons, he says he wants them a quarter of a minute in the legs and nine seconds around the waist.

Two hours from Tabor to Nazareth—and as it was an uncommonly mean, narrow, crooked trail, we necessarily met all the camel trains and jackass caravans between Jericho and Jacksonville in that particular place and nowhere else. The donkeys do not matter so much, because they are so small you can jump your horse over them if he is an animal of spirit, but a camel is not jumpable. A camel is as tall as any ordinary dwelling house in Syria—which is to say a camel is from one to two, and sometimes nearly three feet taller than a good-sized man. In this part of the country his load is oftenest in the shape of colossal sacks—one on each side. He and his cargo take up as much room as a carriage. Think of meeting this style of obstruction in a narrow trail. The camel would not turn out for a King. He stalks serenely along, bringing his cushioned stilts forward with the long, regular swing of a pendulum, and whatever is in the way must get out of the way peaceably, or be wiped out forcibly by the bulky sacks. It was a tiresome ride to us, and perfectly exhausting to the horses. We were compelled to jump over upwards of eighteen hundred donkeys, and only one person in the party was unseated less than thirty-eight times by the camels. This seems like a powerful statement, but the poet has said "things are not what they seem." I cannot think of anything, now, more certain to make one shudder than to have a soft-footed camel sneak up behind him and touch him on the ear with its cold, flabby, hanging under-lip. A camel did this for one of the boys, who was drooping over his saddle in a brown study. He glanced up and saw the homely ostrich-head of the beast hovering above him, and made frantic efforts to get out of the way, but the camel reached out and bit him on the shoulder before he accomplished it. This was the only pleasant incident of the journey. It is soothing yet, to think of that majestic apparition sending Jack's heart to his boots with the touch of its clammy lips.

More Enlightenment

We camped in an olive grove near the Virgin Mary's fountain, and that wonderful Arab "guard" came to collect some bucksheesh for his "services" in following us from Tiberias and warding off invisible dangers with the terrors of his armament. The dragoman had paid his master, but that counted as nothing—if you hire a man to smile on you, here, and another man chooses to help him, you have to pay both. They do nothing whatever without pay. More Scriptural significance! How it must have astounded these vagrants to hear the way of salvation offered to them *"without money and without price!"* If the manners, the people or the customs of this country have changed in any respect since the Savior's time, the figures and metaphors of the Bible are not the evidence to prove it by. It is pretty safe, no doubt, to believe that from Abraham's time till now, Palestine has been peopled only with ignorant, degraded, lazy, unwashed loafers and savages. Arabs they were, they are, and always will be. Palestine would be part of Arabia but for an invisible boundary line that men have drawn on maps—God and nature have drawn no such lines. The countries are one, in that they breed people of like instincts, like customs, complexions, trains of thought and manners. The pure, unadulterated Arab nature crops out all through the Israelitish tribes of Old Testament history. The difference between a prowling varlet of an Arab of to-day and an Israelite of old amounts to nothing more, perhaps, than that you spell the nationality of the one with four letters and of the other with nine.

The City of Nazareth

We paid the bucksheesh and discharged our gunboat just at the very time that he might have begun to be useful, if it were possible for such an epoch as that to break the monotony of his worthless career. A glance at the population of Nazareth must surely suggest that a military escort would not be out of place here. Dirt and rags and squalor; vermin, hunger and wretchedness; savage costumes, savage weapons and looks of hate—these are the things that meet one at every step in Nazareth. Magdala is a miracle of barbarous degradation; Nazareth is worse. Here, numbers of the habitations are mere mud cones, like a magnified bee-hive; they have dirt floors of course; there is a small hole for entrance and exit, and this hole must do duty also as window and chimney; that there is room for a man to stretch out or stand up, inside, does not seem possible. Around the front of the hovel is a mangy pack of ragged, sore-eyed children, turbaned, dilapidated men, and scurvy women who a blessed instinct has taught to hide their criminal ugliness behind a veil, though even their bodies be not wholly concealed; all interstices among the group are filled with hungry dogs and cadaverous cats, and its circumference bounded by reclining camels and pensive donkeys. The streets are usually not wider than a double bed, and reek with an affluence of filth and abomination that surely cannot exist elsewhere unless it be in perdition itself. It would be foolish *now* to wonder that the ancients said, "Can any good thing come out of Nazareth?" This is altogether the most unpromising place to expect a good thing to come from that occurs to my mind just now.

Grotto of the Annunciation

We waded through, however, and entered the great Latin Convent which is built over the traditional dwelling place of the Holy Family. We went down a flight of fifteen steps below the ground level, and stood in a small chapel tricked out with tapestry hangings, silver lamps, and oil paintings. A spot marked by a cross, in the marble floor, under the altar, was exhibited as the place made forever holy by the feet of the Virgin when she stood up to receive the message of the angel. So simple, so unpretending a locality, to be the scene of so mighty an event! The very scene of the Annunciation—an event which has been commemorated by splendid shrines and august temples all over the civilized world, and one which the princes of art have made it their loftiest ambition to picture worthily on their canvas; a spot whose history is familiar to the very children of every house, and city, and obscure hamlet of the remotest lands of Christendom; a spot which myriads of men would toil across the breadth of a Continent to see—would consider it a priceless privilege to look upon. It was easy to think these thoughts. But it was not easy to bring myself up to the magnitude of the situation. I could sit off several thousand miles and imagine the angel appearing, with shadowy wings and lustrous countenance, and note the glory that streamed downward upon the Virgin's head while the message from the Throne of God fell upon her ears—any one can do that, but few can do it here. I saw the little recess from which the angel stepped, but could not fill its void. The angels that I know are creatures of unstable fancy—they will not fit in niches of substantial stone. Imagination labors best in distant fields. I doubt if any man can stand in this Grotto of the Annunciation and people with the phantom images of his mind its too tangible walls of stone.

They showed us a broken granite pillar, depending from the roof, which they said was hacked in two by the Moslem conquerors of Nazareth, in the vain hope of pulling down the sanctuary. But the pillar remained miraculously suspended in the air, and, unsupported itself, supported then and still supports the roof. By dividing this statement up among eight, it was found not difficult to believe it. I could have believed the whole of it by myself, no doubt, if I had been well.

The "Grotto" Business

Mind you, these gifted Latin monks never do anything by halves. If they were to show you the Brazen Serpent that was elevated in the wilderness, you could wager all you are worth that they had on hand the pole it was elevated on also, and even the hole it stood in. They have got the "Grotto" of the Annunciation here; and just as convenient to it as one's throat is to his mouth, they have got also the Virgin's Kitchen, and even her sitting-room, where she and Joseph watched the infant Savior play with Hebrew toys eighteen hundred years ago. All under one roof, and all clean, spacious, comfortable "grottoes." It seems funny that personages intimately connected with the Holy Family always lived in grottoes—in Nazareth, in Bethlehem, in imperial Ephesus—and yet nobody else in their day and generation thought of doing anything of the kind. If they ever did, their grottoes are all gone, and I suppose we ought to wonder at the peculiar marvel of the preservation of these I speak of. When the Virgin fled from

Herod's wrath, she hid in a grotto in Bethlehem, and the same is there to this day. The slaughter of the innocents in Bethlehem was done in a grotto; the Savior was born in a grotto—both are shown to pilgrims yet. It is exceedingly strange that these tremendous events all happened in grottoes—and exceedingly fortunate, likewise, because the strongest houses must crumble to ruin in time, but a grotto in the living rock will last forever. It is a swindle—this grotto stuff—but it is one that all men ought to thank the Catholics for. Wherever they ferret out a lost locality made holy by some scriptural event, they straightway build a massive—almost imperishable church there, and preserve the memory of that locality for the gratification of future generations. If it had been left to Protestants to do this most worthy work, we wouldn't even know where Jesusalem is to-day, and the man that could go and put his finger on delectable Nazareth would be too wise for this world. The world owes the Catholics its good will even for the happy rascality of hewing out these bogus grottoes in the rock; for it is infinitely more satisfactory to look at a grotto, where people have faithfully believed for centuries that the Virgin once lived, than to have to imagine a dwelling place for her somewhere, anywhere, nowhere, loose and at large all over this town of Nazareth. There is too large a scope of country. The imagination cannot work. If you were to select an imperishable boulder in the Bay of San Francisco, and prove by imaginary ancient MSS. that that was the identical boulder on which stout Sir Francis Drake stepped when he landed there in old Elizabeth's time, and so label it, an interest would spring up about that spot that would live for ages, and breed more poetry, and magazine romances, and grave historical disquisitions about Sir Francis and the "early days" he found on our coast, than would fill a library. But with the whole sweep of the Bay to devote to the old navigator, the thing is too much diffused. There is no one particular spot to chain your eye, rivet your interest and make you think. The old monks are wise. They know how to drive a stake through a pleasant tradition that will hold it to its place forever.

This letter, numbered thirty-nine by Twain, appeared in the *Daily Alta California* of February 16, 1868. It was used at the beginning of Chapter XXIII. "Hilly, rocky, villainous" became "hilly, rocky"; "seems to carry" became "carries"; "mean, narrow, crooked" became "narrow, crooked"; "thirty-eight" became "sixty"; "cold, flabby, hanging" became "cold, flabby"; and "homely ostrich-head of the beast" became "majestic apparition." The sentence beginning "It is soothing yet" was deleted. "Smile on" became "sneeze for." "More Scriptural significance" was deleted. "Astounded these vagrants" became "surprised these people." The sentence beginning "It is pretty safe, no doubt, to believe" and the remainder of the paragraph were deleted. Also deleted was the long paragraph headed "The City of Nazareth." "Remotest" became "furthest" and "continent" became "world." "Beyond the ocean" was deleted. The sentence beginning "I could have believed the whole of it by myself" was deleted. "Wager all you are worth" became "depend upon it"; "have got also" became "have also"; "funny" became "curious," and "swindle" became "imposture." After "The imagination cannot work," Twain deleted the next 106 words. After "rivet your interest and make you think," Twain inserted a sentence about Plymouth Rock.

46. Jezreel and Samaria

At Large in Palestine, September, 1867.

As we trotted across the Plain of Jezred [Jezreel], we met half a dozen Digger Indians (Bedouins,) with very long spears in their hands, cavorting around on old crowbait horses, and spearing imaginary enemies; whooping, and fluttering their rags in the wind, and carrying on in every respect like a pack of hopeless lunatics. At last, here were the "wild, free sons of the desert, speeding over the plain like the wind, on their beautiful Arabian mares" we had read so much about and longed so much to see! Here were the "picturesque costumes!" This was the "gallant spectacle!" Tatterdemalion vagrants—pitiful braggadocio—"Arabian mares" spined and necked like the ichthyosaurus in the museum, and humped and cornered like a dromedary! To glance at the genuine son of the desert is to take the romance out of him forever—to behold his steed is to long in charity to strip his harness off and let him fall to pieces.

Thus, one by one, the splendid attractions of Palestine are passing away—gradually, but surely, the paint and the gilding are peeling from its cheap theatrical scenery and exposing the unsightly boards beneath.

Jezreel—or, Logansport

Presently we came to a ruinous old buzzard-roost on a hill, the same being the ancient Jezreel of Bible fame. I am sorry your readers are not acquainted with the history of this place, for then it would not be necessary for me to relate it.

Ahab, King of Samaria (this was a very vast Kingdom, for those days, and was very nearly as large as an ordinary county in the States,) dwelt in the city of Jezreel, which was his capital. Near him lived a man by the name of Naboth—no first name given—John W. Naboth will answer as well as any—and this man had a vineyard. The King asked him for it, and when he would not give it, offered to trade for it, or even buy it at thirty days. But Naboth declined. In those days it was considered a sort of crime to part with one's inheritance at any price—and even if a man did part with it, it reverted to himself or his heirs again at the next jubilee year. So this spoiled child of a King went and pouted over it, and lay down on the bed with his face to the wall, and would not take his regular squills. The Queen, a notorious character in those days, and whose name is a byword and a reproach even in these, came in and asked him wherefore he had renigged, and he told her. Jezebel said that if that was all, she could fix it; and she went forth and forged letters to the nobles and wise men, in the King's name, and ordered them to proclaim a fast and set Naboth on high before the people, and suborn two witnesses to swear that he had blasphemed. They did it, and the people stoned the accused by the city wall, and he died. Then Jezebel came and told the King, and said, Behold, the defendant is no more—rise up and confiscate the vineyard. So Ahab confiscated the vineyard, and went into it to possess it. But the Prophet Elijah came to him there and read his fate to him, and the fate of Jezebel; and said that in the place where dogs licked the blood of Naboth, dogs should also lick his blood—and he said, likewise, the dogs shall eat Jezebel by the wall of Jezreel. In the course of time, the King was killed in battle, and when his chariot wheels were washed in the pool of Samaria, the dogs licked the blood. In after years a gentleman by the name of Jehu, who was King of Israel, marched down against Jezreel, by order of one of the Prophets, and administered one of those mild rebukes so common among the chosen, the highly-favored Israelites, to wit, he finished up a gang of kings and other people, and as he came along he saw Jezebel, painted and tricked out in her finery, looking out of a window, and ordered that she be thrown down to him. An obliging servant did it, and Jehu's horse trampled her under foot. Then Jehu went in and sat down to dinner; and presently he said, Go and bury this cursed woman, for she is a King's daughter. The spirit of politeness came upon him too late, however, for the prophecy had already been fulfilled—the dogs had eaten her, and they "found no more of her than the skull, and the feet, and the palms of her hands." They were such nice, cheerful people, those those [sic] Israelites. Ahab, the late King, had left a helpless family behind him—not a large one for those days, but still enough to adorn a fireside—and Jehu, the King, waltzed into that nursery and scalped seventy of those orphans and otherwise made an end of them. Then he killed all the relatives, and teachers, and servants and friends of the family, and rested from his labors, until he was come near to Samaria, where he met forty-two persons and asked them who they were; they said they were brothers of the King of Judah. To speak after the manner of the vulgar, that let them out. When he got to Samaria, he said he would show his zeal for the Lord; so he gathered all the priests and people together that worshiped Baal, pretending that he was going to join that Church and offer up a great sacrifice; and when they were all shut up where they could not defend themselves, he caused every person of them to be slain. It was better than a circus—much better. Then Jehu, the missionary, rested from his labors once more. He knew how to discourage opposition to the true religion.

"If You Belonged to Gideon's Band"

We went back to the valley, and rode to the Fountain of Ain Jelüd, or Jacksonville, whichever you like best. They call it the Fountain of Jezreel, usually. It is a pond about one hundred feet square and two feet deep, with a stream of water trickling into it from under an overhanging ledge of rocks. It is in the midst of a great solitude. Here Gideon pitched his camp in the old times; behind Shunem lay the "Midianites, the Amalekites, and the Children of the East," who were "as grasshoppers for multitude; both they and their camels were without number, as the sand by the sea-side for multitude." Which means that there were 135,000 men, and that they had transportation service accordingly.

Gideon had only 32,000 men, mostly Home Guard material, no doubt, because when he proclaimed that all those who were cowardly and wanted to go home might go, 22,000 packed their trunks and left. Gideon was instructed that even a further sifting would help the army in the same way, and he made his remaining 10,000 step up to the pool and drink. He had a keen eye for a man without enterprise, and every one that got down on his knees to drink, he paid off and discharged.

Those that dipped up the water in their hands and drank, he retained. This reduced his army to 300 men! He stopped then. He judged that it was not best to go on sifting any more. (The present inhabitants of the country must be a more soldierly-style of people than their ancestors, for they always scoop up the water in their paws and "lap it like a dog.")

Then at dead of night Gideon placed a trumpet in each man's right hand, and a pitcher with a lamp in it in his left, and dividing the little army into three companies of a hundred men each, went softly and surrounded the vast camp of the Children of the East. It is likely that they would have to stand pretty wide apart to do it. At a given signal every man broke his pitcher and tooted his horn; the crash of the crockery awoke the sleeping army, the flash of the exposed lamps dazzled and bewildered them, the chorus of the trumpets made them think a great host had surprised them (they kept no scouts, perhaps, and did not know whether there were armies in their neighborhood or not,) and in the excitement of the time they fell to work and slaughtered each other, while Gideon's band stood still and said never a word. A hundred and twenty thousand of the enemy perished on the field, and Gideon chased the other fifteen thousand out of the country. Your readers will regard these statements as extravagant, but they are attested in the official reports of the battle.

Of all the unheard-of military stratagems ever invented, this of Gideon's was probably the wildest the world has any knowledge of. Considering the astonishing success which distinguished it, it is amazing that no General has ever been shrewd enough to try it since. The commonest sagacity, it would seem, ought to have caused it to be adopted into all codes of military tactics long ago.

Samaria

We camped at Jenin before night, and got up and started again at one o'clock in the morning. Somewhere towards daylight we passed the locality where the best authenticated tradition locates the pit into which Joseph's brethren threw him, and about noon, after passing over a succession of mountain tops, clad with groves of figs and olive trees, with the Mediterranean in sight some forty miles away, and going by many ancient Biblical cities whose inhabitants glowered savagely upon our Christian procession, and were inclined to practice on it with stones, we came to the singularly terraced and unlovely hills that betrayed that we were out of Galilee and into Samaria at last.

We climbed a high hill to visit the city of Samaria, where the woman may have hailed from who conversed with Christ at Jacob's Well, and from whence, no doubt, came also the celebrated Good Samaritan, who was probably the only good Samaritan the province ever produced. Herod the Great is said to have made a magnificent city of this villainous place, and a lot of coarse, ugly limestone columns, twenty feet high and two feet through, that are guiltless of all architectural grace of shape and ornament, are exultingly pointed out by many authors as evidence of the fact. They would not have been considered worthy to build chicken coops of in ancient Greece. They are gay for Israel, though.

The inhabitants of this camp are particularly vicious, and stoned two parties of our pilgrims a day or two ago who brought about the difficulty by showing their revolvers when they did not intend to use them—a thing which is deemed bad judgment in California.

There was nothing to do here but buy handfuls of old Roman coins at a cent a grab, and look at a dilapidated church of the Crusaders and a vault in it which once contained the body of John the Baptist. This relic was long ago carried away, and we had seen fragments of it many times before, more particularly in Genoa, where they have secured a commanding interest of the Saint and keep the same in a chapel in the Church of the Annunciation—a sanctum which women are allowed to visit only once a year, because it was to please one of the sex that John was beheaded.

Samaria stood a heavy siege, once, in the days of Elisha, at the hands of the King of Syria. Provisions reached such a figure that "an ass' head was sold for eighty pieces of silver and the fourth part of a cab of dove's dung for five pieces of silver."

An incident recorded of that heavy time will give one a very good idea of the distress that prevailed within these crumbling walls. As the King was walking upon the battlements one day, "a woman cried out, saying, Help, my lord, O King! And the King said, What aileth thee? and she answered, This woman said unto me, Give thy son, that we may eat him to-day, and we will eat my son to-morrow. So we boiled my son, and did eat him; and I said unto her on the next day, Give thy son that we may eat him; and she hath hid her son."

Maternal love, that sentiment that clings to its object through joy and sorrow, from the cradle even unto the grave, was proof against the claims of justice, and at the critical moment scorned the sacred rights of hospitality. This love rose up before the fond, sad mother, and she would not boil her son.

The prophet Elisha declared that within four and twenty hours the market rates for provisions should go down to nothing, almost, and it was so. The Syrian army broke camp and fled, for some cause or other, the famine was relieved from without, and many a shoddy speculator in dove's dung and ass's meat was ruined. But I can't go on finding out things and telling them to your subscribers all night.

We were glad to leave this hot and dusty old village and hurry on. At two o'clock we stopped to lunch and rest at ancient Shechem, between the historic Mounts of Gerizim and Ebal, where in the old times the books of the law, the curses and the blessings, were read from the heights to the Jewish multitudes below. Amen.

This letter, numbered forty-three by Twain, appeared in the *Daily Alta California* of February 23, 1868. It was used at the end of Chapter XXIV. "Pitiful braggadocio" became "cheap braggadocio." The short paragraph beginning "Thus, one by one" was deleted. "Buzzard-roost" became "town." After "the same being the ancient Jezreel," Twain deleted the next twenty-nine words. "As large as an ordinary county in the States" became "half as large as Rhode Island." Twain deleted "no first name given—John W. Naboth will answer as well as any—and this man" and inserted "who." "Trade for it, or even buy it at thirty days" became "buy it"; "declined" became "refused to sell it"; and "and pouted over it" was deleted. "Would not take his regular squills" became "grieved sorely."

"Had renigged" became "sorrowed"; "that if that was all, she could fix it" became "she could secure the vineyard"; "the defendant is no more—rise up and confiscate" became "Naboth is no more—rise up and seize"; "a gentleman by the name of Jehu" became "Jehu"; "mild rebukes" became "convincing rebukes"; "the chosen, the highly-favored Israelites, to wit, he finished up a gang of kings and other people" became "the people of those days: he killed many kings and their subjects"; "tricked out in her finery" became "finely dressed"; "obliging servant" became "servant"; and "spirit of politeness" became "spirit of charity." The sentence beginning "They were such nice, cheerful people" was deleted. After "Ahab, the late King, had left a helpless family behind him," Twain deleted the next thirty-five words and substituted for them "and Jehu killed seventy of the orphan sons." "He killed them" was substituted for "To speak after the manner of the vulgar, that let them out." "Join that church" became "adopt that worship," and "slain" became "killed." "It was better than a circus—much better" was deleted. "Missionary" became "good missionary." The sentence beginning "He knew how to discourage opposition" was deleted, and also deleted was "or Jacksonville, whichever you like best." "Two feet deep" became "four feet deep."

Twain deleted the paragraph beginning "Gideon had only 32,000 men" and the next two paragraphs—totaling 419 words—and substituted for them a paragraph of thirty-three words. "Were inclined" became "were seemingly inclined." After "Good Samaritan," Twain deleted the remainder of the sentence. "This villainous place" became "this place"; "a lot of course, ugly" became "a great number of coarse";

"guiltless of all" became "almost guiltless of"; "exultingly pointed out" became "pointed out"; "worthy to build chicken coops of in ancient Greece. They are gay for Israel, though" became "handsome in ancient Greece, however"; "deemed bad judgment in California" became "deemed bad judgment in the Far West"—and at this point Twain inserted forty-eight words. "A cent a grab" became "a franc a dozen." After "This relic was long ago carried away," Twain deleted the next sixty-two words and substituted for them "to Genoa." "Heavy siege" became "disastrous siege." The paragraph beginning "Maternal love" was deleted, and the sentence beginning "But I can't go on finding out things" was deleted also.

47. A Curious Remnant of the Past

Jerusalem, September, 1867.

The narrow cañon in which Nablous, or Shechem, is situated, is under high cultivation, and the soil is exceedingly black and fertile. It ought to be so, for it throws all Holy Land writers into spasms of admiration. It is well watered, and its affluent vegetation gains effect by contrast with the barren hills that tower on either side. One of these hills is the ancient Mount of Blessings and the other the Mount of Curses; and wise men who go about seeking for fulfilments of prophecy think they find here a wonder of this kind—to-wit, that the Mount of Blessings is strangely fertile and its mate is strangely unproductive. We could not see that there was much difference between them in this respect—what there was, however, was manifestly in favor of the Hill of Curses.

Shechem is distinguished as one of the residents of the patriarch Jacob; and as the seat of those tribes that cut themselves loose from their brethren of Israel and propagated doctrines not in conformity with those of the original Jewish creed. For thousands of years this clan have dwelt in Shechem under strict *tabu,* and having little commerce or fellowship with their fellow men of any religion or nationality. For generations they have not numbered more than one or two hundred, but they still adhere to their ancient faith and maintain their ancient rites and ceremonies. Talk of family and old descent! Princes and nobles pride themselves upon lineages they can trace back some hundreds of years. What is this trifle to this handful of old first families of Shechem, who can name their fathers straight back without a flaw for thousands—straight back to a period so remote that men reared in a country where the days of two hundred years ago are called "ancient" times grow dazed and bewildered when they try to comprehend it! Here is respectability for your [you]—here is "family"—here is high descent worth talking about. This sad, proud remnant of a once mighty community still hold themselves aloof from all the world; they still live as their fathers lived, labored as their fathers labored, think as they did, feel as they did, worship in the same place, in sight of the same landmarks, and in the same quaint, patriarchal way their ancestors did more than thirty centuries ago. I found myself gazing at any straggling scion of this strange race with a riveted fascination, just as one would stare at a living mastodon, or a megatherium that had moved in the grey dawn of creation and seen the wonders of that mysterious world that was before the flood.

Carefully preserved among the sacred archives of this curious community is a MSS. copy of the ancient Jewish law, which is said to be the oldest document on earth. It is written on vellum, and is some four or five thousand years old. Nothing but bucksheesh can purchase a sight. Its fame is somewhat dimmed, in these latter days, because of the doubts so many authors of Palestine travels have felt themselves privileged to cast upon it. Speaking of this MSS. reminds me that I procured from the high-priest of this ancient Samaritan community, at great expense, a secret document of still higher antiquity and far more extraordinary interest, which I propose to publish as soon as I have finished translating it. The main object of my pilgrimage to the Holy Land was to get hold of this priceless record of a forgotten age of the world.

Joshua gave his dying injunction to the children of Israel at Shechem, and buried a vast treasure secretly under an oak tree there about the same time. Part of my errand to Palestine was to prospect for that jewelry, also, but I could not find it.

Joseph's Tomb

About a mile and a half from Shechem we halted at the base of Mount Ebal, before a little square area, inclosed by a high stone wall, neatly whitewashed. Across one end of this inclosure is a tomb built after the manner of the Moslems. It is the tomb of Joseph. No truth is better authenticated than this.

When Joseph was dying he prophesied that exodus of the Israelites from Egypt which occurred four hundred years afterwards. At the same time he exacted of his people an oath that when they journeyed to the land of Canaan, they would bear his bones with them and bury them in the ancient inheritance of his fathers. The oath was kept.

"And the bones of Joseph, which the children of Israel brought up out of Egypt, buried they in Shechem, in a parcel of ground which Jacob bought of the sons of Hamor the father of Shechem, for a hundred pieces of silver."

Few tombs on earth command the veneration of so many races and men of divers creeds as this of Joseph. "Samaritan and Jew, Moslem and Christian alike, revere it, and honor it with their visits. The tomb of Joseph, the dutiful son, the affectionate, forgiving brother, the virtuous man, the wise Prince and ruler. Egypt felt his influence —the world knows his history."

Jacob's Well

In this same "parcel of ground" which Jacob bought of the sons of Hamor for a hundred pieces of silver and paid at least a hundred times too much for it, is Jacob's celebrated well. It is cut in the solid rock, and is nine feet square and ninety feet deep. The name of this unpretending hole in the ground, which one might pass by and take no notice of, is as familiar as household words to even the children and the peasants of many a far-off country. It is more famous than the Parthenon, it is older than the Pyramids.

It was by this well that Jesus sat and talked with a woman of that strange, antiquated Samaritan community I have been speaking of, and told her of the mysterious water of life. As descendants of old English nobles still cherish in the traditions of their houses how that this king or that king tarried a day with some favored ancestor three hundred years ago, no doubt the descendants of the woman of Samaria, living there in Shechem, still refer with pardonable vanity to this conversation of their ancestor, held some little time gone by, with the Messiah of the Christians. It is not likely that they undervalue a distinction such as this. Samaritan nature is human nature, and human nature remembers contact with the illustrious, always.

For an offence done to the family honor, the sons of Jacob exterminated all Shechem once—but, as I have remarked before, what is the use of my sitting up nights to find out things if I am to squander all the information so obtained immediately? I will husband some of it for another day. Very few people know anything about the matters I am instructing your readers in. I know very well how to appreciate the value of what I am doing.

Camping with the Arabs

We left Jacob's Well and travelled till 8 in the evening, but rather slowly, for we had been in the saddle nineteen hours, and the horses were cruelly tired. We got so far ahead of the tents that we had to camp in an Arab village, and sleep on the ground. We could have slept in the largest of the houses, but there were some little drawbacks; it was populous with vermin, it had a dirt floor, it was in no respect cleanly, and there was a family of goats in the only bedroom, and two donkeys in the parlor. Outside there were no inconveniences, except that the dusky, ragged, earnest-eyed villagers of both sexes and all ages grouped themselves on their haunches all around us, and discussed us and criticized us with noisy tongues till midnight. We did not mind the noise, being tired, but, doubtless, you know that it is almost an impossible thing to go to sleep when you know that people are looking at you. We went to bed at ten, and got up again at two and started once more. Thus are people persecuted by dragomen, whose sole ambition in life is to get ahead of each other.

About daylight we passed Shiloh, where the Ark of the Covenant rested three hundred years, and at whose gates good old Eli fell down and "brake his neck" when the messenger, riding hard from the battle, told him of the defeat of his people, the death of his sons, and, more than all, the capture of Israel's pride, her hope, her refuge, the ancient ark her forefathers brought with them out of Egypt. It is little wonder that under circumstances like these he fell down and brake his neck. But Shiloh had no charms for us. We were so cold that there was no comfort but in motion, and so drowsy we could hardly sit upon the horses.

Jacob's Ladder, etc.

After a while we came to a shapeless mass of ruins, which still bears the name of Beth-el. It was here that Jacob lay down and had that superb vision of angels flitting up and down a ladder that reached from the clouds to earth, and caught glimpses of their blessed home through the open gates of Heaven.

The pilgrims took what was left of the hallowed ruin, and we pressed on toward the goal of our crusade, renowned Jerusalem.

The further we went the hotter the sun got, and the more rocky and bare, repulsive and dreary the landscape became. There could not have been more fragments of stone strewn broadcast over this part of the world, if every ten square feet of the land had been occupied by a separate and distinct stone-cutter's establishment for an age. There was hardly a tree or a shrub anywhere. Even the olive and the cactus, those fast friends of a worthless soil, had almost deserted the country. No landscape exists that is more tiresome to the eye than that which bounds the approaches to Jerusalem. The only difference between the roads and the surrounding country, perhaps, is that there are rather more rocks in the roads than in the surrounding country.

We passed Ramah, and Beroth, and on the right saw the tomb of the prophet Samuel, perched high upon a commanding eminence. Still no Jerusalem came in sight. We hurried on impatiently. We halted a moment at the ancient Fountain of Beira, but its stones, worn deeply by the chafing chins of a hundred generations of thirsty horses, had no interest for us—we longed to see Jerusalem. We spurred up hill after hill, and usually began to stretch our necks minutes before we got to the top—but disappointment always followed:—more stupid hills beyond—more unsightly landscape—no Holy City.

The Pilgrimage Accomplished

At last, away in the middle of the day, ancient bits of wall and crumbling arches began to line the way—we toiled up one more hill, and every pilgrim and every sinner swung his hat on high. Jerusalem!

Perched on its eternal hills, white and domed and solid, massed together and hooped with high gray walls, the venerable city gleamed in the sun. So small! Why, it was no larger than an American village of four thousand inhabitants, and no larger than an ordinary Syrian city of thirty thousand. Jerusalem numbers only fourteen thousand people.

We dismounted and looked, with very few words of conversation, across the wide intervening valley for an hour or more; and noted those prominent features of the city that pictures make familiar to all men from their school days till their death. We could recognize the Tower of Hippicus, the Mosque of Omar, the Damascus Gate, the Mount of Olives, the Valley of Jehoshaphat, the Tower of David and the Garden of Gethsemane—and dating from these landmarks could tell very nearly the localities of many others we were not able to distinguish.

I record it here as a notable but not discreditable fact that not even our pilgrims wept. I think there was no individual in the party whose brain was not teeming with thoughts and images and memories invoked by the grand history of the venerable city that lay before us, but still among them all was no "voice of them that wept." I suppose it was the only detachment that ever entered Jerusalem without crying about it. I have read all the books on Palestine, nearly, that have been printed, and the authors all wept. When Mr. Prime was here, before he wrote his curious "Tent Life in the Holy Land," he wept, and his party all wept, and the dragoman wept, and so did the muleteers, and even a Latin priest, and a Jew that came straggling along. It would have been just as cheap to believe that the camels and the asses wept also, and fully as likely; and he might as well have added them to the water company likewise. Prime got such a start then that he never could shut himself off; and he went through Palestine and irrigated it from one end to the other. No man was ever so easily affected as he, probably. Whenever he found a holy place that was well authenticated, he cried; whenever he found one that was not well authenticated, he cried anyhow, and took the chances; whenever he couldn't find any holy place at all, he just cried "for a flyer," as the wordly [worldly] say. No man ever enjoyed a funeral as Prime did his Sentimental Journey through the Holy Land. How his horse ever kept his health, being exposed to these periodical showers all the time, is a wonder. I never will believe anybody again that says he cried over Jerusalem; the book-makers have created within me a bitter animosity against these boastful Jerusalem-weepers and also a lack of faith in them. If ever a party were peculiarly liable to tears, under such circumstances, it is our pilgrims. They are the very boys to go into sentimental convulsions at the merest shadow of a provocation. Yet they wept not over Jerusalem.

Just after noon we entered these narrow, crooked streets, by the ancient and the famed Damascus Gate, and now for several hours I have been trying to comprehend that I am actually in the illustrious old city where Solomon dwelt and Jesus was crucified, and have not succeeded. And never shall. I know that well enough.

This letter, numbered forty-four by Twain, appeared in the *Daily Alta California* of March 1, 1868. It became Chapter XXV of Volume II. The sentence beginning "It ought to be so" was deleted. "Go about seeking" became "seek," and "much difference" became "really much difference." After "in this respect," Twain inserted "however" and deleted the remainder of the sentence. The sentence beginning "The main object of my pilgrimage" was deleted. The sentence beginning "Part of my errand to Palestine" was deleted and two sentences were substituted for it. "And paid at least a hundred times too much for it" was deleted. The passage beginning with "but, as I have remarked before" and extending to the end of the paragraph was deleted. "Chafing chins of a hundred generations of thirsty horses" became "chins of thirsty animals that are dead and gone centuries ago," and "with very few words of conversation" became "without speaking a dozen sentences."

For the passage beginning "I suppose it was the only detachment that ever entered Jerusalem" and extending to the end of the paragraph (302 words), Twain substituted a short paragraph (forty-one words) more appropriate to the subject. The concluding words of the letter, "and Jesus was crucified, and have not succeeded. And never shall. I know that well enough" became "where Abraham held converse with the Deity, and where walls still stand that witnessed the spectacle of the Crucifixion."

48. Exploring Jerusalem

Jerusalem, September, 1867.

A FAST WALKER could go outside the walls of Jerusalem and walk entirely around the city in an hour. I do not know how else to make one understand how small it is. The appearance of the city is peculiar. It is as knobby with countless little domes as a prison door is with bolt-heads. Every house has from one to half-a-dozen of these white plastered domes of stone, broad and low, sitting in the centre of, or in a cluster upon, the flat roof. Wherefore, when one looks down from an eminence, upon the compact masses of houses (so closely crowded together, in fact, that there is no appearance of streets at all, and so it looks solid), he sees the knobbiest town in the world, except Constantinople. It looks as if it might be roofed, from centre to circumference, with inverted saucers. The monotony of the view is interrupted only by the great Mosque of Omar, the Tower of Hippicus, and one or two other buildings that rise into commanding prominence.

The houses are generally two stories high, built strongly of masonry, whitewashed or plastered outside, and have a cage of wooden latticework projecting in front of every window. To reproduce a Jerusalem street, it would only be necessary to up-end a chicken-coop and hang it before each window in a row of American houses.

The streets are roughly and badly paved with stone, and are tolerably crooked—enough so to make each street appear to close together constantly and come to an end about a hundred yards ahead of a pilgrim as long as he chooses to walk in it. Projecting from the top of the lower story of many of the houses is a very narrow porch-roof or shed, without supports from below; and I have several times seen cats jump across the street from one shed to the other when they were out calling. The cats could have jumped double the distance without extraordinary exertion. I mention these things to give one an idea of how narrow the streets are. Since a cat can jump across them without the least inconvenience, I suppose it will not be worth while for me to state that such streets are too narrow for carriages. These vehicles can not navigate the Holy City.

The population of Jerusalem is composed of Moslems, Jews, Greeks, Latins, Armenians, Syrians, Copts, Abyssinians, Greek Catholics, and a handful of Christians. One hundred of the latter sect are all that dwell now in this birthplace of Christianity. The nationalities of the above list of sects, and the languages spoken by them, are altogether too numerous to mention. It seems to me that all the races and colors and tongues of the earth must be represented among the 14,000 souls that dwell in Jerusalem. Rags, wretchedness, poverty and dirt, those signs and symbols that indicate the presence of Moslem rule more surely than the Crescent flag itself, abound. Lepers, cripples, the blind, and the idiotic, assail you on every hand, and they know but one word of but one language—the eternal "bucksheesh." To see the numbers of maimed, malformed and diseased humanity that throng the holy places and obstruct the gates, one might suppose that the ancient days had come again, and that the angel of the Lord was expected to arrive at any moment to stir the waters of Bethesda. Jerusalem is mournful, and dreary, and lifeless. I would not desire to live here.

The Holy Sepulchre

One naturally goes first to the Holy Sepulchre. It is right in the city, near the western gate; it and the place of the Crucifixion, and, in fact, every other place intimately connected with that tremendous event, are ingeniously massed together and covered by one roof—the dome of the Church of the Holy Sepulchre.

Entering the building, through the midst of the usual assemblage of beggars, one sees on his left a few Turkish guards—for Christians of different sects will not only quarrel, but fight, also, in this sacred place, if allowed to do it. Before you is a marble slab, which covers the Stone of Unction, whereon the Saviour's body was laid to prepare it for burial. It was found necessary to conceal the real stone in this way in order to save it from destruction. Pilgrims were too much given to chipping off pieces of it to carry home. Ours were disappointed—none of them have got a fragment of this famous stone. Near by is a circular railing which marks the spot where the Virgin stood when the Lord's body was anointed.

Entering the great Rotunda, we stand before the most sacred locality in Christendom—the grave of Jesus. It is in the centre of the church, and immediately under the great dome. It is inclosed in a sort of little temple of yellow and white stone, of fanciful design. Within the little temple is a portion of the very stone which was rolled away from the door of the Sepulchre, and on which the angel was sitting when Mary came thither "at early dawn." The stone *was* there, at any rate, day before yesterday. Our pilgrims have been there since. Stooping low, we enter the vault—the Sepulchre itself. It is only about six feet by seven, and the stone couch on which the dead Savior lay extends from end to end of the apartment and occupies half its width. It is covered with a marble slab which has been much worn by the lips of pilgrims. This slab serves as an altar, now. Over it hang some fifty gold and silver lamps, which are kept always burning, and the place is otherwise scandalized by trumpery gew-gaws and tawdry ornamentation.

All sects of Christians have chapels under the roof of the Church of the Holy Sepulchre, and each must keep to itself and not venture upon another's ground. It has been proven conclusively that they cannot worship together around the grave of the Saviour of the World without fighting. The chapel of the Syrians is not handsome; that of the Copts is the humblest of them all. It is nothing but a dismal cavern, roughly hewn in the living rock of the Hill of Cavalry. In one side of it two ancient tombs are hewn, which are claimed to be those in which Nicodemus and Joseph of Aramathea were buried.

As we moved among the great piers and pillars of another part of the Church, we came upon a party of black robed, stupid, animal-looking Italian monks, with candles in their hands, who were chanting something in Latin, and going through some kind of a circus performance around a disk of white marble let into the floor. It was there that the risen Savior appeared to Mary Magdalene in the likeness of a gardener. Near by was a similar stone shaped like a star—here the Magdalene herself stood, at the same time. Monks were performing in this place also. They perform everywhere—all over the vast building, and at all hours. Their candles are always flittering about in the gloom, and making the dim old Church more dismal than there is any necessity that it should be, even though it is a tomb.

The Finding of the Cross

We were shown the place where the Lord appeared to His mother after the Resurrection. Here, also, a marble slab marks the place where St. Helena, the mother of the Emperor Constantine, found the crosses about 300 years after the crucifixion. According to the legend, this great discovery elicited extravagant demonstrations of joy. But they were of short duration. The question intruded itself: "Which bore the blessed Saviour, and which the thieves?" To be in doubt, in so mighty a matter as this—to be uncertain which one to adore and kiss, and steal chips from for keepsakes—was agonizing. It turned the public joy to sorrow. But when lived there a holy priest who could not set so simple a trouble as this at rest? One of these soon hit upon a plan that would be a certain test. A noble lady lay very ill in Jerusalem. The wise priests ordered that the three crosses be taken to her bedside one at a time. It was done. When her eyes fell upon the first one, she uttered a scream that was heard beyond the Damascus Gate, and even upon the Mount of Olives, it was said, and then fell back in a deadly swoon. They recovered her and brought the second cross. Instantly she went into fearful convulsions, and it was with the greatest difficulty that six strong men could hold her. They were afraid, now, to bring in the third cross. They began to fear that possibly they had fallen upon the wrong crosses, and that the true cross was not with this number at all. However, as the woman seemed likely to die with the convulsions that were tearing her, they concluded that the third could do no more than put her out of her misery with a happy despatch. So they brought it, and behold, a miracle! The woman sprang from her bed, smiling and joyful, and perfectly restored to health. When we listen to evidence like this, we cannot but believe. We would be ashamed to doubt, and properly, too. Even the very part of Jerusalem where this all occurred is there yet. So there is really no room for doubt.

The Pillar of Flagellation

The priests showed us, through a small screen, a fragment of the genuine Pillar of Flagellation, to which Christ was bound when they scourged him. We could not see it. This was because it was so dark inside the screen, perhaps. However, a broom handle is kept here, which the pilgrim pokes through a hole in the screen, and then, naturally enough, he no longer doubts that the true Pillar of Flagellation is in there. He cannot have any excuse to doubt it, for he can feel it with the stick. He can feel it as distinctly as he could feel anything.

The Place of a Relic

Not far from here was a niche where they used to preserve a piece of the True Cross, but it is gone, now. Our pilgrims are out of luck since we got here, somehow. They have not been able to make any collections worth having. This piece of the cross was discovered in the sixteenth century. The Latin priests say it was stolen away, long ago, by priests of another sect. That seems like a hard statement to make, but I know very well that it *was* stolen, because I have seen it myself in several of the cathedrals of Italy and France.

Godfrey's Sword

But the relic that touched us most was the plain old sword of that stout Crusader, bold Godfrey of Bouillon—King of Godfrey of Jerusalem. No blade in Christendom wields such enchantment as this—no blade of all that rust in the ancestral halls of Europe is able to invoke such visions of romance in the brain of him who looks upon it—none that can prate of such chivalric deeds or tell such brave tales of the warrior days of old. It stirs within a man every memory of the Holy Wars that has been sleeping in his brain for years, and peoples his thoughts with mail-clad images, with marching armies, with battles and with sieges. It speaks to him of Baldwin, and Tancred, the princely Saladin and gorgeous old Richard of the Lion Heart! It was with just such blades as these that these splendid heroes of romance used to segregate a man, so to speak, and leave the half of him to fall one way and the other half the other. This very sword has cloven hundreds of Saracen Knights from crown to chin in those Knightly times when Godfrey wielded it. It was enchanted, then, by a genius that was under the command of King Solomon. When danger approached its master's tent it always struck the shield and clanged out a fierce alarm upon the startled ear of night. In times of doubt, or in fog or darkness, if it were drawn from its sheath it would point instantly towards the foe, and thus reveal the way—and it would also attempt to start after them of its own accord. A Christian could not be so disguised that it would not know him and refuse to hurt him—nor a Moslem so disguised that it would not leap from its scabbard and take his life. These statements are all well authenticated in many legends that are among the most trustworthy legends the good old monks preserve. I can never forget old Godfrey's sword, now. I tried it on a Moslem, and clove him in twain like a doughnut. The spirit of its ancient owner was upon me, and if I had had a graveyard I would have destroyed all the infidels in Jerusalem. I never like to kill a man when I have no place to bury him in. I wiped the blood off the old sword and handed it back to the priest—I did not want the fresh gore to obliterate those old sacred spots that crimsoned its brightness six hundred years ago and thus gave Godfrey warning that before the sun went down his journey of life would end. And they do say that—

Dinner is ready.

This letter, numbered forty-five by Twain, appeared in the *Daily Alta California* of March 8, 1868. Chapter XXVI, Volume II, begins with this letter. "A row" became "an alley"; "I suppose it will not be worth while for me" became "it is hardly necessary"; "handful of Christians" became "handful of Protestants"; "the nationalities of the above list of sects" became "the nice shades of nationality comprised in the above list"; and "arrive" became "descend." The sentence beginning "Ours were disappointed" was deleted. The sentence beginning "The stone *was* there, at any rate" and the following sentence were deleted. After "all sects of Christians," Twain inserted "(except Protestants)." "Without fighting" became "in peace"; "stupid, animal-looking" became "animal-looking"; "a circus performance" became "religious performance"; "to adore and kiss, and steal chips from for keepsakes—was agonizing" became "to adore—was a grievous misfortune"; "the priest showed us, through a small screen" became "the priest tried to show us through a small screen"; "broom handle" became "baton"; and "pokes" became "thrusts." The sentence beginning "Our pilgrims are out of luck" and the following sentence were deleted. "Gorgeous old Richard" became "great Richard"; "those Knightly times" became "those old times"; and "the spirit of its ancient owner" became "the spirit of Grimes." The sentence beginning "I never like to kill a man" was deleted. The last eight words of the letter were deleted also.

49. More Biblical Landmarks

Jerusalem, September, 1867.

Still moving through the gloom of the Church of the Holy Sepulchre we came to a small chapel, hewn out of the rock—a den which has been known as "The Prison of Our Lord" for many centuries. Tradition says that here the Savior was confined just previously to the crucifixion. Under an altar by the door was a pair of stone stocks for human legs. These things are called the "Bonds of Christ," and the use they were once put to has given them the name they now bear.

"The Centre of the Earth"

This is the most roomy, the richest and the showiest chapel in the Church of the Holy Sepulchre. Its altar, like that of all the Greek Churches, is a lofty screen that extends clear across the chapel, and is gorgeous with gilding and pictures. The numerous lamps that hang before it are of gold and silver, and cost great sums.

But the feature of the place is a short column that rises from the middle of the marble pavement of the chapel, and marks the exact *centre of the earth.* The most reliable traditions inform us that this was known to be the earth's centre, ages ago, and that when Christ was upon earth he set all doubts upon the subject at rest forever, by stating with his own lips that the tradition was correct. Now, mark you, He said that that particular column stood upon the centre of the world. If the centre of the world changes, the column changes its position accordingly. This column has moved three different times, of its own accord. This is because, in great convulsions of nature, at three different times masses of the earth—whole ranges of mountains, probably—have flown off into space, thus lessening the diameter of the earth, and changing the exact locality of its centre by a point or two. This is a very curious and interesting circumstance, and is a withering rebuke to those ignorant philosophers who would make us believe that it is not possible for any portion of the earth to fly off into space.

To satisfy himself that this spot was really the centre of the earth, a sceptic once paid well for the privilege of ascending to the dome of the church to see if the sun gave him a shadow at noon. He came down perfectly convinced. The day was very cloudy and the sun threw no shadows at all; but the man was perfectly satisfied that if the sun had come out and made shadows it could not have made any for him. Proofs like these are not to be set aside by the idle tongues of cavilers. To such as are not bigoted, and are willing to be convinced, they carry a conviction that nothing can ever shake.

If even greater proofs than those I have mentioned are wanted, to satisfy the headstrong and the foolish that this is the genuine centre of the earth, they are here. The greatest of them lies in the fact that from under this very column was taken the *dust from which Adam was made*. This can surely be regarded in the light of a settler. It is not likely that the original first man would have been made from an inferior quality of earth when it was entirely convenient to get first quality dirt from the world's centre. This will strike any reflecting mind forcibly. That Adam was formed of dirt procured in this very spot is amply proven by the fact that in six thousand years no man has ever been able to prove that the dirt was *not* procured here whereof he was made.

It is a singular circumstance that right under the roof of this same great church, and not far away from that illustrious column, old Adam, the father of the human race, lies buried. There is no question that he is actually buried in the grave which is pointed out as his—there can be none—because it has never yet been proven that that grave is not the grave in which he is buried. I could not do less than shed some tender tears over poor old Adam. I could not but feel how much he had lost by dying so young. He had not seen the telegraph, or the locomotive, or the steamboat; he did not even see the flood. He missed the Paris Exposition. There was a roughness about that that cannot be over-estimated. He never had to pay three dollars a dozen for washing, and then have somebody's shirts come home to him that were too tight around the neck—but can a happiness like that atone for the suffering it must have cost him to have to go into company in the meagre costume of his time? When he first put on fig leaves he probably felt innocently gay; and when he finally branched out and got himself up regardless of expense, in a sheep-skin, he must have considered himself positively gorgeous. But think of Adam, with that skin and his long patriarchal beard, and think of him in a claw-hammer coat, white kids, and a moustache. The more I reflected upon what Adam had lost in being taken away so early, the more I was moved and the more I wept. The subject is too painful for contemplation, even now. Let us change it.

The Martyred Soldier

The next place the guide took us to in the holy church was an altar dedicated to the Roman soldier who was of the military guard that attended at the crucifixion to keep order, and who—when the veil of the Temple was rent in the awful darkness that followed; the rock of Golgotha was split asunder by an earthquake; the artillery of heaven thundered, and in the baleful glare of the lightnings the shrouded dead flitted about the streets of Jerusalem—shook with fear and said, "Surely this was the Son of God!" Exactly where this altar stands now, that Roman soldier stood then, in full view of the crucified Savior—in full sight and hearing of all the marvels that were transpiring far and wide about the circumference of the Hill of Calvary. And exactly in this self-same spot the priests of the Temple beheaded him for those blasphemous words he had spoken. There can be no question about these facts, because there is a picture of the whole affair on the front of the altar, where any one can see it who desires to do so. That soldier stood there, and there he was beheaded. I am as well satisfied about that as if there were two pictures of it.

"Inri"

In this altar they used to keep one of the most curious relics that human eyes ever looked upon—a thing that had power to fascinate the beholder in some mysterious way and keep him staring for hours together. It was nothing less than the copper plate Pilate put upon the Savior's cross, and upon which he wrote, "THIS IS THE KING OF THE JEWS." I think St. Helena, the mother of Constantine, found this wonderful memento when she was prospecting here in the third century. She was all over Palestine, and she had a run of luck the like of which was never seen before nor since. Whenever she found a thing mentioned in her Bible, Old or New, she would take her umbrella and start out after that thing and never, never stop until she found it. If it was Adam, she would find Adam; if it was the Ark, she would find the Ark; if it was Goliah, or Joshua or Exodus, or any of those parties, she would tree *them;* if it was a cup of a saint, or the handkerchief of the Virgin, or a painting by St. Luke, a man could risk his shekels that she would raise them; there was not anything she couldn't find. She was starting after Moses when she died; Moses is not found yet. And as for martyrs—why, martyrs were her strong suit, as you might say. She could start a martyr any time. She was pretty much always turning up a martyr somewhere, and dividing him up among the churches—a leg to this great cathedral, an arm to that, the body to the third, and so on, and the toe-nails she gave to the small fry. She meant well, of course, but then she has those martyrs divided up and scattered around so, that fragments of different ones have got mixed together, and there is going to be trouble some day on account of it. She was a most remarkable woman, and very impartial about martyrs.

She did best here on Calvary, no doubt. She had a claim here that she worked as long as she lived, and always had reason to be satisfied with it. She found the inscription here that I was speaking of, I think. She found it in this very spot, close to where the martyred Roman soldier stood. It is but just to say that the circumstance aroused no suspicion concerning the soldier. That copper plate is in one of the churches in Rome, now. I have seen it there. The inscription is very distinct. It is written in English, Italian and Spanish. This fact proves its authenticity, because these languages were not known in Pilate's time.

The Division of the Garments

We passed along a few steps and saw the altar built over the very spot where the soldiers divided the raiment of the Savior. One cannot well doubt that this is the right spot, because he can see with his own eyes that the very same original locality is still here.

The Penitent Thief

Then we went down into a cavern which cavilers say was once a cistern. It is a chapel, now, however—the Chapel of St. Helena. It is

51 feet long by 43 wide. In it is a marble chair which Helena used to sit in while she superintended her workmen when they were digging and delving for the True Cross. In this place is an altar dedicated to St. Dimas, the penitent thief. They have not dedicated anything to the other thief. He has never been popular here, and never deserved to be.

The Invention of the Cross

From the cistern we descended twelve steps into a large roughly shaped grotto, carved wholly out of the living rock. Helena blasted it out when she was searching for the true cross. She had a laborious piece of work, here, but it was richly rewarded. Out of this place she got the crown of thorns, the nails of the cross, the true cross itself and the cross of the penitent thief. When she thought she had found everything and was about to stop, she was told in a dream to continue a day longer. It was very fortunate. She put in one more blast and raised out the cross of the penitent thief.

The walls and roof of this grotto still weep bitter tears in memory of the event that transpired here, and devout pilgrims groan and sob when these sad tears fall upon them from the dripping rock. The Monks call this apartment the "Chapel of the Invention of the True Cross"—a name which is unfortunate, because it leads blockheads to imagine that a tacit acknowledgment is thus made that the tradition that Helena found the true cross here is a fiction—an invention. It is a happiness to know, however, that intelligent people do not doubt the story in any of its particulars.

Priests of any of the chapels and denominations in the Church of the Holy Sepulchre can visit this sacred grotto to weep and pray and worship the gentle Redeemer. Two different congregations are not allowed to enter at the same time, however, because they always fight, and it is not a good place to fight in.

This Church of the Holy Sepulchre is the most interesting place I ever was in. There is more to see in a small space than can be found elsewhere in the world. It is the Vatican of Jerusalem. I have not finished with it yet. People of all branches of Christianity are deeply interested in it, and it will be proper and right to give to it another chapter.

This letter, numbered forty-six by Twain, appeared in the *Daily Alta California* of March 15, 1868. It was also used in Chapter XXVI, immediately following Letter

48. "Den" became "place"; "this is the most roomy" became "the Greek Chapel is the most roomy"; "inform us" became "tell us"; "ignorant philosophers" became "philosophers"; "perfectly satisfied" became "satisfied"; "first quality dirt" became "first quality"; and "old Adam" became "Adam himself." The tomb-of-Adam incident was rather thoroughly rewritten. "Exactly where" and "exactly in" became "where" and "in." The last three sentences in the paragraph headed "The Martyred Soldier" were deleted. "Staring" became "gazing"; "was prospecting here" became "was here"; "was all over" became "traveled all over"; "she had a run of luck the like of which was never seen before nor since" became "was always fortunate"; "whenever she found" became "whenever the good old enthusiast found"; and "take her umbrella and start out after" became "go and search for." "Or Exodus, or any of those parties" was deleted.

"Tree" became "find." After "she would tree *them*," Twain omitted the next 196 words. The sentence beginning "It is but just to say that" was deleted. "I have seen it there" became "Anyone can see it there." "It is written in English, Italian and Spanish" and the following sentence were deleted. "Where the soldiers divided" became "where the good Catholic priests say the soldiers divided." The second sentence under the heading "The Division of the Garments" was deleted. After "St. Dimas, the penitent thief," Twain omitted two sentences and inserted three new ones. "She put in one more blast and raised out the cross of the penitent thief" became "she did so, and found the cross of the other thief," and "blockheads" became "the ignorant." "And it is not a good place to fight in" was deleted. The last paragraph was deleted also.

50. A Holy Place

Jerusalem, September, 1867.

STILL MARCHING through the venerable Church of the Holy Sepulchre, among chanting priests in coarse long robes and sandals; pilgrims of all colors and many nationalities, in all sorts of strange costumes; under dusky arches and by dingy piers and columns; through a sombre cathedral gloom freighted with smoke and incense, and faintly starred with scores of candles that appeared suddenly and as suddenly disappeared, or drifted mysteriously hither and thither about the distant aisles like ghostly jack-o'-lanterns—we came at last to a small chapel which is called the "Chapel of the Mocking." Under the altar was a fragment of a marble column; this was the seat Christ sat on when he was reviled, and mockingly made King, crowned with a crown of thorns and sceptred with a reed. It was here that they blindfolded him and struck him, and said in derision, "Prophesy who it is that smote thee." The tradition that this is the identical spot of the mocking is a very ancient one. The guide said that Saewulf was the first to mention it. I do not know as much about Saewulf as I do about Dickens, but still, I cannot well refuse to receive his evidence—none of us can. Saewulf is sound. We can have no reasonable doubt about that.

Distinguished Dead

They showed us where the great Godfrey and his brother Baldwin, the first Christian Kings of Jerusalem, once lay buried by that sacred sepulchre they had fought so long and so valiantly to wrest from the hands of the infidel. But the niches that had contained the ashes of these renowned crusaders were empty. Even the coverings of their tombs are gone—destroyed by devout members of the Greek Church, because Godfrey and Baldwin were Latin princes, and had been reared in a Christian faith whose creed differed in some unimportant respects from theirs.

We passed on, and halted before the tomb of Melchisedek! You will remember Melchisedek, no doubt; he was the King who came out and levied a tax on Abraham the time that he chased Lot's captors to Dan, and took all their property from them. That was about four thousand years ago, and Melchisedek died shortly afterward. However, his tomb is in a good state of preservation. I wanted very much to have the tombs of Adam and Melchisedek opened—especially Adam's as he was a distant relative of mine—but the priest would not do it. I would have liked very much to see how these ancient celebrities looked. It was only a natural curiosity, and harmless. But we shall never see old Father Adam and Melchisedek any more, because they are dead, now.

Place of the Crucifixion

When one enters the Church of the Holy Sepulchre, the Sepulchre itself is the first thing he desires to see, and really is almost the first thing he does see. The next thing he has a strong curiosity to see is the spot where the Savior was crucified. But this they exhibit last. It is the crowning glory of the place. One is grave and thoughtful when he stands in the little Tomb of the Savior—he could not well be otherwise in such a place—but he has not the slightest possible belief that ever the Lord lay there, and so the interest he feels in the spot is very, very greatly diluted by that reflection. He looks at the place where Mary stood, in another part of the church, and where John stood, and Mary Magdalene; where the mob derided the Lord; where the angel sat; where the crown of thorns was found, and the true cross; where the risen Savior appeared—he looks at all these places with interest, but with the same conviction he felt in the case of the Sepulchre, that there is nothing genuine about them, and that they are imaginary holy places created by the monks. But the place of the Crucifixion affects him differently. He fully believes that he is looking upon the very spot where the Savior gave up his life. He remembers that Christ was very celebrated, long before he came to Jerusalem; he knows that his fame was so great that crowds followed him all the time; he is aware that his entry into the city produced a stirring sensation, and that his reception was a kind of ovation; he cannot overlook the fact that when he was crucified there were very many in Jerusalem who believed that he was the true Son of God. To publicly execute such a personage was sufficient in itself to make the locality of the execution a memorable place for ages; added to this, the storm, the darkness, the earthquake, the rending of the veil of the Temple and the untimely waking of the dead, were events calculated to fix the execution of the scene of it in the memory of even the most thoughtless witness. Fathers would tell their sons about the strange affair, and point out the spot; the sons would transmit the story to their children, and thus a period of three hundred years would easily be spanned—at which time Helena came and built a church upon Calvary to commemorate the death and burial of the Lord and preserve the sacred-place in the memories of men; since that time there has always been a church there. It is not possible that there can be any mistake about the locality of the Crucifixion. Not half a dozen persons knew where they buried the Savior, perhaps, and a burial is not a startling event, anyhow; therefore, we can be pardoned for unbelief in the Sepulchre, but not in the place of the Crucifixion. Five hundred years hence there will be no vestige of Bunker Hill Monument left, but America will still know where the battle was fought and where Warren fell. The crucifixion of Christ was too notable an event in Jerusalem, and the Hill of Calvary made too celebrated by it, to be forgotten in the short space of three hundred years. Thinking after this fashion, I climbed the stairway in the church which brings one to the top of the small inclosed pinnacle of rock, and gazed upon the place where the true cross once stood, with a far more absorbing interest than I had ever felt in anything earthly before. I could not believe that the three holes in the top of the rock were the actual ones the crosses stood in, but I felt satisfied that those crosses had stood so near the place now occupied by them, that the few feet of possible difference were a matter of no consequence.

When one stands where the Savior was crucified, he finds it all he can do to keep it strictly before his mind that Christ was not crucified in a Catholic Church. He must remind himself every now and then that the great event transpired in the open air, and not in a gloomy, candle-lighted cell in a little corner of a vast church, up-stairs—a small cell all bejewelled and bespangled with flashy, tawdry ornamentation, in execrable taste. Under a marble altar like a table, is a circular hole in the marble floor, corresponding with the one just under it in which the true cross stood. The first thing every one does is to kneel down and take a candle and examine this hole. He does this strange prospecting with an amount of gravity that can never be estimated or appreciated by a man who has not seen the operation. Then he pokes his candle against a splendid engraved picture of the Savior, done on a massy slab of gold, and wonderfully rayed and starred with diamonds, which hangs above the hole within the altar, and this solemnity changes to lively admiration. He rises and faces the finely wrought figures of the Savior and the malefactors uplifted upon their crosses behind the altar, and bright with a metallic lustre of many colors. He turns next to the figures close to them of the Virgin and Mary Magdalene; next to the rift in the living rock made by the earthquake at the time of the Crucifixion, and an extension of which he had seen before in the wall of one of the grottoes below; he looks next at the show-case with a figure of the Virgin in it, and is amazed at the princely fortune in precious gems and jewelry that hangs so thickly about the form as to hide it like a garment almost. All about the apartment the gaudy trappings of the Greek Church offend the eye and keep the mind on the rack to remember that this is the Place of the Crucifixion—Golgotha—the Mount of Calvary—and *not* an altar in a Catholic Church. The last thing a man looks at is that which was also the first—the place where the true cross stood. That will chain him to the spot and compel him to look once more, and once again, after he has satisfied all curiosity and lost all interest concerning the other matters pertaining to the locality.

And so I close my chapter on the Church of the Holy Sepulchre—the most sacred locality on earth to millions and millions of God's creatures. In its history from the first, and in its tremendous associations, it is the most illustrious edifice in Christendom. With all its claptrap side-shows and unseemly humbuggery of every kind, it is still grand, reverend, venerable—a God died there; for fifteen hundred years its shrines have been wet with the tears of Pilgrims from the earth's remotest confines; for more than two hundred, the most gallant knights that ever wielded sword wasted their lives away in a struggle to seize it and hold it sacred from infidel pollution. Even in our own day it has been heard of in the politics of Europe. The Crimean War, that cost millions of treasure and rivers of blood, was fought because two rival nations claimed the sole right to put a new dome upon the Church of the Holy Sepulchre; and when they could not agree they went to war. History is full of this old Church of the Holy Sepulchre —full of blood that was shed because of the respect and the veneration in which men held the last resting-place of the meek and lowly, the mild and gentle, Prince of Peace!

This letter, numbered forty-seven by Twain, appeared in the *Daily Alta California* of March 22, 1868. It was used in Chapter XXVI, immediately following Letter 49. "I do not know as much about Saewulf as I do about Dickens" became "I do not know Saewulf." The two short sentences following "none of us can" were deleted. "Tax on Abraham" became "tribute on Abraham," and "chased" became "pursued." The passage beginning "I wanted very much to have the tombs" and extending to the end of the paragraph was deleted. "Curiosity" became "yearning," and "diluted" became "marred." "Thinking after this fashion" was deleted. "Gazed" became "looked." "Tawdry" was deleted. "Pokes his candle against" became "holds his candle before," and "splendidly engraved" became "richly engraved." "And *not* an altar in a Catholic Church" was deleted. "God's creatures" became "men, and women, and children, the noble and the humble, bond and free." "Humbuggery" became "impostures." "It has been heard of in the politics of Europe. "The Crimean War" became "a war," and "upon the Church of the Holy Sepulchre; and when they could not agree they went to war" became "upon it."

51. The Wandering Jew

Jerusalem, September, 1867.

We were standing in a narrow street by the Tower of Antonio. "On these stones, that are crumbling away," the guide said, "the Savior sat and rested before taking up the cross. This is the beginning of the Sorrowful Way, or the Way of Grief." The party took due note of the sacred spot, and moved on. It is curious, but no chapel is built upon that ground, and there is no grotto there. We passed under the "Ecce

Homo Arch," and saw the very window from which Pilate's wife warned her husband to have nothing to do with the persecution of the Just Man. This window is in an excellent state of preservation, considering its great age. They showed us where Jesus rested the second time, and where the mob refused to give him up, and said, "Let his blood be upon our heads and upon our children's children forever." The French Catholics are building a church on this spot, and with their usual veneration for historical relics, are building in the new such scraps of ancient walls as they have found there. Further on, we saw the spot where the fainting Savior fell under the weight of his cross. A great granite column of some ancient temple lay there at the time, and the heavy cross struck it such a blow that it broke in two in the middle. We might have thought this story the idle invention of priests and guides, but the broken column was still there to show for itself. One cannot go behind the evidences.

We crossed a street, and came presently to the former residence of St. Veronica. When the Savior passed there, she came out, full of womanly compassion, and spoke pitying words to him, undaunted by the hootings and threatenings of the mob, and wiped the perspiration from his face with her handkerchief. We had heard so much of St. Veronica, and seen her picture by so many masters, that it was like meeting an old friend unexpectedly to stumble upon her ancient home in Jerusalem. The strangest thing about the incident that has made her so famous, is that, when she wiped the perspiration away, the print of the Savior's face remained upon the handkerchief, a perfect portrait, and so remains unto this day. I know this, because I saw this handkerchief in a cathedral in Paris, in another in Spain, and in two others in Italy. In the Milan Cathedral it costs five francs to see it, and at St. Peter's at Rome, it is almost impossible to see it at any price. No tradition is so amply verified as this of St. Veronica and her handkerchief.

At the next corner we saw a deep indention in the hard stone masonry of the corner of a house, but might have gone heedlessly by it but that the guide said it was made by the elbow of the Savior, who stumbled here and fell. Presently we came to just such another indention in a stone wall. The guide said the Savior fell here, also, and made this depression with his elbow. We believed. We could not disbelieve, with the evidences before our eyes.

There were other places where the Lord fell, and others where he rested; but one of the most curious land-marks of sacred history we found on this morning walk through the crooked lanes that lead toward Calvary, was a certain stone built into a house—a stone that was so seamed and scarred that it bore a sort of grotesque resemblance to the human face. The projections that answered for cheeks were worn smooth by the passionate kisses of generations of pilgrims from distant lands. We asked "Why?" The guide said it was because this was one of "the very stones of Jerusalem" that Christ mentioned when he was reproved for permitting the people to cry "Hosannah!" when he made his memorable entry into the city upon an ass. One of the pilgrims said, " But there is no evidence that the stones *did* cry out—Christ said that if the people [were] stopped from shouting Hosannah, the very stones *would* do it." The guide was perfectly serene. He said, calmly, "This is one of the stones that *would* have cried out." It was of little use to try to shake this fellow's simple faith—it was easy to see that.

House of the Wandering Jew

And so we came at last to another wonder, of deep and abiding interest—the veritable house where the unhappy wretch once lived who has been celebrated in song and story for more than eighteen hundred years as the Wandering Jew. On the memorable day of the Crucifixion he stood in this old doorway with his arms akimbo, looking out upon the struggling mob that was approaching, and when the weary Savior would have sat down and rested him a moment, pushed him rudely away and said, "Move on!" The Lord said, "Move on, thou, likewise," and the command has never been revoked from that day to this. All men know how that the miscreant upon whose head that just curse fell has roamed up and down the broad world, for ages and ages, seeking rest and never finding it—courting death but always in vain—longing to stop, in city, in wilderness, in desert solitudes, yet hearing always that relentless warning to march—march on. They say —do these hoary traditions—that when Titus sacked Jerusalem and slaughtered eleven hundred thousand Jews in her streets and by-ways, the Wandering Jew was seen always in the thickest of the fight and that when battle-axes gleamed in the air, he bowed his head beneath them; when swords flashed their deadly lightnings, he sprang in their way; he bared his breast to whizzing javelins, to hissing arrows, to any and to every weapon that promised death and forgetfulness, and rest. But it was useless—he walked forth out of the carnage without a wound.

And it is said that five hundred years afterward, he followed Mahomet when he carried destruction to the cities of Arabia, and then turned against him. His calculations were wrong again. No quarter was given to any living creature but one, and that was the only one of all the host that did not want it. He sought death five hundred years later, in the wars of the Crusades, and offered himself, with them, to famine and pestilence at Ascalon. He escaped again—he could not die. These repeated annoyances could have at last but one effect—they shook his confidence. Since then the Wandering Jew has carried on a kind of desultory toying with the most promising of the aids and implements of destruction, but with small hope, as a general thing. He has speculated some in cholera, and railroads, and has taken almost a lively interest in infernal machines and patent medicines. He is old, now, and grave; as becomes an age like his; he indulges in no light amusements save that he goes generally to executions, and is fond of funerals.

There is one thing he cannot avoid: go where he will about the world, he must never fail to report in Jerusalem every fiftieth year. Only a year or two ago he was here for the thirty-seventh time since Jesus was crucified on Calvary. They say that many old people, who are here now, saw him then, and had seen him before. He looks always the same—old, and withered, and hollow-eyed, and listless, save that there is about him a something which seems to suggest that he is looking for some one, expecting some one—the friends of his youth, perhaps. But the most of them are dead, now. He always pokes about the old streets, looking lonesome, making his mark on a wall here and there, and eyeing the oldest buildings with a sort of friendly half interest; and he sheds a few tears at the threshold of his ancient dwelling, and bitter, bitter tears they are. Then he collects his rent and leaves again. He has been seen standing near the Church of the Holy Sepulchre on many a starlight night, for he has cherished an idea for many centuries that if he could only enter there, he could rest. But when he approaches, the doors slam to with a crash, the earth trembles, and all the lights in Jerusalem burn a ghastly blue! He does this every fifty years, just the same. It is hopeless, but then it is hard to break habits one has been eighteen hundred years accustomed to. The old tourist is far away on his wanderings, now. How he must smile to see a pack of blockheads like us, galloping about the world, and looking wise, and imagining we are finding out a good deal about it! He must have a consuming contempt for the ignorant, complacent asses that go skurrying about the world in these railroading days and call it travelling. When the guide pointed out where the Wandering Jew had left his familiar mark upon a wall, I was filled with astonishment. It read: "S. T.—1860—X."

All I have revealed about the Wandering Jew can be amply proven by reference to our guide.

Solomon's Temple

The mighty Mosque of Omar, and the paved court around it, occupy a fourth of Jerusalem. They are upon Mount Moriah, where King Solomon's Temple stood. This Mosque is the holiest place the Mohammedan knows, outside of Mecca. Up to within a year or two past, no Christian could gain admission to it or its court for love or money. But the prohibition has been removed, and we entered freely for bucksheesh.

I need not speak of the wonderful beauty and the exquisite grace and symmetry that have made this Mosque so celebrated, because I did not see them. One cannot see such things at an instant glance—one only finds out how really beautiful a really beautiful woman is after considerable acquaintance with her; and the rule applies to Niagara Falls, to majestic mountains and to mosques—especially to mosques.

The great feature of the Mosque of Omar is the prodigious rock in the centre of its rotunda. It was upon this rock that Abraham came so near offering up his son Isaac—this, at least, is authentic—is very much more to be relied on than most of the traditions, at any rate. On this rock, also, the angel stood and threatened Jerusalem, and David persuaded him to spare the city. Mahomet was well acquainted with this stone. From it he ascended to heaven. The stone naturally tried to follow him, and if the angel Gabriel had not happened by the merest good luck to be there to grab it, it would have done it. Very few people have a grip like Gabriel—the prints of his monstrous fingers, two inches deep, are to be seen in that rock to-day. "I suppose he just snaked that vast rock back to its place as easy and unconcerned as another person would nip a dough-nut."—Brown.

This rock, large as it is, is suspended in the air. It does not touch anything at all. The guide said so. This is very wonderful. In the place on it where Mahomet stood, he left his foot-prints in the solid stone. I should judge that he wore about eighteens. But what I was going to say, when I spoke of the rock being suspended, was, that in the floor of the cavern under it they showed us a slab which they said covered a hole which was a thing of extraordinary interest to all Mahommedans, because that hole leads down to purgatory, and every soul that is transferred from thence to Heaven must pass up through this orifice. Mahomet stands there and yanks them out by the hair. All Mahommedans shave their heads, but they are careful to leave a lock of hair for the Prophet to take hold of. Our guide observed that a good Mahommedan would consider himself doomed to stay with the damned forever if he were to lose his scalp-lock and die before it grew again. The most of them that I have seen ought to stay with the damned, anyhow, without reference to how they were barbered. What sort of use they can ever make of them in Heaven is much ahead of me.

For several ages no woman has been allowed to enter the cavern where that important hole is. The simple reason is that one of the sex was once caught there blabbing everything she knew about what was going on above ground, to the rapscallions in purgatory down below. She carried the thing to such an extreme that nothing could be kept private—nothing could be done or said on earth but everybody in hell knew all about it before the sun went down. It was about time to shut off this woman's telegraph, and it was promptly done. Her breath subsided about the same time.

But as I was about to remark concerning the small portion of the genuine King Solomon's Temple that still remains to chain the eye of the visitor, and provoke in him curious trains of thought—

This letter, numbered forty-eight by Twain, appeared in the *Daily Alta California* of March 29, 1868. Chapter XXVII begins with it. "Due note" became "note." The sentence beginning "It is curious, but no chapel" was deleted. "Building in" became "incorporating into." The sentence beginning "We might have thought this story the idle invention" and the following sentence were deleted, and Twain substituted for them, "Such was the guide's story when he halted us before the broken column." "To stumble upon" became "to come upon," and "indention" became "indentation." "We believed" and the following sentence were deleted. "Sacred history" became "ancient history"; "broad world" became "wide world"; and "Mahomet" became "Mohammed." After "and then turned against him," Twain inserted "hoping in this way to win the death of a traitor."

"Goes generally to executions" became "goes sometimes to executions"; "a something" became "something"; "a fourth of Jerusalem" became "*a fourth part* of Jerusalem"; "one only finds out" became "one frequently only finds out"; "the stone naturally tried" became "the stone tried"; and "grab it" became "seize it." Brown's remark was deleted. "Purgatory" became "perdition" and "yanks" became "lifts." The sentence beginning "What sort of use they can ever make" was deleted. "Simple reason" became "reason"; "purgatory" became "the infernal regions"; "carried the thing" became "carried her gossiping"; "in hell" became "in perdition"; and "shut off" became "suppress." The last paragraph of the letter was deleted.

52. Enough of Sights

Jerusalem, September, 1867.

Everywhere about the Mosque of Omar are portions of pillars, curiously wrought altars, and fragments of elegantly carved marble—precious remains of Solomon's Temple. These have been dug from all depths in the soil and rubbish of Mount Moriah, and the Moslems have always shown a disposition to preserve them with the utmost care. At that portion of the ancient wall of Solomon's Temple which is called the Jews' Place of Wailing, and where the Hebrews assemble every Friday to kiss the venerated stones and weep over the fallen greatness of Zion, any one can see a part of the unquestioned and undisputed Temple of Solomon, the same consisting of three or four stones lying one upon the other, (which is an unimportant variation from the prophecy,) each of which is about twice as long as a 7-octave piano, and about as thick as such a piano is high. But it is only a year or two ago that the ancient edict prohibiting Christian rubbish like ourselves to *enter* the Mosque of Omar and see the costly marbles that once adorned the inner Temple was annulled. The designs wrought upon these fragments are all quaint and peculiar, and so the charm of novelty is added to the deep interest they naturally inspire. One meets with these venerable scraps at every turn, especially in the neighboring Mosque el Aksa, in whose inner walls a very large number of them are carefully built for preservation. These pieces of stone, stained and dusty with age, dimly hint at a grandeur we have all been taught to regard as the princeliest ever seen on earth; and they call up pictures of a pageant that is familiar to all imaginations—camels laden with spices and treasure—beautiful slaves, presents for Solomon's harem—a long cavalcade of richly caparisoned beasts and warriors—and Sheba's Queen in the van of this vision of Oriental magnificence. These elegant fragments bear a richer interest than the solemn vastness of the stones the Jews kiss in the Place of Wailing can ever have for the careless sinner.

Underneath the olives and the orange trees that flourish in the court of the great Mosque is a wilderness of pillars—remains of the ancient Temple; they supported it. There are ponderous archways down there, also, over which the destroying "plough" of prophecy passed harmless. It is pleasant to know we are disappointed, in that we never dreamed we might see portions of the actual Temple of Solomon, and experience no shadow of suspicion that they were a monkish humbug and a swindle.

Too Much of a Happiness

We are surfeited completely surfeited with sights. Nothing in Jerusalem has any fascination for us, now, but the Church of the Holy Sepulchre. We have been there every day, and have not grown tired of it; but we are utterly weary of everything else. The sights are too many. They swarm about you at every step; no single foot of ground in all Jerusalem or within its neighborhood seems to be without a stirring and important history of its own. It is a very relief to steal a walk of a hundred yards without a guide along to prate unceasingly about every stone one steps upon and drag you back ages and ages to the day when it achieved celebrity.

It seems hardly real when I find myself leaning for a moment on a ruined wall, whistling gently, and looking listlessly down into the slimy cesspool that lives in history as the Blessed Pool of Bethesda. I did not think such things *could* be so crowded together as to even cheapen their interest, much less take it away altogether. For several days we have been drifting heedlessly about, using our eyes and our ears merely because it was our duty to do it, and for no other reason. We have been glad, always, when it was time to go home and bother no more about illustrious localities.

We have worried through. There is ineffable happiness in the thought. Except that we have not seen the frog-pond they call the Pool of Hezekiah, where David saw the wife of Uriah (I think that was his name) taking her bath, and fell in love with her. When they told us there was Scripture testimony that David sent Uriah to the front of the battle so that he could get him killed off and then marry his wife, we said we didn't care. We visited David's tomb, but we felt no enthusiasm in the knowledge that David had a tomb. I think we felt a resentment toward him for having a tomb at all. If he hadn't had one we need not have gone there.

Well, likewise we went out at the Jaffa Gate, and of course in going out we passed by the Tower of Hippicus. The guide insolently tried to tell us something about it, but we let him know, in a few words, that we did not care anything about Hippicus or his ruinous old property; and we gave him to understand that he must not offend in this way again.

We rode across the Valley of Hinnom, between two of the Pools of Gihon, and by an aqueduct built by Solomon, which still conveys water to the city. We ascended the Hill of Evil Counsel, where Judas received his thirty pieces of silver, and we also lingered a moment under the tree a venerable tradition says he hanged himself on. Were we reflective?—were we emotional? We swabbed the sweat from our faces, and glared up into the tree at some imaginary Judas—but it is likely that the first reflection was, "Why couldn't *you* have hanged yourself in town?"

We descended to the cañon again, and then that guide began to give name and history to every bank and boulder we came to: This was the Field of Blood; these cuttings in the rock were shrines and temples of Moloch; here they sacrificed children; yonder is the Zion Gate; the Tyropean Valley; the Hill of Ophel; fifty other things; here is the junction of the Valley of Jehoshaphat—on your right is the Well of Job—and so on. It was awful. We turned up Jehoshaphat. The tune went on: "This is the Mount of Olives; this is the Hill of Offence; the nest of huts is the Village of Siloam; here, yonder, everywhere, is the King's Garden; under this great tree Zacharias, the high priest, did something to somebody, or somebody did something to Zacharias; yonder is Mount Moriah and the Temple wall; the tomb of Absalom; the tomb of St. James, the tomb of Zacharias; beyond, are the Garden of Gethsemane and the tomb of the Virgin Mary; here is the Pool of Siloam, and—" "Then, let us go in and take a drink and have some respite from this merciless persecution!" exploded from several lips.

We went. The Pool is a deep, walled ditch, through which a clear stream of water runs, that comes from under Jerusalem somewhere, and passing through the Fountain of the Virgin, or being supplied from it, reaches this place by way of a tunnel of heavy masonry. The famous pool looked exactly as it looked in Christ's time, no doubt, and the same rusty looking, dusky Oriental squaws, came down in their old slouchy Oriental way, and carried off jars of the water on their heads, just as they did two thousand years ago, and just as they will do fifty thousand years hence if any of the breed are still left on earth. Pilgrims are always astonished to see them carry the jars on their heads —though I do not see why they should be, the custom is always so represented in the pictures. But your pilgrim that has marked his guide book all up with marks that signify "Here be astonished," is going to be astonished just at every one of those places, if it kills him.

We cleared out from there and stopped at the Fountain of the Virgin. But the water was not good, and there was no comfort or peace anywhere, on account of the regiment of boys and girls and beggars that persecuted us all the time for bucksheesh. The guide wanted us to give them some money, and we did it; but when he went on to say that they were starving to death we could not but feel that we had done a great sin in throwing obstacles in the way of such a desirable consummation, and tried to collect it back, but it could not be done.

But there is no use in my trying to talk about the Garden of Gethsemane—this mood of mine is ill suited to the subject—or about the tomb of the Virgin, for the same reason. I cannot speak now of the Mount of Olives or its view of Jerusalem, the Dead Sea and the mountains of Moab; nor of the Damascus Gate or the tree that was planted by King Godfrey of Jerusalem. One ought to feel pleasantly when he talks of these noted things. I cannot say anything about the stone column that projects over Jehoshaphat from the Temple wall like a cannon, except that the Moslems believe Mahomet will sit astride of it when he comes to judge the world. It is a pity he could not judge it from some roost of his own in Mecca, without trespassing on our holy ground. Close by is the Golden Gate, in the Temple wall—a gate that was an elegant piece of sculpture in the time of the Temple, and is even so yet. From it, in ancient times, the Jewish High Priest turned loose the scape-goat and let him flee to the wilderness and bear away his twelve-month load of the sins of the people. If they were to turn one loose now, he would not get as far the the Garden of Gethsemane till these miserable vagabonds here would gobble him up, sins and all. *They* wouldn't care. Mutton-chops and sin is good enough living for them. The Moslems watch the Golden Gate with a jealous eye, and an anxious one, for they have an honored tradition that when it falls, Islamism will fall, and with it the Ottoman Empire. It did not grieve me any to notice that the old gate was getting a little shaky.

This letter, numbered fifty-three by Twain, appeared in the *Daily Alta California* of April 12, 1868. It was used in Chapter XXVII, following Letter 51 (with two paragraphs intervening). "Which is an unimportant variation of the prophecy" was deleted. "Oriental magnificence" was put in quotes. "Careless sinner" became "heedless sinner." Before "underneath the olives and the orange trees," Twain inserted "down in the hollow ground." "Swindle" became "fraud"; "surfeited, completely surfeited" became "surfeited"; "utterly weary" became "weary"; and "prate" became "talk." "Whistling gently" was deleted. "Slimy cesspool that lives in history as the Blessed Pool of Bethesda" became "historic pool of Bethesda." "Even cheapen their interest, much less take it away altogether. For several days we have been drifting heedlessly about" became "diminish their interest. But, in serious truth, we have been drifting about, for several days." "Merely because it was our duty to do it, and for no other reason" became "more from a sense of duty than any higher and worthier reason"; "we have been glad, always" became "and too often we have been glad"; and "bother" became "be distressed."

The paragraph beginning "We have worried through" and the following paragraph were completely rewritten. The passage beginning "Were we reflective?" and extending to the end of the paragraph was deleted. "Fifty other things" and "and so on. It was awful" were deleted. "Tune" became "recital," and "did something to somebody, or somebody did something to Zacharias" became "was murdered." The sentence beginning "Then, let us go in and take a drink" and the following sentence were completely rewritten. "Christ's time" became "Solomon's time"; "rusty looking, dusky Oriental squaws" became "dusky, Oriental women"; "old slouchy" became "old"; "two thousand" became "three thousand"; and "any of the breed" became "any of them." The passage beginning "Pilgrims are always astonished" and extending to the end of the paragraph was deleted. "Cleared out" became "went away." The sentence beginning "But there is no use in my trying to talk" was rewritten. "Noted things" became "things." To "gobble him up," Twain attached this footnote: "Favorite pilgrim expression."

53. Threatened with Attack

Jerusalem, Sept., 1867.

We cast up the account. It footed up pretty fairly. There was nothing more at Jerusalem to be seen, except the houses of Dives and Lazarus of the parable, and "Moreover the dog;" the Tombs of the Kings; ditto of the Judges; the spot where they stoned one disciple to death, and beheaded another; the room and the table made celebrated by the Last Supper; the fig-tree that Jesus withered; a dozen of historical places about Gethsemane and the Mount of Olives, and fifteen or twenty others in different portions of the city itself. We began to see our way through. It was suggested that we might hire parties to visit these things for us and thus see them by proxy, but after some deliberation it was decided that such a course would be discreditable. Still, we had got altogether enough, for the present. There was open rebellion in the camp—undisguised mutiny. There was a strong disposition to lie around the hotel and smoke. A diversion must be tried, or demoralization would ensue. The Jordan, Jericho and the Dead Sea were suggested. The remainder of Jerusalem would keep till we got back. The journey was approved and the dragoman notified.

I have not overdrawn the picture. There were only two men in our party of eight whose sight-seeing enthusiasm did not thoroughly and completely wear out before we finished Jerusalem, and from what I can learn we held out longer than any other party of the whole army of pilgrims we brought into the Holy Land. The wild enthusiasm of Palestine sight-seers is to be found only in the books they write, I think—not in their actual experience. One of our pilgrims went up and saw the sun rise on Olivet. I did not hear of any other that did it. One is always jaded, here, always languid and weary. His brain is so worn and racked with the day's accumulations of knowledge when he comes home at night, that it is like an overloaded stomach, and he feels as if it would be an unspeakable relief to take a mental emetic and throw up everything he ever learned in his life.

Dismal Rumors

At nine in the morning the caravan was before the hotel door and we were at breakfast. There was a commotion about the place. Rumors of war and bloodshed were flying everywhere. The lawless Bedouins in the Valley of the Jordan and the deserts down by the Dead Sea were up in arms, and were going to destroy all comers. They had had a battle with a troop of Turkish cavalry and defeated them; several men killed. They had shut up the inhabitants of a village and a Turkish garrison in an old fort near Jericho, and were besieging them. They had marched upon a camp of our pilgrims by the Jordan, and they only saved their lives by stealing away and flying to Jerusalem under whip and spur in the darkness of the night. Another of our parties had been fired on from an ambush and then attacked in the open day. Shots were fired on both sides. Fortunately there was no bloodshed. We spoke with the very pilgrim who had fired one of the shots, and learned from his own lips how, in this imminent deadly peril, only the cool courage of the pilgrims, their strength of numbers and imposing display of war material, had saved them from utter destruction. It was reported that the Consul had requested that no more of our pilgrims should go to the

Jordan while this state of things lasted; and further, that he was unwilling that any more should go, at least without an unusually strong military guard. Here was trouble. But with the horses at the door and everybody aware of what they were there for, what would *you* have done? Acknowledge that you were afraid, and backed shamefully out? Hardly. It would not be human nature, where there were so many women. You would have done as we did: said you were not afraid of a million Bedouins—and made your will and proposed quietly to yourself to take up an unostentatious position in the rear of the procession.

I think we must all have determined upon the same line of tactics, for it did seem as if we never would get to Jericho. I had a notoriously slow horse, but somehow I could not keep him in the rear, to save my neck. He was forever turning up in the lead. In such cases I naturally trembled a little, and got down to fix my saddle. But it wasn't of any use. The others all got down to fix their saddles, too. I never saw such a time with saddles. It was the first time any of them had got out of order in three weeks, and now they had all broken down at once. I tried walking, for exercise—I had not had enough in Jerusalem prospecting for holy places. But it was a failure. The whole gang were suffering for exercise, and it was not fifteen minutes till they were all on foot and I had the lead again. It was very discouraging.

Lazarus

This was all after we got beyond Bethany. We stopped at the miserable mud village of Bethany, an hour out from Jerusalem. They showed us the tomb of Lazarus. I had rather live in it than in any house in the town. And they showed us also a large "Fountain of Lazarus," and in the centre of the village the ancient dwelling of Lazarus. Lazarus appears to have been a man of property. The legends of the Sunday Schools do him great injustice; they give one the impression that he was poor. It is because they get him mixed up with that disreputable Lazarus who had no merit but his virtue, and that never has been as respectable as money. The house of Lazarus is a three-story edifice, of stone masonry, but the accumulated rubbish of ages has buried all of it but the upper story. We took candles and descended to the dismal cell-like chambers where Jesus sat at meat with Martha and Mary, and conversed with them about their brother. We could not but look upon these old dingy apartments with a more than common interest.

But we went away from there with increased respect for Lazarus as a man of property. He must have stood high in the village. I love to think of Lazarus, now, as having been Mayor of Bethany at some time or other. If the ancient archives of the village could be found, no doubt they would prove that he had held that office in his time, and flourished gallantly at the head of torchlight processions when the firemen turned out. It is pleasant to me to cherish the harmless fancy that somewhere underneath that mountain of rubbish at Bethany there are stained and mouldering election tickets with "VOTE FOR LAZARUS" on them.

Bedouins!

We had had a glimpse, from a mountain top, of the Dead Sea, lying like a blue shield in the plain of the Jordan, and now we were marching down a close, flaming, rugged, desolate defile, where no living creature could enjoy life except, perhaps, a lizard or a salamander. It was such a dreary, repulsive, horrible solitude! It was the "wilderness" where John preached, with camel's hair about his loins—raiment enough—but he never could have got his locusts and wild honey here. We were poking along down through this villainous place, every man in the rear. Our guards—two gorgeous young Arab shieks, with cargoes of swords, guns, pistols and daggers on board—were loafing ahead.

"Bedouins!"

Every man shrunk up and disappeared in his clothes like a mud-turtle. My first impulse was to dash forward and destroy the Bedouins. My second was to dash to the rear to see if there were any coming in that direction. I acted on the latter impulse. So did all the others. If any Bedouins had approached us, then, from that point of the compass, they would have paid dearly for their rashness. We all remarked that, afterwards. There would have been scenes of riot and blood-shed there that no pen could describe. I know that, because each man told what he would have done, individually; and such a medley of strange and unheard of inventions of cruelty you could not conceive of. One man said he had calmly made up his mind to perish where he stood, if need be; but never yield an inch; he was going to wait, with deadly patience till he could count the stripes upon the first Bedouin's jacket, and then count them and let him have it. Another was going to sit still till the first lance reached within an inch of his breast, and then dodge it and seize it. I forbear to tell what he was going to do to that Bedouin that owned it. It makes my blood run cold to think of it. Another was going to scalp such Bedouins as fell to his share, and take his bald-headed sons of the desert home with him alive for trophies. But the wild-eyed pilgrim rhapsodist was silent. His orbs gleamed with a deadly light, but his lips moved not. Anxiety grew, and he was questioned. If he had got a Bedouin, what would he have done with him—shot him? He smiled a smile of grim contempt and shook his head. Would he have stabbed him? Another shake. Would he have quartered him—flayed him? More shakes. Oh! horror, what would he have done?

"Eat him!"

That was the awful sentence that thundered from his lips. What was grammar to a desperado like that? I was glad in my heart that I had been spared these scenes of malignant carnage. No Bedouins attacked our terrible rear. And none attacked the front. The new-comers were only a reinforcement of cadaverous Arabs, in shirts and bare legs, sent far ahead of us to brandish rusty guns, and shout and brag, and carry on like a pack of lunatics, and thus scare away all bands of marauding Bedouins that might lurk about our path. What a shame it is that armed white Christians must travel under guard of wretched vermin like this as a protection against the prowling vagabonds of the desert who are always going to do something desperate, but never do it. I may as well mention here that on our whole trip we saw no Bedouins, and had no more use for an Arab guard than we could have had for patent leather boots and stove-pipe hats. The Bedouins that attacked the other parties of pilgrims so fiercely were provided for the occasion by the Arab guards of those parties, and shipped from Jerusalem for temporary service as Bedouins. They met together in full view of the pilgrims, after the battle, and took lunch, divided the bucksheesh extorted in the season of danger, and then accompanied the cavalcade home to the city! The nuisance of an Arab guard is one which is created by the Sheiks and the Bedouins together, for mutual profit, it is said, and no doubt there is a good deal of truth in it.

Ancient Jericho, etc.

We visited the fountain that the prophet Elisha sweetened (it is sweet yet); where he remained some time and was fed by the ravens. The ravens got tired of dividing up, perhaps, and left. None are there now.

Ancient Jericho is not very picturesque as a ruin. When Joshua promenaded around it seven times, some three thousand years ago, and blew it down with his trumpet, he gave it such a terrific final blast that he hardly left enough of it to swear by. To re-build it has always been an unpopular move, on account of a curse that is still on record and in force against any speculator that may take a notion to embark in the enterprise. It has never been attempted but once, and then trouble followed. We camped near Jericho.

This letter, numbered fifty-four by Twain, appeared in the *Daily Alta California* of April 26, 1868. In the book, Twain placed it at the beginning of Chapter XXVIII. "Houses" became "traditional houses." "And 'moreover the dog' " was deleted. "Ditto" became "and those"; "one disciple" became "one of the disciples"; and "dozen" became "number." The passage beginning "We began to see our way through" and extending to the end of the following paragraph was completely rewritten. "Naturally trembled" became "trembled"; "prospecting" became "searching"; "gang" became "mob"; "miserable mud village" became "village"; "mixed up" became "confused"; and "disreputable Lazarus" became "Lazarus."

The paragraph beginning "But we went away from there" was deleted. "Poking" became "moping"; "villainous place" became "dreadful place"; "like a pack of lunatics" became "like lunatics"; "wretched vermin" became "vermin"; and "stove-pipe hats" became "white kid gloves." The sentence beginning "The ravens got tired" and the following sentence were deleted. "Promenaded" became "marched." "Gave it such a terrific final blast that he hardly left enough of it to swear by" became "did the work so well and so completely that he hardly left enough of the city to cast a shadow"—and the remainder of the paragraph was rewritten.

54. Bethlehem, the Dead Sea

Jerusalem, Sept., 1867.

At two in the morning they routed us out of bed—another swindle —another stupid effort of our dragoman to get ahead of a rival. It was not two hours to the Jordan. However, we were dressed and under way before any one thought of looking to see what time it was, and so we drowsed on through the chill night air and dreamed of camp fires, warm beds and other comfortable things. We were sorry enough that the Jordan had ever become celebrated.

We reached the famous river before 4 o'clock, and the night was so black that we could have ridden into it without seeing it. Some of us were in a savage frame of mind. We waited and waited for daylight, but it did not come. Finally two of us went away in the dark and slept an hour on the ground, in the bushes, and caught cold. This act incensed the guard. It hurt their dignity to think that any pilgrim should scorn their protection in the worst Bedouin locality in Palestine. We let it go at that, though in reality we had forgotten about the Bedouins or we would not have been so reckless.

With the first suspicion of dawn, every pilgrim snatched off his clothes and darted into the dark torrent, singing:

> *On Jordan's stormy banks I stand,*
> *And cast a wishful eye*
> *Toe Caanyan's fair and happy land,*
> *Where my po-sessions lie.*

But they did not sing long. The water was so fearfully cold that they suddenly throttled down their music valves and waltzed out again. They shivered on the bank, and were deeply chagrined. They had promised themselves all along that they would cross the Jordan where the Israelites crossed it when they entered Caanan [Canaan] from their weary pilgrimage in the desert. They would cross where the twelve stones were placed in memory of that great event. While they did it they would picture to themselves that vast army of pilgrims marching through the cloven waters, bearing the hallowed ark of the covenant and shouting hosannahs, and singing songs of thanksgiving and praise. Each had promised himself that he would be the first to cross. They were at the goal of their hopes at last, but the current was too swift, the water was too cold!

It was sad, very sad, Jack, the youth that was with me, did them a service, then. He got up and went and led the way across the Jordan, and all was happiness again. The pilgrims waded over and stood upon the further bank. I rushed over also, and rushed back, and now I shall never have to cross the Jordan any more in the night. I can always wait till daylight, hereafter. The main thing accomplished, the drooping, miserable gang sat down to wait for the sun again, for all wanted to see the water as well as feel it. But it was too cold a business. Some cans were filled from the historic river, some canes cut from its banks, and then the party mounted and rode reluctantly away to keep from freezing to death. So we saw the Jordan very dimly. The thickets of bushes that bordered its banks threw their shadows across its shallow, turbulent waters ("stormy," the hymn makes them, with a complimentary stretch of fancy), and we could not judge of the width of the stream by the eye. We knew by our wading experience, however, that a good many streets in America are double as wide as the Jordan.

Daylight came, soon after we got under way, and in the course of an hour or two we reached

The Dead Sea

Nothing grows in the flat, burning desert around it but weeds and the poor Dead Sea apple the poets say is beautiful to the eye, but crumbles to ashes and dust when you break it. Such as we found were not handsome, but they were bitter to the taste. They yielded no dust. It was because they were not ripe, perhaps.

The desert and the barren hills gleam painfully in the sun, around the Dead Sea, and there is no pleasant thing or living creature upon it or about its borders to cheer the eye. It is a scorching, arid, repulsive solitude. A silence broods over the scene that is depressing to the spirits. It makes one think of funerals and death.

The little sea is about as large as Lake Bigler. Its waters are very clear, and it has a pebbly bottom and is shallow for some distance out from the shores. It yields quantities of asphaltum; chunks of it lie all about its banks; this stuff gives the place something of an unpleasant smell.

All our reading had taught us to expect that the first plunge into the Dead Sea would be attended with distressing results—our bodies would feel as if they were suddenly pierced by millions of red-hot needles; the dreadful smarting would continue for hours; we might even look to be blistered from head to foot, and suffer miserably for many days. We were infamously disappointed. Our eight sprang in at the same time that another party of pilgrims did, and nobody screamed once. None of them ever did complain of anything more than a slight pricking sensation in places where their skin was abraded, and then only for a short time. My face smarted for a couple of hours, but it was partly because I got it badly sunburned while I was bathing, and staid in so long that it got plastered over with salt.

It was a funny bath. We could not sink. One could stretch himself at full length on his back, with his arms on his breast, and all of his body above a line drawn from the corner of his jaw past the middle of his side, the middle of his leg and through his ancle [ankle] bone would remain out of water. He could lift his head clear out, if he chose. No position can be retained long; you lose your balance and whirl over, first on your back and then on your face, and so on. You can lie comfortably, on your back, with your head out, and your legs out from your knees down, by steadying yourself with your hands. You can sit, with your knees drawn up to your chin and your arms clasped around them, but you are bound to turn over presently because you are top-heavy in that position. You can stand up straight in water that is over your head, and from the middle of your breast upward you will not be wet. But you cannot remain so. The water will soon float your feet to the surface. You cannot swim on your back and make any progress of any consequence, because your feet stick away above the surface, and there is nothing to propel yourself with but your heels. If you swim on your face, you kick up the water like a stern-wheel boat. You make no headway. A horse is so top-heavy that he can neither swim nor stand up in the Dead Sea. He turns over on his side at once. Some of us bathed for more than an hour, and then came out coated with salt till we shone like icicles. We scrubbed it off with a coarse towel and rode off smelling badly. Salt crystals glitter in the sun about the shores of the lake. In places they coat the ground like a brilliant crust of ice.

Bethlehem, etc.

We looked everywhere, as we passed along, but never saw grain or crystal of Lot's wife. It was a great disappointment. For many and many a year we had known her bright, sad story, and taken that interest in her which beauty in misfortune always inspires. But she was gone. Her picturesque form no longer looms above the desert of the Dead Sea to remind the tourist of the doom that fell upon the lost cities, while at the same time it called painful attention to that unhappy trait of curiosity that takes up so much spare room in all her sex. The lowing herds wound slowly o'er the lea, sometime or other, and took her along with them, no doubt.

We stopped at Mars Saba that night and slept in the Convent. At 9 or 10 in the morning we reached the Plain of the Shepherds, and stood in a walled garden of olives where the shepherds were watching their flocks by night, nineteen centuries ago, when the multitude of angels brought them the tidings that the Savior was born. A quarter of a mile away was Bethlehem of Judea, and the pilgrims took some of the stone wall and hurried on.

In the huge Church of the Nativity, in Bethlehem, built fifteen hundred years ago by the inveterate St. Helena, they took us below ground, and into a grotto cut in the living rock. This was the "manger" where Christ was born. A silver star set in the floor bears a Latin inscription to that effect. It is polished with the kisses of many generations of worshipping pilgrims. The grotto was tricked out in the usual tasteless style observable in all the holy places of Palestine. As in the Church of the Holy Sepulchre, envy and uncharitableness were apparent here. The priests and the members of the Greek and Latin Churches cannot come by the same corridor to kneel in the sacred birth-place of the Redeemer, but are compelled to approach and retire by different avenues, lest they quarrel and fight on this holiest ground on earth.

You cannot think in this place any more than you can in any other in Palestine that would be likely to inspire reflection. Beggars, cripples and greasy monks compass you about, and make you think only of bucksheesh when you would rather think of something more in keeping with the character of the spot.

I was glad to get out of there, and glad when we had trotted through the grottoes where Eusebius wrote, and Jerome fasted, and Joseph prepared for the flight into Egypt, and the dozen other distinguished grottoes, and knew we were done. The Church of the Nativity is almost as well packed with exceeding holy places as the Church of the Holy Sepulchre itself. They have even got in it a grotto wherein 20,000 children were slaughtered by Herod when he was seeking the life of the infant Jesus.

We went to the Milk Grotto, of course—a cavern where Mary hid herself for a while before the flight into Egypt. Its walls were black before she entered, but in suckling the child, a drop of her milk fell upon the floor and instantly changed the darkness of the walls to its own snowy hue. We took many little fragments of stone from here, because it is well known in all the East that a barren woman hath need only to touch her lips to one of these and her failing will depart from her. We took many specimens, to the end that we might confer happiness upon certain households that we wot of. Let the distressed apply to me, postage paid, and a stamp extra, for my sands of life are well nigh run out, and I would do good to my fellow man while yet I can.

We got away from Bethlehem and its troops of beggars and relic-peddlers in the afternoon, and spending very little time at Rachel's tomb and the Pool of Solomon, hurried to Jerusalem as fast as possible. I never was as glad to get home again in all my life before. I never have enjoyed rest as I have enjoyed it during these last few hours. The journey to the Dead Sea, the Jordan and Bethlehem was short, but it was an awful one! Such roasting heat, such oppressive solitude, and such dismal desolation cannot surely exist elsewhere on earth. And *such* fatigue! I think I can sleep now.

This letter, numbered fifty-one by Twain, appeared in the *Daily Alta California* of May 17, 1868. It was also used in Chapter XXVIII, following Letter 53. "Swindle" became "piece of unwarranted cruelty." The sentence beginning "We were sorry enough" was deleted and a paragraph was inserted. "A savage" became "an unhappy." The passage beginning "This act incensed the guard" and extending to the end of the paragraph was deleted and another passage was substituted for it. "Snatched" became "took," and "darted" became "waded." Twain corrected the stanza from the hymn. "Suddenly throttled down their music valves and waltzed" became "were obliged to stop singing and scamper."

The sentence beginning "They shivered on the bank" was rewritten in two sentences. "Weary" became "long." In the paragraph beginning "It was sad, very sad," the first five sentences were revised and rewritten. "Thing accomplished" became "object compassed"; "gang" became "party"; "business" became "pastime"; "historic river" became "holy river"; "The little sea is about as large as Lake Bigler" became "The Dead Sea is small"; "chunks" became "fragments"; "infamously disappointed" became "disappointed"; and "got plastered" became "became plastered." After "plastered over with salt," Twain inserted a paragraph (taken from Letter 55). For "smelling badly," Twain substituted thirty-six words. After the paragraph ending "coat the ground like a brilliant crust of ice," Twain inserted two paragraphs (taken mainly, but with revisions, from Letter 55). "Bright, sad" became "sad," and "beauty in misfortune" became "misfortune." That part of the paragraph following "the doom that fell upon the lost cities" was deleted.

For the sentence "We stopped at Mars Saba that night and slept in the Convent," Twain substituted a long passage of more than twelve hundred words. "Nineteen centuries" became "eighteen centuries." After the paragraph ending "took some of the stone wall and hurried on," Twain inserted a paragraph. After the paragraph ending "on this holiest ground on earth," Twain inserted a paragraph. "Greasy monks" became "monks"; "get out of there" became "get away"; "trotted" became "walked"; and "have even got" became "even have." The sentence beginning "Let the distressed apply to me" was deleted. "Spending very little time at Rachel's tomb and the Pool of Solomon" became "after spending some little time at Rachel's tomb"; "as glad" became "*so* glad"; "in all my life before" became "before"; and "awful one" became "exhausting one." "I think I can sleep now" was deleted.

55. Palestine Scenery

Jerusalem, September, 1867.

Of all the lands on earth for dismal scenery, I think Palestine must be the prince. The hills are barren, they are dull of color, they are unpicturesque in shape. The valleys are unsightly deserts fringed with a feeble vegetation that has an expression about it of being ashamed of itself. The Dead Sea and the Sea of Galilee—mere lakes they are—sleep in the midst of a vast stretch of hill and plain wherein the eye rests upon no pleasant tint, no striking object, no soft picture dreaming in a purple haze or mottled with the shadows of the clouds. Every outline is harsh, every feature is distinct, there is no perspective—distance works no enchantment here. It is the most hopeless, dreary, heartbroken piece of territory out of Arizona. I think the sun would skip it if he could make schedule time by going around. What Palestine wants is paint. It will never be a beautiful country until it is painted. Each detachment of pilgrims ought to give it a coat, and build walls at short distances, so that one could not see too much landscape at once. The children of Israel wandered about the desert beyond those Mountains of Moab yonder for forty years, and then crossed the Jordan where we camped, and marched into Canaan with songs of rapture and rejoicing; and it is a wonder to me that they didn't pack up and march out of it again. That they refrained from doing it speaks volumes for the desolation of the wilderness. But then, all those that had seen Egypt were dead. That fact is mildly suggestive. I speak as if Canaan had never been a better country than it is now. I have much better judgment than to say that there is considerable evidence that it has not changed in any respect in four thousand years—evidence that there was not any chance for it to change for the worse—evidence that from the date of its creation the difference between it and a "wilderness" was not more perceptible than the difference between one Chinaman and another. I refrain from saying these things, not because they might not savor somewhat of truth, but because they could not be popular.

But the severest thing that has been said about Palestine was said here in Jerusalem. A pilgrim with his periodical ecstacy upon him (it usually comes in a flush of happiness after dinner) finished his apostrophe with, "O, that I could be here at the Second Advent!"

A grave gentleman said, "It will not occur in Palestine."

"What!"

"The Second Advent will take place elsewhere—possibly in America."

"Blasphemy!"

"I speak reasonably. You are in the Holy Land. You have seen the Holy Land once?"

"Yes."

"Shall you ever want to come here again?"

"Well—no."

"My friend, the Savior has been here once!"

I hope I am not unjust toward the natural scenery of Palestine. And yet I have been so disappointed that such a thing is almost possible. Before the *Quaker City* left New York, the passengers were instructed to bring along an assortment of books. A list of the volumes they ought to have, in order to be posted concerning England, France, Spain and the many other countries they were to visit, was furnished to each, viz.: "Robinson's Holy Land"; "Pilgrim's Progress"; "Dusenberry's Researches in Palestine"; "The Plymouth Collection of Hymns"; "City of the Great King"; "Shepherd of Salisbury Plain"; "Tent Life in the Holy Land"; "Tupper's Poems"; "The Prince of the House of David"; "Whole Duty of Man"; "Jericho and the Jordan"; "Bradshaw's Sermons"; "Walks About Jerusalem"; "Salvation Through Grace."

It was the rarest library that ever was seen. Sixty-four copies of "Dusenberry's Researches," and all the other works in proportion. I shall always remember the first night we camped within the confines of Holy Land. The pilgrims had said on shipboard that we should not want for knowledge of the country we were about to visit—so they told a cabin boy to take a lot of books from the ship's library and pack them in Elder W.'s valise. The boy took them all from one shelf. That memorable night by the camp-fire the Elder got out this valise and said, "Now we will make a list of these books, by number and title, so that they won't get lost. I will pass each book to you and call its number; you set it down, and pass the book to Dan, calling its name; you keep the record, and let Dan take charge of the lot. Here, now, is Number One."

"No. 1—Salvation by Grace."

Dan—"No. 1—Salvation by Grace."

"Number Two."

"No. 2—Salvation by Grace."

Dan—"No. 2—Salvation by Grace."

"Number Three."

"No. 3—Salvation by Grace."

Nobody had laughed. But it was a trying time.

"Number Four," (hesitatingly).

"No. 4—Salvation by Grace."

Dan—"No. 4—Salvation by Grace."

"Number Five," (nervously).

"No. 5—Salvation by —"

Elder—"*Silence*, you infernal idiot! By everything that's sacred, if either of you ever mention this, it shall cost you dearly!" And then he rushed furiously away to tear up the ground or destroy somebody. It was a pity the cabin-boy took all the books from one shelf.

But, as I was going to say when this reminiscence intruded itself upon me, we had nothing much on board the ship to read but travels in Palestine, and very naturally we got Palestine drilled into us thoroughly. All these books of travel managed, somehow, to leave with us a sort of vague notion that Palestine was very beautiful—a notion that we were about to enter a modified form of fairy land. And so a bitter disappointment awaited us. The fairy land was modified too much. It was a howling wilderness instead of a garden. This has incensed us against all our Holy Land authors, and inclines us to say intemperate things about the land itself.

But that was a funny library. When we got to the Azores, not a scrap of paper could be found in the ship that referred to those islands. As we neared Gibraltar we could hardly find out from any book on board whether Gibraltar was a rock, or an island, or a statue, or a piece of poetry. And without meaning any disrespect to the passengers, there were not a great many on board who could tell us. We were bound for France, England, Italy, Germany, Switzerland, Greece, Turkey, Africa, Syria, Palestine, Egypt, and many a noted island in the sea, and yet all our library, almost, was made up of Holy Land, Plymouth Collection and Salvation by Grace! Bear with us if we seem exasperated at Palestine, for we have suffered much.

We bathed in the Dead Sea, but that was only another infamous deception. It did not make our bodies smart as if ten million needles were thrust into them; it did not blister us; it did not cover us with a slimy ooze and confer upon us an atrocious fragrance. It was an aggravating disappointment. It did not hurt at all hardly; it was not very slimy; and I could not discover that we smelt really any worse than we have always smelt since we have been in Palestine. It was only a different kind of smell, but not conspicuous on that account, because we have a great deal of variety in that respect. We don't smell, here on the Jordan, the same as we did in Jerusalem; and we didn't smell in Jerusalem just as we did in Nazareth, or Jacksonport, or Steubenville, or any of those other wretched ancient towns in Galilee. No, we change all the time, and generally for the worse. We do our own washing.

We floundered around in the Dead Sea, but we could not sink. It is utterly impossible. When we stood up in two-fathom water, our heads, our shoulders, and fully one-half of our breasts remained out of the water; we could lie down and clasp our knees up to our chins, with our heads clear out, and nothing of us would be submerged but a portion of our bodies. A man might lie on his back and read or smoke very comfortably as long as he kept still; but the moment he moved he would flirt over on his face. I doubt if he could sink to his chin, however, even with a twenty-pound weight hung to his heels—thus wonderfully buoyant is the water. Do you suppose Sodom and Gomorrah are under there yet? They must have floated to the top. Poor Lot's wife is gone—I never think of her without feeling sad. The cattle must have got her. There is something infinitely touching in the thought. Hers was too sad a history to jest about. I might speak with levity of Lot himself, or of Goliah, or many other of the Patriarchs, but whenever I think of poor Lot's wife I feel no longer in a mood for flippant speeches. Peace to her sediment!

The Jordan is a hard road to travel, I believe. It is true. The road to the Jordan from any place, is a particularly hard one to travel. One cannot find worse—at least out of Palestine. And yet the road from Jerusalem down here to Jericho and the Jordan is the best in Palestine; I am ready to admit that. I always thought the river Jordan was four thousand miles long and thirty-five miles wide, and so I have been miserably disappointed again. It is only ninety miles long, and so crooked that a man don't know which side of it he is on half the time. In going ninety miles it don't get over more than fifty miles of ground. It is not any wider than Broadway in New York. How is it that such a creek as this has imposed itself upon me all my life as a mighty river?

This is a country of disappointments. Nothing in it is as extraordinary as one expects it to be. There is the Sea of Galilee and that shabby Dead Sea—neither of them twenty miles long or thirteen wide. And yet all my life I thought they were sixty-thousand miles in diameter. Woe is me!

MARK TWAIN

NOTE.—This was written in place of No. 51, which was mislaid for a time, but was found subsequently.

M. T.

This letter, numbered fifty-two by Twain, appeared in the *Daily Alta California* of April 5, 1868. As Twain states in the note at the end, it was written to take the place of the preceding letter, which had been temporarily lost. The two letters partly overlap and Twain made more use of the preceding letter than he did of this one. He inserted a few passages from this letter in Letter 54 as used in the second half of Chapter XXVIII.

The first six sentences of the opening paragraph were used in Chapter XXIX, where Twain sums up his impressions of the Holy Land. "On earth" became "there are," and "ashamed of itself" became "sorrowful and despondent." "Mere lakes they are" was deleted. "It is the most hopeless, dreary, heartbroken piece of territory out of Arizona" became "It is a hopeless, dreary, heartbroken land."

In the paragraph beginning "We bathed in the Dead Sea," the passage beginning "it did not blister us" and extending to the end of the paragraph was inserted in Chapter XXVIII, in the account which Twain had taken from Letter 54. "It was an aggravating disappointment. "It did not hurt at all hardly" was deleted since it was mere repetition. "Jacksonport, or Steubenville" became "Tiberias, or Cesarea Philippi," and "wretched" became "ruinous."

In the last paragraph of the letter the passage beginning "I always thought the river Jordan was four thousand miles long" and extending to the end of the paragraph was also used, in revised form, in Chapter XXVIII. "I always thought" became "when I was a boy I somehow got the impression that." "And so I have been miserably disappointed again" was deleted. "Don't" became "does not." "How is it that such a creek" and the next thirty-two words were deleted. "Shabby" was deleted. "All my life" became "when I was in Sunday-school." "Woe is me" was deleted.

56. American Colony in Palestine

Alexandria, Egypt, Oct. 2, 1867.

THE AMERICAN excursion steamer *Quaker City* arrived here to-day from Jaffa, in Palestine. All the passengers are well.

The *Quaker City* brings about 30 or 40 of Old Adams's American-

Colony dupes. Others have deserted before, and 17 have died since the foolish expedition landed in Palestine a year ago. Fifteen still remain outside the walls of Jaffa, with Adams, the prophet. These 15 are all that are left of the original 160 that sailed from Maine 12 months ago, to found a new colony and a new religion in Syria, and wait for the second coming of Christ. The colonists have been sadly disappointed. The colony was a failure, and Christ did not come. The colony failed on account of heavy taxes and poor crops—a discrepancy between the almanac and the Book of Revelations interfered with the Second Advent. Adams, the Prophet of God, got drunk in September, 1866, and remains so to this day. It is to be hoped that he will see the error of his ways when he gets sober.

The famous Adams colonization expedition may be considered as finished, extinguished, and ready for its obituary. The 15 want to go home badly enough, but they have got no money, are in debt to Adams, and must stay and work for him. So ends one of the strangest chapters in American history. This man Adams is a shrewd man, and a seductive talker. He got up a new religion, and went about preaching it in the State of Maine and thereabouts. I have asked several of these colonists on board the ship what its nature was, but they are singularly reticent on the subject. They speak vaguely of a flood which was promised, but turned out to be a drouth; they do not say what the flood had to do with their salvation, or how it was going to prosper their religion. They talk also of the long-prophecied assembling of the Jews in Palestine from the four quarters of the world, and the restoration of their ancient power and grandeur, but they do not make it appear that an immigration of Yankees to the Holy Land was contemplated by the old prophets as a part of that programme; and now that the Jews have not "swarmed," yet one is left at a loss to understand why that circumstance should distress the American colony of Mr. Adams. I can make neither head nor tail of this religion. I have been told all along that there was a strong free-love feature in it, but a glance at the colonists of both sexes on board this ship has swept that notion from my mind.

Mr. Adams preached his new doctrine, and gathered together a little band of 160 men, women and children last year, and sailed for Jaffa, in Syria. They were simple, unpretending country people, nearly all from one county (Washington) in Maine, and received Adams's extravagant account of the beauty of the paradise he was taking them to, and the richness of its soil, with full confidence. Many of the colonists brought horses, and all manner of farming implements, and all seem to have started with a fair amount of money. Adams became custodian of all the funds. They could not have selected a better—he has got them yet. He had no money when he started out as a prophet, but now he is in reasonably comfortable circumstances, and his colonists are reduced to poverty. The first crop of the colonists did not return them even the seed they put in the ground. This year they raised what is considered in Syria a very good crop—seven bushels of wheat to the acre (the natives call a season like this a "blessed year")—but they had sowed two bushels of seed to the acre; they had to save two bushels out for next year's planting, rents and taxes took rather more than the balance, and so no fortunes were made. In Palestine the Government takes one-fourth of the gross yield of the field, the landlord from whom the farm is rented takes one-fifth of the gross yield, and what is left must be saved for seed. Foreigners must rent land; they cannot own it. The colonists who raised the best crop this year lost $500 on it. He thinks if he had raised a better one it would have beggared him. Irrigation would make the rich plain of Jaffa yield astonishing crops of wheat, but at the same time it would make it yield still more astonishing crops of thorns and thistles seven feet high; and, therefore, on the whole, it would be unwise to irrigate, even if one had the facilities for it.

For one year, under the flaming sun of Syria, the colonists have struggled along, moneyless, disappointed, disheartened, and hopeless. The prophet treasurer, Adams, has had to support them most of the time, because he could not help himself. He is glad to get rid of any that leave him, no doubt, and they are glad enough to get away from the filthy, thieving, miserable horde of pauper Arabs that have infested their "paradise" like vermin for so many weary months. Poor Adams himself has suffered much. Our Consul at Jerusalem has been obliged to imprison him twice for various reasons; his lambs, whom he was trying so hard to lead to heaven by a new road, have grumbled sore and sighed for the flesh-pots of America; his crops have come to naught, and even the wife of his bosom, instead of comforting him in his season of affliction, would deprive him of the poor consolation of getting drunk. He has had a harder run of luck than almost any prophet that ever lived, because, in addition to his mere ordinary sufferings, he has had the humiliation of seeing all his prophecies go by default. It cannot be otherwise than disgusting to a prophet when his prophecies don't fit the almanac.

The *Quaker City* has now become an emigrant-ship for fanatical pilgrims *from* the Holy Land. What is to be the next chapter in her eventful history?

What I have said about the Adams expedition I got from the Adams refugees themselves, and I have no doubt it is entirely correct. The names of those who are passengers by the *Quaker City* are as follows:

Mrs. P. W. Tabbatt, E. A. Tabbatt, Miss Drusilla Ward, Moses W. Leighton, Mrs. Nancy S. Leighton, M. B. Leighton, G. W. Ames, Z. Corson, Misses D., E., and L. Corson, Leonard Corson, Mrs. C. M. Corson, Mrs. C. H. Witham, F. M. Witham, E. K. Emerson, John A. Briscoe, Mrs. Charlotte A. Briscoe, Misses Lizzie C. and Julia Briscoe, Charles E. Burns, Mrs. Lucy W. Burns, J. B. Ames and wife, A. Norton and wife, P. Norton, E. C. Norton, E. Norton, L. P. Norton, P. F. Emerson, Mr. Rogers and wife.

About half of the above list pay their own way. The other half are provided with funds raised for the purpose by various United States Consuls in the Levant. The refugees propose to go by English steamer from Alexandria to Liverpool, and thence home to America.

This letter, which appeared in the *New York Tribune* of November 2, 1867, was used in Chapter XXX, but it was greatly condensed and completely rewritten. In the book Twain said that one of the *Quaker City* excursionists, Moses S. Beach of the New York *Sun*, gave the American consul-general in Egypt his check for fifteen hundred dollars to send the colonists home to Maine.

57. Home Again

New York, November 20th.

The steamer *Quaker City* arrived yesterday morning and turned her menagerie of pilgrims loose on America—but, thank Heaven, they came ashore in Christian costume. There was some reason to fear that they would astound the public with Moorish *haiks*, Turkish fezzes, sashes from Persia, and such other outlandish diablerie as their distempered fancies were apt to suggest to them to resurrect from their curious foreign trunks. They have struggled through the Custom

House and escaped to their homes. Their Pilgrim's Progress is ended, and they know more now than it is lawful for the Gods themselves to know. They can talk it from now till January—most of them are too old to last longer. They can tell how they criticised the masterpieces of Reubens, Titian and Murillo, in Paris, Italy and Spain—but they, nor any other man, can tell precisely how competent they were to do it. They can give their opinion of the Emperor of France, the Sultan of Turkey, the Czar of Russia, the Pope of Rome, the King of Italy, and Garibaldi, from personal observation—but, alas! they cannot furnish those gentlemen's opinion of *them*. They can tell how they ascended Mont Blanc—how they tried to snuffle over the tomb of Romeo and Juliet—how they gathered weeds in the Coliseum, and cabbaged mosaics from the Baths of Caracalla—how they explored the venerable Alhambra, and were entranced with the exquisite beauty of the Alcazar—how they infested the bazaars of Smyrna, Constantinople, and Cairo—how they "went through" the holy places of Palestine, and left their private mark on every one of them, from Dan unto the Sea of Galilee, and from Nazareth even unto Jerusalem and the Dead Sea—how they climbed the Pyramids of Egypt and swore that Vesuvius was finer than they; that the Sphynx was foolishness to the Parthenon, and the dreamy panorama of the Nile nonsense to the glories of the Bay of Naples. They can tell all about that, and they will—they can boast about all that, but will they tell the secret history of the trip? Catch them at it! They will blow their horns about the thousand places they have visited and get the lockjaw three times a day trying to pronounce the names of them (they never *did* get any of those names right)—but never, never in the world, will they open the sealed book of the secret history of their memorable pilgrimage. And I won't—for the present, at any rate. Good-bye to the well-meaning old gentlemen and ladies. I bear them no malice, albeit they never took kindly the little irreverent remarks I had occasion to make about them occasionally. We didn't amalgamate—that was all. Nothing more than that. I was exceedingly friendly with a good many of them—eight out of the sixty-five—but I didn't dote on the others, and they didn't dote on me. We were always glad to meet, but then we were just as glad to part again. There was a little difference of opinion between us—nothing more. They thought they could have saved Sodom and Gomorrah, and I thought it would have been unwise to risk money on it. I never failed to make friends on shipboard before—but maybe I was meaner than usual, this trip. Still, I was more placable than they. Every night, in calm or storm, I always turned up in their synagogue, in the after cabin, at seven bells, but they never came near my stateroom. They called it a den of iniquity. But I cared not; there were others who knew it as the home of modest merit. I bear the pilgrims no malice, now, none at all. I *did* give them a little parting blast in the *Herald*, this morning, but I only did that just to see the galled jade wince.

A Model Excursion

People always jump to the conclusion that passengers of diverse natures, occupations and modes of life, thrown together in great numbers on board a ship, must infallibly create trouble and unending dissatisfaction for each other. This idea is wrong. Diverse natures (when they are good, whole-hearted human natures,) blend and dove-tail together on shipboard as neatly as the varicolored fragments of stone in an exquisite mosaic—it is your gang of all-perfection, all-piety, all-economy, all-uncharitableness—like ancient mosaic pavements in the ruins of Rome, the stones all one color, and the cracks between them unpleasantly conspicuous—it is a gang like this that makes a particularly and peculiarly infernal trip. I am tired hearing about the "mixed" character of our party on the *Quaker City*. It was not mixed enough —there were not blackguards enough on board in proportion to the saints—there was not genuine piety enough to offset the hypocrisy. Genuine piety! Do you know what constitutes a legal quorum for prayer? It is in the Bible: "When two or three are gathered together," etc. You observe the number. It means two (or more) honest, sincere Christians, of course. Well, we held one hundred and sixty-five prayer-meetings in the *Quaker City*, and one hundred and eighteen of them were scandalous and illegal, because four out of the five real Christians on board were too sea sick to be present at them, and so there wasn't a quorum. I know. I kept a record—prompted partly by the old reportorial instinct, and partly because I knew that their proceedings were null and void, and ought not to be allowed to pass without a protest. I had seen enough of Legislatures to know right from wrong, and I was sorry enough to see things going as they were. They never could have stood a call of the house, and they resented every attempt of mine to get one.

But I am wandering from my subject somewhat. I was only going to say that people of diverse natures make the pleasantest companionship in long sea voyages, and people all of one nature and that not a happy one, make the worst. If I were going to start on a pleasure excursion around the world and to the Holy Land, and had the privilege of making out her passenger list, I think I could do it right and yet not go out of California. This thought was suggested by a dream I had a month ago, while this pilgrimage was still far at sea. I dreamed that I saw the following placard posted upon the bulletin boards of San Francisco:

Passenger List
of the Steamer *'Constitution,'*
Capt. Ned Wakeman,

Which leaves this day on a pleasure excursion around the world, permitting her passengers to stop forty days in London, forty in Vienna, forty in Rome, ten in Geneva, ten in Naples, ten in its surroundings, twenty in Venice, thirty in Florence, fifty in the cities of Spain, two days in Constantinople, half a day in Smyrna, thirty days in St. Petersburg, five months in the Sandwich Islands, six in Egypt, forever in France, and two hours and a half in the Holy Land:

Rev. Dr. Wadsworth,
James Anthony,
Archbishop Alemany,
Paul Morrill,
Rev. Horatio Stebbins,
John William Skae,
Bishop Kip,
T. J. Lamb,
Gen. W. H. French,
Asa Nudd,
Emperor Norton,
Lewis Leland,
Old Ridgeway,
John McComb,
George Parker,
Frank Pixley,
Barry & Patten,
Admiral Jim Smith, late of Hawaiian Navy,
Captain Pease,
Louis Cohn,
Aleck Badlam,
Charles Low,
Colonel Fry,
Jo. Jones,
Pete Hopkins,
General Drum (absent),
Colonel Catherwood,
Squarza,
Stiggers' Citizen Sam Platt,
Jim Coffroth,
Frank Soulé,
R. B. Swain,
One dozen Doctors, chosen at large,
Five delegates from San Quentin,
And Frank Bret Harte, George Barnes, Mark Twain and 300 other newspaper men, in the steerage.

It was a dream, but still it was a dream with wisdom in it. That tribe could travel forever without a row, and preserve each other's respect and esteem. Keep the steerage passengers out of sight, and nothing could be said against the character of the party, either. The list I dreamt of, as above set down, could travel pleasantly. They would certainly make a sensation wherever they went, but they would as certainly leave a good impression behind. And yet this list is made up of all sorts of people, and people of all ages. Against the impressive solemnity of Jim Coffroth, we have the levity of Dr. Wadsworth; against the boisterousness of R. B. Swain, we have the graveyard silence and decorum of Alex. Badlam; against General Drum's fondness for showing military dress, we have the Emperor Norton's antipathy to epaulettes and soldier-buttons; against the reckless gayety of Bishop Kip, we would bring the unsmiling, puritanical straight-lacedness of Anthony & Morrill; against the questionable purity of the five delegates from San Quentin, we would array the bright virtue of the 300 steerage passengers. Such was the pleasure party I saw in my dream. *There* was a crowd for you that could swing round the circle for six months, and never get home-sick—never fall out—never mope and gossip—never wear out a Napoleon carrying it in their pockets—never show disrespect to honest religion—never bring their nationality into disrepute—never fail to make Europe say, "Lo! these Americans be bricks!"

To Washington

I am going to Washington to-morrow, to stay a month or two—possibly longer. I have a lot of Holy Land letters on the way to you that will arrive some time or other.

This letter, which appeared in the *Daily Alta California* of January 8, 1868, was not used by Twain in the book. The few ideas in it that appear in the book had been expressed in other letters in language closer to that of the book, I believe, than any in this letter.

58. Summing Up the Excursion

To the editor of the *Herald:* The steamer *Quaker City* has accomplished at last her extraordinary voyage and returned to her old pier at the foot of Wall street, after an absence of five months and a half. The expedition was a success in some respects, in some it was not. Originally it was advertised as a "pleasure excursion." Well, perhaps it was a pleasure excursion, but certainly it did not look like one; certainly it did not act like one. Anybody's and everybody's notion of a pleasure excursion is that the parties to it will of a necessity be young and giddy and somewhat boisterous. They will dance a good deal, sing a good deal, make love, and pray very little. Anybody's and everybody's notion of a well conducted funeral is that there must be a hearse and a corpse, and chief mourners and mourners by courtesy, many old people, much solemnity, no levity, and a prayer and a sermon withal. Three fourths of the *Quaker City's* passengers were between forty and seventy years of age! There was a picnic crowd for you! It may be supposed that the other fourth was composed of young girls. But it was not. It was chiefly composed of rusty old bachelors and a child of six years. Let us average the ages of the *Quaker City's* pilgrims and set the figure down at fifty years. Is any man insane enough to imagine that this picnic of patriarchs sang, made love, danced, laughed, told anecdotes, dealt in ungodly levity? In my experience they sinned little in these matters. No doubt it was presumed here at home that these frolicsome veterans laughed and sang and romped all day, and day after day, and kept up a noisy excitement from one end of the ship to the other; and that they played blindman's buff or danced quadrilles and waltzes on moonlight evenings on the quarterdeck; and that at odd moments of unoccupied time they jotted a laconic item or two in the journals they opened on such elaborate plan when they left home, and then skurried off to their whist and euchre labors under the cabin lamps. If these things were presumed, the presumption was at fault. The venerable excursionists were not gay and frisky. They played no blind man's buff; they dealt not in whist; they shirked not the irksome journal, for alas! most of them were even writing books. They never romped, they talked but little, they never sang, save in the nightly prayer meeting. The pleasure ship was a synagogue, and the pleasure trip was a funeral excursion without a corpse. (There is nothing exhilarating about a funeral excursion without a corpse.) A free, hearty laugh was a sound that was not heard oftener than once in seven days about those decks or in those cabins; and when it was heard it met with precious little sympathy. The excursionists danced, on three separate evenings, long, long ago (it seems an age), quadrilles, of a single set, made up of three ladies and five gentlemen (the latter with handkerchiefs around their arms to signify their sex), who timed their feet to the solemn wheezing of a melodeon; but even this melancholy orgie was voted to be sinful and dancing was discontinued.

The pilgrims played dominoes when too much Josephus or Robinson's Holy Land Researches, or book writing, made recreation necessary—for dominoes is about as mild and sinless a game as any in the world perhaps, excepting always the ineffably insipid diversion they call playing at croquet, which is a game where you don't pocket any balls and don't carom on anything of any consequence, and when you are done nobody has to pay, and there are no cigars or drinks to saw off, and, consequently, there isn't any satisfaction whatever about it—they played dominoes till they were rested, and then they backguarded each other privately till prayer time. When they were not seasick they were uncommonly prompt when the dinner gong sounded. Such was our daily life on board the ship—solemnity, decorum, dinner, dominoes, prayers, slander. It was not lively enough for a pleasure trip; but if we had only had a corpse it would have made a gorgeous funeral excursion. It is all over now; but when I look back, the idea of these venerable fossils skipping forth on a six months' picnic, seems exquisitely ludicrous. The advertised title of the expedition—"The Grand Holy Land Pleasure Excursion"—was a ghastly misnomer. "The Grand Holy Land Funeral Procession" would have been better—much better.

As advertised, the "Plymouth Collection of Hymns" was used on board. It was frequently used. We had a prayer meeting every night. On this part of the subject I wish to touch very lightly. I could not quarrel, no one could quarrel, with the prayer meetings. We are all taught to respect these things. I merely mention them as being a unique feature in pleasure excursions, and worthy of imitation in future picnics. There were those in the ship's company who attributed the fact that we had a steady siege of storms and head winds for five mortal months solely to the prayer meetings. But I was not of that faction. There were those who were abandoned enough to believe that some time or other a particularly aggravating and long-drawn prayer meeting would bring down a storm that would sink the ship. I was not of that party either. I said all along that we hadn't prayer meetings enough; we ought to have them before breakfast, and between meals, and every now and then, and pretty much all the time. Those were my sentiments. I do not brag, but those were certainly my sentiments. The argument that they prayed the same old prayers over again every night was nothing to me. I knew that if they only performed oftener and held out long enough, they were bound to start something fresh after a while. There is nothing that gives startling variety to a picnic like prayer meetings. Especially when the "Plymouth Collection" is used, because as a general thing the tunes are a shade too complicated for the excursionists, and so, when they are properly tangled, they are exceedingly lively.

Wherever we went, in Europe, Asia or Africa, we made a sensation, and I suppose I may add, created a famine. None of us had ever been anywhere before; we all hailed from the interior; travel was a wild novelty to us, and we conducted ourselves in accordance with the natural instincts that were in us, and trammelled ourselves with no ceremonies, no conventionalities. We alway took care to make it understood that we were Americans—Americans! When we found that a good many foreigners had hardly even heard of America, and that a good many more knew it only as a barbarous province away off somewhere, that had lately been at war with somebody, we pitied the ignorance of the Old World, but abated no jot of our importance. Many and many a simple community in the Eastern hemisphere will remember for years the incursion of the strange horde in the year of our Lord 1867, that called themselves Americans, and seemed to imagine in some unaccountable way that they had a right to be proud of it. We generally created a famine, partly because the coffee on the *Quaker City* was unendurable and sometimes the more substantial fare was not strictly first class; and partly because one naturally tires of sitting long at the same board and eating from the same dishes.

The people of those foreign countries are very, very ignorant. They looked curiously at the costumes we had brought from the wilds of America. They observed that we talked loudly at table sometimes. They noticed that we looked out for expenses and got what we conveniently could out of a franc, and wondered where in the mischief we came from. In Paris they just simply opened their eyes and stared when we spoke to them in French! We never did succeed in making those idiots understand their own language. One of our passengers said to a shopkeeper, in reference to a proposed return to buy a pair of gloves, "*Allong—re tay trankeel*—maybe ve coom Moonday," and would you believe it, that shopkeeper, a born Frenchman, had to ask what it was that had been said. Sometimes it seems to me, somehow, that there must be a difference between Parisian French and *Quaker City* French.

The people stared at us everywhere and we stared at them. We generally made them feel rather small, too, before we got done with them, because we bore down on them with America's greatness until we crushed them. And yet we took kindly to the manners and customs, and especially the fashions of the various peoples we visited. When we left the Azores, we wore awful capotes and used fine tooth combs—successfully. When we came back from Tangier, in Africa, we were topped with fezzes of the bloodiest hue, and hung with tassels like an Indian's scalp lock. In France and Spain we attracted some attention to these costumes. In Italy they naturally took us for distempered Garibaldians, and set a gunboat to look for anything significant in our changes of uniform. We made Rome howl. We could have made any place howl when we had all our clothes on. We got no fresh raiment in Greece—they had but little there of any kind. But at Constantinople, how we turned out! Turbans, scimetars, fezzes, horse pistols, tunics, sashes, baggy trowsers, yellow slippers—Oh, we were gorgeous! The illustrious dogs of Constantinople barked their under jaws off, and even then failed to do us justice. They are all dead by this time. They could not go through such a run of business as we gave them and survive.

And then we went to see the Emperor of Russia. We just called on him as comfortably as if we had known him a century or so, and when we had finished our visit we variegated ourselves with selections from Russian costumes and sailed away again more picturesque than ever. In Smyrna we picked up camels' hair shawls and other dressy things from Persia; but in Palestine—ah, in Palestine—our splendid career ended. They didn't wear any clothes there to speak of. We were satisfied, and stopped. We made no experiments. We did not try their costume. But we astonished the natives of that country. We astonished them with such eccentricities of dress as we could muster. We prowled through the Holy Land, from Cesarea Philippi to Jerusalem and the Dead Sea, a weird procession of pilgrims, gotten up regardless of expense, solemn, gorgeous, green spectacled, drowsing under blue umbrellas, and astride of a sorrier lot of horses, camels and asses than those that came out of Noah's ark, after eleven months of sea-sickness and short rations. If ever those children of Israel in Palestine forget when Gideon's band went through there from America they ought to be cursed once more and finished. It was the rarest spectacle that ever astounded mortal eyes, perhaps.

Well, we were at home in Palestine. It was easy to see that that was the grand feature of the expedition. We had cared nothing much about Europe. We galloped through the Louvre, the Pitti, the Unzzi, the Vatican—all the galleries—and through the pictured and frescoed churches of Venice, Pica and the cathedrals of Spain; some of us said that certain of the great works of the old masters were glorious creations of genius, (we found it out in the guidebook, though we got hold of the wrong picture sometimes), and the others said they were disgraceful old daubs. We examined modern and ancient statuary with a critical eye in Florence, Rome or anywhere we found it, and praised it if we saw fit, and if we didn't we said we preferred the wooden Indians in front of the cigar stores of America. But the Holy Land brought out all our enthusiasm. We fell into raptures by the barren shores of Galilee; we pondered at Tabor and at Nazareth; we exploded into poetry over the questionable loveliness of Esdraelon; we meditated at Jezreel and Samaria over the zeal of Jehu, who slew seventy sons of one gentleman, massacred all the worshippers of Baal in his district, and performed other meritorious missionary services; we rioted, fairly rioted, among the holy places of Jerusalem; we bathed in Jordan and the Dead Sea, reckless whether our accidental insurance policies were extra hazardous or not, and brought away so many jugs of precious water from both places that all the country from Jericho to the mountains of Moab will suffer from drought this year, I think. Yes, the pilgrimage part of the excursion was its pet feature—there is no question about that. After dismal, desolate, smileless Palestine, beautiful Egypt had few charms for us. We merely glanced at it, and were ready for home.

They wouldn't let us land at Malta—quarantine; they wouldn't let us land in Sardinia; nor at Algiers, Africa; nor at Malaga, Spain; nor at Cadiz; nor at the Madeira Islands. So we got offended at all foreigners and turned our backs upon them and came home. I suppose we only stopped at the Bermudas because they were in the programme. We did not care anything about any place at all. We wanted to go home. Homesickness was abroad in the ship—it was epidemic. If the authorities of New York had known how badly we had it, they would have quarantined us here.

We failed to sell the ship. I mention this because to sell the ship seemed to be as much of an object of the excursion as anything else, and so of course to know that we failed to sell her must necessarily be of interest to the public. We were to sell the ship and then walk home, I suppose. That would have given variety to the pleasure excursion at any rate.

The grand pilgrimage is over. Goodby to it, and a pleasant memory to it, I am able to say in all kindness. I bear no malice, no ill will towards any individual that was connected with it, either as passenger or officer. Such persons as I did not like at all yesterday I like very well to-day, now that I am at home, and always hereafter I shall be able to poke fun at the whole gang if the spirit so moves me to do, without ever saying a malicious word. The expedition accomplished all that its programme promised that it should accomplish, and we ought all to be satisfied with the management of the matter, certainly. But that such pleasure excursions as this are calculated to be suffocated with pleasure, I deny; and that a party more ill-fitted, by age and awful solemnity, for skurrying around the world on a giddy picnic, ever went to sea in a ship since the world began, I deny also, most fervently.

This letter, which appeared in the *New York Herald* of November 20, 1867, was written for this newspaper on Twain's first night in New York (November 19, 1867) after the return of the *Quaker City.* He reprinted it in "A Newspaper Valedictory," following Chapter XXXIII. He admitted that "some of the passengers have abused me for writing it," but he called it "a kind word for the Hadjis—Hadjis are people who have made the pilgrimage—" and added: "I have read it, and read it again; and if there is a sentence in it that is not fulsomely complimentary to captain, ship, and passengers, *I* cannot find it. If it is not a chapter that any company might be proud to have a body write about them, my judgment is fit for nothing."

As always, Twain made some revisions in the letter. "After an absence of five months and a half" was deleted. "And pray very little" became "but sermonize very little"; "playing at croquet" became "croquet"; "cigars or drinks" became "refreshments"; "prayers" became "devotions"; "gorgeous" became "noble"; "ludricrous" became "refreshing"; and "ghastly misnomer" became "misnomer."

The paragraph beginning "As advertised, the 'Plymouth Collection of Hymns' " was deleted. "Pisa" became "Naples" and "zeal of Jehu" became "missionary zeal of Jehu." "Who slew seventy sons of one gentleman, massacred all the worshippers of Baal in his district, and performed other meritorious missionary services" was deleted. "Dismal, desolate, smileless" became "dismal, smileless." The paragraph beginning "We failed to sell the ship" was deleted. "Such persons as" became "things," and the last sentence of the letter was deleted.

Index

Abana River: 195ff., 208
Abraham, the dragoman: 180, 182, 187
Acropolis: 100ff.
Adams, the prophet: 306–309
Ain Jelüd: 256; *see also* Jacksonville
Ain Mellahah (Williamsburgh): 217
Alexander II (Emperor of Russia): 134, 140ff., 149ff., 160ff., 179, 216; address to 144–45, 156; visit mentioned, 317
Algiers: 318
Ames, G. W.: 309
Ames, J. B.: 309
American Colonists in Palestine: 306–309
American Consul in Odessa: 141ff., 151f.
Annunciation (Italian town): 84, 87
"Ape's Hill": 19
Apparition, the: 237–40
Areopagus: 101, 107
Armenians (in Smyrna): 166
Athens: 75, 100–109, 136
Ayassoluk: 173
Azis, Abdul (also Abdul Aziz): 40
Azores: 3–10, 12–18; location of, 3

Baalbec (city of ruin): 179f., 185, 190ff.
Baalbec (Twain's horse): 192–93
Balaklava: 135
Baldwinsville: *see* Cesarea Phillippi
Banias: 208
Basilica of St. Mark: 64
Beach, Mr.: 109
Bedouins, attack by: 294–95
Beersheba: 213
Beirout: 179, 184, 204
Bellaggio: 53
Bermudas: 318
Beroth: 264
Bethany: 293–94
Bethlehem: 300–301
Bethsaida: 228, 231, 240
Birch, Dr.: 58, 101, 107f., 211–12
Bismarck: 40
Black Sea: 137
Blessed Pool of Bethesda: 288
Blucher, Wm.: 11–12, 15, 16
Blue Grotto: 92
Bois de Boulogne: 91
Bridge of Sighs: 60ff.
Briscoe, Mrs. Charlotte A.: 309
Briscoe, John A.: 309
Briscoe, Julia: 309
Briscoe, Lizzie C.: 309
Bronze Horses, the: 61
Brown: 7, 8, 23ff., 29ff., 41, 50–51, 56–58, 94, 117, 127f., 136, 140, 155, 159, 161, 178–79, 180, 187, 285
Bullard, Mr.: 109
Burns, Charles E.: 309
Burns, Mrs. Lucy W.: 309

Cadiz: 318
Campioni, Marco: 52

Capernaum: 226, 228, 240
Capote: 14
Capri: 92–93
Castle of Banias: 206ff.
Cathedral (Milan): 48–52
Cathedral of San Lorenzo: 45–46
Cave of the Seven Sleepers: 175
"Centre of the earth": 272–73
Cesarea Phillippi: 208ff., 227, 240
Chapel of the Mocking: 277–78
Chapel of St. Helena: 275–76
Church of the Annunciation: 46, 258
Church of the Holy Sepulchre: 267–81, 288, 300
Church of the Nativity: 300
"City of Palaces": *see* Genoa
Civita Vecchia: 72–74, 75
Columbus, Christopher: 44
Constantinople: 75, 109–33, 142, 157, 160, 163, 179, 249, 266, 317; amusements of, 122–23; cripples of, 115–16; dogs of, 123–25; fashions in, 113; morals in, 120–22; newspapers in, 126–27
Coressus Mountain: 173
Corson, Mrs. C. M.: 309
Corson, D.: 309
Corson, E.: 309
Corson, Leonard: 309
Corson, Z.: 309
Council of Ten: 61–62
Council of Three: 61–63
Crocker, Timothy D.: 145, 156
Curtin, M.: 148

Dabney, Mr.: 4
Dalgorouki, Prince: 150, 161
Damascus: 179f., 192–204, 241
Damascus Gate: 265, 290
Dan (passenger): 58, 93, 303–304
Dan (city): 213–14, 219, 240; *see also* Dutch Flat
Dancing Dervishes: 118, 131f.
Dardenelles: *see* Hellespont
Dead Sea: 180, 292, 294, 298–99, 304ff.; bathing in, 298–99
Deburich (Deburieh): 245–46
Denny, Colonel: 101f., 104, 107f.
Diogenes: 106
Doctor: 58; *see also* Dr. Birch
Dr. B.: 211–12; *see also* Dr. Birch
Drake's boy (passenger): 159
Ducal Palace: 61
Duomo: 69
Dutch Flat (Dan): 213–18

El Yuba Dam: 206
Emerson, E. K.: 309
Emerson, P. F.: 309
Emperor of Morocco: 30, 33; wives of, 32
Emperor of Russia: *see* Alexander II
Empress of Russia: 144ff., 149, 152f., 158
Ephesus: 164f., 172

Faubourg St. Antoine: 39, 91
Fayal: 24, 75
Festetics, Count: 150
Florence: 66–71
Flores: 12–13
Fountain of Beira: 264
Fountain of Jezreel: 240
Fountain of Lazarus: 293
Fountain of the Virgin: 290

Garden of Gethsemane: 265, 289ff.
Genoa: 41–47, 75, 115; population of, 41
George I (Greece): 110f.
Gibraltar: 18–25, 75
Gibson, Wm.: 145, 156

Governor-General of Odessa: 142–43, 150f., 161
Grand Trianon: 38–39
Great Pico, height of: 3
Great Square of St. Mark: 60–61
Grotto del Cane: *see* Grotto of the Dog
Grotto of the Annunciation: 251–52
Grotto of the Dog: 93–94

Hadji Mohammed Lamartz: 30
Hartley, Sir Charles: 138
Hellespont: 111f., 167
Hill of Ophel: 289
Horta, Fayal: 3–10, 13–15

Inkerman: 135
"Interrogation" (passenger): 24
Ischia Island: 83f., 93

Jack (passenger): 250, 297
Jackson, Dr.: 101, 107–108
Jacksonville (Ain Jelüd): 249, 256
Jacob's Well: 262–63
Jaffa: 306ff.
Jaffa Gate: 288
Jebel el Kuneiyiseh: 185
Jenin: 257
Jericho (city): 292f., 296
Jerico (also Jericho) (Twain's horse): 181, 184–85, 192
Jerusalem: 180, 241, 264–93; population of, 267; streets of, 267
Jesuit Cathedral (Horta): 6–7
Jesuit Church (Venice): 68
Jezreel: 254–57
Jonesborough (Arabic village): 206
Joppa: 180
Jordan River: 219, 240, 292ff., 296–98, 305; crossing of, 297–98
Joseph: story of, 220–24; tomb of, 261–62

Kaf'r Houer: 188–89
Kinney, Col. P.: 145, 156

Lake Agnano: 93
Lake Como: 53–57
Lake Gennesaret: 225f., 231, 241
Lake Huleh: 213f.
Lake Tahoe: 53, 55, 225ff.
Latin Convent (Nazareth): 251–52
Lebanon Mountains: 185
Leghorn: 75
Leighton, M. B.: 309
Leighton, Moses W.: 309
Leighton, Mrs. Nancy S.: 309
Leonardo da Vinci: 57–58
Levant Herald, The: 126–27
Lion of St. Mark: 61
Logansport: *see* Jezreel
Lord High Admiral (Russia): 152
Louis XIV: 37ff.
Louis XV: 38
Louis Napoleon: see Napoleon III

McMath, Mr.: 35
Madeira Islands: 318
Magdala: 232–35, 251
Maintenon, Madame: 38–39
Malaga: 318
Malakoff tower: 135
Malta: 318
Marie Antoinette: 38
Marie, Grand Duchess: 144ff., 152f., 158f.
Mars-hill: 136
Mars Saba: 299
Mary Magdalene, house of: 234
Meander River: 174
Medici family: 69–71

Mediterranean: 257
Mekseh: 185
Michael, Grand Duke: 144ff., 146, 149, 151, 155, 157ff.
Milan: 48–52, 57, 115
Milan Cathedral: 48–52, 58
Milk Grotto: 300
Millerites: 171–72
Mosque el Aksa: 287–88
Mosque of Omar: 265f., 285–88
Mosque of St. Sophia: 116–18
Mosque of the Sultan Selim: 173
Mount Carmel: 243
Mount Ebal: 259, 261
Mount Gerizim: 259
Mount Hattin: 243
Mount Hermon: 185, 204, 240
Mount Moriah: 285, 287, 289
Mount of Olives: 265, 289ff.
Mount Tabor: 220, 242–45, 248f.
Mount Vesuvius: 83–99

Naples: 74–76, 82, 85–92; population of, 90; wages in, 91–92; prices in, 92
Naples Museum: 81
Naples *Observer:* 74–76
Napoleon: 38, 215
Napoleon III: 40, 66, 149, 153, 215
Narghili, Twain's experience with: 122–23
Nazareth: 228, 248–53
Norton, A.: 309
Norton, E. 309
Norton, E. C.: 309
Norton, L. P.: 309
Norton, P.: 309

Odessa: 137–43; bathing in, 139–40
Oracle, the (passenger): 23–24
Order of St. George: 146, 148–49

Pallavicini, Count: 243
Pallavicini Garden: 47, 243–45
Paris: 39–40, 91
Parthenon: 101, 103ff.
Petit Trianon: 38
Pharpar River: 195ff.
Pico: 18
Pillar of Flagellation: 270
Pillars of Hercules: 19
Pion (Prion): 173ff.
Piraeus: 100f., 108–109
Plain of Esdraelon: 243, 245
Plain of Jezreel: 254
Plain of the Shepherds: 299
Pliny the Younger: 82–83
Poet, the (passenger): 24, 160f.
Pompadour: 38
Pompeii: 76–82, 134
Pool of Hezekiah: 288
Pool of Siloam: 289
Portugal: 3, 13
Pozzuoli: 93
Prime, Mr.: 265
Procida: 93
Prodigal Son, story of: 246–48
Pyramids: 75

Queen's chair: 20–21

Ramah: 264
Redan: 135
River of Damascus: *see* Abana River
Rogers, Mr.: 309
Rock of Gibraltar: 19f.
Russ pavement, in Horta: 9

Safed: 240, 243
St. Elmo: 89
Samaria: 258–59

San Carlo Borromeo: 50
San Miguel: 13
Sandwich Islands: 134
Sanford, A. N. (also S. A.): 145, 156
Sardinia: 318
Sea of Galilee: 219, 225ff., 229–37, 240, 243
Sea of Marmora: 125
Sea of Tiberias: 180
Sebastopol: 132–37, 139, 148, 162
"Seven Churches" of Asia: 168–69
Seven Sleepers: 175–78
Shechem: 259ff.
Shiloh: 263
Siberia: 154
Siloam: 289
Smyrna: 163–72, 179
Stamboul: 112, 119
Straight Street (Damascus): 200ff.
Strait of Gibraltar: 18–19
Sultan of Syria: 187
Sultan of Turkey: 149
Syria: 178–204

Tabbatt, E. A.: 309
Tabbatt, Mrs. P. W.: 309
Tangier: 25–36, 72; cats of, 34; population of, 35–36
Temple of Diana: 173
Temple of Jupiter: 190f.
Temple of Solomon: 285–88
Temple of the Sun: 190–91
Temple of Theseus: 106
Theatre of San Carlo: 85
Thebes: 75
Thousand and One Columns: 118–19
Tiberias: 226, 231ff., 240
Todleben, General (also Gen. Todtleben): 148, 162
Tower of Antonio: 281
Tower of David: 265
Tower of Hippicus: 265f., 289
Turkish coffee, Twain's opinion of: 131–32
Tyropean Valley: 289

Ungern-Sternberg, Baron: 149, 162

Valley of Hinnom: 289
Valley of Jehoshophat: 265, 289
Venice: 59–65, 97–99
Versailles: 36–39; description of palace, 37–38
Viceroy of Egypt: 142

W., Elder (passenger): 303–304
Wadsworth, J. C. L.: 35
Wandering Jew, the, story of: 283–85
Webster, Professor: 4
Well of Job: 289
Williamsburgh: 220; *see also* Ain Mellahah
Witham, Mrs. C. H.: 309
Witham, F. M.: 309
Wrangel, Baron: 148, 162

Yalta: 148, 158, 116

Zion Gate: 289